Speaking of America: Readings in U.S. History

VOLUME I: TO 1877
SECOND EDITION

LAURA A. BELMONTE
Oklahoma State University

THOMSON
WADSWORTH

Australia • Brazil • Canada • Mexico • Singapore • Spain
United Kingdom • United States

To the Students Who Inspire Me
In Memory of Karla Frances Smith (1976–2003)

Speaking of America: Readings in U.S. History
Volume I: To 1877
Second Edition
Laura A. Belmonte

Publisher: Clark Baxter
Senior Acquisitions Editor: Ashley Dodge
Assistant Editor: Paul Massicotte
Technology Project Manager: David Lionetti
Marketing Manager: Lori Grebe Cook
Marketing Assistant: Teresa Jessen
Marketing Communications Manager: Tami Strang
Project Manager, Editorial Production: Katy German
Creative Director: Rob Hugel
Art Director: Maria Epes

Print Buyer: Barbara Britton
Permissions Editor: Sue Howard
Production Service: G&S Book Services
Photo Researcher: Sue Howard
Copy Editor: Carrie Andrews
Cover Designer: Lisa Henry
Cover Image: © Corbis. All Rights Reserved
Cover Printer: Phoenix Color Corp
Compositor: Integra
Printer: Courier Westford

Library of Congress Control Number: 200596950

ISBN 0-495-05017-2

Thomson Higher Education
10 Davis Drive
Belmont, CA 94002-3098
USA

For more information about our products,
contact us at:
Thomson Learning Academic Resource Center
1-800-423-0563

For permission to use material from this text or
product, submit a request online at
http://www.thomsonrights.com.
Any additional questions about permissions can be
submitted by e-mail to
thomsonrights@thomson.com.

Contents

3   The Spirit of Revolution   67

4   We the People   103

5   A New Nation   149

6   Antebellum Politics and Reform   197

7   Social and Cultural Change, 1820–1865   229

Preface

When I began *Speaking of America*, I had no idea how deeply it would enrich my appreciation and understanding of the American people. The voices I encountered haunted, moved, and enraged me. In returning to the words of well-known citizens, I was sometimes amazed at how historians have simplified, even distorted, the meanings and contradictions of the original writings. In discovering the perspectives of common people ignored by future generations, I was awed by their extraordinary insights on their communities.

Speaking of America is designed to expose students to a variety of sources on United States history from the colonial era to the present day. The collection includes a wide array of speeches, letters, paintings, artifacts, poems, short stories, photographs, lyrics, book excerpts, articles, and news accounts encompassing multicultural and regional perspectives. The selected readings address important episodes in politics, economics, and foreign policy as well as social and cultural changes. Both famous and "ordinary" Americans are featured.

Speaking of America uses interdisciplinary materials in order to expose students to the broadest perspectives on American history.

- The collection can be used alone or in conjunction with a U.S. history textbook.

- Each chapter begins with an introduction providing a historical overview of a specific era.

- Chapter introductions are followed by a list of key themes addressed by the subsequent documents.

- Biographical sketches and historical context precede the individual primary sources.

- Each reading incorporates questions prompting students to analyze multiple perspectives, change over time, and the relevance of the past to the present.

A Note To The Student

PRIMARY SOURCES

Speaking of America requires students to examine a variety of historical readings and objects. Primary sources are firsthand accounts of historical events (for example, diaries, oral histories, court testimony, laws, newspapers, public records, memoirs, correspondence, official reports). Some of this evidence comes from individuals who actually witnessed or participated in an event and immediately recorded their impressions—for example, James Madison's copious notes on the Constitutional Convention. Primary sources also include cultural or material artifacts created at a certain time. Photographs, maps, films, songs, poems, furniture, clothing, toys, artwork, or literature are examples. Historians use primary sources to determine what happened in the past and to interpret an event or person's historical significance.

In order to use primary sources appropriately, one must pay careful attention to details. First, try to focus on the particular time and place in which it was produced. Remember that historical actors are describing their era, not the contemporary world. Second, keep in mind how other people living at the same time might describe an event differently and how events change over time. By comparing these perspectives and evaluating how the past differs from the present, students can gain a sense of the complexity and progression of history.

Here are some suggestions about issues that readers should consider when assessing primary sources:

1. CONTEXT – Read the introduction of each chapter and the individual document carefully. Keep in mind the events, people, and ideas of a particular era.

2. ARGUMENTS – Identify an author's theses and assess how well he or she develops and supports these claims. At times, I have included parenthetical definitions or modernized spelling and grammar in order to make it easier to understand an author's style.

3. PERSPECTIVE – Ask *who* is writing a specific account. Consider how an individual's background may have affected his or her beliefs. Can you detect a bias? Use the introductory paragraphs for helpful clues about the author's social or political status, race, religion, gender, class, and so on. It is also important to inquire *when* a document was produced. For example, a soldier writing home from the battlefield might portray his or her experience differently than he or she would in a memoir written forty years later. Evaluate whether an individual may be distorting events in order to serve personal interests or to

harm or benefit someone. Assess *why* this person is writing. Is he or she trying to persuade or deceive an audience? What were his or her motivations?

4. AUDIENCE – An author's style will vary greatly depending on his or her intended audience. One will use a different tone in a private letter to a loved one than in a public speech made before Congress. At the same time, keep in mind that a diary, autobiography, or letter may reflect an author's desire to be perceived in a specific way.

5. SIGNIFICANCE – Inquire why a source is *historically important*. Does it reshape our understanding of a particular event or person? Does it offer a perspective that broadens our knowledge about a certain time or place?

INTERPRETING VISUAL SOURCES

Artwork, artifacts, and objects are tangible forms of historical evidence. These materials may give voice to people who had an oral culture or whose written documents may have been damaged or lost. For example, archeologists at Jamestown have discovered earthworks, wooden foundations, weapons, and armor that are revising historians' understanding of the settlement and its inhabitants. Consider how touching or wearing a corset might enrich one's perception of women's lives in the Victorian era. Comparing the furniture, kitchen utensils, and linens of different homes enables us to assess the socio-economic background of their residents. Artists' techniques and subjects can reveal important insights about a certain era and individuals' perceptions of themselves.

ACKNOWLEDGMENTS

It is my great pleasure to thank several people who helped make *Speaking of America* a reality. Susan Oliver spent countless hours scanning and tracking down copyright permissions. Marion Umeno, Shelly Lemons, Lisa Guinn, Stefanie Decker, and Jim Klein were gifted teaching assistants who offered wonderful feedback on readings and questions. Charlene Boyer Lewis, Rebecca B. Edwards, Mark Schultz, Victoria Allison, and the anonymous readers of the first edition shared insights that immeasurably improved these volumes. During the 2002–2003 academic year, my colleagues at the Center for Humanities at Oregon State University provided encouragement and friendship during the final stages of writing. Clark and Abigail Baxter of Thomson Wadsworth championed and enriched this project in ways I cannot enumerate. The skill and insights of Ashley Dodge and Paul Massicotte enriched the second edition.

As I was finishing this collection, I learned that Karla Smith, one of my favorite students at Oklahoma State University, died after a long illness. Her spirit, empathy, and intelligence made her an absolute joy to teach. A few weeks before her death, she thanked me for "helping me see how my life is connected to a bigger picture, past, present, and future." I can only hope that the voices you meet in *Speaking of America* inspire you to draw the same conclusion.

1

Cultures Meet

In 1492, the arrival of Europeans in the Americas sparked radical transformations in world history, including violence, trade, diet, slavery, epidemics, and miscegenation. American Indians adapted to the onslaught of Europeans in a variety of ways. The following readings provide glimpses of the Europeans' motives for colonization, their impressions of the New World, and their interactions with native peoples.

THEMES TO CONSIDER

- The complexities of Euro-Indian interactions
- Ethnocentrism—a group's conviction that its way of life, belief system, culture, religion, etc., is superior to all others
- Differing notions of gender among Europeans and Indians

1.1

Christopher Columbus, Journal (1492)

After 500 years, Christopher Columbus remains a flamboyant and controversial figure in the history of European exploration. Born in Genoa, Italy, in 1451, Columbus became a sailor and moved to Spain following the death of his wife. Like most learned men of his era, Columbus believed that the earth was round. Convinced that Europeans could reach Asia by sailing westward across the Atlantic Ocean, he solicited royal sponsors for a voyage to the Far East. In 1492, Spanish monarchs King Ferdinand and Queen Isabella agreed to subsidize the trip in the hopes of spreading Christianity and competing economically with Portugal. Having greatly underestimated the world's circumference and the open-sea distance from Europe to Asia, Columbus reached the Caribbean Islands. He mistakenly believed that he was in the East Indies and later Cathay (China).

Although his exploits garnered fame, additional royal patronage, and the title "Admiral of the Ocean Sea," Columbus proved a poor colonial administrator and never attained great wealth. In 1506, after making three additional voyages to the Americas, Columbus died. Recently, some critics have vilified Columbus as a symbol of European exploitation of indigenous peoples. In this passage, Columbus describes his "discovery" of the "Indians."

FOCUS QUESTIONS

1. How does Columbus describe his initial interactions with the Indians?
2. Is there evidence of ethnocentrism in his remarks? If so, provide examples.
3. In your opinion, are contemporary celebrations of Columbus Day appropriate or not? Why?

Thursday 11 October 1492

He [sometimes Columbus refers to himself in the third person] steered west-southwest.... They saw petrels and a green bulrush near the ship. The men of the caravel Pinta saw a cane and a stick, and took on board another small stick

SOURCE: E. G. Bourne, ed., *The Northmen, Columbus and Cabot* (New York, 1906).

that appeared to have been worked with iron, and a piece of cane, and other vegetation originating on land, and a small plank. . . . With these signs everyone breathed more easily and cheered up. . . .

At two hours after midnight the land appeared, from which they were about two leagues distant. They hauled down all the sails and kept only the treo, which is the mainsail without bonnets, and jogged on and off, passing time until daylight Friday, when they reached an islet of the Lucayas, which was called Guanaham in the language of the Indians. Soon they saw naked people; and the Admiral went ashore in the armed launch, and Martin Alonso Pinzon and his brother Vicente Anes, who was captain of the Niña.

The Admiral brought out the royal banner and the captains two flags with the green cross, which the Admiral carried on all the ships as a standard, with an F and a Y, and over each letter a crown, one on one side and the other on the other. Thus put ashore they saw very green trees and many ponds and fruits of various kinds. The Admiral called to the two captains and to the others who had jumped ashore and to Rodrigo Descobedo, the escrivano of the whole fleet, and to Rodrigo Sanchez de Segovia; and he said that they should be witnesses that, in the presence of all, he would take, as in fact he did take, possession of the said island for the king and for the queen his lords, making the declarations that were required, and which at more length are contained in the testimonials made there in writing. Soon many people of the island gathered there.

What follows are the very words of the Admiral in his book about his first voyage to, and discovery of, these Indies, he says, in order that they would be friendly to us—because I recognized that they were people who would be better freed and converted to our Holy Faith by love than by force—to some of them I gave red caps, and glass beads which they put on their chests, and many other things of small value, in which they took so much pleasure and became so much our friends that it was a marvel. Later they came swimming to the ships' launches where we were and brought us parrots and cotton thread in balls and javelins and many other things, and they traded them to us for other things which we gave them, such as small glass beads and bells. In sum, they took everything and gave of what they had very willingly. But it seemed to me that they were a people very poor in everything. All of them go around as naked as their mothers bore them; and the women also, although I did not see more than one quite young girl. And all those that I saw were young people, for none did I see of more than 30 years of age. They are very well formed, with handsome bodies and good faces. Their hair coarse—almost like the tail of a horse—and short. They wear their hair down over their eyebrows except for a little in the back which they wear long and never cut. Some of them paint themselves with black, and they are of the color of the Canarians, neither black nor white; and some of them paint themselves with white, and some of them with red, and some of them with whatever they find. And some of them paint their faces, and some of them the whole body, and some of them only the eyes, and some of them only the nose. They do not carry arms nor are they acquainted with them, because I showed them swords and they took them by the edge and through ignorance cut themselves. They have no iron.

Their javelins are shafts without iron and some of them have at the end a fish tooth.... All of them alike are of good-sized stature and carry themselves well. I saw some who had marks of wounds on their bodies and I made signs to them asking what they were; and they showed me how people from other islands nearby came there and tried to take them, and how they defended themselves; and I believed and believe that—they come here from tierra firme to take them captive. They should be good and intelligent servants, for I see that they say very quickly everything that is said to them; and I believe that they would become Christians very easily, for it seemed to me that they had no religion. Our Lord pleasing, at the time of my departure I will take six of them from here to Your Highnesses in order that they may learn to speak...

...I was attentive and labored to find out if there was any gold; and I saw that some of them wore a little piece hung in a hole that they have in their noses. And by signs I was able to understand that, going to the south or rounding the island to the south, there was there a king who had large vessels of it and had very much gold.... This island is quite big and very flat and with very green trees and much water and a very large lake in the middle and without any mountains; and all of it so green that it is a pleasure to look at it. And these people are very gentle, and because of their desire to have some of our things and believing that nothing will be given to them without their giving something, and not having anything, they take what they can and then throw themselves into the water to swim....

1.2

Bartolemé de Las Casas, Brief Account of the Devastation of the Indies (1542)

Bartolemé de Las Casas was born in Seville in 1474. After entering the priesthood at age thirty-six, he accompanied conquistadors to the Caribbean. Horrified by Spanish mistreatment of Indians, Las Casas proposed that African slaves be used as an alternative labor force in the New World. While denying that slavery itself was sinful or evil, Las Casas spent his entire life defending the rights of nonwhite peoples. Ironically, his writings helped perpetuate the "Black

---

SOURCE: Bartolemé de Las Casas, *Brief Account of the Devastation of the Indies* (1542).

Legend." *Fearful of the vast Spanish empire, European Protestants attacked the Spanish as bloodthirsty zealots determined to enrich themselves, destroy indigenous peoples, and spread Catholicism.*

In this reading, Las Casas describes a series of interactions between Spaniards and the inhabitants of Hispaniola (Haiti).

FOCUS QUESTIONS

1. How does Las Casas describe the Indians at the time the Spanish first arrived?

2. According to Las Casas, how did the Spanish treat the Indians? How did the Indians react? How did the condition of the Indians change over time?

3. What might account for the differences in Las Casas and Christopher Columbus's (Document 1.1) depictions of Euro-Indian interactions?

The Indies were discovered in the year one thousand four hundred and ninety-two. In the following year a great many Spaniards went there with the intention of settling the land. Thus, forty-nine years have passed since the first settlers penetrated the land, the first so claimed being the large and most happy isle called Hispaniola [Haiti], which is six hundred leagues in circumference. Around it in all directions are many other islands, some very big, others very small, and all of them were, as we saw with our own eyes, densely populated with native peoples called Indians. This large island was perhaps the most densely populated place in the world. There must be close to two hundred leagues of land on this island, and the seacoast has been explored for more than ten thousand leagues, and each day more of it is being explored. And all the land so far discovered is a beehive of people; it is as though God had crowded into these lands the great majority of mankind.

And of all the infinite universe of humanity, these people are the most guileless, the most devoid of wickedness and duplicity, the most obedient and faithful to their native masters and to the Spanish Christians whom they serve. They are by nature the most humble, patient, and peaceable, holding no grudges, free from embroilments, neither excitable nor quarrelsome. These people are the most devoid of rancors, hatreds, or desire for vengeance of any people in the world. And because they are so weak and complaisant, they are less able to endure heavy labor and soon die of no matter what malady. The sons of nobles among us, brought up in the enjoyments of life's refinements, are no more delicate than are these Indians, even those among them who are of the lowest rank of laborers. They are also poor people, for they not only possess little but have no desire to possess worldly goods. For this reason they are not arrogant, embittered, or greedy. Their repasts are such that the food of the holy fathers in the desert can scarcely be more parsimonious, scanty, and poor. As to their dress, they are generally naked, with only their pudenda covered somewhat. And when they cover their shoulders it is with a square cloth no more than two *varas* in size. They have no beds, but sleep on a kind of matting or else in a kind of suspended net called *bamacas*. They are very clean in their persons, with alert, intelligent minds, docile and open to doctrine, very apt to receive our holy Catholic faith, to be endowed with virtuous customs, and to behave in a godly fashion. And once they begin to hear the tidings of the Faith, they are so insistent on knowing more and on taking the sacraments of the Church and on observing the divine cult that, truly, the missionaries who are here need to be endowed by God with great patience in order to cope with such eagerness. Some of the secular Spaniards who have been here for many years say that the goodness of the Indians is undeniable and that if this gifted people could be brought to know the one true God they would be the most fortunate people in the world.

Yet into this sheepfold, into this land of meek outcasts there came some Spaniards who immediately behaved like ravening wild beasts, wolves, tigers, or lions that had been starved for many days. And Spaniards have behaved in no other way during the past forty years, down to the present time, for they are still acting like ravening beasts, killing, terrorizing, afflicting, torturing, and destroy-ing the native peoples, doing all this with the strangest and most varied new methods of cruelty, never seen or heard of before....

The common ways mainly employed by the Spaniards who call themselves Christian and who have gone there to extirpate those pitiful nations and wipe them off the earth is by unjustly waging cruel and bloody wars. Then, when they have slain all those who fought for their lives or to escape the tortures they would have to endure, that is to say, when they have slain all the native rulers and young men (since the Spaniards usually spare only the women and children, who are subjected to the hardest and bitterest servitude ever suffered by man or beast), they enslave any survivors. With these infernal methods of tyranny they debase and weaken countless numbers of those pitiful Indian nations.

Their reason for killing and destroying such an infinite number of souls is that the Christians have an ultimate aim, which is to acquire gold, and to swell themselves with riches in a very brief time and thus rise to a high estate disproportionate to their merits. It should be kept in mind that their insatiable greed and ambition, the greatest ever seen in the world, is the cause of their villainies. And also, those lands are so rich and felicitous, the native peoples so meek and patient, so easy to subject, that our Spaniards have no more consider-ation for them than beasts. And I say this from my own knowledge of the acts I witnessed. But I should not say "than beasts" for, thanks be to God, they have treated beasts with some respect; I should say instead like excrement on the public squares. And thus they have deprived the Indians of their lives and souls, for the millions I mentioned have died without the Faith and without the benefit of the sacraments. This is a well-known and proven fact which even the tyrant Governors, themselves killers, know and admit. And never have the Indians in all the Indies committed any act against the Spanish Christians, until those Christians have first and many times committed countless cruel aggressions against them or against neighboring nations. For in the beginning the Indians regarded the Spaniards as angels from Heaven. Only after the Spaniards had used violence against them, killing, robbing, torturing, did the Indians ever rise up against them. . . .

On the Island Hispaniola was where the Spaniards first landed, as I have said. Here those Christians perpetrated their first ravages and oppressions against the native peoples. This was the first land in the New World to be destroyed and depopulated by the Christians, and here they began their subjection of the women and children, taking them away from the Indians to use them and ill use them, eating the food they provided with their sweat and toil. The Spaniards did not content themselves with what the Indians gave them of their own free will, according to their ability, which was always too little to satisfy enormous appetites, for a Christian eats and consumes in one day an amount of food that would suffice to feed three houses inhabited by ten Indians for one month. And they committed other acts of force and violence and oppression which made the Indians realize that these men had not come from Heaven. And some of the Indians concealed their foods while others concealed their wives and children and still others fled to the mountains to avoid the terrible transactions of the Christians.

And the Christians attacked them with buffets and beatings, until finally they laid hands on the nobles of the villages. Then they behaved with such temerity and shamelessness that the most powerful ruler of the islands had to see his own wife raped by a Christian officer.

From that time onward the Indians began to seek ways to throw the Christians out of their lands. They took up arms, but their weapons were very weak and of little service in offense and still less in defense. (Because of this, the wars of the Indians against each other are little more than games played by children.) And the Christians, with their horses and swords and pikes began to carry out massacres and strange cruelties against them. They attacked the towns and spared neither the children nor the aged nor pregnant women nor women in childbed, not only stabbing them and dismembering them but cutting them to pieces as if dealing with sheep in the slaughter house. They laid bets as to who, with one stroke of the sword, could split a man in two or could cut off his head or spill out his entrails with a single stroke of the pike. They took infants from their mothers' breasts, snatching them by the legs and pitching them headfirst against the crags or snatched them by the arms and threw them into the rivers, roaring with laughter and saying as the babies fell into the water, "Boil there, you offspring of the devil!" Other infants they put to the sword along with their mothers and anyone else who happened to be nearby. They made some low wide gallows on which the hanged victim's feet almost touched the ground, stringing up their victims in lots of thirteen, in memory of Our Redeemer and His twelve Apostles, then set burning wood at their feet and thus burned them alive. To others they attached straw or wrapped their whole bodies in straw and set them afire. With still others, all those they wanted to capture alive, they cut off their hands and hung them round the victim's neck, saying, "Go now, carry the message," meaning, Take the news to the Indians who have fled to the mountains. They usually dealt with the chieftains and nobles in the following way: they made a grid of rods which they placed on forked sticks, then lashed the victims to the grid and lighted a smoldering fire underneath, so that little by little, as those captives screamed in despair and torment, their souls would leave them. . . .

After the wars and the killings had ended, when usually there survived only some boys, some women, and children, these survivors were distributed among the Christians to be slaves. The *repartimiento* or distribution was made according to the rank and importance of the Christian to whom the Indians were allocated, one of them being given thirty, another forty, still another, one or two hundred, and besides the rank of the Christian there was also to be considered in what favor he stood with the tyrant they called Governor. The pretext was that these allocated Indians were to be instructed in the articles of the Christian Faith. As if those Christians who were as a rule foolish and cruel and greedy and vicious could be caretakers of souls! And the care they took was to send the men to the mines to dig for gold, which is intolerable labor, and to send the women into the fields of the big ranches to hoe and till the land, work suitable for strong men. Nor to either the men or the women did they give any food except herbs and legumes, things of little substance. The milk in the breasts of the women with infants dried up and thus in a short while the infants perished. And since men and women were separated, there could be no marital relations. And the men died in the mines and the women died on the ranches from the same causes, exhaustion and hunger. And thus was depopulated that island which had been densely populated.

1.3

Captain John Smith Describes the Founding of Jamestown (1607)

Preoccupied with economic, political, and religious unrest for much of the sixteenth century, the English began colonization efforts later than many European powers. In 1607, the Virginia Company of London deployed 105 settlers to a site on the James River near Chesapeake Bay. Calling their encampment Jamestown, the men chose a location easily defended against the powerful Powhatan Confederacy but plagued by a lack of fresh water. Convinced that local Indians would feed

SOURCE: John Smith, *The Generall Historie of Virginia, New England & the Summer Isles . . .* [1624] (Glasgow, 1907).

them, most of the settlers searched for gold instead of planting crops. Not surprisingly, the colony did not flourish, and only thirty-eight men survived in January 1608. The Virginia Company hoped that Captain John Smith could rescue the troubled settlement.

A colorful figure, Smith had served as a soldier of fortune in wars against the Turks and the Spanish. Declaring "He who does not work, will not eat," Smith instituted discipline, encouraged farming, and established relations with the Indians. In 1609, a gunpowder accident forced Smith to return to England. In his absence, Jamestown foundered again. Although the cultivation of mild varieties of tobacco provided a lucrative export, the Virginia colony struggled through the 1620s.

In this excerpt, Smith recounts his first months in Jamestown. (Some spelling has been modernized.)

FOCUS QUESTIONS

1. How does Smith describe the initial state of Jamestown?
2. How does Smith improve the situation? How does he seem to view his own contributions to the colony?
3. What enabled Jamestown to survive?

Being thus left to our fortunes, it fortuned that within ten days scarce ten amongst us could either go or well stand, such extreme weakness and sickness oppressed us. And thereat none need marvel, if they consider the cause and reason, which was this:

Whilst the ships stayed, our allowance was somewhat bettered by a daily proportion of biscuit, which the sailors would pilfer to sell, give, or exchange with us for money, sassafras, furs, or love. But when they departed, there remained neither tavern, beer house, nor place of relief but the common kettle. Had we been as free from all sins as gluttony and drunkenness, we might have been canonized for saints. But our President would never have been admitted, for engrossing to his private [i.e., his own use] oatmeal, sack, oil, aquavitae [liquor], beef, eggs, or what not, but the [common] kettle. That, indeed, he allowed equally to be distributed, and that was half a pint of wheat, and as much barley boiled with water for a man a day. And this having fried some 26 weeks in the ship's hold contained as many worms as grains, so that we might truly call it rather so much bran than corn. Our drink was water, our lodgings castles in the air [i.e., in the trees].

With this lodging and diet, our extreme toil in bearing and planting Pallisadoes so strained and bruised us, and our continual labor in the extremity of the heat had so weakened us, as were cause sufficient to have made us as miserable in our native country or any other place in the world.

From May to September those that escaped lived upon sturgeon and sea crabs. Fifty in this time we buried.

The rest seeing the President's projects to escape these miseries in our penance by flight (who all this time had neither felt want nor sickness) so moved our dead spirits that we deposed him and established Ratcliffe in his place (Gosnold being dead), Kendall deposed. Smith newly recovered [from illness], Martin and Ratcliffe was by his care preserved and relieved, and the most of the soldiers recovered with the skillful diligence of Master Thomas Wotton, our surgeon general.

But now was all our provision spent, the sturgeon gone, all hopes abandoned. Each hour expecting the fury of the savages, when God, the patron of all good endeavors, in that desperate extremity so changed the hearts of the savages, that they brought such plenty of their fruits and provisions that no man wanted.

And now, where some, affirmed it was ill done of the Council to send forth men so badly provided, this incontradictable reason will show them plainly they are too ill advised to nourish such ill conceits. First, the fault of our going was our own. What could be thought fitting or necessary we had; but what we should find or want or where we should be we were all ignorant; and supposing to make our passage in two months with victual to live and the advantage of the spring to work, we were at sea five months, where we both spent our victual and lost the opportunity of the time and season to plant. . . .

Such actions have ever since the world's beginning been subject to such accidents, and everything of worth is found full of difficulties; but nothing so difficult as to establish a commonwealth so far remote from men and means, and where men's minds are so untoward as neither do well themselves nor suffer others. But to proceed.

The new President and Martin, being little beloved, of weak judgment in dangers and less industry in peace, committed the managing of all things abroad to Captain Smith; who by his own example, good words, and fair promises set some to mow, others to bind thatch, some to build houses, others to thatch them, himself always bearing the greatest task for his own share, so that in short time he provided most of them lodgings, neglecting any for himself.

This done, seeing the savages' superfluity begin to decrease [Captain Smith] (with some of the workmen) shipped himself in the shallop to search the country for trade. The want of the language, knowledge to manage his boat without sails, the want of a sufficient power (knowing the multitude of the savages), apparel for his men, and other necessaries, were infinite impediments, yet no discouragement.

Being but six or seven in company, he went down the river to Kecoughtan, where at first they scorned him, as a famished man, and would in derision offer him a handful of corn, a piece of bread for their swords and muskets, and such like proportions also for their apparel.

But seeing by trade and courtesy there was nothing to be had, he made bold to try such conclusions as necessity enforced, though contrary to his commission. [He] let fly his muskets, ran his boat on shore, whereat they all fled into the woods. So marching towards their houses, they might see great heaps of corn: much ado he had to restrain his hungry soldiers from present taking of it, expecting as it happened that the savages would assault them; as not long after they did with a most hideous noise.

Sixty or seventy of them, some black, some red, some white, some parti-colored came in a square order, singing and dancing out of the woods, with their Okee (which was an idol made of skins, stuffed with moss, all painted and hung with chains and copper) borne before them. And in this manner, being well armed with clubs, targets, bows and arrows, they charged the English, that so kindly received them with their muskets loaden with pistol shot, that down fell their god and divers lay on the ground.

The rest fled again to the woods and ere long sent one of the Quiyoughka-soucks to offer peace and redeem their Okee. Smith told them if only six of them would come unarmed and load his boat, he would not only be their friend, but restore them their Okee, and give them beads, copper, and hatchets besides: which on both sides was to their contents performed: and then they brought him venison, turkeys, wild fowl, bread, and what they had, singing and dancing in sign of friendship till they departed. . . .

Smith, perceiving (notwithstanding their late misery) not any regarded but from hand to mouth (the company being well recovered), caused the penance to be provided with things fitting to get provision for the year following. . . .

1.4

John Winthrop, Reasons for Emigrating to New England (1629)

John Winthrop was born in Suffolk, England, in 1587. An only child, Winthrop expected to inherit his father's estate, Groton Manor. He received an education befitting an aspiring country gentleman. But his conversion to Puritanism profoundly altered the course of Winthrop's life.

Often misunderstood today, the Puritans were Protestants who opposed the corruption in the Church of England and the increasing materialism and individualism engulfing their nation. They hoped to purify their church in order to make their society more pleasing to God. Through hard work, moderation, and faith, they aspired to build a moral and charitable community. In 1628, several Puritan merchants received a charter to establish a colony in New England. Organized as the Massachusetts Bay Company, the colonists elected John Winthrop governor.

SOURCE: R. C. Winthrop, *Life and Letters of John Winthrop*, 2 vols. (Boston, 1869), 1:309–11.

In this passage, Winthrop explains why devoted Christians should follow the Puritans to New England. (Spelling has been modernized.)

FOCUS QUESTIONS

1. What are the major reasons Winthrop provides for moving to the New World?
2. Do you see similarities between the conditions Winthrop describes and modern society? If so, provide examples.
3. If you had lived in England in 1629, would you have joined the Puritans? Why or why not?

Reasons to be considered for justifying the undertakers of the intended Plantation in New England, & for encouraging such whose hearts God shall move to join with them in it.

1. It will be a service to the Church of great consequence to carry the Gospel into those parts of the world . . . & to raise a Bulwark against the kingdom of Anti-Christ which the Jesuits labor to rear up in those parts.

2. All other churches of Europe are brought to desolation, & our sins, for which the Lord begins already to frown upon us & to cut us short, do threaten evil times to be coming upon us, & who knows, but that God hath provided this place to be a refuge for many whom he means to save out of the general calamity, & seeing the Church hath no place left to fly into but the wilderness, what better work can there be, than to go & provide tabernacles & food for her against she comes thither:

3. This Land grows weary of her Inhabitants, so as man, who is the most precious of all creatures, is here more vile & base than the earth we tread upon, & of less price among us than an horse or a sheep: masters are forced by authority to entertain servants, parents to maintain their own children, all towns complain of the burthen of their poor, though we have taken up many unnecessary yea unlawful trades to maintain them, & we use the authority of the Law to hinder the increase of our people. . . .

4. The whole earth is the Lord's garden & he hath given it to the Sons of men with a general Commission: Gen 1:28: increase & multiply, & replenish the earth & subdue it, . . . why then should we stand striving here for places of habitation . . . & in the meantime suffer a whole Continent as fruitful & convenient for the use of man to lie waste without any improvement?

5. . . . All arts & Trades are carried in that deceitful & unrighteous course, as it is almost impossible for a good & upright man, to maintain his charge & live comfortably in any of them.

6. The fountains of Learning & Religion are so corrupted as . . . most children (even the best wits & of fairest hopes) are perverted, corrupted, & utterly overthrown by the multitude of evil examples. . . .

7. What can be a better work, & more honorable & worthy a Christian than to help raise & support a particular Church while it is in the Infancy, & to join his forces with such a company of faithful people. . . .

1.5

William Bradford on Sickness among the Natives (1633)

The arrival of Europeans in North America had devastating consequences for American Indians. Lacking resistance to European and African infections, many tribes were decimated by disease, especially the highly contagious smallpox. In some regions, 90 percent of the indigenous population perished. But Europeans were also affected by disease. After some explorers contracted syphilis in the New World, the venereal disease ravaged the Old World for centuries.

After the Pilgrims arrived in New England on the Mayflower, *William Bradford was elected governor of the Plymouth colony. In addition to his political duties, Bradford served as Plymouth's historian.*

In this excerpt from his A History of Plimouth Plantation *(1651), Bradford describes the catastrophic impact of smallpox on New England tribes. (Some spelling has been modernized.)*

FOCUS QUESTIONS

1. How did these Indians contract smallpox? How did the disease affect them?

2. How did the English react to the Indians' plight?

3. Why does Bradford believe the Indians became ill? Do you agree with his conclusions? Explain your answers.

SOURCE: William Bradford, *History of Plimouth Plantation* (Boston, 1898), 388–389.

I am now to relate some strange and remarkable passages. There was a company of people [who] lived in the country, up above in the river of Connecticut, a great way from their trading house there, and were enemies to those Indians which lived about them, and of whom they stood in some fear of being a stout people. About a thousand of them had enclosed themselves in a fort, which they had strongly palisaded. About 3 or 4 Dutch men went up in the beginning of winter to live with them, to get their trade, and prevent them for bringing it to the English, or to fall into amity with them; but at spring to bring all down to their place. But their enterprise failed, for it pleased God to visit these Indians with a great sickness, and such a mortality that of a 1000 above 900 and a half of them died, and many of them did rot above ground for want of burial, and the Dutch men almost starved before they could get away because of the ice and snow. But about Feb: they got with much difficulty to their trading house; whom they kindly relieved, being almost spent with hunger and cold. Being thus refreshed by them diverse days, they got their own place, and the Dutch were very thankful for this kindness.

This spring, also those Indians that lived about their trading house there fell sick of the small pox and died most miserably; for a sorer disease cannot befall them; they fear it more than the plague; for usually they that have this disease have them in abundance, and for want of bedding and lining and other helps, they fall into lamentable condition, as they lie on their hard mats, the pox breaking and mattering, and running one into another, their skin cleaving (by reason thereof) to the mats they lie on; when they turn them, a whole side will flee off at once, (as it were) and they will be all of a gore blood, most fearful to behold; and then being very sore, what with cold and other distempers, they die like rotten sheep. The condition of this people was so lamentable, and they fell down so generally of this disease, as they were (in the end) not able to help one another; no, not to make a fire, not to fetch a little water to drink, nor any to bury the dead; but would strive as long as they could, and when they could procure no other means to make fire, they would burn the wooden trays and dishes they ate their meat in, and their very bows and arrows; and some would crawl out on all four to get a little water, and some times die by the way, and not be able to get in again. But those of the English house, (though at first they were afraid of the infection,) yet seeing their woeful and sad condition, and hearing their pitiful cries and lamentations, they had compassion of them, and daily fetched them wood and water, and made them fires, got them victuals whilst they lived, and buried them when they died. For very few of them escaped, notwithstanding they did what they could for them, to the hazard of them selves. The chief Sachem himself now died, and almost all his friends and kindred. But by the marvelous goodness and providence of God not one of the English was so much as sick, or in the least measure tainted with this disease, though they daily did these offices for them for many weeks together. And this mercy which they showed them was kindly taken, and thankfully acknowledged of all the Indians that knew or heard of the same; and their mrs. here did much commend and reward them for the same.

1.6

The Indians of the Six Nations to William & Mary College (1744)

Despite devastating losses from disease and warfare, Indians fought to preserve their culture amidst European settlement. At first, many Indians and whites engaged in mutually beneficial commercial relationships. But as the white population grew, Indians resisted encroachment on their farming and hunting grounds. Tensions often exploded in horrific violence perpetrated by both sides. Many Indians particularly resented whites' attempts to convert them to Christianity and European customs.

In this passage, Indians living in the Chesapeake respond to an overture from their white neighbors.

FOCUS QUESTIONS

1. What have the whites offered the Indians of the Six Nations?
2. How do the Indians respond?
3. How did relations between the settlers and the Indians change over time? Do you think peaceful coexistence was possible? Why or why not?

Sirs,

We know that you highly esteem the kind of learning taught in Colleges, and that the Maintenance of our young Men, while with you, would be very expensive to you. We are convinced, therefore, that you mean to do us Good by your Proposal; and we thank you heartily. But you, who are wise, must know that different Nations have different Conceptions of things; and you will therefore not take it amiss, if our Ideas of this kind of Education happen not to be the same with yours. We have had some Experience of it. Several of our Young People were formerly brought up at the Colleges of the Northern Provinces; they were instructed in all your Sciences; but, when they came back to us, they were bad Runners, ignorant

SOURCE: Samuel G. Drake, *Biography and History of the Indians of North America*, Third edition, O. L. Perkins and Hillard, Gray & Company, Boston, 1834, Vol.1, p. 27.

of every means of living in the Woods, unable to bear either Cold or Hunger, knew neither how to build a Cabin, take a Deer, or kill an Enemy, spoke our Language imperfectly, were therefore neither fit for Hunters, Warriors, nor Counsellors; they were totally good for nothing. We are, however, not the less obliged by your kind Offer, tho' we decline accepting it; and, to show our grateful Sense of it, if the Gentlemen of Virginia will send us a Dozen of their Sons, we will take care of their Education; instruct them in all we know, and make Men of them.

1.7

Jesuit Comparison of French and Native Life (1657–1658)

Hoping to spread Roman Catholicism and to increase trade, the French established several outposts in North America. By the 1670s, French settlers in Canada had built a lucrative fur trade, and missionaries had converted many local tribes. Most of the priests were Jesuits, members of a Catholic order devoted to education. Founded in 1534, the Jesuits pledged to strengthen Roman Catholicism against Protestant expansion. After years of rigorous study, Jesuits were often sent alone to live among potential converts. Jesuit missionaries in Canada produced extensive accounts of their experiences. Published as Jesuit Relations, *their writings provide invaluable information about the meeting of cultures in the New World.*

In this passage, a Jesuit priest compares French and Indian customs.

FOCUS QUESTIONS

1. What are some of the ways that the French and the Indians differed?

2. What does the priest appear to admire about the Indians? What does he seem to condemn?

3. How are the Indians adapting to French ways?

SOURCE: *The Jesuit Relations and Allied Documents*, Vol. 44, *Iroquois, Lower Canada*, 1656–58, ed. Reuben G. Thwaites (Cleveland, 1899), 277–309. Republished by Pageant Books, New York (1959).

Although they have a tenderer and more delicate skin than the French—... [one] ascribes this delicacy to the oil and grease with which they anoint and rub themselves,—yet those good people have none of our Europeans' softness and delicacy. They find sleep sweeter upon the earth for a bed, with a pillow of wood, than do many upon down.... The Savages go almost half naked during the Winter, while the French dress as warmly as they can.

Concerning the sense of sight, it is quite certain that, in general, it is more perfect among the Savages than among the French.... I would readily believe that the superiority enjoyed by them, over us, in this particular, is due to their not drinking wine or eating salt, spices, or other things capable of drying up the humors of the eye and impairing its tone. However it may be regarding the excellence of their eyesight, it must be admitted that it often finds beauty where ours sees only ugliness....

In France, to make a face more beautiful, it is cleansed of oil and washed as carefully as possible. The Savages, on the contrary, anoint and grease it as much as they can, thinking it more pleasing the more shiny it is with their grease or oil. To make one's self hideous in Europe, one daubs himself with black, yellow, and blue; and that is the very thing that makes a Savage handsome and of very pleasing appearance....

Each thinks his own fashion the most beautiful....

The beard is held to add grace and adornment to man, but this opinion is not everywhere received. In that new world, a beard is the greatest disfigurement that a face can have....

In Europe, if a boy should dress up like a girl, he would be a masquerader. In new France, a woman's dress is not improper for a man....

In Europe, the seam of stockings is behind the leg.... Among the Savages it is otherwise; the seam of stockings worn by men is between the legs, and here they fasten little ornaments—made of porcupine quills, stained scarlet, and in the form of fringe or of spangles—which meet when they walk, and make ... a pretty effect, not easily described. The women wear this ornamentation on the outer side of the leg.

In France, patterns and raised shoes are considered the most beautiful.... The Savages' shoes are as flat as tennis-shoes, but much wider, especially in winter, when they stuff and line them amply to keep away the cold.

Shirts are in Europe worn next to the skin, under the other garments. The Savages wear them usually over their dress, to shield it from snow and rain....

The end of a shirt protruding from under the coat is an indecorous thing; but not so in Canadas. You will see Savages dressed in French attire, with worsted stockings and a cloak, but without any breeches; while before and ... behind are seen two large shirt-flaps hanging down below the cloak.... That fashion seems all the more tasteful in their eyes because they regard our breeches as an encumbrance....

Politeness and propriety have taught us to carry handkerchiefs. In this matter the Savages charge us with filthiness—because, they say, we place what is unclean in a fine white piece of linen, and put it away in our pockets as something very precious, while they throw it upon the ground....

Most Europeans sit on raised seats, using round or square tables. The Savages eat from the ground....

In France, food and drink are taken together. The Algonquins follow quite the contrary custom in their feasts, first eating what is served to them, and then drinking, without touching food again. . . .

We wash meat to cleanse it of blood and impurities; the Savages do not wash it, for fear of losing its blood and a part of its fat. . . . We usually begin dinner with soup, which is the last dish among the Savages, the broth of the pot serving them for drink. Bread is eaten here with meat and other courses; if you give some to a Savage, he will make a separate course of it and very often eat it last. Yet they are gradually adapting themselves to our way.

In most parts of Europe, when any one makes a call he is invited to drink; among the Savages he is invited to eat. . . .

When the Savages are not hunting or on a journey, their usual posture is to recline or sit on the ground. They cannot remain standing, maintaining that their legs become swollen immediately. Seats higher than the ground they dislike; the French, on the contrary, use chairs, benches, or stools, leaving the ground and litter to the animals.

A good dancer in France does not move his arms much, and holds his body erect, moving his feet so nimbly that, you would say, he spurns the ground and wishes to stay in the air. The Savages, on the contrary, bend over in their dances, thrusting out their arms and moving violently as if they were kneading bread, while they strike the ground with their feet so vigorously that one would say they were determined to make it tremble, or to bury themselves in it up to the neck. . . .

In France, children are carried on the arm, or clasped to the breast; in Canadas, the mothers bear them behind their backs. In France, they are kept as well covered as possible. . . . The cradle, in France, is left at home; there the women carry it with their children; it is composed merely of a cedar board, on which the poor little one is bound like a bundle. . . .

In France, a Workman does not expect his pay until he completes his task; the Savages ask it in advance. . . .

Europeans have no hesitation about telling their names and conditions, but you embarrass a Savage by asking him his name; if you do ask him, he will say that he does not know, and will make a sign to someone else to tell it.

In France, when a father gives his daughter in marriage, he allows her a dowry. There, it is given to the girl's father.

In Europe, the children inherit from their parents; among the Hurons the nephews, sons of the father's sister, are their uncle's heirs; and the Savage's small belongings will be given to friends of the deceased, rather than to his children. . . .

In France, the man usually takes to his house the woman he marries; there the man goes to the woman's house to dwell.

In France, if any one fall into a fit of anger, or harbor some evil purpose, or meditate some harm, he is reviled, threatened, and punished; there, they give him presents, to soothe his ill-humor, cure his mental ailment, and put good thoughts into his head. This custom, in the sincerity of their actions, is not a bad one; for if he is angry, or is devising some ill to resent an offense—touch this present, his anger and his evil purpose are immediately effaced from his mind.

In a large part of Europe, ceremonies and compliments are indulged in to such an excess as to drive out sincerity. There, quite the contrary, sincerity is entirely naked. . . .

In Europe, we unclothe the dead as much as we can, leaving them only what is necessary to veil them and hide them from our eyes. The Savages, however, give them all that they can, anointing and attiring them as if for their wedding, and burying them with all their favorite belongings.

The French are stretched lengthwise in their graves, while the Savages, in burying their dead make them take in the grave the position which they held in their mothers' wombs. In some parts of France, the dead are placed with their heads turned toward the East; the Savages make them face the West.

1.8

Jesuit Observations on the "Enslavement" of Native American Women (1610–1614)

Gender greatly affected how European settlers and Native Americans perceived one another. Whereas sex refers to male and female biological characteristics, gender describes the roles and traits identifying sexual differences. Conceptions of gender can vary widely across time and place. Gender interconnects with how societies define work, education, property ownership, appearance, fashion, and parenting.

In the following readings, we see several examples of how white settlers' views of gender influenced their impressions of tribal customs.

FOCUS QUESTIONS

1. How do these passages describe the roles of men and women in tribal life?

2. How might Indians have disagreed with this writer's conclusions?

SOURCE: Reuben Gold Thwaites, ed. *The Jesuit Relations and Allied Documents* (Cleveland, 1896–1901), Vol 1, *Acadia: 1610–1613*, pp. 257, 259; Vol 2, *Acadia: 1612–1614*, pp. 77, 79. Republished by Pageant Books, New York (1959).

3. How do these readings differ from the portrayal of gender found in
    Document 1.9?

[1610–1613]

The care of household affairs, and whatever work there may be in the family, are
placed upon the women. They build and repair the wigwams, carry water and
wood, and prepare the food; their duties and position are those of slaves, laborers,
and beasts of burden. The pursuits of hunting and war belong to the men.
Thence arise the isolation and numerical weakness of the race. For the women,
although naturally prolific, cannot, on account of their occupation in these labors,
either bring forth fully developed offspring, or properly nourish them after they
have been brought forth; therefore they either suffer abortion, or forsake their
newborn children, while engaged in carrying water, procuring wood, and other
tasks, so that scarcely one infant in thirty survives until youth. To this there is
added their ignorance of medicine, because of which they seldom recover from
illnesses which are at all severe.

[1612–1614]

To obtain the necessaries of life they [the Indians of Acadia] endure cold
and hunger in an extraordinary manner. During eight or ten days, if the
necessity is imposed on them, they will follow the chase in fasting, and they
hunt with the greatest ardor when the snow is deepest and the cold most
severe. And yet these same Savages, the offspring, so to speak, of Boreas [the
North Wind] and the ice, when once they have returned with their booty and
installed themselves in their tents, become indolent and unwilling to perform
any labor whatever, imposing this entirely upon the women. The latter,
besides the onerous role of bearing and rearing the children, also transport
the game from the place where it has fallen; they are the hewers of wood and
drawers of water; they make and repair the household utensils; they prepare
food; they skin the game and prepare the hides like fullers; they sew garments;
they catch fish and gather shellfish for food; often they even hunt; they make
the canoes, that is, skiffs of marvelous rapidity, out of bark; they set up the
tents wherever and whenever they stop for the night—in short, the men
concern themselves with nothing but the more laborious hunting and the
waging of war. For this reason almost every one has several wives, and
especially the Sagamores, since they cannot maintain their power and keep
up the number of their dependents unless they have not only many children to
inspire fear or conciliate favor, but also many slaves to perform patiently the
menial tasks of every sort that are necessary. For their wives are regarded and
treated as slaves.

1.9

Reverend John Heckewelder Challenges European Stereotypes of Native American Gender Relations (1819)

In this passage, Reverend John Heckewelder (1743–1823) offers another interpretation of gender roles in Indian life. Born in Bedford, England, Heckewelder emigrated to America with his family as a boy. After studying at a Moravian school in Pennsylvania, he worked as a cooper's apprentice until he seized the opportunity to travel to the Ohio country with a Moravian missionary. He later became a missionary himself and spent years working among the Delaware Indians. After returning to Pennsylvania upon retiring in 1786, Heckewelder advised the U.S. government on Indian affairs and wrote numerous accounts of Indian life. In this selection from his History, Manners, and Customs of the Indian Nations Who Once Inhabited Pennsylvania and the Neighboring States *(1819), Heckewelder recalls the daily lives of Indian men and women.*

FOCUS QUESTIONS

1. What are some of the writer's observations about the tribal duties of Indian men and women?

2. How do these conclusions differ from those found in Document 1.8? With which document do you most agree? Explain why.

There are many persons who believe, from the labor that they see the Indian women perform, that they are in a manner treated as slaves. These labors, indeed, are hard, compared with the tasks that are imposed upon families in civilized society; but they are no more than their fair share, under every consideration and due allowance, of the hardships attendant on savage life. Therefore they are not only voluntarily, but cheerfully submitted to; and as women are not obliged to

SOURCE: Rev. John Heckewelder, *History, Manners, and Customs of the Indian Nations Who Once Inhabited Pennsylvania and the Neighboring States*, rev. ed., by Rev. William Reichel (Philadelphia: Historical Society of Pennsylvania, 1876), pp. 154–158.

live with their husbands any longer than suits their pleasure or convenience, it cannot be supposed that they would submit to be loaded with unjust or unequal burdens. . . .

When a marriage takes place, the duties and labors incumbent on each party re well known to both. It is understood that the husband is to build the house for them to dwell in, to find the necessary implements of husbandry, as axes, hoes, &c., to provide a canoe, and also dishes, bowls, and other necessary vessels for housekeeping. The woman generally has a kettle or two, and some other articles of kitchen furniture, which she brings with her. The husband, as master of the family, considers himself bound to support it by his bodily exertions, as hunting, trapping, &c.; the woman as his help-mate, takes upon herself the labors of the field, and is far from considering them as more important than those to which her husband is subjected, being well satisfied that with his gun and traps he can maintain a family in any place where game is to be found; nor do they think it any hardship imposed upon them; for they themselves say, that while their field labor employs them at most six weeks in the year, that of the men continues the whole year round. . . .

The work of the women is not hard or difficult. They are both able and willing to do it, and always perform it with cheerfulness. Mothers teach their daughters those duties which common sense would otherwise point out to them when grown up. Within doors, their labor is very trifling; there is seldom more than one pot or kettle to attend to. There is no scrubbing of the house, and but little to wash, and that not often. Their principal occupations are to cut and fetch in the fire wood, till the ground, sow and reap the grain, and pound the corn in mortars for their pottage, and to make bread which they bake in the ashes. When going on a journey, or to hunting camps with their husbands, if they have no horses, they carry a pack on their backs which often appears heavier than it really is; it generally consists of a blanket, a dressed deer skin for moccasins, a few articles of kitchen furniture, as a kettle, bowl, or dish with spoons, and some bread, corn, salt &c., for their nourishment. I have never known an Indian woman to complain of the hardship of carrying this burden, which serves for their own comfort and support as well as of their husbands.

The tilling of the ground at home, getting of the fire wood, and pounding of corn in mortars, is frequently done by female parties, much in the manner of those husking, quilting, and other *frolics* (as they are called), which are so common in some parts of the United States [among whites], particularly to the eastward. The labor is thus quickly and easily performed. . . .

When the harvest is in, which generally happens by the end of September, the women have little else to do than to prepare the daily victuals, and get fire wood, until the latter end of February or beginning of March, as the season is more or less backward, when they go to their sugar camps, where they extract sugar from the maple tree. The men having built and repaired their temporary cabin, and made all the troughs of various sizes, the women commence making sugar, while the men are looking out for meat, at this time generally fat bears, which are still in their winter quarters. When at home, they will occasionally assist their wives in gathering sap, and watch the kettles in their absence, that the syrup may not boil over.

A man who wishes his wife to be with him while he is out hunting in the woods, needs only tell her, that on such a day they will go to such a place, where he will hunt for a length of time, and she will be sure to have provisions and every thing else that is necessary in complete readiness, and well packed up to carry to the spot; . . .

The husband generally leaves the skins and poultry which he has procured by hunting to the care of his wife, who sells or barters them away to the best advantage for such necessaries as are wanted in the family; not forgetting to supply her husband with what he stands in need of, who, when he receives it from her hands never fails to return her thanks in the kindest manner. If debts had been previously contracted, either by the woman, or by her and her husband jointly, or if a horse should be wanted, as much is laid aside as will be sufficient to pay the debts or purchase the horse.

2

✳

Colonial Society

During the seventeenth century, thousands of Europeans settled in North America. Their reasons for emigrating varied widely. Some came for religious freedom. Some sought economic opportunities. Others arrived as indentured servants or slaves. The migration created a multicultural society characterized by accommodation and tension. While some people found personal freedom and economic advancement in the colonies, others suffered deprivation and discrimination.

THEMES TO CONSIDER

- How a colonist's daily experiences might have differed depending on where he or she lived
- Family life and gender roles
- Labor, class, and poverty
- Interconnections among race, gender, and the law
- The role of religion in colonists' lives
- Conflicts between Europeans and Indians
- Regional differences among the colonies
- The origins and importance of unfree labor and slavery in the colonies

2.1

The London Company Instructs the Governor in Virginia (1622)

In 1606, James I granted charters to two commercial trading companies, one based in London and the other in Plymouth. Charged with colonizing the eastern seaboard of North America, the companies received overlapping land grants extending from contemporary Maine to Cape Fear. The company to succeed first would receive the disputed territory. Colonists worked for the companies and were subject to stockholders.

While the Plymouth Company failed quickly, the London Company sustained a struggling settlement in Jamestown. Harsh living conditions and clashes with the Powhatan Confederacy stymied the colony's growth. But after John Rolfe perfected a mild variety of tobacco, Virginians gained a valuable export. By 1619, the London Company was dispatching resources and people to the colony. The same year also marked the establishment of the first representative government in America, the House of Burgesses.

To attract investors and settlers, the London Company awarded fifty-acre plots ("headrights") to anyone paying for his or her passage or that of a worker. By subsidizing the voyages of indentured servants, Virginia planters began accruing large tracts of land. With desperate economic conditions in England, thousands of young people were willing to sell their labor in order to reach the New World.

Despite Virginia's increasing prosperity, the colony was plagued by infighting, debt, diseases, and continuing conflicts with the Indians. In 1622, after Indians killed 347 of Jamestown's 1,200 residents, the London Company sponsored a successful war against the local tribes. But the effort bankrupted the London Company. Dismayed by the colony's mismanagement, James I dissolved the London Company and made Virginia a royal colony in 1624.

With a 4 to 1 sex ratio in the colony, women were in great demand as laborers and as potential wives. Associating marriage with stability and maturity, colonial Virginians were eager to build families. This passage describes the London Company's efforts to populate its Virginia settlement.

SOURCE: "Letter to the Governor and Council in Virginia," August 12, 1622, *Records of the Virginia Company of London*, ed. S. M. Kingsbury (Washington, DC, 1933).

FOCUS QUESTIONS

1. What specific instructions pertained to the women arriving on this voyage?
2. What do such directives indicate about colonial Virginia?

There come now in this ship, and are immediately to follow in some others many hundreds of people, to whom as we here think ourselves bound to give the best encouragement for their going, there is no way left to increase the plantation [Jamestown], but by abundance of private undertakers; so we think you obliged to give all possible furtherance and assistance for the good entertaining and well settling of them, that they may both thrive and prosper and others by their welfare be drawn after them. This is the way that we conceive most effectual for the engaging of this state, and securing of Virginia, for in the multitude of people is the strength of a kingdom. . . .

We send you in this ship one widow and eleven maids for wives for the people in Virginia: there hath been especial care had in the choice of them; for there hath not any one of them been received but upon good commendations. We pray you all therefore in general to take them into your care; and more especially we recommend that at their first landing, they may be housed, lodged, and provided for of diet till they be married; for such was the haste of sending them away, as that straightened with time we had no means to put provisions aboard. And in case they cannot be presently married we desire they may be put to several households that have wives till they can be provided of husbands. There are nearly fifty more which are shortly to come, are sent by certain worthy gentlemen, who taking into their consideration that the plantation can never flourish till families be planted, and the respect of wives and children fix the people on the soil. Therefore have given this fair beginning: for the reimbursing of whose charges it is ordered that every man that marries them give 120 weight of the best leaf tobacco for each of them, and in case any of them die, that proportion must be advanced to it upon those who survive. That marriage be free according to the laws of nature, yet would we not have these maids deceived and married to servants, but only to such free men or tenants as have means to maintain them. We pray you therefore to be fathers to them in this business, not enforcing them to marry against their wills; neither send we them to be servants, save in case of extremity, for we would have their condition so much bettered as multitudes may be allured thereby to come unto you. And you may assure such men as marry those women that the first servants sent over by the company shall be consigned to them; it being our intent to preserve families, and to prefer married men before single persons.

2.2

The Experiences of an Indentured Servant in Virginia (1623)

Throughout the eighteenth century, thousands of whites arrived in North America as indentured servants. Depending on his or her age, a servant was obliged to serve from four to seven years. The prices of indentured servants varied according to skill. In exchange for their labor, servants received paid passage from Europe, as well as food, clothing, and shelter once they arrived in the colonies. When the contract expired, a servant was supposed to receive provisions and occasionally land in order to begin life as a freeman.

During the indenture, servants were subject to their master. A master could sell or rent his servants. Servants were prohibited from marrying and having children. They could receive severe punishments for misbehavior. In many instances, servants lived and worked in conditions virtually identical to those of slaves. Sickness, hunger, and exhaustion killed many servants before they completed their terms.

In this passage, Richard Frethorne describes the hardships many indentured servants endured. Although historians know very little about Frethorne's life, his story provides insight into the lives of unfree laborers in the colonies. (Some spelling and syntax have been modernized.)

FOCUS QUESTIONS

1. Why do you think Frethorne chose to become an indentured servant?
2. How does he describe his life as an indentured servant? What does he ask his parents to send him?
3. What do you think happened to Frethorne?
4. If you had lived in this era, would you have been willing to become an indentured servant? Why or why not?

SOURCE: Richard Frethorne, "Letter to His Parents," March 20, April, *The Records of the Virginia Company of London*, vol. IV (Washington, D.C.: Government Printing Office, 1935), ed. Susan M. Kingsbury.

Loving and kind father and mother:

My most humble duty remembered to you hoping in God of your good health, as I my self am at the making hereof, this is to let you understand that I your Child am in a most heavy Case by reason of the nature of the Country [which] is such that it causeth much sickness, [such as] scurvy and "the bloody flux" and diverse other diseases, which maketh the body very poor and weak. And when we are sick there is nothing to comfort us; for since I came out of the ship, I never ate anything but peas, and loblollie (that is water gruel). As for deer or venison I never saw any since I came into this land. There is indeed some foul, but we are not allowed to go, and get it, but must work hard both early and late for a mess of water gruel, and a mouthful of bread, and beef. A mouthful of bread for a penny loaf must serve for four men which is most pitiful.

[I]f you did know as much as I, when people cry out day, and night—Oh that they were in England without their limbs—and would not care to lose any limb to be in England again, yea though they beg from door to door. For we live in fear of the enemy every hour, yet we have had combat with them . . . and we took two alive and made slaves of them. But it was by policy, for we are in great danger, for our plantation is very weak by reason of the death and sickness of company. For we came but twenty for the merchants, and they are half dead just; and we look every hour when two more should go. Yet there came some four other men yet to live with us, of which there is but one alive; and our Lieutenant is dead, and [also] his father and his brother. And there was some five or six of the last year's twenty, of which there is but three left, so that we are fain to get other men to plant with us; and yet we are but 32 to fight against 3000 if they should come. . . .

And I have nothing to comfort me. . . . I have nothing at all—no, not a shirt to my back but two rags, nor no clothes but one poor suit, nor but one pair of shoes, but one pair of stockings, but one cap, but two bands [collars]. My cloak is stolen by one of my own fellows, and to his dying hour [he] would not tell me what he did with it; but some of my fellows saw him buy butter and beef from a ship, which my cloak, [no] doubt, paid for.

So that I have not a penny, nor a penny worth to help me to either spice or sugar or strong waters, without which one cannot live here. For as strong beer in England doth fatten and strengthen them, so water here doth wash and weaken these here. . . . But I am not half a quarter so strong as I was in England, and all is for want of victuals, for I do protest unto you, that I have eaten more in a day at home than I have allowed me here for a week. You have given more than my day's allowance to a beggar at the door; and if Mr. Jackson had not relieved me, I should be in a poor case. But he like a father and she like a loving mother doth still help me. . . .

And he [Mr. Jackson] much marveled that you would send a servant to the Company; he saith I had been better knocked on the head. And indeed so I find it now, to my great grief and misery; and saith if you love me you will redeem me suddenly, and for which I do entreat and beg. And if you cannot get the merchants to redeem me for some little money, then for God's sake get a gathering or entreat some good folks to lay out some little sum of money in meal and cheese and butter and beef. Any eating meat will yield great profit. Oil and vinegar is very good; but, father, there is great loss in leaking. But for God's sake send beef and cheese and butter, or the more of one sort and none of another. . . .

Good father, do not forget me, but have mercy and pity my miserable case. I know if you did but see me, you would weep to see me. . . . I pray you to remember my love to all my friends and kindred. I hope all my brothers and sisters are in good health, and as for my part I have down my resolution that certainly will be; that is, that the answer of this letter will be life or death to me. Therefore, good father, send as soon as you can; and if you send me anything let this be the mark.

ROT
Richard Frethorne
Martin's Hundred [Virginia, 1623]

2.3

Race, Gender, and Servitude in Virginia Law (1661–1691)

Racial slavery evolved slowly in colonial America. Although Africans first arrived in 1619, their status was virtually identical to that of indentured servants. Africans and poor whites performed similar jobs under the same circumstances. Since slavery was not yet a lifelong condition, both races were able to earn their freedom. A slave could earn his or her freedom by converting to Christianity.

But growing tensions between planters and freemen prompted whites to substitute black slaves for white servants. In 1641, Massachusetts became the first colony to legally recognize slavery. Other colonies soon followed. After 1660, revised statutes defined slavery as a lifelong, inheritable condition inextricably linked to race and no longer voided (stripped of legal force) by conversion to

SOURCE: Assembly of Virginia, Act XVI, April 1691, in William Waller Henning, *The Statutes at Large: Being a Collection of All the Laws of Virginia, from the First Session of the Legislature, in the Year 1619*, 13 vols. (New York: 1823), vol. 3: 86–87.

Christianity. New laws on sexual behavior and reproduction fostered white supremacy and patriarchy (a social system in which the father is the supreme authority). By 1705, rigid legal codes governed almost every aspect of the lives of slaves.

This passage includes examples of slave laws in Virginia. (Some spelling is modernized.)

FOCUS QUESTIONS

1. How could one's race and/or sex determine one's fate under these laws?
2. How did the laws change over time?
3. What impact do you think these laws had on slave families?
4. What do these laws suggest about life in colonial Virginia?

The Laws of Virginia (1661, 1662, 1691, 1705)

[March 1661]

For restraint of the filthy sin of fornication [sexual intercourse between partners who are not married], Be it enacted that what man or woman soever shall commit fornication, he and she so offending, upon proof thereof by confession or evidence shall pay each of them five hundred pounds of tobacco fine, (a) to the use of the parish or parishes they dwell in, and be bound to their good behavior, and be imprisoned until they find security to be bound with them, and if they or either of them committing fornication as aforesaid be servants then the master of such servant so offending shall pay the said five hundred pounds of tobacco as aforesaid to the use of the parish aforesaid, for which the said servant shall serve half a year after the time by indenture or custom is expired, and if the master shall refuse to pay the fine then the servant to be whipped; and if it happen a bastard child to be gotten in such fornication then the woman if a servant in regard of the loss and trouble her master doth sustain by her having a bastard shall serve two years after her time by indenture is expired or pay two thousand pounds of tobacco to her master besides the fine or punishment for committing the offence and the reputed father to put in security to keep the child and save the parish harm.

[December 1662]

Whereas by act of Assembly every woman servant having a bastard is to serve two years, and late experience show that some dissolute masters have gotten their maids with child, and yet claim the benefit of their service, and on the contrary if a woman got with child by her master should be freed from that service it might probably induce such loose persons to lay all their bastards to their masters; it is therefore thought fit and accordingly enacted, and be it enacted henceforward that each woman servant got with child by her master shall after her time by indenture or custom is expired be by the churchwardens of the parish where she lived when she was brought to bed of such bastard, sold for two years, and the tobacco to be employed by the vestry for the use of the parish. . . .

Whereas some doubts have arisen whether children got by any Englishman upon a negro woman should be slave or free, Be it therefore enacted and declared by this present grand assembly, that all children bourn in this country shall be held bond or free only according to the condition of the mother, And that if any Christian shall commit fornication with a negro man or woman, he or she so offending shall pay double the fines imposed by the former act.

[April 1691]

. . . For prevention of that abominable mixture and spurious issue which hereafter may increase in this dominion, as well as by negroes, mulattos, and Indians intermarrying with English, or other white women, as by their unlawful accompanying with one another, Be it enacted . . . that . . . whatsoever English or other white man or woman being free, shall intermarry with a negro, mulatto or Indian man or woman bond or free shall within three months after such marriage be banished and removed from this dominion forever. . . .

And be it further enacted . . . That if any English woman being free shall have a bastard child by any negro or mulatto, she pay the sum of fifteen pounds sterling, within one month after such bastard child shall be born, to the Church wardens of the parish . . . and in default of such payment she shall be taken into the possession of the said Church wardens and disposed of for five years, and the said fine of fifteen pounds, or whatever the woman shall be disposed of for, shall be paid, one third part to their majesties . . . and one other third part to the use of the parish . . . and the other third part to the informer, and that such bastard child be bound out as a servant by the said Church wardens until he or she shall attain the age of thirty years, and in case such English woman that shall have such bastard child be a servant, she shall be sold by the said church wardens (after her time is expired that she ought by law serve her master), for five years, and the money she shall be sold for divided as if before appointed, and the child to serve as aforesaid.

[1705]

And be it further enacted, That no minister of the church of England, or other minister, or person whatsoever, within this colony and dominion, shall hereafter willingly presume to marry a white man with a negro or mulatto woman; or to marry a white woman with a negro or mulatto man, upon paid of forfeiting or paying, for every such marriage the sum of ten thousand pounds of tobacco; one half to our sovereign lady the Queen . . . and the other half to the informer.

2.4

Trial and Interrogation
of Hutchinson (1637)

*The founders of Massachusetts Bay hoped to build a community based on
religious ideals. In his 1630 sermon, "A Model of Christian Charity,"
Governor John Winthrop announced that the colony would be "a city upon a
hill" that would inspire other nations. Adhering to a covenant that bound them
to God and to each other, the Puritans were disciplined and motivated. They
quickly established a network of well-organized towns, each centering on a
congregation. Before one could attain full church membership, the Puritans
required a public account of conversion.*

*Not all Puritans agreed with their leaders' religious and political views. In
1635, Puritan authorities banished Roger Williams for arguing that church and
state should be completely separate. Anne Hutchinson, another dissident, organized weekly theological discussions for the women of Boston. Arguing that individuals possessed the ability to interpret and preach the Scriptures, Hutchinson
questioned clerical authority and began drawing both male and female followers.
In 1637, Hutchinson's critics charged her with sedition and heresy. After she
was convicted and banished, Hutchinson settled on Long Island Sound. In
1643, she and most of her children were killed by Indians, an event some
Puritans viewed as divine retribution.*

*In this selection, Hutchinson testifies before her accusers at the Massachusetts
Bay legislature (the General Court). (Some spelling has been modernized.)*

FOCUS QUESTIONS

1. How do Hutchinson's accusers treat her? How does Hutchinson
   respond?
2. Why was Hutchinson's sex so significant in these proceedings?
3. What were the charges levied against Hutchinson? Why was she found
   guilty?

SOURCE: Thomas Hutchinson, *History of the Colony and Province of Massachusetts*
(Boston, 1767).

The Examination of Mrs. Anne Hutchinson at the Court at Newtown.

Mr. John Winthrop, Governor. Mrs. Hutchinson, you are called here as one of those that have troubled the peace of the commonwealth and the churches here; you are known to be a woman that hath had a great share in the promoting and divulging of those opinions that are causes of this trouble, and . . . you have spoken diverse things as we have been informed very prejudicial to the honour of the churches and ministers thereof, and you have maintained a meeting and an assembly in your house that hath been condemned by the general assembly as a thing not tolerable nor comely in the sight of God nor fitting for your sex, and notwithstanding that was cried down you have continued the same, therefore we have thought good to send for you to understand how things are, that if you be in an erroneous way we may reduce you that so you may become a profitable member here among us, otherwise if you be obstinate in your course that then the court may take such course that you may trouble us no further, therefore I would intreat you to express whether you do not hold and assent in practice to those opinions and factions that have been handled in court already. . . .

HUTCHINSON: What have I said or done?

WINTHROP: Why for your doings, this you did harbour and countenance those that are parties in this faction that you have heard of.

HUTCHINSON: That's matter of conscience, Sir.

WINTHROP: Your conscience you must keep or it must be kept for you.

HUTCHINSON: Must not I then entertain the saints because I must keep my conscience?

WINTHROP: Say that one brother should commit felony or treason and come to his other brother's house, if he knows him guilty and conceals him he is guilty of the same. It is his conscience to entertain him, but if his conscience comes into act in giving countenance and entertainment to him that hath broken the law he is guilty too. So if you do countenance those that are transgressors of the law you are in the same fact . . .

HUTCHINSON: What law have I broken?

WINTHROP: Why the fifth commandment . . .

HUTCHINSON: But put the case Sir that I do fear the Lord and my parents, may not I entertain them that fear the Lord because my parents will not give me leave?

WINTHROP: If they be the fathers of the commonwealth, and they of another religion, if you entertain them then you dishonor your parents and are justly punishable . . .

HUTCHINSON: I may put honor upon them as the children of God and as they do honor the Lord.

WINTHROP: We do not mean to discourse with those of your sex but only this; you do adhere unto them and do endeavor to set forward this faction and so you do dishonor us.

HUTCHINSON: I do acknowledge no such thing neither do I think that I ever put any dishonor upon you.

WINTHROP: Why do you keep such a meeting at your house as you do every week upon a set day?

HUTCHINSON: It is lawful for me so to do, as it is all your practices and can you find a warrant for yourself and condemn me for the same thing? The ground of my taking it up was, when I first came to this land because I did not go to such meetings as those were, it was presently reported that I did not allow of such meetings but held them unlawful and therefore in that regard they said I was proud and did despise all ordinances, upon that a friend came unto me and told me of it and I to prevent such aspersions took it up, but it was in practice before I came therefore I was not the first . . .

WINTHROP: Well, admit there was no man at your meeting and that you was sorry for it, there is no warrant for your doings, and by what warrant do you continue such a course?

HUTCHINSON: I conceive there lies a clear rule in Titus, that the elder women should instruct the younger [Titus 2:3–5] and then I must have a time wherein I must do it. . . .

WINTHROP: [S]uppose that a man should come and say Mrs. Hutchinson I hear that you are a woman that God hath given his grace unto and you have knowledge in the word of God I pray instruct me a little, ought you not to instruct this man?

HUTCHINSON: I think I may.—Do you think it not lawful for me to teach women and why do you call me to teach the court?

WINTHROP: We do not call you to teach the court but to lay open yourself. . . . Your course is not to be suffered for, besides that we find such a course as this to be greatly prejudicial to the state, besides the occasion that it is to seduce many honest persons that are called to those meetings and your opinions being known to be different from the word of God may seduce many simple souls that resort unto you, besides that the occasion which hath come of late hath come from none but such as have frequented your meetings, so that now they are flown off from magistrates and ministers and this since they have come to you, and besides that it will not well stand with the commonwealth that families should be neglected for so many neighbors and dames and so much time spent, we see no rule of God for this, we see not that any should have authority to set up any other exercises besides what authority hath already set up and so what hurt comes of this you will be guilty of and we for suffering you.

HUTCHINSON: Sir I do not believe that to be so . . .

WINTHROP: We are your judges, and not you ours and we must compel you to it.

HUTCHINSON: If it please you by authority to put it down I will freely let you for I am subject to your authority....

WINTHROP: Let us state the case and then we may know what to do. That which is laid to Mrs. Hutchinson's charge is this, that she hath traduced the magistrates and ministers of this jurisdiction, that she hath said the ministers preached a covenant of works and Mr. Cotton a covenant of grace, and that they were not able ministers of the gospel, and she excuses it that she made it a private conference and with a promise of secrecy....

HUTCHINSON: If you please to give me leave I shall give you the ground of what I know to be true. Being much troubled to see the falseness of the constitution of the church of England, I had like to have turned separatist; whereupon I kept a day of solemn humiliation and pondering of the thing; this scripture was brought unto me—he that denies Jesus Christ to be come in the flesh is antichrist—This I considered of and in considering found that the papists did not deny him to become in the flesh nor we did not deny him—who then was antichrist?... The Lord knows that I could not open scripture; he must by his prophetical office open it unto me.... I bless the Lord, he hath let me see which was the clear ministry and which the wrong. Since that time I confess I have been more choice and he hath let me to distinguish between the voice of my beloved and the voice of Moses, the voice of John Baptist and the voice of antichrist, for all those voices are spoken of in scripture. Now if you do condemn me for speaking what in my conscience I know to be truth I must commit myself unto the Lord.

MR. NOWELL: How do you know that that was the spirit?

HUTCHINSON: How did Abraham know that it was God that bid him offer his son, being a breach of the sixth commandment?

MR. DUDLEY, DEPUTY GOVERNOR: By an immediate voice.

HUTCHINSON: So to me by an immediate revelation.... Ever since that time I have been confident of what he hath revealed unto me ... You have power over my body but the Lord Jesus hath power over my body and soul, and assure yourselves thus much, you do as much as in you lies to put the Lord Jesus Christ from you, and if you go on in this course you begin you will bring a curse upon you and your posterity, and the mouth of the Lord hath spoken it....

WINTHROP: The court hath already declared themselves satisfied concerning the things you hear, and concerning the troublesomeness of her spirit and the danger of her course amongst us, which is not to be suffered. Therefore if it be the mind of the court that Mrs. Hutchinson for these things that appear before us is unfit for our society, and if it be the mind of the court that she shall be banished out of our liberties and imprisoned till she be sent away, let them hold up their hands. . . .

WINTHROP: Mrs. Hutchinson, the sentence of the court you hear is that you are banished from out of our jurisdiction as being a woman not fit for our society, and are to be imprisoned till the court shall send you away . . .

2.5

Edward Randolph, the Causes and Results of King Philip's War (1675)

In contrast to colonial Virginians, New England settlers encountered little resistance from local Indian tribes, many of which had already been decimated by disease. Although initial Anglo-Indian contacts were mutually beneficial, the Puritans eventually outlawed tribal religions and attempted to convert Indians to Christianity. By the 1650s, many Indians surrendered and moved to "praying towns," reservations created by Massachusetts Bay officials.

But English attempts to migrate farther inland sparked ferocious Indian resistance. In 1637, the Puritans had waged a successful campaign to suppress the Pequots. As English attempts to expand their lands continued, the colonists dramatically changed the environment of New England. Faced with population losses, food shortages, and debt, some Indians became demoralized or addicted to alcohol. Others blended aspects of Indian religion and Christianity, stirring the resentment of Puritan missionaries who viewed the Indians as hopelessly "uncivilized" and heathen.

By the 1670s, tensions in New England were ready to explode. English efforts to coerce the Indians into selling their lands and embracing white culture infuriated local tribes, especially the Wampanoag in Plymouth. The

SOURCE: Thomas Hutchinson, *A Collection of Original Papers Relative to the History of the Colony of Massachusetts Bay* (Boston, 1769), 490–494.

Wampanoags' leader, Metacom (King Philip), vowed to fight further English expansion and organized a confederation of New England tribes, including the formidable Narraganset. In 1675, after the Puritans hanged three Wampanoags for murdering a Christian Indian, Anglo-Indian violence rapidly escalated. Whites and Indians throughout New England incurred devastating losses. After King Philip died in August 1676, Indian resistance collapsed. Thereafter, English settlers were unimpeded in their expansion across New England.

In this passage, Edward Randolph, a British royal official, assesses the war. (Some spelling has been modernized.)

FOCUS QUESTIONS

1. What does Randolph believe caused King Philip's War?
2. How does Randolph regard the Indians? What is his opinion of the government of Massachusetts Bay?
3. What impact did the war have upon New England?
4. What are the terms of the proposed peace settlement? Do you think they were fair? Explain your answer.

What hath been the original cause of the present war with the natives? What are the advantages or disadvantages arising thereby and will probably be the End?

Various are the reports and conjectures of the causes of the present Indian war. Some impute it to an impudent zeal in the magistrates of Boston to christianize those heathens before they were civilized and enjoining them the strict observation of their laws, which, to a people so rude and licentious, hath proved even intolerable, and that the more, for that while the magistrates, for their profit, put the laws severely in execution against the Indians, the people, on the other side, for lucre and gain, entice and provoke the Indians to the breach thereof, especially to drunkenness, to which those people are so generally addicted....

Some believe there have been vagrant and jesuitical priests, who have made it their businesses, for some years past, to go from Sachim to Sachim, to exasperate the Indians against the English and to bring them into a confederacy, and that they were promised supplies from France and other parts to extirpate the English nation out of the continent of America. Others impute the cause to some injuries offered to the Sachim Philip; for he being possessed of a tract of land called Mount Hope, a very fertile, pleasant and rich soil, some English had a mind to dispossess him thereof, who never wanting one pretence or other to attain their end, complained of injuries done by Philip and his Indians to their stock and cattle, whereupon Philip was often summoned before the magistrate, sometimes imprisoned, and never released but upon parting with a considerable part of his land.

But the government of the Massachusetts (to give it in their own words) do declare these are the great evils for which God hath given the heathen commission to rise against them: The woeful breach of the 5th commandment, in contempt of their authority, which is a sin highly provoking to the Lord: For men wearing long hair and wigs made of women's hair; for women wearing borders of hair and for cutting, curling, and laying out the hair, and disguising themselves by following strange fashions in their apparel: For profaneness in the people not frequenting their meetings, and others going away before the blessing be pronounced: For suffering the Quakers to live amongst them . . ., contrary to their old laws and resolutions.

With many such reasons, but whatever be the cause, the English have contributed much to their misfortunes, for they first taught the Indians the use of arms, and admitted them to be present at all their musters and trainings, and showed them how to handle, mend, and fix their muskets, and have been furnished with all sorts of arms by permission of the government, so that the Indians are become excellent firemen. . . .

No advantage but many disadvantages have arisen to the English by the war, for about 600 men have been slain, and 12 captains, most of them brave and stout persons and of loyal principles, while the church members had liberty to stay at home and not hazard their persons in the wilderness.

The loss to the English in the several colonies, in their habitations and stock, is reckoned to amount to 150,000*l.* There having been about 1200 houses burned, 8000 head of cattle, great and small, killed, and many thousands of bushels of wheat, peas, and other grain burned . . . and upward of 3000 Indians men women and children destroyed, who if well managed would have been very serviceable to the English, which makes all manner of labor dear.

The war at present is near an end . . . .

The government of Boston have concluded a peace upon these terms.

1. That there be henceforward a firm peace between the Indians and English.

2. That after publication of the articles of peace by the general court, if any English shall willfully kill an Indian upon due proof, he shall die, and if an Indian kill an Englishman and escape, the Indians are to produce him, and he to pass trial by the English laws.

     That the Indians shall not conceal any known enemies to the English but shall discover them and bring them to the English.

     That upon all occasions the Indians are to aid and assist the English against their enemies, and to be under English command.

     That all Indians have liberty to sit down at their former habitation without let. . . .

2.6

Mary Rowlandson, Captivity Narrative (1682)

Violent confrontations with Indians intensified negative stereotypes held by English settlers. Most Europeans characterized Indians as barbaric heathens or, less frequently, as "noble savages." Captivity narratives, an early genre of American literature, reinforced these stereotypes.

Mary Rowlandson (1637–1710) wrote one of the most famous captivity narratives. Raised in New England, Rowlandson married the Reverend Joseph Rowlandson in 1756. They lived with their three children in Lancaster, Massachusetts. In February 1676, as King Philip's War raged, an Indian raiding party stormed Lancaster and captured twenty-four townspeople, including Rowlandson and her children, one of whom died shortly thereafter. Although she adapted to the Indians' diet and earned special privileges because of her sewing skills, Rowlandson suffered greatly during her three months of captivity. In May 1676, her husband secured her release with a £20 ransom payment. Her two surviving children were freed several weeks later. In 1682, Rowlandson published an account of her experiences awkwardly titled The Sovereignty and Goodness of God, Together with the Faithfulness of His Promises Displayed; Being a Narrative of the Captivity and Restoration of Mrs. Mary Rowlandson. *better known as "The Narrative of Mary Rowlandson." The narrative went through thirty editions and remains a powerful example of early American literature.*

FOCUS QUESTIONS

1. What are the major events in Rowlandson's story?

2. How does she portray the Indians? Do her views seem to change during her ordeal? Explain your answers.

3. What does Rowlandson's narrative tell us about the condition of the Indians?

SOURCE: Mary Rowlandson, *The Narrative of the Captivity and the Restoration of Mrs. Mary Rowlandson* (1682). The complete narrative appears online at http://www.library.csi.cuny.edu/dept/history/lavender/rowlandson.html.

4. How does Rowlandson's account of King Philip's War differ from Edward Randolph's account (Document 2.5)?

5. Why do you think that captivity narratives like Rowlandson's were so popular among early Americans? How did such narratives reinforce stereotypes about Indians?

On the tenth of February 1675, came the Indians with great numbers upon Lancaster: their first coming was about sunrising; hearing the noise of some guns, we looked out; several houses were burning, and the smoke ascending to heaven.... At length they came and beset our own house, and quickly it was the dolefullest day that ever mine eyes saw. The house stood upon the edge of a hill; some of the Indians got behind the hill, others into the barn, and others behind anything that could shelter them; from all which places they shot against the house, so that the bullets seemed to fly like hail; and quickly they wounded one man among us, then another, and then a third. About two hours (according to my observation, in that amazing time) they had been about the house before they prevailed to fire it (which they did with flax and hemp, which they brought out of the barn, and there being no defense about the house, only two flankers at two opposite corners and one of them not finished); they fired it once and one ventured out and quenched it, but they quickly fired it again, and that took.... No sooner were we out of the house, but my brother-in-law (being before wounded, in defending the house, in or near the throat) fell down dead, whereat the Indians scornfully shouted, and hallowed, and were presently upon him, stripping off his clothes, the bullets flying thick, one went through my side, and the same (as would seem) through the bowels and hand of my dear child in my arms. One of my elder sisters' children, named William, had then his leg broken, which the Indians perceiving, they knocked him on [his] head. Thus were we butchered by those merciless heathen, standing amazed, with the blood running down to our heels.... The Indians laid hold of us, pulling me one way, and the children another, and said, "Come go along with us"; I told them they would kill me: they answered, if I were willing to go along with them, they would not hurt me....

Now away we must go with those barbarous creatures, with our bodies wounded and bleeding, and our hearts no less than our bodies....

After this it quickly began to snow, and when night came on, they stopped, and now down I must sit in the snow, by a little fire, and a few boughs behind me, with my sick child in my lap; and calling much for water, being now (through the wound) fallen into a violent fever. My own wound also growing so stiff that I could scarce sit down or rise up; yet so it must be, that I must sit all this cold winter night upon the cold snowy ground, with my sick child in my arms, looking that every hour would be the last of its life; and having no Christian friend near me, either to comfort or help me....

Thus nine days I sat upon my knees, with my babe in my lap, till my flesh was raw again; my child being even ready to depart this sorrowful world, they bade me carry it out to another wigwam (I suppose because they would not be troubled with such spectacles) whither I went with a very heavy heart, and down

I sat with the picture of death in my lap. About two hours in the night, my sweet babe like a lamb departed this life on Feb. 18, 1675. It being about six years, and five months old. It was nine days from the first wounding, in this miserable condition, without any refreshing of one nature or other, except a little cold water. . . .

I cannot but take notice of the wonderful mercy of God to me in those afflictions, in sending me a Bible. One of the Indians that came from Medfield fight, had brought some plunder, came to me, and asked me, if I would have a Bible, he had got one in his basket. I was glad of it, and asked him, whether he thought the Indians would let me read? He answered, yes. So I took the Bible. . . .

The first week of my being among them I hardly ate any thing; the second week I found my stomach grow very faint for want of something; and yet it was very hard to get down their filthy trash; but the third week, though I could think how formerly my stomach would turn against this or that, and I could starve and die before I could eat such things, yet they were sweet and savory to my taste. I was at this time knitting a pair of white cotton stockings for my mistress; and had not yet wrought upon a Sabbath day. When the Sabbath came they bade me go to work. I told them it was the Sabbath day, and desired them to let me rest, and told them I would do as much more tomorrow; to which they answered me they would break my face. And here I cannot but take notice of the strange providence of God in preserving the heathen. They were many hundreds, old and young, some sick, and some lame; many had papooses at their backs. The greatest number at this time with us were squaws, and they traveled with all they had, bag and baggage, and yet they got over this river aforesaid; and on Monday they set their wigwams on fire, and away they went. On that very day came the English army after them to this river, and saw the smoke of their wigwams, and yet this river put a stop to them. God did not give them courage or activity to go over after us. We were not ready for so great a mercy as victory and deliverance. . . .

We traveled on till night; and in the morning, we must go over the river to Philip's crew. When I was in the canoe I could not but be amazed at the numerous crew of pagans that were on the bank on the other side. When I came ashore, they gathered all about me, I sitting alone in the midst. I observed they asked one another questions, and laughed, and rejoiced over their gains and victories. Then my heart began to fail: and I fell aweeping, which was the first time to my remembrance, that I wept before them. . . . There one of them asked me why I wept. I could hardly tell what to say: Yet I answered, they would kill me. "No," said he, "none will hurt you." Then came one of them and gave me two spoonfuls of meal to comfort me, and another gave me half a pint of peas; which was more worth than many bushels at another time. Then I went to see King Philip. He bade me come in and sit down, and asked me whether I would smoke it (a usual compliment nowadays amongst saints and sinners) but this no way suited me. . . . During my abode in this place, Philip spake to me to make a shirt for his boy, which I did, for which he gave me a shilling. I offered the money to my master, but he bade me keep it; and with it I bought a piece of horse flesh. Afterwards he asked me to make a cap for his boy, for which he invited me to dinner. I went, and he gave me a pancake, about as big as two fingers. It was made of parched wheat, beaten, and fried in bear's grease, but I thought I never tasted pleasanter meat in my life. . . .

One bitter cold day I could find no room to sit down before the fire. I went out, and could not tell what to do, but I went in to another wigwam, where they were also sitting round the fire, but the squaw laid a skin for me, and bid me sit down, and gave me some ground nuts, and bade me come again; and told me they would buy me, if they were able, and yet these were strangers to me that I never saw before. . . .

Now must we pack up and be gone from this thicket, bending our course toward the Baytowns; I having nothing to eat by the way this day, but a few crumbs of cake, that an Indian gave my girl the same day we were taken. She gave it me, and I put it in my pocket; there it lay, till it was so moldy (for want of good baking) that one could not tell what it was made of; it fell all to crumbs, and grew so dry and hard, that it was like little flints; and this refreshed me many times, when I was ready to faint. It was in my thoughts when I put it into my mouth, that if ever I returned, I would tell the world what a blessing the Lord gave to such mean food. As we went along they killed a deer, with a young one in her, they gave me a piece of the fawn, and it was so young and tender, that one might eat the bones as well as the flesh, and yet I thought it very good. When night came on we sat down; it rained, but they quickly got up a bark wigwam, where I lay dry that night. I looked out in the morning, and many of them had lain in the rain all night, I saw by their reeking. Thus the Lord dealt mercifully with me many times, and I fared better than many of them. In the morning they took the blood of the deer, and put it into the paunch, and so boiled it. I could eat nothing of that, though they ate it sweetly. . . .

It was thought, if their corn were cut down, they would starve and die with hunger, and all their corn that could be found, was destroyed, and they driven from that little they had in store, into the woods in the midst of winter; and yet how to admiration did the Lord preserve them for His holy ends, and the destruction of many still amongst the English! Strangely did the Lord provide for them; that I did not see (all the time I was among them) one man, woman, or child, die with hunger. Though many times they would eat that, that a hog or a dog would hardly touch; yet by that God strengthened them to be a scourge to His people.

The chief and commonest food was ground nuts. They eat also nuts and acorns, artichokes, lilly roots, ground beans, and several other weeds and roots, that I know not. They would pick up old bones, and cut them to pieces at the joints, and if they were full of worms and maggots, they would scald them over the fire to make the vermine come out, and then boil them, and drink up the liquor, and then beat the great ends of them in a mortar, and so eat them. They would eat horse's guts, and ears, and all sorts of wild birds which they could catch; also bear, venison, beaver, tortoise, frogs, squirrels, dogs, skunks, rattlesnakes; yea, the very bark of trees; besides all sorts of creatures, and provision which they plundered from the English. I can but stand in admiration to see the wonderful power of God in providing for such a vast number of our enemies in the wilderness, where there was nothing to be seen, but from hand to mouth. . . .

2.7

The Examination and Confession of Ann Foster at Salem Village (1692)

By the late 1600s, many Puritans were becoming more individualistic and materialistic. They began to question the founders' vision of an egalitarian and charitable community. Several New England towns split into class factions.

In late 1691, Salem, Massachusetts, was such a place. Comprised of the port of Salem Town and the farms of Salem Village, the town was experiencing economic and political changes. The affluent merchants of Salem Town controlled local politics while the farmers of Salem Village struggled.

After discussing voodoo with a West Indian slave, Tituba, several Salem Village girls claimed that they were possessed by the devil. They subsequently accused three Salem women, including Tituba, of practicing witchcraft. As their charges multiplied, they most often named older women in prosperous circumstances. Formerly dismissed as mere servants, the girls gained temporary influence by articulating anxieties about social change.

As public hysteria increased, civil magistrates established a tribunal in Salem. Almost 400 men and women were accused and imprisoned. Many tried to save themselves by making false confessions or implicating others. Twenty people were executed. In October 1692, as the furor waned, Governor William Phips abolished the special court and eventually pardoned the accused.

This excerpt features Ann Foster's testimony against Martha Carrier in the Salem witchcraft trials. Carrier was hanged. Foster died in prison. (Some spelling has been modernized.)

FOCUS QUESTIONS

1. Of what does Ann Foster accuse Goody Carrier?

2. Why do you think people were so willing to believe these accusations?

3. Could we have anything similar to the Salem witchcraft trials in our own society? Explain your answer.

SOURCE: *The Colonial Horizon: America in the Sixteenth and Seventeenth Centuries*, 1969, ed. William H. Goetzmann (Reading, MA: Addison Wesley Publishing Company).

16 July 1692

Ann Foster Examined confessed that it was Goody Carrier that made her a witch that she came to her in person about Six years ago & told her if she would not be a witch ye devil should tear her in pieces & carry her away at which time she promised to Serve the devil that she had bewitched a hog of John Lovejoy's to death & that she had hurt some persons in Salem Village, that Goody Carrier came to her & would have her bewitch two children of Andrew Allins & that she had then two puppets made & stuck pins in them to bewitch ye said children by which one of them died [the] other very sick, that she was at the meeting of the witches at Salem Village, that Goody Carrier came & told her of the meeting and would have her go, so they got upon Sticks & went said Jorny & being there did see Mr. Buroughs ye minister who spake to them all, & this was about two months ago that there was then twenty five persons meet together, that she tied a knot in a Rage & threw it into the fire to hurt Tim Swan & that she did hurt the rest that complained of her by Squeezing puppets like them & so almost choked them.

18 July 1692

Ann Foster Examined confessed that the devil in shape of a man appeared to her with Goody Carrier about six year since when they made her a witch & that she promised to serve the devil two years, upon which the devil promised her prosperity and many things but never performed it, that she & Martha Carrier did both ride on a stick or pole when they went to the witch meeting at Salem Village & that the stick broke: as they were carried in the air above the tops of the trees, & they fell but she did hang fast about the neck of Goody Carrier & were presently at the village, that she was then much hurt of her Leg, she further saith that she heard some of the witches say there was three hundred & five in the whole Country & that they would ruin that place the Village, also said there was present at that meeting two men besides Mr. Burroughs the minister & one of them had gray hair, she saith that she formerly frequented the public meeting to worship god, but the devil had such power over her that she could not profit there & that was her undoing: she saith that about three or four years ago Martha Carrier told her she would bewitch James Hobbs child to death & the child died in twenty four hours.

21 July 1692

Ann Foster Examined Owned her former confession being read to her and further confessed that the discourse amongst the witches at the meeting at Salem village was that they would afflict there to set up the Devil's Kingdome. This confession is true as witness my hand.

Ann Foster Signed & Owned the above Examination & Confession before me
Salem 10th September 1692
John Higginson, Just Peace

2.8

"Pennsylvania, the Poor Man's Paradise" (1698)

In 1681, in order to pay a substantial debt owed to William Penn's father, Charles II appointed Penn the sole proprietor of a large tract of American land. A Quaker, Penn founded a colony based on religious freedom and economic opportunity. Penn publicized his venture throughout Western Europe and drew scores of Quakers and other religious groups to Pennsylvania. Fertile lands and lengthy growing seasons attracted many others. With a reputation for tolerance and organization, Pennsylvania flourished.

In this excerpt, Gabriel Thomas, a Quaker who lived in Pennsylvania from 1682 to 1697, describes conditions in the new settlement. (Some spelling has been modernized.)

FOCUS QUESTIONS

1. What does Thomas claim draws people to Pennsylvania? How did conditions in Pennsylvania differ from much of Europe?

2. Do you agree that Pennsylvania was a "poor man's paradise"? Explain your answer.

And now for their Lots and Lands in City and Country, in their great Advancement since they were first laid out, which was within the compass of about Twelve Years, that which might have been bought for Fifteen or Eighteen Shillings, is now sold for Fourscore Pounds in ready Silver; and some other Lots, that might have been then Purchased for Three Pounds, within the space of Two Years, were sold for a Hundred Pounds a piece....

Now the true Reason why this Fruitful Country and Flourishing City [Philadelphia] advance so considerably in the Purchase of Lands both in the one and the other, is their great and extended Traffic and Commerce both by Sea and Land, viz. to New-York, New-England, Virginia, Maryland, Carolina,

SOURCE: Gabriel Thomas, *An Historical and Geographical Account of the Province and Country of Pennsilvania* (London, 1698), 23–45.

Jamaica, Barbadoes, Nevis, Monsserat, Antigua, St. Christophers, Bermuda, New-Foundland, Madeiras, Saltetudeous, and Old-England; besides several other places. Their Merchandize chiefly consists in Horses, Pipe-Staves, Pork and Beef Salted and Barreled up, Bread, and Flour, all sorts of Grain, Peas, Beans, Skins, Furs, Tobacco, or Pot-Ashes, Wax, &c. which are Barter'd for Rum, Sugar, Molasses, Silver, Negroes, Wine, Linen, Household-Goods, &c....

... The Country at the first, laying out, was void of Inhabitants (except the Heathens, or very few Christians worth naming) and not many People caring to abandon a quiet and easy (at least tolerable) Life in their Native Country (usually the most agreeable to all Mankind) to seek out a new hazardous, and careful one in a Foreign Wilderness or Desert Country, wholly destitute of Christian Inhabitants, and even to arrive at which, they must pass over a vast Ocean, exposed to some Dangers, and not a few Inconveniences: But now all those Cares, Fears and Hazards are vanished, for the Country is pretty well Peopled, and very much Improved, and will be more every Day, now the Dove is returned with the Olive-branch of Peace in her Mouth.

I must needs say, even the Present Encouragements are very great and inviting, for Poor People (both Men and Women) of all kinds, can here get three times the Wages for their Labor they can in England or Wales....

Corn and Flesh, and what else serves Man for Drink, Food and Rayment, is much cheaper here than in England, or elsewhere; but the chief reason why Wages of Servants of all sorts is much higher here than there, arises from the great Fertility and Produce of the Place; besides, if these larger Stipends were refused them, they would quickly set up for themselves, for they can have Provision very cheap, and Land for a very small matter, or next to nothing in comparison of the Purchase of Lands in England; and the Farmers there, can better afford to give that great Wages than the Farmers in England can, for several Reasons very obvious.

As first, their Land costs them (as I said but just now) little or nothing in comparison, of which the Farmers commonly will get twice the increase of Corn for every Bushel they sow, that the Farmers in England can from the richest Land they have.

In the Second place, they have constantly good price for their Corn, by reason of the great and quick vent into Barbados and other Islands; through which means Silver is become more plentiful than here in England, considering the Number of People, and that causes a quick Trade for both Corn and Cattle; and that is the reason that Corn differs now from the Price formerly, else it would be at half the Price it was at then; for a Brother of mine (to my own particular knowledge) sold within the compass of one Week, about One Hundred and Twenty fat Beasts, most of them good handsome large Oxen.

Thirdly, They pay no Tithes, and their Taxes are inconsiderable; the Place is free for all Persuasions, in a Sober and Civil way; for the Church of England and the Quakers bear equal Share in the Government. They live Friendly and Well together; there is no Persecution for Religion, nor ever like to be; 'tis this that knocks all Commerce on the Head, together with high Imposts, strict Laws, and cramping Orders. Before I end this Paragraph, I shall add another Reason why Women's Wages are so exorbitant; they are not yet very numerous, which makes them stand upon high Terms for their several Services, in Sempstering, Washing, Spinning, Knitting, Sewing, and in all the other parts of their Employments; for they have for Spinning either Worsted of Linen, Two Shillings a Pound, and commonly for Knitting a very Coarse pair of Yarn Stockings, they have half a Crown a pair; moreover, they are usually Married before they are Twenty Years of Age, and when once in that Noose, are for the most part a little uneasy, and make their Husbands so too, till they procure them a Maid Servant to bear the burden of the Work, as also in some measure to wait on them too. . . .

What I have here written, is not a Fiction, Flam, Whim, or any sinister Design, either to impose upon the Ignorant, or credulous, or to curry Favor with the Rich and Mighty, but in mere Pity and Pure Compassion to the Numbers of Poor Laboring Men, Women, and Children in England, half starve'd, visible in their meager looks, that are continually wandering up and down looking for Employment without finding any, who here need not lie idle a moment. . . . Here are no Beggars to be seen (it is a shame and Disgrace to the State that there are so many in England) not indeed have any here at least Occasion or Temptation to take up that Scandalous Lazy Life . . .

2.9

Images of the Rise of a Consumer Society (1729–1750)

During the 1700s, Americans made their wealth much more obvious to the casual observer. Eager to emulate British styles, elites constructed lavish homes stocked with elegant furnishings. The gentry also wore expensive clothing and drove ornate carriages. To exhibit their social status, they cultivated sophisticated tastes in literature, studied foreign languages, and adopted strict codes of etiquette. The following images demonstrate some of these trends.

FOCUS QUESTIONS

1. What do these images suggest about class structure in colonial America?
2. How might the possessions of less wealthy Americans, such as those described by Gabriel Thomas (Document 2.8), have compared to those featured here?

John Smibert, *Dean Berkeley and His Entourage* (The Bermuda Group), d. 1729. Oil on Canvas, 61 in. × 93 in. (176.5 × 236.2 cm) unframed. Yale University Art Gallery; gift of Isaac Lathrop.

Born in Scotland, Smibert (1688–1751) was the first formally trained artist to come to the American colonies. After studying art in London, Smibert traveled to Italy, where he met the Protestant bishop George Berkeley. In 1728, Smibert accompanied Berkeley on an unsuccessful mission to train missionaries in Bermuda. Never reaching the Caribbean, the duo remained in Boston. There, local elites extolled Smibert's painting of his traveling companions. Flooded with re-quests for personal portraits, Smibert stayed in New England, and greatly influenced several later American artists including John Singleton Copley and Robert Feke.

Like their counterparts in England, American gentry copied the designs of Andrea Palladio, a noted architect in Renaissance Italy. Drayton Hall's two-story, temple-like form, columns, and triangular pediment exemplify Georgian-Palladian architecture. Carefully preserved by several generations of the Drayton family, the plantation is now a historic site of the National Trust for Historic Preservation.

The third image shows an example of Queen Anne style furniture, produced from the 1720s until approximately 1750. This highboy dresser is made of maple and offers examples of the graceful lines and intricate carvings dominating Queen Anne designs.

Drayton Hall (1738–1742), plantation house in Charleston, South Carolina. Photograph by Ronald Blunt for the National Trust, 1994. http://www.ronbluntphoto.com/Draytonh.html.

Highboy. Watercolor by Leonard Battee c. 1939. Colored pencil and graphite on paper board, 55.5 × 36.4 cm (21-13/16 in. × 14-15/16 in.). Photograph © Board of Trustees, National Gallery of Art, Washington. Index of American Design, 1943.8.5928, http://www.nga.gov/collection/gallery/iadfurn/iadfurn-18142.0.html.

2.10

John Lawson, *A New Voyage to Carolina* (1709)

Prior to the 1690s, most Carolina residents were independent farmers who worked their own land. The introduction of rice drastically changed the colony. Although quite lucrative, rice cultivation required complicated waterworks and intensive labor. Within twenty years, rice planters pushed out many small landholders and imported thousands of African slaves. As blacks became a majority of the Carolina population, the colony instituted brutal slave codes. Whites also captured thousands of Indians and sold them to West Indian planters. Not surprisingly, many tribes such as the Yamasee and Tuscarora fought back. In 1715, 400 whites died in a vicious but victorious war against the Yamasee. Many of the surviving Indians fled to Florida or the Creek Nation. By the 1720s, white Carolinians exhausted by years of violence and eager to protect their flourishing economy asked the British government to end proprietary rule. In 1729, Carolina was divided into two colonies under royal jurisdiction and protection.

John Lawson (1674–1711) offers a strikingly placid portrait of Carolina during this chaotic time. An explorer, surveyor, naturalist, and writer, Lawson arrived in Charleston in 1700. He spent the next eleven years traveling through Carolina. In 1709, he published A New Voyage to Carolina, *excerpted here. Two years later, he was captured and killed by Tuscarora Indians in the Neuse River region. (Some spelling is modernized.)*

FOCUS QUESTIONS

1. Why does Lawson believe that so many people are moving to Carolina?
2. How does he describe the local Indians? Why can one consider these remarks ironic?
3. What does this selection tell us about the colonial economy and natural environment?

SOURCE: John Lawson, *A New Voyage to Carolina* (London, 1709). The complete text is published at http://rla.unc.edu/Archives/accounts/Lawson/Lawson.html.

4. How does Lawson describe the men and women he encounters?
5. How does Lawson's account of Carolina differ from that of Charles Wood-mason (Document 2.11)?

When we consider the Latitude and convenient Situation of *Carolina*, had we no farther Confirmation thereof, our Reason would inform us, that such a Place lay fairly to be a delicious Country, being placed in that Girdle of the World which affords Wine, Oil, Fruit, Grain, and Silk, with other rich Commodities, besides a sweet Air, moderate Climate, and fertile Soil; these are the Blessings (under Heaven's Protection) that spin out the Thread of Life to its utmost Extent, and crown our Days with the Sweets of Health and Plenty, which, when joined with Content, renders the Possessors the Happiest Race of Men upon Earth.

The Inhabitants of *Carolina*, through the Richness of the Soil, live an easy and pleasant Life. The Land being of several sorts of Compost, some stiff, others light, some marl, others rich black Mould; here barren of Pine, but affording Pitch, Tar, and Masts; there vastly rich, especially on the Fresh [freshwater, not salty] Rivers, one part bearing great Timbers, others being Savannas or natural Meads, where no Trees grow for several Miles, adorned by Nature with a pleasant Verdure, and beautiful Flowers, frequent in no other Places, yielding abundance of Herbage for Cattle, Sheep, and Horse.

The Country in general affords pleasant Seats, the Land (except in some few Places) being dry and high Banks, parceled out into most convenient Necks, (by the Creeks) easy to be fenced in for securing their Stocks to more strict Boundaries, whereby, with a small trouble of fencing, almost every man may enjoy, to himself, an entire Plantation, or rather Park. These, with the other Benefits of Plenty of Fish, Wild-Fowl, Venison, and the other Conveniences which this Summer-Country naturally furnishes, has induced a great many Families to leave the more Northerly Plantations, and sit down under one of the mildest Governments in the World; in a Country that, with moderate Industry, will afford all the Necessaries of Life.

We have yearly abundance of Strangers come among us, who chiefly strive to go Southerly to settle, because there is a vast Tract of rich Land betwixt the Place we are seated in, and *Cape-Fair*, and upon that River, and more Southerly which is inhabited by none but a few *Indians*, who are at this time well affected to the *English*, and very desirous of their coming to live among them. The more Southerly, the milder Winters, with the Advantages of purchasing the Lords Land at the most easy and moderate Rate of any Lands in *America*, nay (allowing all Advantages thereto annexed) I may say, the Universe does not afford such another; Besides, Men have a great Advantage of choosing good and commodious Tracts of Land at the first Seating of a Country or River, whereas the Later Settlers are forced to purchase smaller Dividends of the old Standers, and sometimes at very considerable Rates; as now in *Virginia* and *Maryland*, where a thousand Acres of good Land cannot be bought under twenty Shillings an Acre, besides two Shillings yearly Acknowledgment for every hundred Acres; which Sum, be it more or less, will serve to put the Merchant or Planter here into a good posture of Buildings, Slaves, and other Necessaries, when the Purchase of his Land comes to him on such easy Terms. And as our Grain . . . thrives with us to admiration, no less do our Stocks of Cattle, Horses, Sheep, and Swine multiply. . . .

Our Produce for Exportation to *Europe* and the Islands in *America*, are Beef, Pork, Tallow, Hides, Deer-Skins, Furs, Pitch, Tar, Wheat, *Indian*-Corn, Pease, Masts, Staves, Heading, Boards and all sorts of Timber and Lumber for *Madera* and the *West-Indies*; Rosin, Turpentine, and several sorts of Gums and Tears, with some medicinal Drugs, are here produced; Besides Rice, and several other foreign Grains, which thrive very well. Good Bricks and Tiles are made, and several sorts of useful Earths, as Bole, Fullers-Earth, Oaker, and Tobacco-Pipe-Clay, in great plenty; Earths for the Potters Trade, and fine Sand for the Glass-Makers. In building with Bricks, we make our Lime of Oyster-Shells, though we have great Store of Lime-Stone, towards the Heads of our Rivers, where are Stones of all sorts that are useful, besides vast Quantities of excellent Marble. Iron-Stone we have plenty of, both in the Low-Grounds and on the Hills; Lead and Copper has been found, so has Antimony [a metallic element]; But no Endeavors have been used to discover those Subterraneous Species; otherwise we might, in all probability, find out the best Minerals, which are not wanting in *Carolina*. . . .

It must be confessed, that the most noble and sweetest Part of this Country, is not inhabited by any but the Savages; and a great deal of the richest Part thereof, has no Inhabitants but the Beasts of the Wilderness: For, the *Indians* are not inclinable to settle in the richest Land, because the Timbers are too large for them to cut down, and too much burdened with Wood for their Laborers to make Plantations of; besides, the Healthfulness of those Hills is apparent, by the Gigantic Stature, and Gray-Heads, so common amongst the Savages that dwell near the Mountains. The great Creator of all things, having most wisely diffused his Blessings, by parceling out the Vintages of the World, into such Lots, as his wonderful Foresight saw most proper, requisite, and convenient for the Habitations of his Creatures. . . .

As for those of our own Country in *Carolina*, some of the Men are very laborious, and make great Improvements in their Way; but I dare hardly give them that Character in general. The Easy way of living in that plentiful Country, makes a great many Planters very negligent, which, were they otherwise, that Colony might now have been in a far better Condition than it is, (as to Trade, and other Advantages) which an universal Industry would have led them into.

The Women are the most industrious Sex in that Place, and, by their good Housewifery, make a great deal of Cloth of their own Cotton, Wool and Flax; some of them keeping their Families (though large) very decently appareled, both with Linens and Woolens, so that they have no occasion to run into the Merchant's Debt, or lay their Money out on Stores for Clothing.

The *Christian* Natives of *Carolina* are a straight, clean-limbed People; the Children being seldom or never troubled with Rickets, or those other Distempers, that the *Europeans* are visited withal. 'Tis next to a Miracle, to see one of them deformed in Body. The Vicinity of the Sun makes Impression on the Men, who labor out of doors, or use the Water. As for those Women, that do not expose themselves to the Weather, they are often very fair, and generally as well featured, as you shall see anywhere, and have very brisk charming Eyes, which sets them off to Advantage. They marry very young; some at Thirteen or Fourteen; and She that stays till Twenty, is reckoned a stale Maid; which is a very indifferent Character in that warm Country. The Women are very fruitful; most Houses being full of Little Ones. It has been observed, that Women long married, and without Children, in other Places, have removed to *Carolina*, and become joyful Mothers. They have very easy Travail in their Child-bearing, in which they are so happy, as seldom to miscarry. Both Sexes are generally spare of Body, and not Choleric, nor easily cast down at Disappointments and Losses, seldom immoderately grieving at Misfortunes, unless for the Loss of their nearest Relations and Friends, which seems to make a more than ordinary Impression upon them. Many of the Women are very handy in Canoes, and will manage them with great Dexterity and Skill, which they become accustomed to in this watery Country. They are ready to help their Husbands in any servile Work, as Planting, when the Season of the Weather requires Expedition; Pride seldom banishing good Housewifery. The Girls are not bred up to the Wheel, and Sewing only; but the Dairy and affairs of the House they are very well acquainted withal; so that you shall see them, whilst very young, manage their Business with a great deal of Conduct and Alacrity. The Children of both Sexes are very docile, and learn any thing with a great deal of Ease and Method; and those that have the Advantages of Education, write good Hands, and prove good Accountants, which is most coveted, and indeed most necessary in these Parts. . . .

All these things duly weighed, any rational Man that has a mind to purchase Land in the Plantations for a Settlement of himself and Family, will soon discover the Advantages that attend the Settlers and Purchasers of Land in *Carolina*, above all other Colonies in the *English* Dominions in *America*. . . .

2.11

Reverend Charles Woodmason on Religion in the Carolina Backcountry (1767–1768)

While the New England and Chesapeake colonies developed, political and religious tumult rocked England. In 1660, with the ascension of Charles II to the monarchy, a new period of stability began. To reward his political supporters, Charles established new colonies in North America. In 1663, he gave eight proprietors a huge tract of land claimed by Spain and populated by thousands of Indians. The proprietors named the colony Carolina. Aware that many English settlers were eager to flee the crowded conditions in the British West Indies, the proprietors offered attractive enticements, including land and religious freedom. Carolina's founders hoped to build a society based on aristocratic privilege and the Church of England (also known as the Anglican Church).

It proved quite difficult to realize these aims. Many people came to Carolina to escape the domination of wealthy planters. They had their own religious and cultural traditions. In this reading, Reverend Charles Woodmason describes life in the colony. An Anglican missionary, Woodmason traveled the region widely seeking converts among the religiously diverse population. His journals provide a vivid portrait of backcountry colonists. (Some spelling has been modernized.)

FOCUS QUESTIONS

1. How does Woodmason portray the people and living conditions in the Carolina backcountry?

2. How does Woodmason's account of Carolina differ from John Lawson's account (Document 2.10)?

3. How do the backcountry residents respond to Woodmason and his ministry?

SOURCE: *The Carolina Backcountry on the Eve of Revolution: The Journal and Other Writings of Charles Woodmason, Anglican Itinerant*, edited by Richard J. Hooker. Copyright ©1953 by the University of North Carolina Press, renewed 1981 by Richard J. Hooker. Published for the Omohundro Institute of Early American History and Culture. Used by permission of the Publisher.

4. How do Woodmason's experiences reflect the religious diversity among the Carolinians?

5. How does religious life in this region differ from Puritan New England?

February 1767, Friday 19

Journeyed upwards to Lynch's Creek, and did Duty there on Sunday the 21. A Crowd of People assembled, the Major Part Episcopals—Married several Couple on the Proclamation and Baptized 30 or 40 children and 2 Adults—A Great Number of Adults present—but all of them totally ignorant of the first Principles of things—So cannot baptize them—And what is worse, being obliged to be in perpetual Motion, I cannot have Time to instruct them, which is great Grief to me. In this Congregation was not a Bible or Common Prayer—None to respond. All very poor and extremely ignorant—Yet desirous of the Knowledge of God and of Christ. Their Case is truly pitiable. . . .

From the lower part of Lynch's Creek I proceeded to the upper—and from the Greater to the Lesser; The Weather was exceeding Cold and piercing—And as these People live in open Log Cabins with hardly a Blanket to cover them, or Clothing to cover their Nakedness, I endured Great Hardships and my Horse more than his Rider—they having no fodder, nor a Grain of Corn to spare.—[total] miles 1470

I had appointed a Congregation to meet me at the Head of Hanging Rock Creek—Where I arrived on Tuesday Evening—Found the Houses filled with debauched licentious fellows, and Scot Presbyterians who had hired these lawless Ruffians to insult me, which they did with Impunity—Telling me, they wanted no D—d Black Gown Sons of Bitches among them—and threatening to lay me behind the Fire, which they assuredly would have done had not some travelers alighted very opportunely, and taken me under Protection—These Men sat up with, and guarded me all the Night—In the Morning the lawless Rabble moved off on seeing the Church People appear, of whom had a large Congregation. But the Service was greatly interrupted by a Gang of Presbyterians who kept hallooing and whooping without Door like Indians.—30 [miles] . . .

1768. How dismal the Case—How hard the Lot of any Gentleman in this Part of the World! No Physician—No Medicines—No Necessaries—Nurses, or Care in Sickness. If You are taken in any Disorder, there You must lie till Nature gets the better of the Disease, or Death relives You. 'Tis the fashion of these People to abandon all Persons when Sick, instead of visiting them—So that a Stranger who has no Relatives or Connections, is in a most Terrible Situation!—1779 [total miles]

The same as for Society and converse—I have not yet met with one literate, or traveled Person—No ingenious Mind—None of any Capacity—Only some few well disposed Religious Persons, but whose Knowledge is very circumscribed. . . .

In all these Excursions, I am obliged to carry my own Necessaries with me—A Biskit—Cheese—A Pint of Rum—Some Sugar—Chocolate—Tea, or Coffee—With Cups Knife Spoon Plate Towels and Linen. So that I go alway[s] heavy loaded like a Trooper. If I did not, I should starve. Never will I be Out again from home for a Month together to take the Chance of things—As in many Places they have naught but a Gourd to drink out of Not a Plate Knife or Spoon, a Glass, Cup, or any thing—It is well if they can get some Body Linen, and some have not even that. They are so burdened with Young Children, that the Women cannot attend both House and Field—And many live by Hunting, and killing of Deer—There's not a Cabin but has 10 or 12 Young Children in it—When the Boys are 18 and Girls 14 they marry—so that in many Cabins You will see 10 or 15 Children. Children and Grand Children of one Size—and the mother looking as Young as the Daughter. Yet these Poor People enjoy good Health; and are generally cut off by Endemic or Epidemic Disorders, which when they happen, makes Great Havoc among them.—1894 [total miles]

You may ask how it is that I imagine to compose, or compile Discourses? This is a hard Task on me, as what suits one Congregation and Set of People, will not another. One Class shall be a vile disorderly Crew. The Address to them will not suit a serious Moral Community—It is this Midnight Work of Study and Writing that much impairs me—for when I come off a Journey of 100 Miles jaded, sweated, and exhausted, Instead of resting and refreshing I must go to the Desk, and write for the next Sunday, or meeting of some particular Congregation—Or, as the Season calls.

As to Itinerant Ministers: You must understand that all (or greatest Part) of this Part of the Province w[h]ere I am, has been settled within these 5 Years by Irish Presbyterians from Belfast, or Pennsylvania and they imagined that they could secure this large Tract of fine Country to themselves and their Sect. Hereon, they built Meeting Houses, and got Pastors from Ireland, and Scotland. But with these there has also a Great Number of New Lights and Independents come here from New England, and many Baptists from thence, being driven from, and not able to live there among the Saints [The Puritans]—Some of these maintain their Teachers. But to keep up their Interests, and preserve their People from falling off to the Church established, and to keep them in a Knot together, the Synods of Pennsylvania and New England send out a Set of Rambling fellows Yearly—who do no Good to the People, no Service to Religion—but turning of their Brains and picking of their Pockets of every Pistreen the Poor Wretches have, return back again, with double the Profits I can make—for though the Law gives me 12/6 Currency for every Baptism, I never yet took one farthing—and of near 100 Couple that I've married, I have not been paid for 1/3. Their Poverty is so Great, that were they to offer me a fee, my Heart would not let me take it.

'Tis these roving Teachers that stir up the Minds of the People against the Established Church [The Church of England], and her Ministers—and make the Situation of any Gentleman extremely uneasy, vexatious, and disagreeable. I would sooner starve in England on a Currency of 20[sterling] p ann, than to live here on 200 Guineas, did not the Interests of Religion and the Church absolutely require it—Some few of these Itinerants have encountered me—I find them a Set of Rhapsodists—Enthusiasts—Bigots—Pedantic, illiterate, impudent Hypocrites—Straining at Gnats, and swallowing Camels, and making Religion a Cloak for Covetousness Detraction, Guile, Impostures and their particular Fabric of Things.

Among these Quakers and Presbyterians, are many concealed Papists—They are not tolerated in this Government—And in the Shape of New Light Preachers, I've met with many Jesuits. We have too here a Society of *Dunkards*—these resort to hear me when I am over at Jackson Creek.

Among this Medley of Religions—True Genuine Christianity is not to be found. And the perverse persecuting Spirit of the Presbyterians, displays it Self much more here than in Scotland. It is dangerous to live among, or near any of them—for if they cannot cheat, rob, defraud or injure You in Your Goods—they will belie, defame, lessen, blacken, disparage the most valuable Person breathing, not of their Communion in his Character, Good Name, or Reputation and Credit. They have almost wormed out all the Church People—who cannot bear to live among such a Set of Vile unaccountable Wretches. . . .

June 16. Came up from St. Marks to Pine Tree, and next Day went down to Swift Creek, where married 2 Couple and baptized several Adults and Young Children—Sunday the 19th at the Meeting House at Pine Tree—The Presbyterians carried off the Key—But some Persons got in and opened the Doors—The Magistrate attended—but had but a small Congregation the Principal People generally riding abroad every Sunday for Recreation.—20 [miles]

The open profanation of the Lords Day in this Province is one of the most crying Sins in it—and is carried to a great height—Among the low Class, it is abused by Hunting fishing fowling, and Racing—By the Women in frolicking and Wantonness. By others in Drinking Bouts and Card playing—Even in and about Charlestown, the Taverns have more Visitants than the Churches.

2.12

Olaudah Equiano Recalls the Horrors of the Middle Passage (1756)

Beginning in 1619, the transatlantic slave trade brought millions of Africans to North America. In 1755, at the age of 11, Olaudah Equiano (Gustavus Vassa) was kidnapped from Benin (now Nigeria). He was sold in the West Indies, where he received some education and was eventually freed. After arriving in England, he

SOURCE: Olaudah Equiano, *The Life of Olaudah Equiano, or Gustavus Vassa, the African* (Boston, 1837), 43–52.

became an active abolitionist. British antislavery activists financed the publication of his autobiography, The Interesting Narrative of the Life of Olaudah Equiano, *or* Gustavus Vassa, the African *(1789). The book was well-received and printed in several editions. In this account, Equiano describes the Middle Passage.*

FOCUS QUESTIONS

1. What are Equiano's initial responses to the slave traders?
2. How does he describe conditions on the slave ship?
3. What happened when the ship reached Barbados?
4. How do you think accounts like this affected public opinions about slavery?

The first object which saluted my eyes when I arrived on the coast was the sea, and a slave ship then riding at anchor, and waiting for its cargo. These filled me with astonishment, which was soon converted into terror, when I was carried on board. I was immediately handled, and tossed up, to see if I were sound, by some of the crew; and I was now persuaded that I had got into a world of bad spirits, and that they were going to kill me. Their complexions too differing so much from ours, their long hair, and the language they spoke (which was very different from any I had ever heard) united to confirm me in this belief. Indeed such were the horrors of my views and fears at the moment, that, if ten thousand worlds had been my own, I would have freely parted with them all to have exchanged my condition with that of the meanest slave in my own country. When I looked round the ship too and saw a large furnace or copper boiling, and a multitude of black people of every description chained together, every one for their countenances expressing dejection and sorrow, I no longer doubted my fate; and, quite overpowered with horror and anguish, I fell motionless on the deck and fainted. When I recovered a little I found some black people about me, who I believed were some of those who had brought me on board, and had been receiving their pay; they talked to me in order to cheer me, but all in vain. I asked them if we were not to be eaten by those white men with horrible looks, red faces, and loose hair. They told me I was not ...

I now saw myself deprived of all chance of returning to my native country, or even the least glimpse of hope of gaining the shore, which I now considered as friendly; and I even wished for my former slavery in preference to my present situation. ... I was soon put down under the decks, and there I received such a salutation in my nostrils as I had never experienced in my life: so that, with the loathsomeness of the stench, and crying together, I became so sick and low that I was not able to eat, nor had I the desire to taste any thing. I now wished for the last friend, death, to relieve me, but soon, to my grief, two of the white men offered me eatables; and, on my refusing to eat, one of them laid me across I think the windlass, and tied my feet, while the other flogged me severely. I had never experienced anything of this kind before; and although, not being used to the water, I naturally feared that element the first time I saw it, yet nevertheless, could I have got over the nettings, I would have jumped over the side, but could not; and, besides, the crew used to watch us very closely who were not chained down to the decks, lest we should leap into the water: and I have seen some of these poor African prisoners most severely cut for attempting to do so, and hourly whipped for not eating. This indeed was often the case with myself. In a little time after, amongst the poor chained men, I found some of my own nation, which in a small degree gave ease to my mind. I inquired of these what was to be done with us; they gave me to understand we were to be carried to these white people's country to work for them. I then was a little revived, and thought, if it were no worse than working, my situation was not so desperate: but still I feared I should be put to death, the white people looked and acted, as I thought, in so savage a manner; for I had never seen among any people such instances of brutal cruelty; and this not only shown toward us blacks, but also to some of the whites themselves. . . .

The stench of the hold while we were on the coast was so intolerably loathsome, that it was dangerous to remain there for any time, and some of us had been permitted to stay on the deck for the fresh air; but now that the whole ship's cargo were confined together, it became absolutely pestilential. The closeness of the place, and the heat of the climate, added to the number in the ship, which was so crowded that each had scarcely room to turn himself, almost suffocated us. This produced copious perspiration, so that the air soon became unfit for respiration, from a variety of loathsome smells, and brought on a sickness amongst the slaves, of which many died, thus falling victims to the improvident avarice, as I may call it, of their purchasers. This wretched situation was again aggravated by the galling of the chains, now become insupportable; and the filth of the necessary tubs, into which the children often fell, and were almost suffocated. The shrieks of the women, and the groans of the dying, rendered the whole a scene of horror almost inconceivable. Happily perhaps for myself, I was soon reduced so low here that it was thought necessary to keep me always on deck; and from my extreme youth I was not put in fetters. . . .

One day, when we had a smooth sea and a moderate wind, two of my wearied countrymen who were chained together (I was near them at the time), preferring death to such a life of misery, somehow made it through the nettings and jumped into the sea: immediately another quite dejected fellow . . . followed their example. . . .

At last we came in sight of the island of Barbados, at which the whites on board gave a great shout, and made many signs of joy to us. . . . Many merchants and planters now came on board, though it was evening. They put on in separate parcels, and examined us attentively. They also made us jump, and pointed to the land, signifying we were to go there. . . . We were not many days in the merchant's custody before we were sold after their usual manner, which is this:—On a signal given, (as the beat of the drum) the buyers rush at once into the yard where the slaves are confined, and make choice of that parcel they like best. The noise and clamor with which this is attended, and the eagerness visible in the countenances of the buyers, serve not a little to increase the apprehension of terrified Africans, who may well be supposed to consider them as the ministers of that destruction to which they think themselves devoted. In this manner, without scruple, are relations and friends separated, most of them never to see each other again. . . .

2.13

Alexander Falconbridge, the African Slave Trade (1788)

At several trading posts along the coast of West Africa, Europeans traded rum, clothing, and other goods for human beings captured by Africans. After enduring brutal conditions at coastal forts, potential slaves spent two to three months in the horrifying Middle Passage to the New World. As slave traders grew rich, a series of wars devastated African culture and family life. By 1750, ships brought 45,000 slaves a year to the British colonies. England surpassed Portugal and Spain as the world's leading slave trader.

In this passage, Alexander Falconbridge, ship surgeon, describes the barbaric conditions on slave ships.

FOCUS QUESTIONS

1. How does Falconbridge's description of the Middle Passage compare to Olaudah Equiano's (Document 2.12)?

2. How does Falconbridge view the Africans? Do you think his opinions were common among slave traders? Explain your answer.

As soon as the wretched Africans, purchased at the fairs, fall into the hands of the black traders, they experience in earnest those dreadful sufferings which they are doomed in future to undergo. And there is not the least room to doubt, but that

SOURCE: Alexander Falconbridge, *An Account of the Slave Trade on the Coast of Africa* (London: 1788).

even before they can reach the fairs, great numbers perish from cruel usage, want of food, traveling through inhospitable deserts, etc. They are brought from the places where they are purchased to Bonny, etc. in canoes; at the bottom of which they lie, having their hands tied with a kind of willow twigs, and a strict watch is kept over them. Their usage in other respects, during the time of passage, which generally lasts several days, is equally cruel. Their allowance of food is so scanty, that it is barely sufficient to support nature. They are, besides, much exposed to the violent rains which frequently fall here, being covered only with mats that afford but a slight defense; and as there is usually water at the bottom of the canoes, from their leaking, they are scarcely ever dry.

Nor do these unhappy beings, after they become the property of the Europeans (from whom as a more civilized people, more humanity might naturally be expected), find their situation in the least amended. Their treatment is no less rigorous. The men Negroes, on being brought aboard the ship, are immediately fastened together, two and two, by handcuffs on their wrists, and irons riveted on their legs. They are then sent down between the decks, and placed in an apartment partitioned off for that purpose. The women likewise are placed in a separate room, on the same deck, but without being ironed. And an adjoining room, on the same deck is besides appointed for the boys. Thus are they placed in different apartments.

But at the same time, they are frequently stowed so close, as to admit of no other posture than lying on their sides. Neither will the height between decks, unless directly under the grating, permit them the indulgence of an erect posture; especially where there are platforms, which is generally the case. These platforms are a kind of shelf, about eight or nine feet in breadth, extending from the side of the ship towards the center. They are placed nearly midway between the decks, at the distance of two or three feet from each deck. Upon these the Negroes are stowed in the same manner as they are on the deck underneath.

... About eight o'clock in the morning the Negroes are generally brought upon deck. Their irons being examined, a long chain, which is locked to a ring-bolt, fixed in the deck, is run through the rings of the shackles of the men, and then locked to another ring-bolt, fixed also in the deck. By this means fifty or sixty, and sometimes more, are fastened to one chain, in order to prevent them from rising, or endeavoring to escape. If the weather proves favorable, they are permitted to remain in that situation till four or five in the afternoon, when they are disengaged from the chain, and sent down. ...

... Upon the Negroes refusing to take sustenance, I have seen coals of fire, glowing hot, put on a shovel, and placed so near their lips, as to scorch and burn them. And this has been accompanied with threats, of forcing them to swallow the coals, if they any longer persisted in refusing to eat. These means have generally had the desired effect. I have also been credibly informed that a certain captain in the slave trade poured melted lead on such of the Negroes as obstinately refused their food.

Exercise being deemed necessary for the preservation of their health, they are sometimes obligated to dance, when the weather will permit their coming on deck. If they go about it reluctantly, or do not move with agility, they are flogged; a person standing by them all the time with at cat-o'-nine-tails in his hand for that purpose. Their music, upon these occasions, consists of a drum, sometimes with only one head; and when that is worn out, they do not scruple to make use of the bottom of one of the tubs before described. The poor wretches are frequently compelled to sing also; but when they do so, their songs are generally, as may naturally be expected, melancholy lamentations of their exile from their native country.

. . . On board some ships, the common sailors are allowed to have intercourse with such of the black women whose consent they can procure. And some of them have been known to take the inconstancy of their paramours so much to heart, as to leap overboard and drown themselves. The officers are permitted to indulge their passions among them at pleasure, and sometimes are guilty of such brutal excesses as disgrace human nature.

The hardships and inconveniences suffered by the Negroes during the passage are scarcely to be enumerated or conceived. They are far more violently affected by the seasickness than the Europeans. It frequently terminates in death, especially among the women. But the exclusion of the fresh air is among the most intolerable. For the purpose of admitting this needful refreshment, most of the ships in the slave trade are provided, between the decks, with five or six airports on each side of the ship, of about six inches in length, and four in breadth; in addition to which, some few ships, but not one in twenty, have what they denominate wind-sails. But whenever the sea is rough and the rain heavy, it becomes necessary to shut these, and every other conveyance by which the air is admitted. The fresh air being thus excluded, the Negroes' rooms very soon grow intolerably hot. The confined air, rendered noxious by the effluvia exhaled from their bodies, and by being repeatedly breathed, soon produces fevers and fluxes, which generally carries off great numbers of them.

. . . One morning, upon examining the place allotted for the sick Negroes, I perceived that one of them, who was so emaciated as scarcely to be able to walk, was missing, and was convinced that he must have gone overboard in the night, probably to put a more expeditious period to his sufferings. And, to conclude on this subject, I could not help being sensibly affected, on a former voyage, at observing with what apparent eagerness a black woman seized some dirt from off an African yam, and put it into her mouth, seeming to rejoice at the opportunity of possessing some of her native earth.

From these instances I think it may have been clearly deduced that the unhappy Africans are not bereft of the finer feelings, but have a strong attachment to their native country, together with a just sense of the value of liberty. And the situation of the miserable beings above described, more forcibly urges the necessity of abolishing a trade which is the source of such evils, than the most eloquent harangue, or persuasive arguments could do.

2.14

A Puritan Prescription for Marital Concord (1712)

The Puritans considered nuclear families essential to preserving social order and community. The well-ordered family was one in which wives, children, and servants dutifully obeyed the man of the house. The "good wife" submitted to her husband's authority. This is not to say that Puritan marriages were not happy and loving unions. Many were.

Despite the religious nature of their settlements, the Puritans considered marriage a civil contract, not a sacrament. Although divorce was rare, courts did dissolve marriages in instances of bigamy, desertion, adultery, or physical abuse. Courts and churches also disciplined people who failed to maintain tranquil households.

New England wives enjoyed far more legal protection from domestic violence and abandonment than their English counterparts. Yet they remained subject to English laws that granted husbands control of their property except in cases where a premarital agreement existed. A widow inherited her husband's estate only when no children existed or when a husband made special provisions in his will. Widows were entitled to use one-third of the estate for the duration of their lives.

In this excerpt from Benjamin Wadsworth's The Well-Ordered Family *(1712), Puritan couples are advised about their marital duties.*

FOCUS QUESTION

1. What does Wadsworth consider essential to a successful marriage? Would you want a marriage like the one he recommends? Explain your answer.

Christians should endeavor to please and glorify God, in whatever capacity or relation they sustain.

Under this doctrine, my design is (by God's help) to say something about relative duties, particularly in families. I shall therefore endeavor to speak as

SOURCE: Benjamin Wadsworth, *A Well-Ordered Family* (Boston, 1712), 2d. ed., pp. 22–59, *passim.*

briefly and plainly as I can about: (1) family prayer; (2) the duties of husbands and wives; (3) the duties of parents and children; (4) the duties of masters and servants. . . .

ABOUT THE DUTIES OF HUSBANDS AND WIVES

Concerning the duties of this relation we may assert a few things. It is their duty to dwell together with one another. Surely they should dwell together, if one house cannot hold them, surely they are not affected to each other as they should be. They should have a very great and tender love and affection to one another. This is plainly commanded by God. This duty of love is mutual; it should be performed by each, to each of them. When, therefore, they quarrel or disagree, then they do the Devil's work; he is pleased at it, glad of it. But such contention provokes God; it dishonors Him; it is a vile example before inferiors in the family; it tends to prevent family prayer.

As to outward things. If the one is sick, troubled, or distressed, the other should manifest care, tenderness, pity, and compassion, and afford all possible relief and succor. They should likewise unite their prudent counsels and endeavors, comfortable to maintain themselves and the family under their joint care.

Husband and wife should be patient one toward another. If both are truly pious, yet neither of them is perfectly holy, in such cases a patient, forgiving, forbearing spirit is very needful. . . .

The husband's government ought to be gentle and easy, and the wife's obedience ready and cheerful. The husband is called the head of the woman. It belongs to the head to rule and govern. Wives are part of the house and family, and ought to be under the husband's government. Yet his government should not be with rigor, haughtiness, harshness, severity, but with the greatest love, gentleness, kindness, tenderness that may be. Though he governs her, he must not treat her as a servant, but as his own flesh; he must love her to himself.

Those husbands are much to blame who do not carry it lovingly and kindly to their wives. O man, if your wife is not so young, beautiful, healthy, well-tempered, and qualified as you would wish; if she did not bring a large estate to you, or cannot do so much for you, as some other women have done for their husbands; yet she is your wife, and the great God commands you to love her, not be bitter, but kind to her. What can be more plain and expressive than that?

Those wives are much to blame who do not carry it lovingly and obediently to their own husbands. O woman, if your husband is not as young, beautiful, healthy, so well-tempered, and qualified as your could wish; if he has not such abilities, riches, honors, as some others have; yet he is your husband, and the great God commands you to love, honor, and obey him. Yea, though possibly you have greater abilities of the mind than he has, was of some high birth, and he of a more common birth, or did bring more estate, yet since he is your husband, God has made him your head, and set him above you, and made it your duty to love and revere him.

Parents should act wisely and prudently in the matching of their children. They should endeavor that they may marry someone who is most proper for them, most likely to bring blessings to them.

2.15

Jane Colman Turell, "Lines on Childbirth" (1741)

In colonial America, families often dealt with death. Infant mortality rates were nearly 50 percent in some regions. Some historians speculate that the dangers of childbirth inspired many women to become avid church members.

Jane Colman Turell (1708–1735) wrote extensively about daily life in rural Massachusetts. After her death, her husband Ebenezer gathered her writings and had them published as Some Memoirs of the Life and Death of Mrs. Jane Turell *(1741).*

In this poem, Turell writes about her pregnancies.

FOCUS QUESTIONS

1. How does Turell describe her pregnancies? What is her fondest wish?

2. What does this poem suggest about family life in colonial America?

Phoebus has thrice his yearly circuit run,
The winter's over, and the summer's done;
Since that bright day on which our hands were join'd,
And to Philander I my all resign'd.
Thrice in my womb I've found the pleasing strife,
In the first struggles of my infant's life:
But O how soon by Heaven I'm call'd to mourn,
While from my womb a lifeless babe is torn?

SOURCE: Published in *The Heath Anthology of American Literature*, Paul Lauter et al., eds. (Lexington, MA: D.C. Heath and Company, 1990), pp. 642–43.

Born to the grave ere it had seen the light,
Or with one smile had cheer'd my longing sight.
Again in travail pains my nerves are wreck'd,
My eye balls start, my heart strings almost crack'd;
Now I forget my pains,
and now I press Philander's image to my panting breast.
Ten days I hold him in my joyful arms,
And feast my eyes upon his infant charms.
But then the King of Terrors does advance,
To pierce its bosom with his iron lance.
Its soul releas'd, upward it takes its flight,
Oh never more below to bless my sight!
Farewell sweet babes I hope to meet above,
And there with you sing the Redeemer's love.
And now O gracious Savior lend thine ear,
To this my earnest cry and humble prayer,
That when the hour arrives with painful throes,
Which shall my burden to the world disclose;
I may deliverance have, and joy to see,
A living child, to dedicate to Thee.

Phoebus in Greek mythology is Apollo, god of sunlight.
Philander is a pseudonym for Turell's husband, Ebenezer.

3

✳

The Spirit of Revolution

Throughout the eighteenth century, demographic, economic, religious, and intellectual factors led to the rise of a uniquely American identity. Fueled by natural reproduction, the slave trade, and immigration, the population grew dramatically. Booming transatlantic markets enabled people to participate in the world economy as producers and consumers. While not all Americans enjoyed prosperity, many colonists purchased consumer goods and began living more genteel, social lifestyles. Inspired by the European Enlightenment, intellectuals embraced an optimistic worldview based on rational thought and self-improvement. At the same time, the Great Awakening reminded individuals of Man's sinful nature, while emphasizing the equality of all in the eyes of the Lord. Both movements reflected the individualism shaping American society.

As Americans defined themselves, they began to clash with British authorities. After the Seven Years' War, the British government imposed a series of laws and taxes to defray its debts and to consolidate its imperial holdings. Used to legislating for themselves, many colonists viewed these measures as attacks on their independence and economic security. As collective protests escalated, deep divisions emerged between those embracing republican political ideals and those remaining loyal to Britain. The eruption of the American Revolution intensified these conflicts.

THEMES TO CONSIDER

- The religious and political importance of the Great Awakening
- Justifications for and attacks on British authority in the American colonies
- How political protests changed the political and social roles of American women

- The principles of republicanism and their significance in shaping colonial protests, the American Revolution, and the political and social history of the United States

- The impact of the American Revolution upon American Indians, women, and slaves

- The ways that republicanism and the American Revolution broadened notions of civic life and challenged traditional ideas on race and gender

3.1

Jonathan Edwards, "Sinners in the Hands of an Angry God" (1741)

The Great Awakening profoundly changed American religious history. Part of a larger evangelical movement that began in Western Europe, the Great Awakening was a series of religious revivals held throughout the American colonies beginning in the 1730s. In contrast to staid preaching, revivalist ministers offered emotionally charged sermons stressing the corruption of Man, the wrath of God, and the need for repentance.

Jonathan Edwards brilliantly articulated such views. After rigorous theological training at Yale, he returned to Northampton, Massachusetts, to become a colleague of his grandfather, the Congregationalist pastor Solomon Stoddard. Incorporating Enlightenment philosophy into traditional religious doctrine, Edwards preached justification by faith alone. After Stoddard's death in 1729, Edwards became the Northampton pastor. His teachings soon sparked a religious revival throughout the Connecticut River Valley.

But other ministers spread revivalism throughout America. The most influential was George Whitefield, an Englishman who inspired thousands to seek salvation. The Great Awakening created deep divisions between "Old Light" rationalists and "New Light" evangelicals. Many "New Lights" left their traditional churches, such as the Congregationalists and Anglicans, and joined sects like the Baptists and Methodists. The Great Awakening proved particularly powerful among women and African Americans. It also may have contributed to the American Revolution by making ordinary people more willing to question authority.

This selection features portions of "Sinners in the Hands of an Angry God," Jonathan Edwards's most famous sermon.

SOURCE: Jonathan Edwards, *Works* 2 (1840): 10–11.

FOCUS QUESTIONS

1. What are the central themes of "Sinners in the Hands of an Angry God"?
2. Why do you think sermons like this inspired so many people? How would you have reacted to this sermon?

The God that holds you over the pit of hell, much as one holds a spider or some loathsome insect over the fire, abhors you, and is dreadfully provoked. His wrath towards you burns like fire; he looks upon you as worthy of nothing else but to be cast into the fire. He is of purer eyes than to bear you in his sight; you are ten thousand times as abominable in his eyes as the most hateful, venomous serpent is in ours.

You have offended him infinitely more than ever a stubborn rebel did his prince, and yet it is nothing but his hand that holds you from falling into the fire every moment. It is to be ascribed to nothing else that you did not go to hell last night; that you were suffered to awake again in this world, after you closed your eyes to sleep. And there is no other reason to be given why you have not dropped into hell since you arose in the morning, but that God's hand has held you up. There is no other reason to be given why you have not gone to hell since you have sat here in the house of God provoking his pure eye by your sinful, wicked manner of attending his solemn worship. Yea, there is nothing else that is to be given as a reason why you do not this very moment drop down into hell.

O sinner! Consider the fearful danger you are in! It is a great furnace of wrath, a wide and bottomless pit, full of fire and of wrath that you are held over in the hand of that God whose wrath is provoked and incensed as much against you as against many of the damned in hell. You hang by a slender thread, with the flames of Divine wrath flashing about it, and ready every moment to singe it and burn it asunder. . . .

It would be dreadful to suffer this fierceness and wrath of Almighty God one moment; but you must suffer it to all eternity. There will be no end to this exquisite, horrible, misery. . . .

How dreadful is the state of those that are daily and hourly in danger of this great wrath and infinite misery! But this is the dismal case of every soul in this congregation that has not been born again, however moral and strict, sober and religious, they may otherwise be. Oh! that you would consider it, whether you be young or old!

There is no reason to think that there are many in this congregation, now hearing this discourse, that will actually be the subjects of this very misery to all eternity. We know not who they are, or in what seats they sit, or what thoughts they now have. It may be they are now at ease, and hear all these things without much disturbance, and are now flattering themselves that they are not the persons, promising themselves that they shall escape.

If we knew that there was one person, and but one in the whole congregation, that was to be the subject of this misery, what an awful thing it would be to think of! If we knew who it was, what an awful sight would it be to see such a person! How might the rest of the congregation lift up a lamentable and bitter cry over him!

But, alas! Instead of one, how many is it likely will remember this discourse, in hell! And it would be a wonder if some that are now present should not be in hell in a very short time before this year is out. And it would be no wonder if some persons that now sit here in some seats of this meeting-house, in health, and quiet and secure, should be there before tomorrow morning!

3.2

Thomas Hutchinson Recounts the Mob Reaction to the Stamp Act in Boston (1765)

After costly victories in the Seven Years' War and Pontiac's Rebellion (1763–1764), Great Britain was in a financial crisis. Because British citizens paid annual taxes twenty-five times higher than Americans, British officials turned to the colonies for additional sources of revenue. After the Sugar Act (1764) failed to offset the costs of defending North America, Parliament passed the Stamp Act (1765). The Stamp Act required the purchase of royal seals on all commercial and legal papers, newspapers, playing cards, and dice. Where the Sugar Act primarily affected shippers and merchants, the Stamp Act had a far bigger impact.

Insistent in their rights as Englishmen to be taxed only by their consent through directly elected representatives, colonists bitterly protested the Stamp Act. Boston was the epicenter of discontent. Members of groups like the Loyal Nine and the Sons of Liberty began rioting and intimidating imperial stamp distributors. Many blamed the Stamp Act on Thomas Hutchinson, royal lieutenant governor of Massachusetts Bay and chief justice of the Superior Court.

SOURCE: Reprinted by permission of the publisher from Vol. 3, pp. 86–88, *The History of the Colony and Province of Massachusetts Bay*, 3 vols. (Boston, 1764–1828) by Thomas Hutchinson, edited by Lawrence Haw Mayo, Cambridge, Mass.: Harvard University Press, Copyright © 1936 by the President and Fellows of Harvard College.

Increasingly hostile to those protesting British rule, Hutchinson became one of the most prominent Loyalists in the colonies.

In this selection, Hutchinson describes the Stamp Act riots.

FOCUS QUESTIONS

1. What were some of the ways Bostonians responded to the Stamp Act? How was Hutchinson personally affected by the protests?

2. Why have protesters targeted Hutchinson? How does he respond to their accusations?

3. Were the Stamp Act riots an effective way to convey colonists' dissatisfaction with British policies? Explain your answer.

The distributor of stamps for the colony of Connecticut arrived in Boston from London; and having been agent for that colony, and in other respect of a very reputable character, received from many gentlemen of the town such civilities as were due to him. When he set out from Connecticut, Mr. Oliver, the distributor for Massachusetts Bay, accompanied him out of town. This occasioned murmuring among the people, and an inflammatory piece in the next Boston Gazette. A few days after, early in the morning, a stuffed image was hung upon a tree, called the great tree of the south part of Boston [subsequently called Liberty Tree]. Labels affixed denoted it to be designed for the distributor of stamps....

Before night, the image was taken down, and carried through the townhouse, in the chamber whereof the governor and council were sitting. Forty or fifty tradesmen, decently dressed, preceded; and some thousands of the mob followed down King street to Oliver's dock, near which Mr. Oliver had lately erected a building, which, it was conjectured, he designed for a stamp office. This was laid flat to the ground in a few minutes. From thence the mob preceded for Fort Hill, but Mr. Oliver's house being in the way, they endeavoured to force themselves into it, and being opposed, broke the windows, beat down the doors, entered, and destroyed part of his furniture, and continued in riot until midnight, before they separated....

Several of the council gave it as their opinion, Mr. Oliver being present, that the people, not only of the town of Boston, but of the country in general, would never submit to the execution of the stamp act, let the consequence of an opposition to it be what it would. It was also reported, that the people of Connecticut had threatened to hang their distributor on the first tree after he entered the colony; and that, to avoid it, he had turned aside to Rhode Island.

Despairing of protection, and finding his family in terror and great distress, Mr. Oliver came to a sudden resolution to resign his office before another night....

The next evening, the mob surrounded the house of the lieutenant-governor and chief justice [Hutchinson]. He was at Mr. Oliver's house when it was assaulted, and had excited the sheriff, and the colonel of the regiment, to attempt to suppress the mob. A report was soon spread, that he was a favourer of the stamp act, and had encouraged it by letters to the ministry. Upon notice of the approach of the people, he caused the doors and windows to be barred; and remained in the house. . . .

Certain depositions had been taken, many months before these transactions, by order of the governor, concerning the illicit trade carrying on; and one of them, made by the judge of the admiralty, at the special desire of the governor, had been sworn to before the lieutenant-governor, as chief justice. They had been shown, at one of the offices in England, to a person who arrived in Boston just at this time, and he had acquainted several merchants, whose names were in some of the depositions as smugglers, with the contents. This brought, though without reason, the resentment of the merchants against the persons who, by their office were obliged to administer the oaths, as well as against the officers of the customs and admiralty, who had made the depositions; and the leaders of the mob contrived a riot, which, after some small efforts against such officers, was to spend its principal force upon the lieutenant-governor. And, in the evening of the 26th of August, such a mob was collected in King street, drawn there by a bonfire, and well supplied with strong drink. After some annoyance to the house of the registrar of the admiralty, and somewhat greater to that of the comptroller of the customs, whose cellars they plundered of the wine and spirits in them, they came, with intoxicated rage, upon the house of the lieutenant-governor. The doors were immediately split to pieces with broad axes, and a way made there, and at the windows, for the entry of the mob; which poured in, and filled, in an instant, every room in the house.

The lieutenant-governor had very short notice of the approach of the mob. He directed his children, and the rest of his family, to leave the house immediately, determining to keep possession himself. His eldest daughter, after going a little way from the house, returned, and refused to quit it, unless her father would do the like.

This caused him to depart from his resolutions, a few minutes before the mob entered. They continued their possession until day-light; destroyed, carried away, or cast into the street, every thing that was in the house; demolished every part of it, except the walls, as far as lay in their power; and had begun to break away the brickwork.

The damage was estimated at about twenty-five hundred pounds sterling, without any regard to a great collection of public as well as private papers, in the possession and custody of the lieutenant-governor.

This town was, the whole night, under the awe of this mob; many of the magistrates, with the field of officers of the militia, standing by as spectators; and nobody daring to oppose, or contradict.

3.3

Benjamin Franklin, Testimony Against the Stamp Act (1766)

The violent nature of many Stamp Act protests alarmed colonial moderates. Hoping to voice their grievances peacefully, nine colonies sent representatives to New York in October 1765. Following the Stamp Act Congress, colonists began flooding Parliament with petitions to repeal the detested tax. They also organized boycotts on British imports. By late 1765, many stamp collectors had resigned their posts, and British manufacturers and merchants were suffering devastating losses. Parliament finally repealed the Stamp Act in 1766. Simultaneously, however, Parliament issued the Declaratory Act, reiterating its right to legislate and tax anywhere in the British empire "in all cases whatsoever." The Stamp Act crisis compelled many Americans to contemplate their relationship to the British government.

Benjamin Franklin (1706–1790) is one of the most colorful figures in American history. A publisher, author, inventor, scientist, and diplomat, Franklin gained international fame. He became the colonists' chief spokesperson in debates with the British officials. In 1776, he helped draft the Declaration of Independence. During the American Revolution, he persuaded France to extend military and economic assistance to the United States. In 1787, he played a vital role in framing the Constitution.

In this reading, Franklin testifies before a committee of the House of Commons.

FOCUS QUESTIONS

1. What types of taxes were the American colonists paying?
2. Why did the colonists find the Stamp Act so objectionable?
3. According to Franklin, how were American attitudes toward Britain changing? What were Americans willing to do in order to get the Stamp Act repealed?
4. Would you have joined the Stamp Act protests? Explain your answer.

SOURCE: *The Examination of Doctor Benjamin Franklin . . . relating to the Repeal of the Stamp Act* (Philadelphia, 1766), 1–23 *passim*; *The Parliamentary History of England* (London: 1813), XVI, 138–159.

Q: What is your name, and place of abode?

A: Franklin, of Philadelphia.

Q: Do the Americans pay any considerable taxes among themselves?

A: Certainly many, and very heavy taxes.

Q: What are the present taxes in Pennsylvania, laid by the laws of the colony?

A: There are taxes on all estates, real and personal; a poll tax; a tax on all offices, professions, trades, and businesses, according to their profits; an excise on all wine, rum, and other spirits; and a duty of ten pounds per head on all Negroes imported, with some other duties.

Q: For what purposes are those taxes laid?

A: For the support of the civil and military establishments of the country, and to discharge the heavy debt contracted in the last [Seven Years'] war. . . .

Q: Are not all the people very able to pay those taxes?

A: No. The frontier counties, all along the continent, have been frequently ravaged by the enemy and greatly impoverished, and are able to pay very little tax. . . .

Q: Are not the colonies, from their circumstances, very able to pay the stamp duty?

A: In my opinion there is not gold and silver enough in the colonies to pay the stamp duty for one year.

Q: Don't you know that the money arising from the stamps was all to be laid out in America?

A: I know it is appropriated by the act to the American service; but it will be spent in the conquered colonies, where the soldiers are, not in the colonies that pay it. . . .

Q: Do you think it right that America should be protected by this country and pay no part of the expense?

A: That is not the case. The colonies raised, clothed, and paid, during the last war, near 25,000 men, and spent many millions.

Q: Were you not reimbursed by Parliament?

A: We were only reimbursed what, in your opinion, we had advanced beyond our proportion, or beyond what might reasonably be expected from us; and it was a very small part of what we spent. Pennsylvania, in particular, disbursed about 500,000 pounds, and the reimbursements, in the whole, did not exceed 60,000 pounds. . . .

Q: Do you think the people of America would submit to pay the stamp duty, if it was moderated?

A: No, never, unless compelled by force of arms. . . .

Q: What was the temper of America towards Great Britain before the year 1763?

A: The best in the world. They submitted willingly to the government of the Crown, and paid, in all their courts, obedience to acts of Parliament. Numerous as the people are in the several old provinces, they cost you nothing in forts, citadels, garrisons or armies, to keep them in subjection. They were governed by this country at the expence only of a little pen, ink and paper. They were led by a thread. They had not only respect, but an affection, for Great Britain, for its laws, its customs and manners, and even a fondness for its fashions, that greatly increased the commerce. Natives of Britain were always treated with particular regard; to be an Old England-man, was, of itself, a character of some respect, and gave a kind of rank among us.

Q: And what is their temper now?

A: O, very much altered.

Q: Did you ever hear the authority of Parliament to make laws for America questioned till lately?

A: The authority of Parliament was allowed to be valid in all laws, except such as should lay internal taxes. It was never disputed in laying duties to regulate commerce. . . .

Q: What is your opinion of a future tax, imposed on the same principle with that of the Stamp Act? How would the Americans receive it?

A: Just as they do this. They would not pay it.

Q: Have not you heard of the resolutions of this House, and of the House of Lords, asserting the right of Parliament relating to America, including a power to tax the people there?

A: Yes, I have heard of such resolutions.

Q: What will be the opinion of the Americans on those resolutions?

A: They will think them unconstitutional and unjust.

Q: Was it an opinion in America before 1763 that the Parliament had no right to lay taxes and duties there?

A: I never heard any objection to the right of laying duties to regulate commerce; but a right to lay internal taxes was never supposed to be in Parliament, as we are not represented there. . . .

Q: Did the Americans ever dispute the controlling power of Parliament to regulate the commerce?

A: No.

Q: Can anything less than a military force carry the Stamp Act into execution?

A: I do not see how a military force can be applied to that purpose.

Q: Why may it not?

A: Suppose a military force sent into America; they will find nobody in arms; what are they then to do? They cannot force a man to take stamps who chooses to do without them. They will not find a rebellion; they may indeed make one.

Q: If the act is not repealed, what do you think will be the consequences?

A: A total loss of the respect and affection the people of America bear to this country, and of all the commerce that depends on that respect and affection.

Q: How can the commerce be affected?

A: You will find that, if the act is not repealed, they will take very little of your manufactures in a short time.

Q: Is it in their power to do without them?

A: I think they may very well do without them.

Q: Is it their interest not to take them?

A: The goods they take from Britain are either necessaries, mere conveniences, or superfluities. The first, as cloth, etc., with a little industry they can make at home; the second they can do without till they are able to provide them among themselves; and the last, which are mere articles of fashion, purchased and consumed because [it is] the fashion in a respected country, but will now be detested and rejected. The people have already struck off, by general agreement, the use of all goods fashionable in mourning. . . .

Q: If the Stamp Act should be repealed, would it induce the assemblies of America to acknowledge the right of Parliament to tax them, and would they erase their resolutions [against the Stamp Act]?

A: No, never.

Q: Is there no means of obliging them to erase those resolutions?

A: None that I know of; they will never do it, unless compelled by force of arms.

Q: Is there a power on earth that can force them to erase them?

A: No power, how great soever, can force men to change their opinions. . . .

Q: What used to be the pride of the Americans?

A: To indulge in the fashions and manufactures of Great Britain.

Q: What is now their pride?

A: To wear their old clothes over again, till they can make new ones.

3.4

Milcah Martha Moore, "The Female Patriots Address'd to the Daughters of Liberty in America" (1768)

Despite their lack of formal political power, women played a vital role in colonial protests against Britain. Responsible for most of the shopping, patriot women ensured that their families adhered to nonimportation agreements. Nonconsumption agreements were even more effective than boycotts. Led by elite women's groups like the Daughters of Liberty, women of all ranks refused to use British goods such as tea and clothing. In this context, domestic tasks, such as spinning cloth, were invested with political virtue.

Milcah Martha Moore (1740–1829), a Philadelphia Quaker, wrote the following poem in order to inspire women to protest British rule.

FOCUS QUESTIONS

1. What types of actions does Moore hope to inspire? How would such activities possibly affect the British?

2. How did actions such as those Moore advocated challenge ideas about women's roles in public life and politics? What were the long-term ramifications of women's participation in colonial protests against British rule?

Since the men, from a party or fear of a frown,
Are kept by a sugar-plum quietly down,
Supinely asleep, and depriv'd of their sight,
Are stripp'd of their freedom, and robb'd of their right;
If the sons, so degenerate! The blessings despise,
Let the Daughters of Liberty nobly arise;
And though we've no voice but a negative here,
The use of the taxables, let us forbear:—
(Then merchants import till your stores are all full,

SOURCE: Published in Lauter, *Heath Anthology of American Literature*, Vol. 1, p. 658.

May the buyers be few, and your traffic be dull!)
Stand firmly resolv'd, and bid Grenville to see,
That rather than freedom we part with our tea,
And well as we love the dear draught when a dry,
As American Patriots our taste we deny—
Pennsylvania's gay meadows can richly afford
To paper our fancy or furnish our board;
And paper sufficient at home still we have,
To assure the wiseacre, we will not sign slave;
When this homespun shall fail, to remonstrate our grief,
We can speak viva voce, or scratch on a leaf;
Refuse all their colors, though richest of dye,
When the juice of a berry our paint can supply,
To humor our fancy—and as for our houses,
They'll do without painting as well as our spouses;
While to keep out the cold of a keen winter morn;
We can screen the northwest with a well polished horn;
And trust me a woman, by honest invention,
Might give this state doctor a dose of prevention.
Join mutual in this, and but small as it seems,
We may jostle a Grenville, and puzzle his schemes;
But a motive more worthy our patriot pen,
Thus acting—we point out their duty to men;
And should the bound-pensioners tell us to hush,
We can throw back the satire, by biding them blush.

3.5

Captain Thomas Preston's Account of the Boston Massacre (1770)

After Parliament enacted the Townshend duties in 1767, scores of British officials strictly enforced trade regulations throughout the colonies. Customs officials and

SOURCE: Captain Thomas Preston's Account of the Boston Massacre (13 March 1770), from British Public Records Office, C.O. 5/759. Reprinted in Merrill Jensen (editor) *English Historical Documents*, Volume IX (London, 1964) pp. 750–53.

British soldiers became the focus of Americans' growing hostility toward British rule. In Boston, hundreds of soldiers frequently clashed with local residents. The most famous of these incidents occurred on March 5, 1770. After being pelted with ice by a small mob, a British soldier accidentally fired his weapon. His comrades followed his lead and five Bostonians, including free black sailor Crispus Attucks, were killed. Samuel Adams, a skillful propagandist and political radical, publicized the "Boston Massacre." Hoping to defuse tensions, the British government tried the soldiers who had fired. Defended by John Adams, the accused received light sentences, further inflaming colonial fears of unrestrained British authority.

In this excerpt, a British soldier gives his perspective on the Boston Massacre.

FOCUS QUESTIONS

1. How does Preston describe the events leading to the Boston Massacre?
2. Does Preston believe that the soldiers responded reasonably to this situation? Do you agree with him? Explain your answer.

It is [a] matter of too great notoriety to need any proofs that the arrival of his Majesty's troops in Boston was extremely obnoxious to its inhabitants. They have ever used all means in their power to weaken the regiments, and to bring them into contempt by promoting and aiding desertions . . . and by grossly and falsely propagating untruths concerning them. . . .

On Monday night about 8 o'clock two soldiers were attacked and beat. But the party of the townspeople in order to carry matters to the utmost length, broke into two meeting houses and rang the alarm bells, which I supposed was for fire as usual, but was soon undeceived. About 9 some of the guard came to and informed me the town inhabitants were assembling to attack the troops, and that the bells were ringing as the signal for that purpose and not for fire, and the beacon intended to be fired to bring in the distant people of the country. This, as I was captain of the day, occasioned my repairing immediately to the main guard. On my way there I saw the people in great commotion, and heard them use the most cruel and horrid threats against the troops. In a few minutes after I reached the guard, about 100 people passed it and went towards the custom house where the king's money is lodged. They immediately surrounded the sentry posted there, and with clubs and other weapons threatened to execute their vengeance on him. I was soon informed by a townsman their intention was to carry off the soldier from his post and probably murder him. On which I desired him to return for further intelligence, and he soon came back and assured me he heard the mob declare they would murder him. This I feared might be a prelude to their plundering the king's chest. I immediately sent a non-commissioned officer and 12 men to protect both the sentry and the king's money, and very soon followed myself to prevent, if possible, all disorder, fearing lest the officer and soldiers, by the insults and provocations of the rioters, should be thrown off their guard and commit some rash act. They soon rushed through the people, and by charging their bayonets in half-circles, kept them at a little distance. Nay, so far was I from intending the death of any person that I suffered the troops to go to the spot where the unhappy affair took place without any loading in their pieces; nor did I ever give orders for loading them. This remiss conduct in me perhaps merits censure; yet it is evidence, resulting from the nature of things, which is the best and surest that can be offered, that my intention was not to act offensively, but the contrary part, and that not without compulsion. The mob still increased and were more out-rageous, striking their clubs or bludgeons one against another, and calling out, come on you rascals, you bloody backs, you lobster scoundrels, fire if you dare, G–d damn you, fire and be damned, we know you dare not, and much more such language was used. At this time I was between the soldiers and the mob, parleying with, and endeavouring all in my power to persuade them to retire peaceably, but to no purpose. They advanced to the points of the bayonets, struck some of them and even the muzzles of the pieces, and seemed to be endeavouring to close with the soldiers. On which some well behaved persons asked me if the guns were charged. I replied yes. They then asked me if I intended to order the men to fire. I answered no. . . . While I was thus speaking, one of the soldiers having received a severe blow with a stick, stepped a little on one side and instantly fired, on which turning to and asking him why he fired without orders, I was struck with a club on my arm, which for some time deprived me of the use of it, which blow had it been placed on my head, most probably would have destroyed me. On this a general attack was made on the men by a great number of heavy clubs and snowballs being thrown at them, by which all our lives were in imminent danger, some persons at the same time from behind calling out, damn your bloods—why don't you fire. Instantly three or four of the soldiers fired, one after another, and directly after three more in the same confusion and hurry. . . . The whole of this melancholy affair was transacted in almost 20 minutes. On my asking the soldiers why they fired without orders, they said they heard the word fire and supposed it came from me. This might be the case as many of the mob called out fire, fire, but I assured the men that I gave no such order; that my words were, don't fire, stop your firing. In short, it was scarcely possible for the soldiers to know who said fire, or don't fire, or stop your firing. . . .

3.6

Paul Revere, Image of *The Bloody Massacre* (1770)

The Boston Massacre culminated months of tensions between colonists and British troops. In 1768, when 2,000 British soldiers arrived to enforce the Townshend duties, Boston was already economically depressed and politically volatile. Many residents resented having to compete for jobs with British soldiers allowed to work after completing their morning duties. To capitalize on the growing disdain for royal officials, Sam Adams began publishing a journal packed with accounts of British verbal and physical harassment of local residents. In late February 1770, after a customs assessor shot a boy who had been throwing rocks at his house, Adams orchestrated a burial procession that fueled anti-British sentiment. Although the British army was not responsible for the boy's death, soldiers drew the colonists' ire. Days later, a mob attacked sentries posted outside a royal customs house, and nervous troops shot into the crowd, killing five Bostonians. Recognizing a priceless opportunity to advance the patriot cause, Sam Adams and others widely publicized the "Boston Massacre" in artwork and writings. Under this barrage of criticism, the British government repealed most of the Townshend duties within a few weeks.

One of colonial America's greatest silversmiths, Paul Revere (1735–1818) was a leader among Boston's artisans and was an enthusiastic supporter of republican ideals. Using his artistic genius to protest British rule, Revere reproduced a copper engraving originally created by Henry Pelham. Printed in scores of colonial newspapers, Revere's image became a famous symbol of British tyranny. In 1775, his notoriety grew after he and William Dawes rode to warn of an impending British attack on Lexington, Massachusetts. After serving in the Continental Army, Revere ran a successful copper mill.

FOCUS QUESTIONS

1. How does Revere's engraving portray the Boston Massacre?

2. How does Revere's version of events differ from that of Captain Thomas Preston (Document 3.5)? Whose story is more accurate? Why?

3. Why do you think images like this one were so effective in fostering anti-British dissent?

Paul Revere, The Bloody Massacre Perpetrated in King Street Boston on March 5th 1770 by a Party of the 29th Regt. *Engraving with watercolor, on laid paper, Boston, 1770. Library of Congress Prints and Photographs Division.*

3.7

Samuel Adams, "The Rights of the Colonists" (1772)

A combination of religious and political elements formed republicanism, the ideology fueling colonial protests of British rule. Republicanism fused Enlightenment political philosophy, English oppositionist views on British government, ancient history, and Protestant religious fervor. Its major themes included belief in natural rights, support for contractual government, and fear of unchecked power. Scores of pamphlets, speeches, and sermons drew on these arguments and inspired American resistance to British tyranny and corruption.

Samuel Adams fervently believed in republicanism. A leading figure among Massachusetts political radicals, Adams was one of the first colonists to denounce taxation without representation. He helped foment the Stamp Act riots. Elected to the lower house of the Massachusetts general court in 1766, Adams became one of the first advocates of American independence. Even after the repeal of the Townshend Acts in 1770, Adams remained committed to radical politics. In 1772, he founded the committees on correspondence so that colonies and towns could spread word of continuing British abuses. Following passage of the Tea Act in 1773, Adams organized the Boston Tea Party. A member of the Continental Congress (1774–81) and a signer of the Declaration of the Independence, Adams was later governor of Massachusetts (1794–97).

In this extract, Adams outlines his political views.

FOCUS QUESTIONS

1. What are Adams's major arguments?
2. What does he perceive as the proper roles of government?
3. Why does he claim that Britain is trying to enslave the colonies?
4. How are Adams's ideas a radical critique of British rule in the colonies?

SOURCE: *Old South Leaflets* no. 173 (Boston: Directors of the Old South Work, 1906)
7: 417–428.

I. NATURAL RIGHTS OF THE COLONISTS AS MEN

Among the natural rights of the Colonists are these: First, a right to life; Secondly, to liberty; Thirdly, to property; together with the right to support and defend them in the best manner they can. These are evident branches of, rather than deductions from, the duty of self-preservation, commonly called the first law of nature. . . .

When men enter into society, it is by voluntary consent; and they have a right to demand and insist upon the performance of such conditions and previous limitations as form an equitable original compact. . . .

In regard to religion, mutual toleration in the different professions thereof is what all good and candid minds in all ages have ever practiced, and, both by precept and example, inculcated on mankind. . . .

Insomuch that Mr. [John] Locke has asserted and proved, beyond the possibility of contradiction on any solid ground, that such toleration ought to be extended to all whose doctrines are not subversive of society. The only sects which he thinks ought to be . . . excluded from such toleration, are those who teach doctrines subversive of the civil government under which they live. The Roman Catholics or Papists are excluded by reason of such doctrines as these, that princes excommunicated may be deposed, and those that they call heretics may be destroyed without mercy; besides their recognizing the Pope in so absolute a manner, in subversion of government . . . leading directly to the worst anarchy and confusion, civil discord, war, and bloodshed. . . .

Governors have no right to seek and take what they please; by this, instead of being content with the station assigned them, that of honorable servants of the society, they would soon become absolute masters, despots, and tyrants. Hence, as a private man has a right to say what wages he will give in his private affairs, so has a community to determine what they will give and grant of their substance for the administration of public affairs. . . .

In short, it is the greatest absurdity to suppose it in the power of one, or any number of men, at the entering into society, to renounce their essential natural rights, or the means of preserving those rights; when the grand end of civil government, from the very nature of its institution, is for the support, protection, and defence of those very rights; the principal of which, as is before observed, are Life, Liberty, and Property. If men, through fear, fraud, or mistake, should in terms renounce or give up any essential natural right, the eternal law of reason and the grand end of society would absolutely vacate such renunciation. The right to freedom being the gift of God Almighty, it is not in the power of man to alienate this gift and voluntarily become a slave.

II. THE RIGHTS OF THE COLONISTS AS SUBJECTS

A commonwealth or state is a body politic, or civil society of men, united together to promote their mutual safety and prosperity by means of their union.

The absolute rights of Englishmen and all freemen, in or out of civil society, are principally personal security, personal liberty, and private property.

All persons born in the British American Colonies are, by the laws of God and nature and by the common law of England, exclusive of all charters from the Crown, well entitled, and by acts of the British Parliament are declared to be entitled, to all the natural, essential, inherent, and inseparable rights, liberties, and privileges of subjects born in Great Britain or within the realm. Among those rights are the following, which no man, or body of men, consistently with their own rights as men and citizens, or members of society, can for themselves give up or take away from others.

. . . The Legislative has no right to absolute, arbitrary power over the lives and fortunes of the people; nor can mortals assume a prerogative not only too high for men, but for angels, and therefore reserved for the exercise of the Deity alone. . . .

The supreme power cannot justly take from any man any part of his property, without his consent in person or by his representative.

. . . Now what liberty can there be where property is taken away without consent? Can it be said with any color of truth and justice, that this continent of three thousand miles in length, and of a breadth as yet unexplored, in which, however, it is supposed there are five millions of people, has the least voice, vote, or influence in the British Parliament? . . .

. . . if the breath of a British House of Commons can originate an act for taking away all our money, our lands will go next, or be subject to rack rents from haughty and relentless landlords, who will ride at ease, while we are trodden in the dirt. The Colonists have been branded with the odious names of traitors and rebels only for complaining of their grievances. How long such treatment will or ought to be borne, is submitted.

3.8

"Plain English," *Reign of King Mob* (1775)

Following passage of the Tea Act in 1773, colonial resistance to the British rapidly escalated. Designed to save the East India Company from bankruptcy, the act lowered the cost of East India Company tea sold in the American colonies. But colonists perceived the measure as yet another attempt to tax them without

SOURCE: *Revington's Gazette*, March 9, 1775. Reprinted in Frank Moore, *Diary of the American Revolution* (New York, etc., 1860), I, 37–42, *passim*.

their consent. In several cities, colonists barred ships bearing tea from landing. In Boston, protestors heaved chests of tea into the sea. The colonies were rife with political tensions.

After Britain enacted the Coercive Acts in 1774, American protestors increasingly harassed those remaining loyal to the Crown. Attacks on "Tories" included vandalism, tarring and feathering, and other means of intimidation. Such tactics sparked charges that the protestors were vigilantes, not political idealists.

In this reading, "Plain English," a loyalist describes the changing political climate in America.

FOCUS QUESTIONS

1. What actions does "Plain English" attribute to the protestors? How does he appear to regard the protestors?

2. What does the use of such tactics suggest about the colonists' commitment to political liberty?

3. How do you think Samuel Adams (Document 3.7) would have responded to Plain English's characterization of the anti-British protestors?

... [S]ome of those people, who, from a sense of their duty to the king, and a reverence for his laws, have behaved quietly and peaceably; and for which reason they have been deprived of their liberty, abused in their persons, and suffered such barbarous cruelties, insults, and indignities, besides the loss of their property, by the hands of lawless mobs and riots, as would have been disgraceful even for savages to have committed. The courts of justice being shut up in most parts of the province, and the justices of those courts compelled by armed force, headed by some who are members of your Congress, to refrain from doing their duties, at present it is rendered impracticable for those sufferers to obtain redress. ...

A particular enumeration of all the instances referred to is apprehended unnecessary, as many of your members are personally knowing of them, and for the information of any of you who may pretend ignorance of them, the following instances are here mentioned.

In August, a mob in Berkshire forced the justices of the Court of Common Pleas from their seats, and shut up the courthouse. They also drove David Ingersoll from this house, and damaged the same, and he was obliged to leave his estate; after which his enclosures were laid waste. At Taunton, Daniel Leonard was driven from his house, and bullets fired into it by the mob, and he [was] obliged to take refuge in Boston, for the supposed crime of obeying His Majesty's requisition as one of his council for this province. ...

Brigadier Ruggles was also attacked by another party, who were routed after having painted and cut the hair off of one of the horses' mane and tail. ... He had another time a very valuable English horse, which was kept as a stallion, poisoned, his family disturbed, and himself obliged to take refuge in Boston, after having been insulted in his own house, and twice in this way, by a mob....

In February, at Plymouth, a number of ladies attempted to divert themselves at their assembly room, but the mob collected...and flung stones which broke the shutters and windows, and endangered their lives. They were forced to get out of the hall, and were pelted and abused to their own homes....

To recount the suffering of all from mobs, rioters, and trespassers, would take more time and paper than can be spared for that purpose. It is hoped the foregoing will be sufficient to put you upon the use of upper means and measures for giving relief to all that have been injured by such unlawful and wicked practices.

3.9

Thomas Paine, Introduction to *Common Sense* (1776)

In April 1775, Massachusetts militia units and British soldiers clashed at Lexington and Concord. After rebel forces began a siege of Boston, 2,200 British and 311 colonists perished in the battles of Breed's Hill and Bunker Hill. In December 1775, Parliament declared that the colonies were in open rebellion. Nonetheless, most Americans hoped to reconcile their differences with Britain. They held corrupt British officials, not George III, responsible for the current political crisis.

Thomas Paine shattered this illusion. Born in Britain, Paine was unsuccessful in several occupations and had two failed marriages before arriving in Philadelphia in November 1774. He began writing numerous articles. In January 1776, he published Common Sense. *In the forty-seven-page treatise, Paine blamed the institutions of monarchy and imperialism, not individuals, for America's travails. Denying that the colonies needed Great Britain, Paine called for the creation of a new nation built on true liberty. Paine's clear arguments and approachable language resonated with all levels of colonial society. Selling more than 100,000 copies,* Common Sense *persuaded thousands of Americans to support independence from Britain.*

SOURCE: Thomas Paine, *Common Sense* (Philadelphia: W. and T. Bradford, 1791).

FOCUS QUESTIONS

1. Why does Paine claim that the American cause is a universal one?
2. How does Paine justify American independence?
3. How do Paine's arguments differ from those of John Dickinson's "A Speech Against American Independence" (Document 3.10)? Which author do you find most convincing? Explain your answer.

The cause of America is, in a great measure, the cause of all mankind. Many circumstances have, and will arise, which are not local, but universal, and through which the principles of all lovers of mankind are affected, and in the event of which, their affections are interested. The laying a country desolate with fire and sword, declaring war against the natural rights of all mankind, and extirpating the defenders thereof from the face of the earth, is the concern of every man to whom nature hath given the power of feeling. . . .

Government, namely, [is] a mode rendered necessary by the inability of moral virtue to govern the world; here too is the design and end of government, viz. freedom and security. And however our eyes may be dazzled with snow, or our ears deceived by sound; however prejudice may warp our wills, or interest darken our understanding, the simple voice of nature and reason will say, 'tis right. . . .

The sun never shined on a cause of greater worth. 'Tis not the affair of a city, a country, a province, or a kingdom, but of a continent—of at least one eighth part of the habitable globe. 'Tis not the concern of a day, a year, or an age; posterity are virtually involved in the contest, and will be more or less affected, even to the end of time, by the proceedings now. Now is the seed time of continental union, faith and honor. The least fracture now will be like a name engraved with the point of a pin on the tender rind of a young oak; the wound will enlarge with the tree, and posterity read it in full grown characters.

By referring the matter from argument to arms, a new area for politics is struck; a new method of thinking hath arisen. All plans, proposals, &c. prior to the nineteenth of April, i.e., to the commencement of hostilities, are like the almanacs of the last year; which, though proper then, are superseded and useless now. Whatever was advanced by the advocates on either side of the question then, terminated in one and the same point, viz., a union with Great Britain; the only difference between the parties was the method of effecting it; the one proposing force, the other friendship; but it hath so far happened that the first hath failed, and the second hath withdrawn her influence.

As much hath been said of the advantages of reconciliation, which, like an agreeable dream, hath passed away and left us as we were, it is but right, that we should examine the contrary side of the argument, and inquire into some of the many material injuries which these colonies sustain, and always will sustain, by being connected with, and dependant on Great Britain. To examine that connection and dependence, on the principles of nature and common sense, to see what we have to trust to, if separated, and what we are to expect, if dependant.

I have heard it asserted by some, that as America hath flourished under her former connection with Great Britain, that the same connection is necessary towards her future happiness, and will always have the same effect. Nothing can be more fallacious than this kind of argument. . . . America would have flourished as much, and probably much more, had no European power had any thing to do with her. The commerce by which she hath enriched herself are the necessaries of life, and will always have a market while eating is the custom of Europe. . . .

We have boasted the protection of Great Britain, without considering, that her motive was interest not attachment; that she did not protect us from our enemies on our account, but from her enemies on her own account, from those who had no quarrel with us on any other account, and who will always be our enemies on the same account. Let Britain wave her pretensions to the continent, or the continent throw off the dependence, and we should be at peace with France and Spain were they at war with Britain. The miseries of Hanover last war [The Seven Years' War], ought to warn us against connections. . . .

But Britain is the parent country, say some. Then the more shame upon her conduct. Even brutes do not devour their young; nor savages make war upon their families; wherefore the assertion, if true, turns to her reproach; but it happens not to be true, or only partly so, and the phrase parent or mother country hath been jesuitically adopted by the king and his parasites, with a low papistical design of gaining an unfair bias on the credulous weakness of our minds. Europe, and not England, is the parent country of America. This new world hath been the asylum for the persecuted lovers of civil and religious liberty from every part of Europe. Hither have they fled, not from the tender embraces of the mother, but from the cruelty of the monster; and it is so far true of England, that the same tyranny which drove the first emigrants from home pursues their descendants still.

In this extensive quarter of the globe, we forget the narrow limits of three hundred and sixty miles (the extent of England) and carry our friendship on a larger scale; we claim brotherhood with every European Christian, and triumph in the generosity of the sentiment. . . .

This is not inflaming or exaggerating matters, but trying them by those feelings and affections which nature justifies, and without which, we should be incapable of discharging the social duties of life, or enjoying the felicities of it. I mean not to exhibit horror for the purpose of provoking revenge, but to awaken us from fatal and unmanly slumbers, that we may pursue determinately some fixed object. It is not in the power of Britain or of Europe to conquer America, if she do not conquer herself by delay and timidity. . . .

3.10

John Dickinson, A Speech Against Independence (1776)

Not all Americans were eager to break away from the British empire. John Dickinson was among those reluctant to embrace independence. A prominent lawyer, Dickinson had represented Pennsylvania at the Stamp Act Congress (1765). In 1767–68, he wrote "Letters from a Farmer in Pennsylvania," an attack on Parliament's plan to use the Townshend Duties in order to pay the salaries of royal officials in the colonies. As a member of the Continental Congress (1774–76), Dickinson voted against the Declaration of Independence. He eventually supported independence and was one of the signers of the U.S. Constitution.

In this passage, Dickinson explains his opposition to the Declaration of Independence.

FOCUS QUESTIONS

1. Why does Dickinson feel that the colonies should resolve their differences with the British?
2. What advantages does he see in remaining part of the British empire?
3. What dangers does he perceive in an independent America?
4. How do Dickinson's views differ from those of Thomas Paine (Document 3.9)? Which author do you find more convincing? Explain your answer.

I know the name of liberty is dear to each one of us; but have we not enjoyed liberty even under the English monarchy? Shall we this day renounce that to go and seek it in I know not what form of republic, which will soon change into a licentious anarchy and popular tyranny? In the human body the head only sustains and governs all the members, directing them, with admirable harmony, to the same object, which is self-preservation and happiness; so the head of the

SOURCE: "Speech of John Dickinson of Pennsylvania, Favoring a Condition of Union with England, Delivered, July 1, 1776," *Principles and Acts of the Revolution in America*, ed. Hezekiah Niles (Baltimore, 1822), 493–495.

body politic, that is the king, in concert with the Parliament, can alone maintain the union of the members of this Empire, lately so flourishing, and prevent civil war by obviating all the evils produced by variety of opinions and diversity of interests. And so firm is my persuasion of this that I fully believe the most cruel war which Great Britain could make upon us would be that of not making any; and that the surest means of bringing us back to her obedience would be that of employing none. For the dread of the English arms, once removed, provinces would rise up against provinces and cities against cities; and we shall be seen to turn against ourselves the arms we have taken up to combat the common enemy.

Insurmountable necessity would then compel us to resort to the tutelary authority which we should have rashly abjured, and, if it consented to receive us again under its aegis, it would be no longer as free citizens but as slaves. Still inexperienced and in our infancy, what proof have we given of our ability to walk without a guide?

...Our union with England...is no less necessary to procure us, with foreign powers, that condescension and respect which is so essential to the prosperity of our commerce, to the enjoyment of any consideration, and to the accomplishment of any enterprise....From the moment when our separation shall take place, everything will assume a contrary direction. The nations will accustom themselves to look upon us with disdain; even the pirates of Africa and Europe will fall upon our vessels, will massacre our seamen, or lead them into a cruel and perpetual slavery....

Independence, I am aware, has attractions for all mankind; but I am maintaining that, in the present quarrel, the friends of independence are the promoters of slavery, and that those who desire to separate would but render us more dependent, ...to change the condition of English subjects for that of slaves to the whole world is a step that could only be counseled by insanity....

But here I am interrupted and told that no one questions the advantages which America derived at first from her conjunction with England; but that the new pretensions of the ministers have changed all, have subverted all. If I should deny that, ...I should deny not only what is the manifest truth but even what I have so often advanced and supported. But is there any doubt that it already feels a secret repentance? These arms, these soldiers it prepares against us are not designed to establish tyranny upon our shores but to vanquish our obstinacy, and to compel us to subscribe to conditions or accommodation.

...To pretend to reduce us to an absolute impossibility of resistance, in cases of oppression, would be, on their part, a chimerical project.... [But only] an uninterrupted succession of victories and of triumphs could alone constrain England to acknowledge American independence; which, whether we can expect, whoever knows the instability of fortune can easily judge.

If we have combated successfully at Lexington and at Boston, Quebec and all Canada have witnessed our reverses. Everyone sees the necessity of opposing the extraordinary pretensions of the ministers; but does everybody see also that of fighting for independence?

...By substituting a total dismemberment to the revocation of the laws we complain of, we should fully justify the ministers; we should merit the infamous name of rebels, and all the British nation would arm, with an unanimous impulse, against those who, from oppressed and complaining subjects, should have become all at once irreconcilable enemies. The English cherish the liberty we defend; they respect the dignity of our cause; but they will blame, they will detest our recourse to independence, and will unite with one consent to combat us.

The propagators of the new doctrine are pleased to assure us that, out of jealousy toward England, foreign sovereigns will lavish their succors upon us, as if these sovereigns could sincerely applaud rebellion; as if they had not colonies, even here in America, in which it is important for them to maintain obedience and tranquility . . . under the most benevolent pretexts they will despoil us of our territories, they will invade our fisheries and obstruct our navigation, they will attempt our liberty and our privileges. We shall learn too late what it costs to trust those European flatteries, and to place that confidence in inveterate enemies which has been withdrawn from long tried friends.

There are many persons who, to gain their ends, extol the advantages of a republic over monarchy. I will not here undertake to examine which of these two forms of government merits the preference. I know, however, that the English nation, after having tried them both, has never found repose except in monarchy. I know, also, that in popular republics themselves, so necessary is monarchy to cement human society, it has been requisite to institute monarchial powers. . . . Nor should I here omit an observation, the truth of which appears to me incontestable—the English constitution seems to be the fruit of the experience of all anterior time, in which monarchy is so tempered that the monarch finds himself checked in his efforts to seize absolute power; and the authority of the people is so regulated that anarchy is not to be feared. But for us it is to be apprehended that, when the counterpoise of monarchy shall no longer exist, the democratic power may carry all before it and involve the whole state in confusion and ruin. Then an ambitious citizen may arise, seize the reins of power, and annihilate liberty forever. . . .

3.11

Joseph Brant Pledges Mohawk Loyalty to Britain (1776)

The American Revolution greatly affected Native Americans. Although Indians participated in other imperial wars in North America, most tribes tried to remain neutral in the Revolution. As the war progressed, staying out of the conflict became difficult. Dependent on Britain for many vital supplies and cognizant of British attempts to restrain American encroachment on tribal lands, most Indians supported England. Others, including the Oneidas and the Catawbas, fought with the Americans. In the end, few Indians benefited from the Revolution. The peace treaty between England and America did not address Indian concerns. Some tribes fled west or to Canada, but most could not escape the new and powerful threat posed by the United States.

Joseph Brant (1742–1807) was a prominent Indian ally of the British. After spending two years (1761–1763) at Moor's Charity School for Indians in Connecticut, Brant converted to the Anglican Church. Upon leaving school, he worked as an interpreter for an Anglican missionary and helped to translate prayers and biblical texts into Mohawk. He fought for the British in the Seven Years' War. In 1774, he served as secretary for Sir William Johnson, the British superintendent for northern Indian affairs. During the American Revolution, Brant led the four tribes of the Iroquois Confederacy that remained loyal to England. With the aid of British regulars and Loyalists, Brant's forces fought throughout New York and Pennsylvania. He also thwarted rival Iroquois efforts to forge a separate peace with the Americans. After the war, the British awarded Brant land in Ontario. Making the best of a bad situation, Brant took several Iroquois with him to Canada and spent the remainder of his life performing missionary work.

This selection features a speech Brant made during a 1776 trip to England. Meeting with Lord George Germain, the royal Secretary for the Colonies, Brant expresses his concerns for the future of his people. (Some spelling has been modernized.)

SOURCE: E. B. O'Callaghan, ed. *Documents Relative to the Colonial History of the State of New York* 15 vols. (Albany: Weed, Parsons, 1853–87), 8:670–71.

FOCUS QUESTIONS

1. What evidence does Brant offer to prove that his people are loyal to the British?
2. How does Brant claim that the British government has treated the Mohawks?
3. Do you think Brant's faith in the British was justified? Explain your answer.

We have crossed the great Lake and come to this kingdom with our Superintendent Col. Johnson from our Confederacy the Six Nations and their Allies, that we might see our Father the Great King, and join in informing him, his Councilors and wise men, of the good intentions of the Indians our brethren, and of their attachment to His Majesty and his Government.

Brother. The Disturbances in America give great trouble to all our Nations, as many strange stories have been told to us by the people in that country. The Six Nations who always loved the King, sent a number of their Chiefs and Warriors with their Superintendent to Canada last summer, where they engaged their allies to join with them in the defense of that country, and when it was invaded by the New England people, they alone defeated them.

Brother. In that engagement we had several of our best Warriors killed and wounded, and the Indians think it very hard they should have been so deceived by the White people in that country, the enemy returning in great numbers, and no White people supporting the Indians, they were obliged to retire to their villages and sit still. We now Brother hope to see these bad children chastised, and that we may be enabled to tell the Indians, who have always been faithful and ready to assist the King, what His Majesty intends.

Brother. The Mohawks our particular Nation, have on all occasions shown their zeal and loyalty to the Great King; yet they have been very badly treated by his people in that country, the City of Albany laying an unjust claim to the lands on which our Lower Castle is built, as one Clock and others do to those of Conijoharrie our Upper Village. We have been often assured by our late great friend Sir William Johnson who never deceived us, and we know he was told so that the King and wise men here would do us justice; but this notwithstanding all our applications have never been done, and it makes us very uneasy. We also feel for the distress in which our Brethren on the Susquehanna are likely to be involved by a mistake made in the Boundary we settled in 1768. This also our Superintendent has laid before the King, and we beg it may be remembered. And also concerning Religion and the want of Ministers of the Church of England, he knows the designs of those bad people and informs us he has laid the same before the King. We have only therefore to request that his Majesty will attend to this matter: it troubles our Nation & they cannot sleep easy in their beds. Indeed it is very hard when we have let the King's subjects have so much of our lands for so little value, they should want to cheat us in this manner of the small spots we have left for our women and children to live on. We are tired out in making complaints & getting no redress. We therefore hope that the Assurances now given us by the Superintendent may take place, and that he may have it in his power to procure us justice.

Brother. We shall truly report all that we hear from you, to the Six Nations at our return. We are well informed there have been many Indians in this Country who came without any authority, from their own, and gave much trouble. We desire Brother to tell you this is not our case. We are warriors known to all the Nations, and are now here by approbation of many of them, whose sentiments we speak.

Brother. We hope these things will be considered and that the King or his great men will give us such an answer as will make our hearts light and glad before we go, and strengthen our hands, so that we may join our Superintendent Col. Johnson in giving satisfaction to all our Nations, when we report to them, on our return; for which purpose we hope soon to be accommodated with a passage.

Dictated by the Indians and taken down by
Jo: Chew. Secretary

3.12

Abigail and John Adams on Women's Rights (1776)

The Revolution permanently changed American society. Profoundly affected by republican ideals, people of all races, classes, and sexes challenged forms of hierarchy. Thousands of women supported the Continental Army as "camp followers," nurses, and in rare instances, as soldiers. But most Americans still believed that women's primary roles were wife and mother. While New Jersey allowed women to vote until 1807, no other state granted women suffrage. Women were barred from formal politics.

Nonetheless, many Americans modified their views. They increasingly accepted the notion of marrying for love instead of familial obligation. Divorce became more readily available to women with abusive husbands. Believing that women were responsible

SOURCE: Abigail Adams to John Adams, March 31, 1776 and May 7, 1776; John Adams to Abigail Adams, April 14, 1776, in L. H. Butterfield et al, eds. *The Book of Abigail and John* (Cambridge: Harvard University Press, 1975), pp. 120–122, 127.

for teaching children moral and political virtues, schools and academies began offering women improved educations to prepare them for their role as "republican mothers."

Abigail and John Adams witnessed such changes. A major figure in the Continental Congress who later became the nation's second president (1797– 1801), John Adams was a brilliant and volatile man. In 1764, he married the lively and intelligent Abigail Smith. They considered their marriage an ideal intellectual and intimate partnership. Often separated by Adams's political duties, the duo shared impassioned letters.

In this exchange, Abigail and John Adams share opinions on women's rights

---

FOCUS QUESTIONS

1. Describe the letters between Abigail and John Adams.
2. What do these letters suggest about women's roles in the new republic and the long-range impact of the American Revolution upon society?

Abigail Adams to John Adams
Braintree March 31, 1776

I long to hear that you have declared an independency—and by the way in the new Code of Laws which I suppose it will be necessary for you to make I desire you would Remember the Ladies, and be more generous and favorable to them than your ancestors. Do not put such unlimited power into the hands of the Husbands. Remember all Men would be tyrants if they could. If particular care and attention is not paid to the Ladies we are determined to foment a Rebellion, and will not hold ourselves bound by any Laws in which we have no voice, or Representation.

That your Sex are Naturally Tyrannical is a Truth so thoroughly established as to admit of no dispute, but such of you as wish to be happy willingly give up the harsh title of Master for the more tender and endearing one of Friend. Why then, not put it out of the power of the vicious and the Lawless to use us with cruelty and indignity with impunity. Men of Sense in all Ages abhor those customs which treat us only as the vassals of your Sex. Regard us then as Beings placed by providence under your protection and in imitation of the Supreme Being make use of that power only for our happiness.

John to Abigail
April 14, 1776

As to Declarations of Independency, be patient. Read our Privateering Laws, and our Commercial Laws. What signifies a Word.

As to your extraordinary Code of Laws, I cannot but laugh. We have been told our Struggle has loosened the bands of Government everywhere. That Children and Apprentices were disobedient—that school and Colleges were grown turbulent—that Indians slighted their Guardians and Negroes grew insolent to their Masters. But your Letter was the first Intimation that another Tribe more numerous and powerful than all the rest were grown discontented.—This is rather too coarse a Compliment but you are so saucy, I wont blot it out.

Depend upon it, We know better than to repeal our Masculine systems. Although they are in full Force, you know they are little more than Theory. We dare not exert our Power in its full Latitude. We are obliged to go fair, and softly, and in Practice you know We are the subjects. We have only the Name of Masters, and rather than give up this, which would completely subject Us to the Despotism of the Petticoat, I hope General Washington, and all our brave Heroes would fight. I am sure every good Politician would plot, as long as he would against Despotism, Empire, Monarchy, Aristocracy, Oligarchy, and Ochlocracy,—A fine Story indeed. I begin to think the Ministry as deep as they are wicked. After stirring up Tories, Landjobbers, Trimmers, Bigots, Canadians, Indians, Negroes, Hanoverians, Hessians, Russians, Irish Roman Catholics, Scots Renegades, at last they have stimulated them to demand new Privileges and threaten to rebel.

Abigail to John
B[raintre]e May 7, 1776

I can not say that I think you very generous to the Ladies, for whilst you are proclaiming peace and goodwill to Men, Emancipating all Nations, you insist upon retaining an absolute power over Wives. But you must remember that Arbitrary power is like most other things which are very hard, very liable to be broken—and notwithstanding all your wise Laws and Maxims we have it in our power not only to free ourselves but to subdue our Masters, and without violence throw both your natural and legal authority at our feet—

"Charm by accepting, by submitting sway
Yet have our Humor most when we obey."

3.13

James Thacher Describes the Battle of Trenton (1777)

The American war effort against Britain began inauspiciously. In March 1776, British forces evacuated Boston and occupied New York. Within a few months, British troops led by General William Howe were crushing the poorly trained and outnumbered Continental Army led by George Washington. By December, American troops had retreated through New Jersey. With his soldiers' enlistments set to expire, Washington took a bold gamble. On Christmas night, he dispatched his ragged army across the frozen Delaware River and mounted a surprise attack on Hessian mercenaries. While losing only four men, Washington's troops captured almost 1,000. By January 3, 1777, Washington scored impressive victories in Trenton and Princeton. The successful campaigns in New Jersey revitalized American morale.

In this excerpt, James Thacher, a surgeon in the Continental Army, describes the battle of Trenton.

FOCUS QUESTIONS

1. How does troop morale change throughout Thacher's account?
2. What types of military tactics did Washington use? Were they successful?

January 5th

At the close of the last year, the situation of our main army was gloomy and discouraging: a large proportion of the troops had retired from service, as their term of enlistment expired, and the small remains of our army was retreating before the enemy, and passed the Delaware for safety. It is now announced in our general orders, to our inexpressible joy and satisfaction, that the scene is in some degree changed, the fortune of war is reversed, and Providence has been pleased to crown the efforts of our commander-in-chief with a splendid victory.

SOURCE: James Thacher, *Military Journal During the American Revolutionary War.* Published at http://www.americanrevolution.org/t1777.html.

His excellency, having obtained information that the advanced party of the enemy, consisting of about fifteen hundred Hessians and British light-horse, under command of Colonel Rahl, was stationed at the village of Trenton, concerted a plan for taking them by surprise. For this purpose he made choice of Christmas night, under the idea that in consequence of the festivity, they might be less vigilantly guarded. At this time the whole force under his immediate command did not exceed three thousand men. At the head of about two thousand four hundred men, one division being commanded by General Greene and the other by General Sullivan, he crossed the river Delaware in boats, in the night of the 25th of December, during a severe storm of snow and rain.

The passage of the boats was rendered extremely difficult and hazardous by the ice, and part of the troops and cannon actually failed in the attempt.

Having landed on the Jersey shore, he had nine miles to march, and he reached the village about seven o'clock in the morning with such promptitude and secrecy, as to attack the enemy almost as soon as his approach was discovered. A smart firing ensued, which continued but a few minutes, when the enemy, finding themselves surrounded, threw down their arms and surrendered as prisoners. Colonel Rahl, the commanding officer, was mortally wounded, and seven other officers were wounded and left at Trenton on their parole. About thirty-five soldiers were killed, sixty wounded, and nine hundred and forty-eight, including thirty officers, were taken prisoners, amounting in all to one thousand and forty-eight. Of the Continentals not more than ten, it is supposed, were killed and wounded. General Washington recrossed the Delaware the same day in triumph, bringing off six excellent brass cannon, about one thousand two hundred small arms, and three standards, with a quantity of baggage, &c.

This very brilliant achievement is highly honorable to the commander-in-chief, and to all that were engaged in the enterprise. We are sanguine in the hope that this most auspicious event will be productive of the happiest effects, by inspiriting our dejected army, and dispelling that panic of despair into which the people have been plunged.

General Washington allowed the Hessian prisoners to retain their baggage, and sent them into the interior of Pennsylvania, ordering that they be treated with favor and humanity. This conduct, so contrary to their expectations, excited their gratitude and veneration for their amiable conqueror, whom they styled, "a very good rebel."

3.14

An Act for the Gradual Abolition
of Slavery (1780)

The American Revolution brought mixed blessings to both free and slave African Americans. Because republican ideals called for freedom and individual rights, the contradiction posed by slavery grew increasingly troubling. Yet, racism and economic concerns complicated white responses to free blacks and slaves.

African Americans played an important role in the Revolution. In 1775, black soldiers fought at Concord, Lexington, and Bunker Hill. Nonetheless, when George Washington became commander of the Continental Army in July 1775, he barred additional African Americans from enlisting and expelled those already serving. Several months later, mass desertions forced Washington to rescind these orders. By the war's end, all states except Georgia and South Carolina had recruited black soldiers, and 5,000 African Americans fought in integrated units.

At the same time, the Revolution marked the beginning of the emancipation movement. In 1776, approximately 475,000 of the 500,000 African Americans were slaves. Even free blacks lacked voting privileges and civil rights. Republican ideology, however, inspired Americans to reconsider their commitment to slavery and to pass laws like the Pennsylvania statute included here. In 1804, every Northern state except for New Hampshire had abolished slavery. Nonetheless, fears that total abolition could bankrupt the country or spark a race war destroyed efforts to end slavery nationwide.

FOCUS QUESTIONS

1. Why is Pennsylvania passing this law? How is the law connected to the ideals of the Revolution?

2. What are the provisions of the law?

3. How do you think this law affected slaves who were living in Pennsylvania at the time?

SOURCE: Published at the Avalon Project of the Yale Law School,
http://www.yale.edu/lawweb/avalon/states/statutes/pennst01.htm.

SECTION 1

When we contemplate our abhorrence of that condition to which the arms and tyranny of Great Britain were exerted to reduce us; when we look back on the variety of dangers to which we have been exposed, and how miraculously our wants in many instances have been supplied, and our deliverances wrought, when even hope and human fortitude have become unequal to the conflict; we are unavoidably led to a serious and grateful sense of the manifold blessings which we have undeservedly received from the hand of that Being from whom every good and perfect gift comes. Impressed with these ideas, we conceive that it is our duty, and we rejoice that it is in our power to extend a portion of that freedom to others, which has been extended to us; and a release from that state of thralldom [slavery] to which we ourselves were tyrannically doomed, and from which we have now every prospect of being delivered. It is not for us to inquire why, in the creation of mankind, the inhabitants of the several parts of the earth were distinguished by a difference in feature or complexion. It is sufficient to know that all are the work of an Almighty Hand. We find in the distribution of the human species, that the most fertile as well as the most barren parts of the earth are inhabited by men of complexions different from ours, and from each other; from whence we may reasonably, as well as religiously, infer, that He who placed them in their various situations, has extended equally his care and protection to all, and that it becomes not us to counteract his mercies. We esteem it a peculiar blessing granted to us, that we are enabled this day to add one more step to universal civilization, by removing as much as possible the sorrows of those who have lived in undeserved bondage, and from which, by the assumed authority of the kings of Great Britain, no effectual, legal relief could be obtained....

SECTION 2

And whereas the condition of those persons who have heretofore been denominated Negro and Mulatto slaves, has been attended with circumstances which not only deprived them of the common blessings that they were by nature entitled to, but has cast them into the deepest afflictions, by an unnatural separation and sale of husband and wife from each other and from their children; an injury, the greatness of which can only be conceived by supposing that we were in the same unhappy case. In justice therefore to persons So unhappily circumstanced, and who, having no prospect before them whereon they may rest their sorrows and their hopes, have no reasonable inducement to render their service to society, which they otherwise might; and also in grateful commemoration of our own happy deliverance from that state of unconditional submission to which we were doomed by the tyranny of Britain.

SECTION 3

Be it enacted, and it is hereby enacted, by the representatives of the freeman of the commonwealth of Pennsylvania, in general assembly met, and by the authority of the same, That all persons, as well Negroes and Mulattoes as others, who shall be born within this state from and after the passing of this act, shall not be deemed and considered as servants for life, or slaves; and that all servitude for life, or slavery of children, in consequence of the slavery of their mothers, in the case of all children born within this state, from and after the passing of this act as aforesaid, shall be, and hereby is utterly taken away, extinguished and for ever abolished.

SECTION 4

Provided always, and be it further enacted by the authority aforesaid, That every Negro and Mulatto child born within this state after the passing of this act as aforesaid (who would, in case this act had not been made, have been born a servant for years, or life, or a slave) shall be deemed to be and shall be by virtue of this act the servant of such person or his or her assigns, who would in such case have been entitled to the service of such child, until such child shall attain unto the age of twenty eight years, in the manner and on the conditions whereon servants bound by indenture for four years are or may be retained and holder; and shall be liable to like correction and punishment, and entitled to like relief in case he or she be evilly treated by his or her master or mistress, and to like freedom dues and other privileges as servants bound by indenture for four years are or may be entitled, unless the person to whom the service of any such child shall belong shall abandon his or her claim to the fame; in which case the overseers of the poor of the city, township or district respectively, where such child shall be So abandoned, shall by indenture bind out every child so abandoned, as an apprentice for a time not exceeding the age herein before limited for the service of such children. . . .

John Bayard, Speaker
Enabled into a law at Philadelphia, on Wednesday, the first day of March,
    A.D. 1780
Thomas Paine, clerk of the general assembly.

4

✳

We the People

The Revolution sparked changes and contradictions. Although republican ideals of freedom and equality motivated Americans in the war against Great Britain, these principles proved difficult to translate into political realities. Class differences, racial prejudice, and gender inequality persisted in the new nation. Nonetheless, the Revolution prompted unprecedented social changes. No longer willing to defer to their "betters," common people earned new respect and courtesy from elites. Northern states began abolishing slavery. Recognition of women's importance in shaping future citizens spurred legal reforms and increased educational opportunities.

Throughout the era, political leaders tried to protect their infant nation from economic instability and international hostilities. Ensuring such security proved difficult under the Articles of Confederation. Reflecting popular fears of centralized authority, the Articles gave the states greater powers than the national government. Lacking an executive branch, a judicial system, and taxation powers, the central government soon faced a host of financial, diplomatic, and political problems. Hoping to resolve these issues, the states appointed delegates charged with revising the Articles.

Ultimately, these representatives abandoned the Articles and began formulating a new frame of government. After a series of compromises between large and small states, the delegates approved the Constitution in September 1787. The document created a strong national government composed of executive, judicial, and legislative branches. The central authority was responsible for the imposition and collection of taxes, the regulation of trade, and the conduct of foreign policy. The framers designed checks and balances to ensure that none of the three branches of government dominated the others. Furthermore, they implemented a federalist system in which the states and the national government shared power and lawmaking duties.

Because the Constitution represented a radical departure from the Confederation of virtually independent states, many Americans greeted the document with dismay. Throughout the ratification process, there were heated debates on centralized authority and individual rights. While Federalists extolled the virtues of the Constitution, Anti-Federalists warned of the threats posed by a strong national government. Despite their defeat, the Anti-Federalists generated widespread support for the adoption of a bill of rights guarding individual freedoms.

Ratification of the Constitution was only the first step in building an effective national government. Indians and whites were fighting in the west. Foreign countries were restricting U.S. commerce and threatening American territory. With a bankrupt treasury and poor credit, the new government's failure was a distinct possibility.

George Washington led the nation through this delicate situation. He clarified the duties of the president and his cabinet. His administration established boundaries for executive, legislative, and judicial powers. While Washington usually deferred to Congress on domestic matters and focused on military and foreign affairs, his caution did not prevent the emergence of political factions. Profound divisions on economic issues, political philosophies, and foreign relations split Americans into Federalists and Republicans. By 1794, these parties hotly debated the meaning of republicanism and the proper structure of government. Where Federalists sought to limit public office to elites who ruled on behalf of the masses, Republicans called for a political system in which ordinary citizens participated extensively. When Federalists claimed that Republicans supported mob rule, Republicans accused Federalists of trying to establish a monarchy and an aristocracy. Disturbed by such inflammatory rhetoric, Washington retired and warned his countrymen that partisanship could destroy the republic.

Ignoring Washington's caveat, Federalists and Republicans intensified their political dispute during the election of 1796. After Federalist John Adams narrowly prevailed, he did little to unify the country. The eruption of international tensions with France created new conflicts. When the Federalists passed the Alien and Sedition Acts, Republicans charged them with violating the Bill of Rights and the system of checks and balances. As the election of 1800 grew closer, Americans hoped that a new leader could reunite the embattled nation.

THEMES TO CONSIDER

- The relationship between church and state
- The importance of western expansion and land ownership in the growth of the United States

- The strengths and weaknesses of the Articles of Confederation
- The justifications for and debates about the U.S. Constitution
- The delicate balance between centralized authority and individual rights
- The contradictions posed by the practice of slavery in the new republic
- Demands for racial and gender equality
- The development of the U.S. economy
- The emergence of political parties and the impact of partisanship
- The United States's role in international relations
- Conflicts over states' rights vs. federal power

4.1

Thomas Jefferson Calls for Religious Freedom in Virginia (1786)

The Revolution prompted reevaluation of the relationship between church and state. Cognizant of the religious diversity of the United States, many statesmen embraced "public religion," a broad interpretation of spirituality transcending individual sects. Seeking to establish boundaries between religious and civil life, most states stopped sponsoring specific churches. Although New Hampshire, Connecticut, and Massachusetts resisted this policy until 1817, 1818, and 1833, respectively, the other states separated church and state by 1786.

Thomas Jefferson (1743–1826) was one of the nation's foremost advocates of religious freedom. As early as 1777, he began calling for Virginia to end its privileging of the Anglican (Episcopal) church. Under this system, the state jailed people who refused to pay church taxes and required ministers of non-Anglican sects to obtain licenses from the state church. Afraid of the effects that established religion could have on atheists and the irreligious and convinced that faith was a personal matter, Jefferson spent years promoting a bill separating church and state in Virginia. Enacted in 1786, Jefferson's law became an important precedent for the First Amendment, the amendment guaranteeing religious freedom for the

SOURCE: Thomas Jefferson, A Bill for Establishing Religious Freedom in Virginia (1786).

individual while erecting a wall of separation between church and government. Along with drafting the Declaration of Independence and founding the University of Virginia, Jefferson considered the act one of his three greatest achievements.

FOCUS QUESTIONS

1. What are the major objectives of Jefferson's bill?
2. Why is Jefferson opposed to state-sponsored religion? Do you find his arguments persuasive? Explain your answer.
3. To what extent do you believe that church and state should be separate? Support your response with examples.

SECTION I

Well aware that the opinions and belief of men depend on their own will, but follow involuntarily the evidence proposed to their minds; that Almighty God hath created the mind free, and manifested his supreme will that free it shall remain by making it altogether insusceptible of restraint; that all attempts to influence it by temporal punishments, or burthens, or by civil incapacitations, tend only to beget habits of hypocrisy and meanness, and are a departure from the plan of the holy author of our religion, who being lord both of body and mind, yet chose not to propagate it by coercions on either, as was in his Almighty power to do, but to exalt it by its influence on reason alone; that the impious presumption of legislature and ruler, civil as well as ecclesiastical, who, being themselves but fallible and uninspired men, have assumed dominion over the faith of others, setting up their own opinions and modes of thinking as the only true and infallible, and as such endeavoring to impose them on others, hath established and maintained false religions over the greatest part of the world and through all time: That to compel a man to furnish contributions of money for the propagation of opinions which he disbelieves and abhors, is sinful and tyrannical; that even the forcing him to support this or that teacher of his own religious persuasion, is depriving him of the comfortable liberty of giving his contributions to the particular pastor whose morals he would make his pattern, and whose powers he feels most persuasive to righteousness; and is withdrawing from the ministry those temporary rewards, which proceeding from an approbation of their personal conduct, are an additional incitement to earnest and unremitting labors for the instruction of mankind; that our civil rights have no dependence on our religious opinions, any more than our opinions in physics or geometry; and therefore the proscribing any citizen as unworthy the public confidence by laying upon him incapacity of being called to offices of trust or emolument, unless he profess or renounce this or that religious opinion, is depriving him injudiciously of those privileges and advantages to which, in common with his fellow-citizens, he has a natural right; that it tends also to corrupt the principles of that very religion it is meant to encourage, by bribing with a monopoly of worldly honors and emoluments, those who will externally profess and conform to it; that though indeed these are criminals who do not withstand such temptation, yet neither are those innocent who lay the bait in their way; that the opinions of men are not the object of civil government, nor under its jurisdiction; that to suffer the civil magistrate to intrude his powers into the field of opinion and to restrain the profession or propagation of principles on supposition of their ill tendency is a dangerous fallacy, which at once destroys all religious liberty, because he being of course judge of that tendency will make his opinions the rule of judgment, and approve or condemn the sentiments of others only as they shall square with or suffer from his own; that it is time enough for the rightful purposes of civil government for its officers to interfere when principles break out into overt acts against peace and good order; and finally, that truth is great and will prevail if left to herself; that she is the proper and sufficient antagonist to error, and has nothing to fear from the conflict unless by human interposition disarmed of her natural weapons, free argument and debate; errors ceasing to be dangerous when it is permitted freely to contradict them.

SECTION II

We the General Assembly of Virginia do enact that no man shall be compelled to frequent or support any religious worship, place, or ministry whatsoever, nor shall be enforced, restrained, molested, or burthened in his body or goods, nor shall otherwise suffer, on account of his religious opinions or belief; but that all men shall be free to profess, and by argument to maintain, their opinions in matters of religion, and that the same shall in no wise diminish, enlarge, or affect their civil liberties.

SECTION III

And though we well know that this Assembly, elected by the people for their ordinary purposes of legislation only, have no power to restrain the acts of succeeding Assemblies, constituted with powers equal to our own, and that therefore to declare this act to be irrevocable would be of no effect in law; yet we are free to declare, and do declare, that the rights hereby asserted are of the natural rights of mankind, and that if any act shall be hereafter passed to repeal the present or to narrow its operations, such act will be an infringement of natural right.

4.2

The Northwest Ordinance (1787)

The Articles of Confederation (1781–1789) served as an important transition in American self-governance. Fearful of centralized authority, Congress adopted a loose grouping of independent states. Approved in 1777, the Articles required the unanimous consent of all thirteen states. A dispute over land claims north of the Ohio River delayed their ratification until 1781. The Articles granted Congress limited powers over the states. Although marred by several weaknesses, the Confederation paved the way to a stronger federal government as outlined by the U.S. Constitution ratified in 1789.

The Northwest Ordinances were the Confederation's most enduring legacy. After several states abandoned their claims to the 160 million acres west of Pennsylvania, Congress instituted procedures for the surveying, settlement, and political incorporation of the Northwest Territory. The Northwest Ordinance of 1787 was the most significant of these measures. It provided for the division of the territory into states and prohibited slavery in the territory. Under this act, Congress appointed a governor and judges to rule a district until its population reached 5,000 adult free men. At that point, the people adopted a temporary constitution and a legislature. After attaining a population of 60,000, a territory could gain statehood in the Union.

The Northwest Ordinances established important precedents. They fulfilled republican hopes of preventing an increase in impoverished tenant farmers and laborers living in the East. Through land ownership and western expansion, the drafters of these measures believed, the future growth of a property-owning, politically engaged citizenry could be assured. The decision to prevent slavery in these territories informed political discussions on westward expansion for decades to come. Finally, the U.S. government's decision to open the Northwest Territory to white settlement made conflicts with Indians living in the region inevitable.

FOCUS QUESTIONS

1. What are some of the major provisions of the Northwest Ordinance? How could a territory become a state?

SOURCE: Charles C. Tansill, ed. *Documents Illustrative of the Formation of the Union of the American States* (Washington, D.C.: Government Printing Office, 1927), House Document No. 398.

2. What rights must territorial governments grant their citizens? Why are these guarantees significant?

3. Why were land ownership and westward expansion so important to the future of the United States?

SECTION I

Be it ordained by the United States in Congress assembled, That the said territory, for the purposes of temporary government, be one district, subject, however, to be divided into two districts, as future circumstances may, in the opinion of Congress, make it expedient....

SECTION 3

Be it ordained by the authority aforesaid, That there shall be appointed from time to time by Congress, a governor, whose commission shall continue in force for the term of three years, unless sooner revoked by Congress; he shall reside in the district, and have a freehold estate therein in 1,000 acres of land, while in the exercise of his office.

SECTION 4

...There shall also be appointed a court to consist of three judges, any two of whom to form a court, who shall have a common law jurisdiction, and reside in the district, and have each therein a freehold estate in 500 acres of land while in the exercise of their offices; and their commissions shall continue in force during good behavior.

SECTION 5

The governor and judges, or a majority of them, shall adopt and publish in the district such laws of the original States, criminal and civil, as may be necessary and best suited to the circumstances of the district, and report them to Congress from time to time: which laws shall be in force in the district until the organization of the General Assembly therein, unless disapproved of by Congress; but afterwards the Legislature shall have authority to alter them as they shall think fit....

SECTION 7

Previous to the organization of the general assembly, the governor shall appoint such magistrates and other civil officers in each county or township, as he shall find necessary for the preservation of the peace and good order in the same . . .

SECTION 9

So soon as there shall be five thousand free male inhabitants of full age in the district, upon giving proof thereof to the governor, they shall receive authority, with time and place, to elect a representative from their counties or townships to represent them in the general assembly. Provided, That, for every five hundred free male inhabitants, there shall be one representative, and so on progressively with the number of free male inhabitants shall the right of representation increase, until the number of representatives shall amount to twenty five; after which, the number and proportion of representatives shall be regulated by the legislature: Provided, That no person be eligible or qualified to act as a representative unless he shall have been a citizen of one of the United States three years, and be a resident in the district, or unless he shall have resided in the district three years; and, in either case, shall likewise hold in his own right, in fee simple, two hundred acres of land within the same; Provided, also, That a freehold in fifty acres of land in the district, having been a citizen of one of the states, and being resident in the district, or the like freehold and two years residence in the district, shall be necessary to qualify a man as an elector of a representative.

SECTION 10

The representatives thus elected, shall serve for the term of two years. . . .

SECTION 14

It is hereby ordained and declared by the authority aforesaid, That the following articles shall be considered as articles of compact between the original States and the people and States in the said territory and forever remain unalterable, unless by common consent, to wit:

> Art. 1. No person, demeaning himself in a peaceable and orderly manner, shall ever be molested on account of his mode of worship or religious sentiments, in the said territory.

Art. 2. The inhabitants of the said territory shall always be entitled to the benefits of the writ of habeas corpus, and of the trial by jury; of a proportionate representation of the people in the legislature; and of judicial proceedings according to the course of the common law. All persons shall be bailable, unless for capital offenses, where the proof shall be evident or the presumption great. All fines shall be moderate; and no cruel or unusual punishments shall be inflicted. . . .

Art. 3. Religion, morality, and knowledge, being necessary to good government and the happiness of mankind, schools and the means of education shall forever be encouraged. The utmost good faith shall always be observed towards the Indians; their lands and property shall never be taken from them without their consent; and, in their property, rights, and liberty, they shall never be invaded or disturbed, unless in just and lawful wars authorized by Congress; but laws founded in justice and humanity, shall from time to time be made for preventing wrongs being done to them, and for preserving peace and friendship with them.

Art. 4. The said territory, and the States which may be formed therein, shall forever remain a part of this Confederacy of the United States of America, subject to the Articles of Confederation, and to such alterations therein as shall be constitutionally made; and to all the acts and ordinances of the United States in Congress assembled, conformable thereto. . . .

Art. 5. There shall be formed in the said territory, not less than three nor more than five States. . . . And, whenever any of the said States shall have sixty thousand free inhabitants therein, such State shall be admitted, by its delegates, into the Congress of the United States, on an equal footing with the original States in all respects whatever . . .

Art. 6. There shall be neither slavery nor involuntary servitude in the said territory, otherwise than in the punishment of crimes whereof the party shall have been duly convicted. . . .

4.3

General Benjamin Lincoln Recalls Shays's Rebellion (1786)

Winning the American Revolution had serious economic consequences for the United States. Now barred from the lucrative trade in the British West Indies and burdened with war debts and shaky finances, the nation plunged into economic depression. The crisis was particularly grave in Massachusetts. Eager to dissolve the state's war debts, the legislature imposed high taxes and required payment in hard currency (gold and silver coins). The measures soon triggered a wave of foreclosures and property seizures. Although several other states printed paper money to ease the economic crisis, the elites who controlled Massachusetts politics obstinately refused to do so.

The situation soon became explosive. In September 1786, Daniel Shays, a Revolutionary War veteran and struggling farmer, led several hundred men in forcing the state Supreme Court in Springfield to suspend debt collection proceedings. Similar protests spread to other towns. In January 1787, Shays led 1,200 men in a raid on the federal arsenal in Springfield. After the state militia crushed the uprising, Shays and fourteen others were arrested and sentenced to death. The following year, the state legislature reduced taxes and Shays secured a pardon.

Although Shays's Rebellion was short-lived, it generated fear that the nation was on the verge of mob rule and economic ruin. It also added momentum to efforts to revise the Articles of Confederation. In this letter, General Benjamin Lincoln, the commander of the Massachusetts militia that suppressed Shays's insurrection, describes the uprising to President George Washington.

FOCUS QUESTIONS

1. How does Lincoln describe Shays's Rebellion?
2. What does he believe has caused the protests? Do you find his explanation convincing? Why or why not?

SOURCE: Albert Bushnell Hart, ed. *American History Told by Contemporaries*, Vol. III: *Building of the Republic* (New York, MacMillan, 1901), pp. 191–194.

3. Why did Shays's Rebellion alarm Americans? Why did it increase popular demands for the revision of the Articles of Confederation?

Hingham, December 4th, 1786

I cannot . . . be surprised to hear your Excellency inquire, "Are your people getting mad? Are we to have the goodly fabric, that eight years were spent in raising, pulled over our heads? What is the cause of all these commotions? When and how will they end?" Although I cannot pretend to give a full and complete answer to them, yet I will make some observations which shall involve in them the best answers to the several questions in my power to give.

"Are your people getting mad?" Many of them appear to be absolutely so, if an attempt to annihilate our present constitution and dissolve the present government can be considered as evidences of insanity.

"Are we to have the goodly fabric, that eight years were spent in rearing, pulled over our heads?" There is great danger that it will be so, I think, unless the tottering system shall be supported by arms, and even then a government which has no other basis than the point of the bayonet, should one be suspended thereon, is so totally different from the one established, at least in idea, by the different States that if we must have recourse to the sad experiment of arms it can hardly be said that we have supported "the goodly fabric." In this view of the matter, it may be "pulled over our heads." This probably will be the case, for there doth not appear to be virtue enough among the people to presence a perfect republican government.

"What is the cause of all these commotions?" The causes are too many and too various for me to pretend to trace and point them out. I shall therefore only mention some of those which appear to be the principal ones. Among those I may rank the ease with which property was acquired, with which credit was obtained, and debts were discharged in the time of the war. Hence people were diverted from their usual industry and economy. A luxuriant mode of living crept into vogue, and soon that income, by which the expenses of all should as much as possible be limited, was no longer considered as having any thing to do with the question at what expense families ought to live, or rather which they ought not to have exceeded. The moment the day arrived when all discovered that things were fast returning back into their original channels, that the industrious were to reap the fruits of their industry, and that the indolent and improvident would soon experience the evils of their idleness and sloth, very many startled at the idea, and instead of attempting to subject themselves to such a line of conduct, which duty to the public and a regard to their own happiness evidently pointed out, they contemplated how they should evade the necessity of reforming their system and of changing their present mode of life, they first complained of commutation, of the weight of public taxes, of the insupportable debt of the Union, of the scarcity of money, and of the cruelty of suffering the private creditors to call for their just dues. This catalogue of complaints was listened to by many. County conventions were formed, and the cry for paper money, subject to depreciation, as was declared by some of their public resolves, was the clamor of the day. But notwithstanding instructions to members of the General Court and petitions from different quarters, the majority of that body were opposed to the measures. Failing of their point, the disaffected in the first place attempted, and in many instances succeeded [,] to stop the courts of law, and to suspend the operations of government. This they hoped to do until they could by force sap the foundations of our constitution, and bring into the Legislature creatures of their own by which they could mould a government at pleasure, and make it subservient to all their purposes, and when an end should thereby be put to public and private debts, the agrarian law might follow with ease. In short, the want of industry, Economy, and common honesty seem to be the causes of the present commotions.

It is impossible for me to determine "when and how they will end;" as I see little probability that they will be brought to a period, and the dignity of government supported, without bloodshed. When a single drop is drawn, the most prophetic spirit will not, in my opinion, be able to determine when it will cease flowing. The proportion of debtors runs high in this State. Too many of them are against the government. The men of property and the holders of the public securities are generally supporters of our present constitution. Few of these have been in the field, and it remains quite problematical whether they will in time so fully discover their own interests as they shall be induced thereby to lend for a season part of their property for the security of the remainder. If these classes of men should not turn out on the broad scale with spirit, and the insurgents should take the field and keep it, our constitution will be overturned, and the federal government broken in upon by lopping off one branch essential to the well being of the whole. This cannot be submitted to by the United States with impunity. They must send force to our aid: when this shall be collected, they will be equal to all purposes....

4.4

James Madison, *Federalist* Number 10 (1788)

When the Philadelphia Convention ended in September 1787, its delegates had approved the Constitution, a document that differed greatly from the Articles of Confederation. Because they knew that it would generate heated discussion, the framers of the Constitution established procedures for its ratification. The states

SOURCE: "The Numerous Advantages of the Union," *The Federalist* (New York, 1901), 44–51.

would convene special conventions comprised of popularly elected representatives. When nine state conventions ratified the Constitution, it would become the new national government.

When first published, the Constitution had minimal support. Still wary of centralized authority, many Americans were reluctant to embrace a radically restructured government. Opponents of the Constitution, stuck with the unwieldy name Anti-Federalists, doubted that the proposed system of checks and balances could work in such a large and diverse republic. They also feared that a strong national government would imperil the states and individual liberties.

To address these concerns, the Federalists, the supporters of the Constitution, began a well-funded publicity campaign. During the ratification process, it became apparent that populous New York and Virginia would be crucial to the new government's success. To bolster support for the Constitution in New York, Alexander Hamilton, James Madison, and John Jay published a series of essays under the pseudonym Publius. Known collectively as The Federalist, *the eighty-five essays became an eloquent expression of American political philosophy. In 1788, New Yorkers voted in favor of ratification.*

James Madison (1751–1836) wrote the most important of the essays, Federalist 10. A brilliant lawyer, Madison helped to draft the Virginia state constitution and advocated religious freedom. While serving in the Continental Congress, Madison was a staunch critic of the Confederation. In 1787, at the Constitutional Convention in Philadelphia, Madison's Virginia Plan provided the basic framework and major themes of the Constitution. Upon entering the House of Representatives, Madison sponsored the first ten amendments to the U.S. Constitution. Known as the Bill of Rights, the amendments protected individual and states' rights. Between 1809 and 1817, he served as the nation's fourth president.

FOCUS QUESTIONS

1. How does Madison define "faction"? Why does he feel that factions arise? Why do factions pose a challenge to legislators?

2. What is Madison's opinion of democracy? How does he compare democratic and republican governments? Which system does he prefer? Why?

3. Compare Madison's arguments to those of Patrick Henry (Document 4.5). Whose assertions do you find most persuasive and why?

4. Do you believe our current government works as Madison claimed it would? Explain your answer.

By a faction, I understand a number of citizens, whether amounting to a majority or minority of the whole, who are united and actuated by some common impulse of passion, or of interest, adverse to the rights of other citizens, or to the permanent and aggregate interests of the community.

There are two methods of curing the mischiefs of faction: the one, by removing its causes; the other, by controlling its effects.

There are again two methods of removing the causes of faction: the one, by destroying the liberty which is essential to its existence; the other, by giving to every citizen the same opinions, the same passions, and the same interests.

It could never be more truly said than of the first remedy that it was worse than the disease. Liberty is to faction what air is to fire, an ailment without which it instantly expires. But it could not be less folly to abolish liberty, which is essential to political life, because it nourishes faction, than it would be to wish the annihilation of air, which is essential to animal life. . . .

The second expedient is as impracticable as the first would be unwise. As long as the reason of man continues fallible, and he is at liberty to exercise it, different opinions will be formed. . . . The diversity in the faculties of men, from which the rights of property originate, is not less an insuperable obstacle to a uniformity of interest. The protection of these faculties is the first object of government. . . .

The latent causes of faction are thus sown in a nature of man; and we see them everywhere brought into different degrees of activity, according to the different circumstances of civil society. . . . But the most common and durable source of factions has been the various and unequal distribution of property.

Those who hold and those who are without property have ever formed distinct interests in society. Those who are creditors and those who are debtors fall under a like discrimination. A landed interest, a manufacturing interest, a mercantile interest, a moneyed interest, with many lesser interests, grow up of necessity in civilized nations and divide them into different classes, actuated by different sentiments and views. The regulation of these various and interfering interests forms the principal task of modern legislation and involves the spirit of party and faction in the necessary and ordinary operations of the government. . . .

It is in vain to say that enlightened statesmen will be able to adjust these clashing interests and render them all subservient to the public good. Enlightened statesmen will not always be at the helm. Nor, in many cases, can such an adjustment be made at all without taking into view indirect and remote considerations, which will rarely prevail over the immediate interest which one party may find in disregarding the right of another or the good of the whole.

The inference to which we are brought is that the causes of faction cannot be removed and that relief is only to be sought in the means of controlling its effects.

If a faction consists of less than a majority, relief is supplied by the republican principal, which enables the majority to defeat its sinister views by regular vote. . . . When a majority is included in a faction, the form of popular government, on the other hand, enables it to sacrifice to its ruling passion or interest both the public good and the rights of other citizens. To secure the public good and private rights against the danger of such a faction, and at the same time to preserve the spirit and the form of popular government, is then the great object to which our inquiries are directed. . . .

From this view of the subject it may be concluded that a pure democracy, by which I mean a society consisting of a small number of citizens who assemble and administer the government in person, can admit of no cure for the mischiefs of faction. A common passion or interest will, in almost every case, be felt by a majority of the whole; a communication and concert result from the form of government itself; and there is nothing to check the inducements to sacrifice the weaker party or an obnoxious individual. Hence it is that such democracies have ever been spectacles of turbulence and contention; have ever been found incompatible with personal security or the rights of property; and have in general been as short in their lives as they have been violent in their deaths. Theoretic politicians, who have patronized this species of government, have erroneously supposed that by reducing mankind to perfect equality in their political rights, they would, at the same time, be perfectly equalized and assimilated in their possessions, their opinions, and their passions.

A republic, by which I mean a government in which the scheme of representation takes place, opens a different prospect and promises the cure for which we are seeking. . . .

The two great points of difference between a democracy and a republic are: first, the delegation of the government in the latter, to a small number of citizens elected by the rest; secondly, the greater sphere of country, over which the latter may be executed.

The effect of the first difference is, on the one hand, to refine and enlarge the public views by passing them through the medium of a chosen body of citizens, whose wisdom may best discern the true interest of their country, and whose patriotism and love of justice will be least likely to sacrifice it to temporary or partial considerations. . . . Men of factious tempers, of local prejudices, or of sinister designs may, by intrigue, by corruption, or by other means, first obtain the suffrages, and then betray the interests of the people. The question resulting is, whether small or extensive republics are more favorable to the election of proper guardians of the public weal; and it is clearly decided in favor of the latter by two obvious considerations:

In the first place, it is to be remarked that, however small the republic may be, the representatives must be raised to a certain number, in order to guard against the cabals of a few; and that, however large it may be, they must be limited to a certain number, in order to guard against the confusion of the multitude. . . .

In the next place, as each representative will be chosen by a greater number of citizens in the large than in the small republic, it will be more difficult for unworthy candidates to practice with success the vicious arts by which elections are too often carried; and the suffrages of the people being more free, will be more likely to center in men who possess the most attractive merit and the most diffusive and established character.

By enlarging too much the number of electors, you render the representative too little acquainted with all their local circumstances and lesser interests; as by reducing it too much, you render him unduly attached to these and too little fit to comprehend and pursue great and national objects. The federal Constitution forms a happy combination in this respect: the great and aggregate interests being referred to the national, the local and particular to the state legislatures.

The other point of difference is the greater number of citizens and the extent of territory which may be brought within the compass of republican than of democratic government; and it is this circumstance principally which renders factious combinations less to be dreaded in the former than in the latter. The smaller the society, the fewer probably will be the distinct parties and interests composing it; . . . the more easily will they concert and execute their plans of oppression. Extend the sphere and you take in a greater variety of parties and interests; you make it less probable that a majority of the whole will have a common motive to invade the rights of their citizens; or if such a common motive exists, it will be more difficult for all who feel it to discover their own strength and to act in unison with each other. . . .

Hence, it clearly appears that the same advantage which a republic has over a democracy, in controlling the effects of factions, is enjoyed by a large over a small republic—is enjoyed by the Union over the states composing it. . . .

In the extent, and proper structure of the Union, therefore, we behold a republican remedy for the diseases most incident to republican government. And according to the degree of pleasure and pride we feel in being republicans, ought to be our zeal in cherishing the spirit and supporting the character of Federalists.

4.5

Patrick Henry, Speech to the Virginia Ratifying Convention (1788)

Afraid that the Constitution did not balance the power of the states and the national government or adequately protect individual liberties, the Anti-Federalists staunchly opposed its ratification. Their concerns reflected many of the same issues that had driven American protests against Great Britain.

The Anti-Federalists faced an uphill battle. The Federalists, the supporters of the Constitution, included several of America's richest and most respected men. Most newspapers were biased toward Federalist views. Lacking the national stature and political experience of their opponents, the Anti-Federalists were not able to generate much interest in their cause. Indeed, only about a quarter of

SOURCE: Patrick Henry, Speech to the Virginia Ratifying Convention, June 5, 1788, published at http://www.wfu.edu/~zulick/340/henry.html.

eligible voters participated in electing delegates to the state ratifying conventions, the majority of whom were Federalists. Only two states, Rhode Island and North Carolina, initially rejected the Constitution—and both adopted it by 1790.

Patrick Henry (1736–1799) was a leading Anti-Federalist. A brilliant orator, Henry is perhaps best known for his 1775 "Give Me Liberty or Give Me Death" speech. After helping to draft Virginia's first state constitution, he served as its governor from 1776 to 1779 and again from 1784 to 1786.

After attending the Philadelphia Convention in 1787, Henry became a passionate opponent of the U.S. Constitution. In this speech to the Virginia ratifying convention in June 1788, he tries to persuade his colleagues to embrace his views. Although Virginia ultimately adopted the Constitution by an 89 to 79 vote, Henry's ideas profoundly influenced the Bill of Rights (1791).

FOCUS QUESTIONS

1. What are Henry's major objections to the Constitution? Do you think his fears were reasonable? Explain your answer.

2. Compare Henry's arguments to those of James Madison (Document 4.4). Whose assertions do you find most persuasive and why?

3. Do any of Henry's ideas still affect American political debates? If so, provide examples.

I rose yesterday to ask a question which arose in my own mind. When I asked that question, I thought the meaning of my interrogation was obvious. The fate of this question and of America may depend on this. Have they said, *We, the states*? Have they made a proposal of a compact between states? If they had, this would be a confederation. It is otherwise most clearly a consolidated government.

The question turns, sir, on that poor little thing—the expression, *We, the people*, instead of the states, of America. I need not take much pains to show that the principles of this system are extremely pernicious, impolitic, and dangerous. Is this a monarchy, like England—a compact between prince and people, with checks on the former to secure the liberty of the latter? Is this a confederacy, like Holland—an association of a number of independent states, each of which retains its individual sovereignty? It is not a democracy, wherein the people retain all their rights securely.

Had these principles been adhered to, we should not have been brought to this alarming transition, from a confederacy to a consolidated government. . . . Here is a resolution as radical as that which separated us from Great Britain. It is radical in this transition; our rights and privileges are endangered, and the sovereignty of the states will be relinquished: and cannot we plainly see that this is actually the case?

The rights of conscience, trial by jury, liberty of the press, all your immunities and franchises, all pretensions to human rights and privileges, are rendered insecure, if not lost, by this change, so loudly talked of by some, and inconsiderately by others. Is this tame relinquishment of rights worthy of freemen? Is it worthy of that manly fortitude that ought to characterize republicans?

It is said eight states have adopted this plan. I declare that if twelve states and a half had adopted it, I would, with manly firmness, and in spite of an erring world, reject it. You are not to inquire how your trade may be increased, nor how you are to become a great and powerful people, but how your liberties can be secured; for liberty ought to be the direct end of your government.

Having premised these things, I shall, with the aid of my judgment and information, which, I confess, are not extensive, go into the discussion of this system more minutely....

The Confederation, this same despised government, merits, in my opinion, the highest encomium [praise]: it carried us through a long and dangerous war; it rendered us victorious in that bloody conflict with a powerful nation; it has secured us a territory greater than any European monarch possesses: and shall a government which has been thus strong and vigorous, be accused of imbecility, and abandoned for want of energy? Consider what you are about to do before you part with the government. Take longer time in reckoning things; revolutions like this have happened in almost every country in Europe; similar examples are to be found in ancient Greece and ancient Rome—instances of the people losing their liberty by their carelessness and the ambition of a few.

We are cautioned by the honorable gentleman, who presides, against faction and turbulence. I acknowledge that licentiousness is dangerous, and that it ought to be provided against; I acknowledge, also, the new form of government may effectually prevent it: yet there is another thing it will as effectually do—it will oppress and ruin the people....

If you make the citizens of this country agree to become the subjects of one great consolidated empire of America, your government will not have sufficient energy to keep them together. Such a government is incompatible with the genius of republicanism. There will be no checks, no real balances, in this government. What can avail your specious, imaginary balance, your rope-dancing, chain-rattling, ridiculous ideal checks and contrivances? ...

When I thus profess myself an advocate for the liberty of the people, I shall be told I am a designing man, that I am to be a great man, that I am to be a demagogue; and many similar illiberal insinuations will be thrown out: but, sir, conscious rectitude outweighs those things with me. I see great jeopardy in this new government. I see none from our present one....

Besides the expenses of maintaining the Senate and other house in as much splendor as they please, there is to be a great and mighty President, with very extensive powers—the powers of a king. He is to be supported in extravagant magnificence; so that the whole of our property may be taken by this American government, by laying what taxes they please, giving themselves what salaries they please, and suspending our laws at their pleasure.

I might be thought too inquisitive, but I believe I should take up very little of your time in enumerating the little power that is left to the government of Virginia; for this power is reduced to little or nothing: their garrisons, magazines, arsenals, and forts, which will be situated in the strongest places within the states; their ten miles square, with all the fine ornaments of human life, added to their powers, and taken from the states, will reduce the power of the latter to nothing. . . .

In this scheme of energetic government, the people will find two sets of tax-gatherers—the state and the federal sheriffs. This, it seems to me, will produce such dreadful oppression as the people cannot possibly bear. The federal sheriff may commit what oppression, make what distresses, he pleases, and ruin you with impunity; for how are you to tie his hands? Have you any sufficiently decided means of preventing him from sucking your blood by speculations, commissions, and fees? . . .

If they perpetrate the most unwarrantable outrage on your person or property, you cannot get redress on this side of Philadelphia or New York; and how can you get it there? If your domestic avocations could permit you to go thither, there you must appeal to judges sworn to support this Constitution, in opposition to that of any state, and who may also be inclined to favor their own officers. When these harpies are aided by excise men, who may search, at any time, your houses, and most secret recesses, will the people bear it? If you think so, you differ from me. . . .

This Constitution is said to have beautiful features; but when I come to examine these features, sir, they appear to me horribly frightful. Among other deformities, it has an awful squinting; it squints toward monarchy; and does not this raise indignation in the breast of every true American?

Your President may easily become king. Your Senate is so imperfectly constructed that your dearest rights may be sacrificed by what may be a small minority; and a very small minority may continue forever unchangeably this government, although horridly defective. Where are your checks in this government? Your strongholds will be in the hands of your enemies. It is on a supposition that your American governors shall be honest, that all the good qualities of this government are founded; but its defective and imperfect construction puts it in their power to perpetrate the worst of mischiefs, should they be bad men; and, sir, would not all the World, from the eastern to the western hemisphere, blame our distracted folly in resting our rights upon the contingency of our rulers being good or bad?

Show me that age and country where the rights and liberties of the people were placed on the sole chance of their rulers being good men, without a consequent loss of liberty! I say that the loss of that dearest privilege has ever followed, with absolute certainty, every such mad attempt. . . .

What can be more defective than the clause concerning the elections? The control given to Congress over the time, place, and manner of holding elections, will totally destroy the end of suffrage. The elections may be held at one place, and the most inconvenient in the state; or they may be at remote distances from those who have a right of suffrage: hence nine out of ten must either not vote at all, or vote for strangers; for the most influential characters will be applied to, to know who are the most proper to be chosen.

I repeat, the control of Congress over the manner, &c., of electing, well warrants this idea. The natural consequence will be, that this democratic branch will possess none of the public confidence; the people will be prejudiced against representatives chosen in such an injudicious manner. . . .

Another beautiful feature of this Constitution is, the publication from time to time of the receipts and expenditures of the public money. This expression, from time to time, is very indefinite and indeterminate: it may extend to a century. Grant that any of them are wicked; they may squander the public money so as to ruin you, and yet this expression will give you no redress.... They may go without punishment, though they commit the most outrageous violation on our immunities. That paper may tell me they will be punished. I ask, By what law? They must make the law, for there is no existing law to do it. What! will they make a law to punish themselves?...

The Senate, by making treaties, may destroy your liberty and laws for want of responsibility. Two thirds of those that shall happen to be present, can, with the President, make treaties that shall be the supreme law of the land; they may make the most ruinous treaties; and yet there is no punishment for them. Whoever shows me a punishment provided for them will oblige me....

We have a right to have time to consider: we shall therefore insist upon it. Unless the government be amended, we can never accept it. The adopting states will doubtless accept our money and our regiments; and what is to be the consequence, if we are disunited? I believe it is yet doubtful, whether it is not proper to stand by a while, and see the effect of its adoption in other states. In forming a government, the utmost care should be taken to prevent its becoming oppressive; and this government is of such an intricate and complicated nature, that no man on this earth can know its real operation.

The other states have no reason to think, from the antecedent conduct of Virginia, that she has any intention of seceding from the Union, or of being less active to support the general welfare....

Before you abandon the present system, I hope you will consider not only its defects, most maturely, but likewise those of that which you are to substitute for it. May you be fully apprized of the dangers of the latter, not by fatal experience, but by some abler advocate than I!

4.6

The Bill of Rights (1791)

Several states had ratified the U.S. Constitution with the understanding that it would be amended to safeguard basic individual freedoms. Written largely by James Madison, the ten amendments were adopted on December 15, 1791.

SOURCE: Published by the U.S. Historical Documents Archive at http://w3.one.net/~mweiler/ushda/ushda.htm.

Known collectively as the Bill of Rights, the amendments guarantee personal liberties and limit governmental power. To many Americans, they embody the most important principles of democracy.

FOCUS QUESTIONS

1. What are the major themes of the Bill of Rights?
2. How does the Bill of Rights reflect the issues raised by Patrick Henry (Document 4.5)?
3. What do you think is the most important amendment in the Bill of Rights? Which do you believe is the least important? Explain your answers.

AMENDMENT I

Congress shall make no law respecting an establishment of religion, or prohibiting the free exercise thereof; or abridging the freedom of speech, or of the press; or the right of the people peaceably to assemble, and to petition the Government for a redress of grievances.

AMENDMENT II

A well-regulated Militia, being necessary to the security of a free State, the right of the people to keep and bear Arms, shall not be infringed.

AMENDMENT III

No Soldier shall, in time of peace be quartered in any house, without the consent of the Owner, nor in time of war, but in a manner to be prescribed by law.

AMENDMENT IV

The right of the people to be secure in their persons, houses, papers, and effects, against unreasonable searches and seizures, shall not be violated, and no Warrants shall issue, but upon probable cause, supported by Oath or affirmation, and particularly describing the place to be searched, and the persons or things to be seized.

AMENDMENT V

No person shall be held to answer for a capital, or otherwise infamous crime, unless on a presentment or indictment of a Grand Jury, except in cases arising in the land or naval forces, or in the Militia, when in actual service in time of War or public danger; nor shall any person be subject for the same offence to be twice put in jeopardy of life or limb; nor shall be compelled in any criminal case to be a witness against himself, nor be deprived of life, liberty, or property, without due process of law; nor shall private property be taken for public use, without just compensation.

AMENDMENT VI

In all criminal prosecutions, the accused shall enjoy the right to a speedy and public trial, by an impartial jury of the State and district wherein the crime shall have been committed, which district shall have been previously ascertained by law, and to be informed of the nature and cause of the accusation; to be confronted with the witnesses against him; to have compulsory process for obtaining witnesses in his favor, and to have the Assistance of Counsel for his defense.

AMENDMENT VII

In Suits at common law, where the value in controversy shall exceed twenty dollars, the right of trial by jury shall be preserved, and no fact tried by a jury, shall be otherwise re-examined in any Court of the United States, than according to the rules of the common law.

AMENDMENT VIII

Excessive bail shall not be required, nor excessive fines imposed, nor cruel and unusual punishments inflicted.

AMENDMENT IX

The enumeration in the Constitution, of certain rights, shall not be construed to deny or disparage others retained by the people.

AMENDMENT X

The powers not delegated to the United States by the Constitution, nor prohibited by it to the States, are reserved to the States respectively, or to the people.

4.7

Thomas Jefferson on Slavery and Race (1781–1787)

Thomas Jefferson ranks among the most enigmatic figures in American history. As a legal scholar, political philosopher, and architect, Jefferson demonstrated brilliance and eloquence. His achievements included drafting the Declaration of Independence, serving as the nation's third president (1801–09), and founding the University of Virginia. To many, he remains an inspirational if paradoxical individual. Although he often preached the virtues of frugality, he died $100,000 in debt (equivalent to $10 million today). While abhorring the institution of slavery, he owned over 600 slaves during his lifetime. Convinced of the biological inferiority of African Americans, he may have fathered at least one child with Sally Hemings, one of his slaves. Although the Jefferson-Hemings relationship is still disputed, DNA tests indicate a link between male descendants in the two families.

In this passage from Notes on the State of Virginia *(1781), Jefferson articulates his views on race and slavery. He wrote the book in response to a Frenchman's inquiry about the physical geography, society, and political institutions of Jefferson's home state. It did not become widely available until an English translation was published in 1787.*

FOCUS QUESTIONS

1. What does Jefferson believe should be done with former slaves? Why?
2. What does he perceive as the major differences between the white and black races?
3. How does he describe American Indians?
4. What is his opinion of slavery?
5. Given Jefferson's paradoxical nature, how should modern Americans evaluate his historical legacy?

SOURCE: Thomas Jefferson, *Notes on the State of Virginia* (London, 1787), 227–273.

It will probably be asked, Why not retain and incorporate the blacks into the state, and thus save the expense of supplying, by importation of white settlers, the vacancies they will leave? Deep rooted prejudices entertained by the whites; ten thousand recollections, by the blacks, of the injuries they have sustained; new provocations; the real distinctions which nature has made; and many other circumstances, will divide us into parties, and produce convulsions, which will probably never end but in the extermination of the one or the other race.

To these objections, which are political, may be added others, which are physical and moral. The first difference which strikes us is that of color. Whether the black of the negro resides in the reticular membrane between the skin and scarf-skin, or in the scarf-skin itself; whether it proceeds from the color of the blood, the color of the bile, or from that of some other secretion, the difference is fixed in nature, and is as real as if its seat and cause were better known to us. And is this difference of no importance? Is it not the foundation of a greater or lesser share of beauty in the two races? Are not the fine mixtures of red and white, the expressions of every passion by greater or less suffusions of color in the one, preferable to that eternal monotony, which reigns in the countenances, that immovable veil of black which covers all the emotions of the other race? Add to these, flowing hair, a more elegant symmetry of form, their own judgment in favor of the whites, declared by their preference of them, as uniformly as is the preference of the Oranootan for the black women over those of his own species. The circumstance of Superior beauty, is thought worthy attention in the propa- gation of our horses, dogs, and other domestic animals; why not in that of man?

Besides those of color, figure, and hair, there are other physical distinctions proving a difference of race. They have less hair on the face and body. They secrete less by the kidneys, and more by the glands of the skin, which gives them a very strong and disagreeable odor. This greater degree of transpiration renders them more tolerant of heat, and less so of cold than the whites. . . . They seem to require less sleep. A black after hard labor through the day, will be induced by the slightest amusements to sit up till midnight, or later, though knowing he must be out with the first dawn of the morning. They are at least as brave, and more adventuresome. But this may perhaps proceed from a want of forethought, which prevents their seeing a danger till it be present. When present, they do not go through it with more coolness or steadiness than the whites. They are more ardent after their female: but love seems with them to be more an eager desire, than a tender delicate mixture of sentiment and sensation. Their griefs are transient. Those numberless afflictions, which render it doubtful whether heaven has given life to us in mercy or in wrath, are less felt, and sooner forgotten with them. In general, their existence appears to participate more of sensation than reflection. . . .

Comparing them by their faculties of memory, reason, and imagination, it appears to me that in memory they are equal to the whites; in reason much inferior, as I think one could scarcely be found capable of tracing and comprehend- ing the investigations of Euclid; and that in imagination they are dull, tasteless, and anomalous. It would be unfair to follow them to Africa for this investigation.

We will consider them here, on the same stage with the whites, and where the facts are not apocryphal on which a judgment is to be formed. It will be right to make great allowances for the difference of condition, of education, of conversation, of the sphere in which they move. . . . Some have been liberally educated, and all have lived in countries where the arts and sciences are cultivated to a considerable degree, and have had before their eyes samples of the best works from abroad.

The Indians, with no advantages of this kind, will often carve figures on their pipes not destitute of design and merit. They will crayon out an animal, a plant, or a country, so as to prove the existence of a germ in their minds which only wants cultivation. They astonish you with strokes of the most sublime oratory; such as prove their reason and sentiment strong, their imagination glowing and elevated. But never yet could I find that a black had uttered a thought above the level of plain narration; never saw even an elementary trait of painting or sculpture. In music they are more generally gifted than the whites with accurate ears for tune and time. . . . Whether they will be equal to the composition of a more extensive run of melody, or of complicated harmony, is yet to be proved. . . . Misery is often the parent of the most affecting touches in poetry. Among the blacks is misery enough, God knows, but no poetry. . . .

The improvement of the blacks in body and mind, in the first instance of their mixture with the whites, has been observed by every one, and proves that their inferiority is not the effect merely of their condition of life. . . . It is not their condition then, but nature, which has produced the distinction. Whether further observation will or will not verify the conjecture, that nature has been less bountiful to them in the endowments of the head, I believe that in those of the heart she will be found to have done them justice. That disposition to theft with which they have been branded, must be ascribed to their situation, and not to any depravity of the moral sense. The man, in whose favor no laws of property exist, probably feels himself less bound to respect those made in favor of others. . . .

Notwithstanding these considerations which must weaken their respect for the laws of property, we find among them numerous instances of the most rigid integrity, and as many as among their better instructed masters, of benevolence, gratitude and unshaken fidelity. The opinion, that they are inferior in the faculties of reason and imagination, must be hazarded with great diffidence. . . . To our reproach it must be said, that though for a century and a half we have had under our eyes the races of black and of red men, they have never yet been viewed by us as subjects of natural history. I advance it therefore as a suspicion only, that the blacks, whether originally a distinct race, or made distinct by time and circumstances, are inferior to the whites in the endowments both of body and mind. . . .

This unfortunate difference of color, and perhaps of faculty, is a powerful obstacle to the emancipation of these people. Many of their advocates, while they wish to vindicate the liberty of human nature are anxious also to preserve its dignity and beauty. . . . There must doubtless be an unhappy influence on the manners of our people produced by the existence of slavery among us. The whole commerce between master and slave is a perpetual exercise of the most boisterous passions, the most unremitting despotism on the one part, and degrading submissions on the other. Our children see this, and learn to imitate it; for man is an imitative animal. . . . If a parent could find no motive either in his philanthropy or his self love, for restraining the intemperance of passion towards his slave, it should always be a sufficient one that his child is present. But generally it is not sufficient. . . . The man must be a prodigy who can retain his manners and morals undepraved by such circumstances.

And with what execration should the statesman be loaded, who, permitting one half the citizens thus to trample on the rights of the other, transforms those into despots, and these into enemies, destroys the morals of the one part, and the *amor patriae* of the other. . . .

And can the liberties of a nation be thought secure when we have removed their only firm basis, a conviction in the minds of the people that these liberties are of the gift of God? That they are not to be violated but with his wrath? Indeed I tremble for my country when I reflect that God is just: that his justice cannot sleep for ever: that considering numbers, nature and natural means only, a revolution of the wheel of fortune, an exchange of situation is among possible events: that it may become probable by supernatural interference! The almighty has no attribute which can take side with us in such a contest.

But it is impossible to be temperate and to pursue this subject through the various considerations of policy, of morals, of history natural and civil. We must be contented to hope they will force their way into every one's mind. I think a change already perceptible, since the origin of the present revolution. The spirit of the master is abating, that of the slave rising from the dust, his condition mollifying, the way I hope preparing, under the auspices of heaven, for a total emancipation, and that this is disposed, in the order of events, to be with the consent of the masters, rather than by their extirpation.

4.8

Benjamin Banneker to Thomas Jefferson (1791)

Many Americans were not blind to the contradiction of slavery in a free society, yet most believed in the inherent superiority of the white race. While millions of African Americans remained enslaved, free blacks faced formidable political, economic, and educational obstacles. Benjamin Banneker (1731–1806), a free

SOURCE: Published at Documentary Sources Database, American Multiculturalism Series, Unit One: Documenting the African-American Experience, Electronic Text Center, University of Virginia Library, http://etext.lib.virginia.edu/readex/24073.html.

black from Maryland, triumphed over these adversities and became a noted intellectual. Largely self-taught, Banneker mastered mathematics and astronomy. In 1790, George Washington appointed him to the team of surveyors laying out Washington, D.C. Banneker's almanacs were acclaimed throughout the United States and Europe.

In the following excerpt, Banneker challenges the assertions on race and slavery expressed by Thomas Jefferson in Notes on the State of Virginia *(1781).*

FOCUS QUESTIONS

1. Why does Banneker send this letter to Thomas Jefferson?
2. How does Banneker dispute prevailing racial attitudes?
3. How does Banneker want American society to change?

Maryland, Baltimore County, August 19, 1791

I am fully sensible of the greatness of that freedom, which I take with you on the present occasion; a liberty which seemed to me scarcely allowable, when I reflected on that distinguished and dignified station in which you stand, and the almost general prejudice and prepossession, which is so prevalent in the world against those of my complexion.

I suppose it is a truth too well attested to you, to need a proof here, that we are a race of beings, who have long labored under the abuse and censure of the world; that we have long been looked upon with an eye of contempt; and that we have long been considered rather as brutish than human, and scarcely capable of mental endowments.

Sir, I hope I may safely admit, in consequence that report which hath reached me, that you are a man less inflexible in sentiments of this nature, than many others; that you are measurably friendly, and well disposed towards us; and that you are willing and ready to lend your aid and assistance to our relief, from those many distresses, and numerous calamities, to which we are reduced.

Now Sir, if this is founded in truth, I apprehend you will embrace every opportunity, to eradicate that train of absurd and false ideas and opinions, which so generally prevails with respect to us; and that your sentiments are concurrent with mine, which are, that one universal Father hath given being to us all; and that he hath not only made us all of one flesh, but that he hath also, without partiality, afforded us all the same sensations and endowed us all with the same faculties; and that however variable we may be in society and religion, however diversified in situation or color, we are all of the same family, and stand in the same relation to him.

Sir, if these are sentiments of which you are fully persuaded, I hope you cannot but acknowledge, that it is the indispensable duty of those, who maintain for themselves the rights of human nature, and who possess the obligations of

Christianity, to extend their power and influence to the relief of every part of the human race, from whatever burden or oppression they may unjustly labor under. . . .

Sir, I have long been convinced, that if your love for yourselves, and for those inestimable laws, which preserved to you the rights of human nature, was founded on sincerity, you could not but be solicitous, that every individual, of whatever rank or distinction, might with you equally enjoy the blessing thereof; neither could you rest satisfied short of the most active effusion of your exertions, in order to their promotion from any state of degradation, to which the unjustifiable cruelty and barbarism of men may have reduced them.

Sir, I freely and cheerfully acknowledge, that I am of the African race, and in the color which is natural to them of the deepest dye; and it is under a sense of the most profound gratitude to the Supreme Ruler of the Universe, that I now confess to you, that I am not under that state of tyrannical thralldom, and inhuman captivity, to which too many of my brethren are doomed, but that I have abundantly tasted of the fruition of those blessings, which proceed from that free and unequaled liberty with which you are favored; and which, I hope, you will willingly allow you have mercifully received, from the immediate have of that Being, from whom proceedeth every good and perfect Gift.

Sir, suffer me to recall to your mind that time, in which the arms and tyranny of the British crown were exerted, with every powerful effort, in order to reduce you to a state of servitude: look back, I entreat you, on the variety of dangers to which you were exposed; reflect on that time, in which every human aid appeared unavailable, and in which even hope and fortitude wore the aspect of inability to the conflict, and you cannot but be led to a serious and grateful sense of your miraculous and providential preservation. . . .

This, sir, was a time when you clearly saw into the injustice of a state of slavery, and in which you had just apprehensions of the horrors of its condition. It was not that your abhorrence thereof was so excited, that you publicly held forth this true and invaluable doctrine, which is worthy to be recorded, and remembered in all succeeding age: "We hold these truths to be self-evident, that all men are created equal; that they are endowed by their Creator with certain unalienable rights, and among these are life, liberty, and the pursuit of happiness."

Here was a time, in which your tender feelings for yourselves had engaged you thus to declare, you were then impressed with proper ideas of the great violation of liberty, and the free possession of these blessings, to which you were entitled by nature; but, Sir, how pitiable is to reflect, . . . that you should at the same time counteract his [God's] mercies, in detaining by fraud and violence so numerous a part of my brethren, under groaning captivity and cruel oppression, that you should at the same time be found guilty of the most criminal act, which you professedly detested in others, with respect to yourselves.

I suppose that your knowledge of the situation of my brethren, is too extensive to need a recital here; neither shall I presume to prescribe methods by which they may be relieved, otherwise than by recommending to you and all others, to wean yourselves from those narrow prejudices which you have imbibed with respect to them, and as Job proposed to his friends, "put your soul in their souls' stead;" thus shall your hearts be enlarged with kindness and benevolence towards them; and thus shall you need neither the direction of myself or others, in what manner to proceed herein.

. . . I ardently hope, that your candor and generosity will plead with you in my behalf, when I make known to you, that it was not originally my design; but having taken up my pen in order to direct to you, as a present, a copy of an Almanac, which I have calculated for the succeeding year, I was unexpectedly and unavoidably led thereto. . . .

And now, Sir, I shall conclude, and subscribe myself, with the most profound respect,

Your most obedient and humble servant,
Benjamin Banneker

4.9

Judith Sargent Murray, "On the Equality of the Sexes" (1790)

Although the Revolution prompted few changes in women's legal status, it inspired debate on the subordination of women. Aware that women exerted tremendous influence on the moral and intellectual development of children, Americans recognized their importance in shaping the nation's future citizens. "Republican mothers" would teach their loved ones the values of liberty and independence. To ensure that women were prepared for these tasks, schools and academies began offering girls improved educations. Such changes laid the foundation for the women's rights movement of the nineteenth century.

Judith Sargent Murray (1751–1820) was one of the earliest advocates of gender equality. Born in Gloucester, Massachusetts, Judith Sargent was the daughter of a wealthy merchant. After receiving a rigorous education unusual for women of the era, she married John Stevens, a sea captain. She continued to educate herself and wrote poetry. In the 1770s, she turned her intellectual energies toward politics. Using assumed names so that her ideas would be taken seriously, she started publishing essays on public affairs. After the Revolution, she immersed

SOURCE: Published at the Judith Sargent Murray Society,
http://www.hurdsmith.com/judith/.

*herself in the Universalist church and married John Murray (after the death of her
first husband). She remained a highly prolific writer of plays, verse, letters, and
political essays.*

*As early as 1779, Murray drafted an essay addressing the equality of the
sexes. But it was not until 1790 that she published "On the Equality of the
Sexes" using the pen name Constantia. (Some spelling and grammar have been
modernized.)*

FOCUS QUESTIONS

1. On what bases does Murray challenge the notion of women's inferiority?
2. What measures does Murray propose for fostering gender equality? What
   advantages does she see in instituting such changes?
3. How do you think Murray's contemporaries reacted to this essay?
4. Do you see any similarities between the arguments of Murray and Benjamin
   Banneker (Document 4.8)? How did the Revolution influence their ideas?

Is it upon mature consideration we adopt the idea, that nature is thus partial in
her distributions? Is it indeed a fact, that she hath yielded to one half of the
human species so unquestionable a mental superiority? I know that to both sexes
elevated understandings, and the reverse, are common. But, suffer me to ask, in
what the minds of females are so notoriously deficient, or unequal. May not the
intellectual powers be ranged under these four heads—imagination, reason,
memory and judgment. The province of imagination hath long since been
surrendered up to us, and we have been crowned undoubted sovereigns of the
regions of fancy. Invention is perhaps the most arduous effort of the mind; this
branch of imagination hath been particularly ceded to us. . . . Observe the variety
of fashions (here I bar the contemptuous smile) which distinguish and adorn the
female world; how continually are they changing. . . . Now, what a playfulness,
what an exuberance of fancy, what strength of inventive imagination, doth this
continual variation discover? . . . Another instance of our creative powers, is our
talent for slander; how ingenious are we at inventive scandal? What a formidable
story can we in a moment fabricate merely from the force of a prolific imagination? How many reputations, in the fertile brain of a female, have been utterly
despoiled? How industrious are we at improving a hint? Suspicion how easily do
we convert into conviction, and conviction, embellished by the power of
eloquence, stalks abroad to the surprise and confusion of unsuspecting innocence.

Perhaps it will be asked if I furnish these facts as instances of excellency in our
sex. Certainly not; but as proofs of a creative faculty, of a lively imagination.
Assuredly great activity of mind is thereby discovered, and was this activity
properly directed, what beneficial effects would follow. Is the needle and kitchen
sufficient to employ the operations of a soul thus organized? I should conceive

not. Nay, it is a truth that those very departments leave the intelligent principle vacant, and at liberty for speculation. Are we deficient in reason? We can only reason from what we know, and if opportunity of acquiring knowledge hath been denied us, the inferiority of our sex cannot fairly be deduced from thence. Memory, I believe, will be allowed us in common, since every one's experience must testify, that a loquacious old woman is as frequently met with, as a communicative old man; their subjects are alike drawn from the fund of other times and the transactions of their youth, or of maturer life, entertain, or perhaps fatigue you, in the evening of their lives....

Yet it may be questioned, from what doth this superiority, in this determining faculty of the soul, proceed. May we not trace its source in the difference of education, and continued advantages? Will it be said that the judgment of a male of two years old, is more sage than that of a female's of the same age? I believe the reverse is generally observed to be true. But from that period what partiality! How is the one exalted and the other depressed, by the contrary modes of education which are adopted! The one is taught to aspire, and the other is early confined and limited. As their years increase, the sister must be wholly domesticated, while the brother is led by the hand through all the flowery paths of science. Grant that their minds are by nature equal, yet who shall wonder at the apparent superiority, if indeed custom becomes second nature; nay if it taketh place of nature, and that it doth the experience of each day will evince. At length arrived at womanhood, the uncultivated fair one feels a void, which the employments allotted her are by no means capable of filling. What can she do? To books she may not apply; or if she doth, to those only of the novel kind, lest she merit the appellation of a learned lady; and what ideas have been affixed to this term, the observation of many can testify. Fashion, scandal, and sometimes what is still more reprehensible, are then called in to her relief; and who can say to what lengths the liberties she takes may proceed. Meantime she herself is most unhappy; she feels the want of a cultivated mind. Is she single, she in vain seeks to fill up time from sexual employments or amusements. Is she united to a person whose soul nature made equal to her own, education hath set him so far above her, that in those entertainments which are productive of such rational felicity, she is not qualified to accompany him. She experiences a mortifying consciousness of inferiority, which embitters every enjoyment. Doth the person to whom her adverse fate hath consigned her, possess a mind incapable of improvement, she is equally wretched, in being so closely connected with an individual whom she cannot but despise. Now, was she permitted the same instructors as her brother, (with an eye however to their particular departments) for the employment of a rational mind an ample field would be opened....

A mind, thus filled, would have little room for the trifles with which our sex are, with too much justice, accused of amusing themselves, and they would thus be rendered fit companions for those, who should one day wear them as their crown. Fashions, in their variety, would then give place to conjectures, which might perhaps conduce to the improvement of the literary world; and there would be no leisure for slander or detraction. Reputation would not then be blasted, but serious speculations would occupy the lively imaginations of the sex.

Unnecessary visits would be precluded, and that custom would only be indulged by way of relaxation, or to answer the demands of consanguinity and friendship. Females would become discreet, their judgments would be invigorated, and their partners for life being circumspectly chosen. . . .

Will it be urged that those acquirements would supersede our domestic duties. I answer that every requisite in female economy is easily attained; and, with truth I can add, that when once attained, they require no further mental attention. Nay, while we are pursuing the needle, or the superintendency of the family, I repeat, that our minds are at full liberty for reflection; that imagination may exert itself in full vigour; and that if a just foundation is early laid, our ideas will then be worthy of rational beings. If we were industrious we might easily find time to arrange them upon paper, or should avocations press too hard for such an indulgence, the hours allotted for conversation would at least become more refined and rational. . . .

Yes, ye lordly, ye haughty sex, our souls are by nature equal to yours; the same breath of God animates, enlivens, and invigorates us; and that we are not fallen lower than yourselves, let those witness who have greatly towered above the various discouragements by which they have been so heavily oppressed. . . . I dare confidently believe, that from the commencement of time to the present day, there hath been as many females, as males, who, by the mere force of natural powers, have merited the crown of applause; who, thus assisted, have seized the wreath of fame. I know there are [those] who assert, that as the animal powers of the one sex are superior, of course their mental faculties also must be stronger; thus attributing strength of mind to the transient organization of this earth born tenement. But if this reasoning is just, man must be content to yield the palm to many of the brute creation, since by not a few of his brethren of the field, he is far surpassed in bodily strength. Moreover, was this argument admitted, it would prove too much, for ocular demonstration evinceth [demonstrates], that there are many robust masculine ladies, and effeminate gentlemen. . . . Besides, were we to grant that animal strength proved any thing, taking into consideration the accustomed impartiality of nature, we should be induced to imagine, that she had invested the female mind with superior strength as an equivalent for the bodily powers of man. But waving this however palpable advantage, for equality only, we wish to contend.

Constantia

4.10

Alexander Hamilton, Report on Manufactures (1791)

The nation's faltering economy presented the Washington administration with one of its greatest challenges. The task of improving the country's financial health fell to Alexander Hamilton (1755–1804), the first secretary of the U.S. Treasury. Formulating a sweeping program for national economic development, he laid the foundation for modern American capitalism.

Little in Hamilton's background suggested he would become such an influential figure. The illegitimate son of a West Indian trader, Hamilton grew up in poverty. After his father abandoned his mother, he went to work at the age of eleven. Employed as a clerk in the countinghouse of two New York merchants, Hamilton's genius and industry drew notice. After his mother died, friends eventually sent him to a New Jersey preparatory school. In 1773, he entered King's College (now Columbia University.) He became very involved in the struggle against Great Britain and wrote influential political tracts. When war erupted in 1775, he enlisted in the Continental Army and distinguished himself in battle. He soon earned an appointment to George Washington's staff. The two men forged a close intellectual and emotional bond.

After the Revolution, Hamilton studied law and started practicing in New York. At the same time, he wrote several pieces analyzing the weaknesses of the Articles of Confederation. After serving as a delegate to the Philadelphia Convention, he became one of the Constitution's most eloquent advocates. He collaborated with James Madison and John Jay on The Federalist, *a series of eighty-five essays defending the Constitution and republican government.*

In 1789, when Hamilton assumed his duties at the Treasury, the country was in desperate economic condition. With the possibility of war against Great Britain, Spain, or both imminent, Hamilton outlined a plan to establish public credit and strengthen the national government. He presented Congress with four reports. In the first two, he devised a program for improving the country's credit and paying its debts. His third report advocated a national bank. Although Congress adopted these proposals, Hamilton's efforts to forge a partnership between the wealthy and the government provoked heated debates.

SOURCE: Published at http://www.oberlin.edu/~gkornbl/Hist258/ReportMfres.html.

Unfazed, Hamilton submitted his Report on Manufactures to Congress. Hoping to encourage industrialization and economic self-sufficiency, he proposed protective tariffs on imports in order to aid the growth of domestic factories. Successful manufacturers, he asserted, would lure immigrants and generate national wealth. James Madison and Thomas Jefferson vehemently opposed Hamilton's plan. They argued that protective tariffs were unfair to consumers and viewed industrialization as a threat to the republic. Land-owning farmers, they claimed, were more virtuous citizens and more economically independent than unruly urban masses. Although Congress did not act on the Report on Manufactures, the political differences between Hamilton and his critics soon split Americans into rival political parties.

FOCUS QUESTIONS

1. How does Hamilton propose to develop the U.S. economy?
2. What advantages does he believe an industrial economy will bring?
3. In what ways is today's economy similar to Hamilton's vision?

The expediency of encouraging manufactures in the United States, which was not long since deemed very questionable, appears at this time to be pretty generally admitted. The embarrassments, which have obstructed the progress of our external trade, have led to serious reflections on the necessity of enlarging the sphere of our domestic commerce: the restrictive regulations, which in foreign markets abridge the vent of the increasing surplus of our Agricultural produce, serve to beget an earnest desire, that a more extensive demand for that surplus may be created at home. . . .

It ought readily to be conceded that the cultivation of the earth—as the primary and most certain source of national supply—as the immediate and chief source of subsistence to man—as the principal source of those materials which constitute the nutriment of other kinds of labor—as including a state most favourable to the freedom and independence of the human mind—one, perhaps, most conducive to the multiplication of the human species—has intrinsically a strong claim to preeminence over every other kind of industry.

But, that it has a title to any thing like an exclusive predilection, in any country, ought to be admitted with great caution. That it is even more productive than every other branch of Industry requires more evidence than has yet been given in support of the position. . . .

It is now proper to proceed a step further, and to enumerate the principal circumstances, from which it may be inferred—that manufacturing establishments not only occasion a positive augmentation of the Produce and Revenue of the Society, but that they contribute essentially to rendering them greater than they could possibly be, without such establishments; These circumstances are—

1. The division of labour.
2. An extension of the use of Machinery.

3. Additional employment to classes of the community not ordinarily engaged in the business.

4. The promoting of emigration from foreign Countries.

5. The furnishing greater scope for the diversity of talents and dispositions which discriminate men from each other.

6. The affording a more ample and various field for enterprise.

7. The creating in some instances a new, and securing in all, a more certain and steady demand for the surplus produce of the soil.

Each of these circumstances has a considerable influence upon the total mass of industrious effort in a community: Together, they add to it a degree of energy and effect, which are not easily conceived. Some comments upon each of them, in the order in which they have been stated, may serve to explain their importance.

I. AS TO THE DIVISION OF LABOUR

It has justly been observed, that there is a scarcely any thing of greater moment in the economy of a nation than the proper division of labour. The separation of occupations causes each to be carried to a much greater perfection, than it could possibly acquire, if they were blended. This arises principally from three circumstances—

1st. The greater skill and dexterity naturally resulting from a constant and undivided application to a single object....

2nd. The economy of time, by avoiding the loss of it, incident to a frequent transition from one operation to another of a different nature....

3rd. An extension of the use of Machinery. A man occupied on a single object will have it more in his power, and will be more naturally led to exert his imagination in devising methods to facilitate and abridge labour, than if he were perplexed by a variety of independent and dissimilar operations....

II. AS TO AN EXTENSION OF THE USE OF MACHINERY, A POINT WHICH, THOUGH PARTLY ANTICIPATED REQUIRES TO BE PLACED IN ONE OR TWO ADDITIONAL LIGHTS

The employment of Machinery forms an item of great importance in the general mass of national industry. 'Tis an artificial force brought in aid of the natural force of man; and, to all the purposes of labour, is an increase of hands; an accession of strength, unencumbered too by the expence of maintaining the laborer. May it not therefore be fairly inferred, that those occupations, which give greatest scope to the use of this auxiliary, contribute most to the general Stock of industrious effort, and, in consequence, to the general product of industry? . . .

III. AS TO THE ADDITIONAL EMPLOYMENT OF CLASSES OF THE COMMUNITY NOT ORIGINALLY ENGAGED IN THE PARTICULAR BUSINESS

This is not among the least valuable of the means, by which manufacturing institutions contribute to augment the general stock of industry and production. In places where those institutions prevail, besides the persons regularly engaged in them, they afford occasional and extra employment to industrious individuals and families, who are willing to devote the leisure resulting from the intermissions of their ordinary pursuits to collateral labours, as a resource for multiplying their acquisitions or their enjoyments. The husbandman himself experiences a new source of profit and support; from the increased industry of his wife and daughters; invited and stimulated by the demands of the neighboring manufactories.

Besides this advantage of occasional employment to classes having different occupations, there is another, of a nature allied to it, and of a similar tendency. This is—the employment of persons who would otherwise be idle (and in many cases a burthen on the community) either from the bias of temper, habit, infirmity of body, or some other cause, indisposing or disqualifying them for the toils of the Country. It is worthy of particular remark, that, in general, women and Children are rendered more useful, and the latter more early useful by manufacturing establishments, than they would otherwise be. Of the number of persons employed in the Cotton Manufactories of Great Britain, it is computed that four sevenths nearly are women and children; of whom the greatest proportion are children, and many of them of a very tender age. . . .

IV. AS TO THE PROMOTING OF EMIGRATION FROM FOREIGN COUNTRIES

Men reluctantly quit one course of occupation and livelihood for another, unless invited to it by very apparent and proximate advantages. Many who would go from one country to another, if they had a prospect of continuing with more benefit the callings, to which they have been educated, will often not be tempted to change their situation, by the hope of doing better, in some other way. Manufacturers, who, listening to the powerful invitations of a better price for their fabrics, or their labour, of greater cheapness of provisions and raw materials, of an exemption from the chief part of the taxes, burthens and restraints, which they endure in the old world, of greater personal independence and consequence, under the operation of a more equal government, and of what is far more precious than mere religious toleration—a perfect equality of religious privileges; would probably flock from Europe to the United States to pursue their own trades or professions, if they were once made sensible of the advantages they would enjoy, and were inspired with an assurance of encouragement and employment, will, with difficulty, be induced to transplant themselves, with a view to becoming Cultivators of Land. . . .

V. AS TO THE FURNISHING GREATER SCOPE FOR THE DIVERSITY OF TALENTS AND DISPOSITIONS, WHICH DISCRIMINATE MEN FROM EACH OTHER . . .

If there be any thing in a remark often to be met with—namely that there is, in the genius of the people of this country, a peculiar aptitude for mechanic improvements, it would operate as a forcible reason for giving opportunities to the exercise of that species of talent, by the propagation of manufactures. . . .

VII. AS TO THE CREATING, IN SOME INSTANCES, A NEW, AND SECURING IN ALL A MORE CERTAIN AND STEADY DEMAND FOR SURPLUS PRODUCE OF THE SOIL

This is among the most important of the circumstances which have been indicated. It is a principal means, by which the establishment of manufactures contributes to an augmentation of the produce or revenue of a country, and has an immediate and direct relation to the prosperity of Agriculture.

It is evident, that the exertions of the husbandman will be steady or fluctuating, vigorous or feeble, in proportion to the steadiness or fluctuation, adequateness or inadequateness, of the markets on which he must depend, for the vent of the surplus, which may be produced by his labor; and that such surplus in the ordinary course of things will be greater or less in the same proportion.

For the purpose of this vent, a domestic market is greatly to be preferred to a foreign one; because it is in the nature of things, far more to be relied upon. It is a primary object of the policy of nations, to be able to supply themselves with subsistence from their own soils; and manufacturing nations, as far as circumstances permit, endeavor to procure from the same source, the raw materials necessary for their own fabrics. This disposition, urged by the spirit of monopoly, is sometimes even carried to an injudicious extreme. It seems not always to be recollected, that nations who have neither mines nor manufactures, can only obtain the manufactured articles, of which they stand in need, by an exchange of the products of their soils; and that, if those who can best furnish them with such articles are unwilling to give a due course to this exchange, they must of necessity, make every possible effort to manufacture for themselves; the effect of which is that the manufacturing nations abridge the natural advantages of their situation, through an unwillingness to permit the Agricultural countries to enjoy the advantages of theirs, and sacrifice the interests of a mutually beneficial intercourse to the vain project of *selling every thing and buying nothing.*

But it is also a consequence of the policy, which has been noted, that the foreign demand for the products of Agricultural countries is, in a great degree, rather casual and occasional, than certain or constant. To what extent injurious interruptions of the demand for some of the staple commodities of the United States, may have been experienced from that cause, must be referred to the judgment of those who are engaged in carrying on the commerce of the country; but it may be safely affirmed, that such interruptions are at times very inconveniently felt, and that cases not unfrequently occur, In which markets are so confined and restricted as to render the demand very unequal to the supply.

Independently likewise of the artificial impediments, which are created by the policy in question, there are natural causes tending to render the external demand for the surplus of Agricultural nations a precarious reliance. The differences of seasons, in the countries, which are the consumers, make immense differences in the produce of their own soils, in different years; and consequently in the degrees of their necessity for foreign supply. Plentiful harvests with them, especially if similar ones occur at the same time in the countries, which are the furnishers, occasion of course a glut in the markets of the latter.

Considering how fast and how much the progress of new settlements in the United States must increase the surplus produce of the soil, and weighing seriously the tendency of the system, which prevails among most of the commercial nations of Europe, whatever dependence may be placed on the force of natural circumstances to counteract the effects of an artificial policy, there appear strong reasons to regard the foreign demand for that surplus as too uncertain a reliance, and to desire a substitute for it, in an extensive domestic market.

To secure such a market, there is no other expedient, than to promote manufacturing establishments. Manufacturers who constitute the most numerous class, after the Cultivators of land, are for that reason the principal consumers of the surplus of their labour.

This idea of an extensive domestic market for the surplus produce of the soil is of the first consequence. It is, of all things, that which most effectually conduces to a flourishing state of Agriculture. If the effect of manufactories should be to detach a portion of the hands, which would otherwise be engaged in Tillage, it might possibly cause a smaller quantity of lands to be under cultivation; but, by their tendency to procure a more certain demand for the surplus produce of the soil, they would, at the same time, cause the lands which were in cultivation to be better improved and more productive. And while, by their influence, the condition of each individual farmer would be meliorated, the total mass of Agricultural production would probably be increased. For this must evidently depend as much, if not more, upon the degree of improvement than upon the number of acres under culture.

It merits particular observation, that the multiplication of manufactories not only furnishes a Market for those articles which have been accustomed to be produced in abundance in a country, but it likewise creates a demand for such as were either unknown or produced in Inconsiderable quantities. The bowels as well as the surface of the earth are ransacked for articles which were before neglected. Animals, Plants and Minerals acquire a utility and a value which were before unexplored.

The foregoing considerations seem sufficient to establish, as general propositions, that it is the interest of nations to diversify the industrious pursuits of the individuals who compose them—that the establishment of manufactures is calculated not only to Increase the general stock of useful and productive labour; but even to improve the state of Agriculture in particular, certainly to advance the interests of those who are engaged in it.

4.11

George Washington's "Farewell Address" (1796)

One of the most beloved Americans, George Washington was commander-in-chief of the Continental Army and later served as the nation's first president (1789–97). Although the Constitution did not create political parties, bitter factions emerged during Washington's presidency. Clashes over the size of the federal government, the national debt, and the capacity of the general populace for political thought soon hardened into partisan distinctions. The Federalists advocated a strong national government ruled by elites independent of direct popular influence. Fearful of tyranny and corruption, the Republicans wanted a government responsive to an informed citizenry. Washington tried to remain nonpartisan.

SOURCE: George Washington, "Farewell Address," *Compilation of the Messages and Papers of the Presidents*, ed. James D. Richardson (Washington, D.C., 1903), 1:213–214.

A volatile international environment complicated matters. When the French Revolution began in 1789, Americans initially cheered the collapse of another monarchy. But, when the French republic descended into the Reign of Terror, the U.S. response was decidedly mixed. While Republicans defended the French (America's ally in the Revolution), Federalists were horrified by news of riots and public executions. When war erupted between France and Britain in 1793, the Federalists supported the British. After Washington declared American neutrality, Republicans accused him of betraying France.

The warring European nations did not respect U.S. neutrality. They restricted American trade, encouraged hostile Indians along the frontier, and expanded their North American empires. Highly reliant on economic exports and vulnerable to military attack, Washington could not ignore these threats. Siding with the Federalists, he advocated a pro-British diplomacy and strong federal government. Such policies enraged his Republican critics.

Exhausted by the political infighting, President Washington decided to retire after two terms. In 1796, he issued a farewell address on the problems facing the nation.

FOCUS QUESTIONS

1. What effect did Washington believe foreign affairs could have on domestic politics?

2. What type of foreign policy does Washington advocate for the United States? Were his suggestions practical? Explain your answer.

3. How has U.S. foreign policy departed from the principles Washington proposed?

Against the insidious wiles of foreign influence (I conjure you to believe me, fellow-citizens,) the jealousy of a free people ought to be constantly awake; since history and experience prove, that foreign influence is one of the baneful foes of Republican Government. But that jealousy, to be useful, must be impartial; else it becomes the instrument of the very influence to be avoided, instead of a defense against it. Excessive partiality for one nation, and excessive dislike for another, cause those whom they actuate to see danger only on one side, and serve to veil and even second the arts of influence on the other. Real patriots, who may resist the intrigues of the favorite, are liable to become suspended and odious; while its tools and dupes usurp the applause and confidence of the people, to surrender their interests.

The great rule of conduct for us, in regard to foreign nations is, extending our commercial relations, to have with them as little political connection as possible. So far as we have already formed engagements, let them be fulfilled with perfect good faith. Here let us stop.

Europe has her own set of primary interests, which to us have none, or a very remote relation. Hence she must be engaged in frequent controversies, the causes of which are essentially foreign to our concerns. Hence, therefore, it must be unwise in us to implicate ourselves, by artificial ties, in the ordinary vicissitudes of her politics, or the ordinary combinations and collisions of her friendships or enmities.

Our detached and distant situation invites and enables us to pursue a different course. If we remain one free people, under an efficient government, the period is not far off, when we may defy material injury from external annoyance; when we may take such an attitude as will cause the neutrality, we may at any time resolve upon, to be scrupulously respected; when belligerent nations, under the impossibility of making acquisitions upon us, will not lightly hazard the giving us provocation; when we may choose peace or war, as our interest, guided by justice, shall counsel.

Why forego the advantages of so peculiar a situation? Why quit our own to stand upon foreign ground? Why, by interweaving our destiny with that of any part of Europe, entangle our peace and prosperity in the toils of European ambition, rivalship, interest, humor, or caprice?

It is our true policy to steer clear of permanent alliances with any portion of the foreign world; so far, I mean, as we are now at liberty to do it; for let me not be understood as capable of patronizing infidelity to existing engagements. I hold the maxim no less applicable to public than to private affairs, that honesty is always the best policy. I repeat it, therefore, let those engagements be observed in their genuine senses. But, in my opinion, it is unnecessary and would be unwise to extend them.

Taking care always to keep ourselves, by suitable establishments, on a respectable defensive posture, we may safely trust to temporary alliances in extraordinary emergencies.

Harmony, liberal intercourse with all nations, are recommended by policy, humanity, and interest. But even our commercial policy should hold an equal and impartial hand; neither seeking nor granting exclusive favors or preferences; consulting the natural course of things; diffusing and diversifying by gentle means the streams of commerce, but forcing nothing; establishing, with powers so disposed, in order to give trade a stable course, to define the rights of our merchants, and to enable the government to support them, conventional rules of intercourse, the best the present circumstances and mutual opinion will permit, but temporary, and liable to be from time to time abandoned or varied, as experience and circumstances shall dictate; constantly keeping in view, that it is folly in one nation to look for disinterested favors from another; that it must pay with a portion of its independence for whatever it may accept under that character; that, by such acceptance, it may place itself in the condition of having given equivalents for nominal favors, and yet of being reproached with ingratitude for not giving more. There can be no greater error than to expect or calculate upon real favors from nation to nation. It is an illusion, which experience must cure, which a just pride ought to discard....

4.12

A Republican Broadside (1796)

When the framers wrote the Constitution, they made no provisions for political parties. They believed that parties would place unscrupulous men into public office and corrupt republican virtues. Within a short time, however, a host of issues prompted Americans to reconsider these views. Opposing philosophies on economic issues, the role of government, the political participation of ordinary citizens, and foreign affairs split Americans into rival factions, Federalists and Republicans.

Federalists favored a strong government run by the wealthy and influential. Suspicious of "mob rule," they believed that public officials should rule on behalf of the masses, not be directly swayed by them. They supported a "loose interpretation" of the Constitution in which the only unconstitutional actions were those expressly forbidden in the document. Many Federalists benefited greatly from Alexander Hamilton's program for economic development and advocated close diplomatic relations with Great Britain. In general, the moneyed classes of the North were the staunchest Federalists.

The Republicans espoused different views. They called for informed citizens to participate widely in political affairs in order to guard against despotism. They adhered to a "strict interpretation" of the Constitution in which governmental powers could not exceed those expressly stated in the document. Republicans feared that Hamilton's economic plans would leave the government beholden to special interests and favored a continuing alliance with France. Southerners, artisans, and farmers were some of the Republicans' strongest supporters.

In 1793, new Democratic (or Republican) societies organized to mobilize opposition to the Federalists. Their efforts escalated after President George Washington associated himself with the Federalists. In response to the widening political divisions in the Washington administration, Thomas Jefferson resigned as Secretary of State. In 1794, Jefferson's supporters began calling themselves Republicans and won a narrow majority in the House of Representatives.

When Washington announced his retirement in 1796, the Republicans and Federalists rushed to solidify their constituencies and win new voters. Highly partisan newspapers helped to shape popular opinions. Stressing their anti-British views, Republicans made special appeals to thousands of recent French and Irish immigrants. Ultimately, however, the Federalist presidential candidate, John Adams, triumphed over Thomas Jefferson. Due to a quirk in the Constitution

SOURCE: Printed at http://www.perno.com/history/docs/broad.htm.

(soon fixed by the Twelfth Amendment), Jefferson became vice president as the candidate receiving the second highest number of votes for president.

This reading features a Republican broadside disseminated in Pennsylvania during the 1796 presidential campaign.

FOCUS QUESTIONS

1. What are some of the Republican's key political positions?
2. Why do the Republicans believe that Thomas Jefferson will be a better president than John Adams?
3. Are similar themes present in modern political campaigns? If so, give examples.

FELLOW CITIZENS!

The first concern of Freemen, calls you forth into action. Pennsylvania was never yet found wanting when Liberty was at stake; she cannot then be indifferent when the question is, Who shall be President of the United States? The citizen who now holds the office of President, has publicly made known to his fellow citizens that he declines to serve in it again. Two candidates are offered to your choice, as his successor; THOMAS JEFFERSON of Virginia, and JOHN ADAMS of New England. No other candidate is proposed, you cannot therefore mistake between them. THOMAS JEFFERSON is the man who was your late Secretary of State, and Minister of the United States to the French nation; JOHN ADAMS is the man who is now Vice President of the United States, and was late the Minister to the king of Great Britain. THOMAS JEFFERSON is a firm REPUBLICAN, JOHN ADAMS is an avowed MONARCHIST. . . .

Thomas Jefferson first drew the declaration of American independence; he first framed the sacred political sentence that all men are born equal. John Adams says this is all a farce and a falsehood; that some men should be born Kings, and some should be born Nobles. Which of these, freemen of Pennsylvania, will you have for your President? Will you, by your votes, contribute to make the avowed friend of monarchy, President? Or will you, by neglectfully staying at home, permit others to saddle you with Political Slavery? Adams has Sons who might aim to succeed their father; Jefferson like Washington, has no Son. Adams is a fond admirer of the British Constitution, and says it is the first wonder of the world. Jefferson likes better our Federal Constitution, and thinks the British full of deformity, corruption and wickedness. Once more, fellow citizens! Choose ye between those two, which you will have for President, Jefferson or Adams. Remember Friday the fourth of November; attend your elections on that day; put in your tickets for fifteen good REPUBLICANS, and let the watch word be LIBERTY and INDEPENDENCE!

4.13

James Madison, the Virginia Resolutions (1798)

During the presidency of John Adams (1797–1801), clashes between the Federalists and Republicans intensified. While the Federalists dominated Congress, the Republicans mobilized ordinary Americans, particularly French and Irish immigrants incensed by the pro-British attitudes of the Federalists. When the Quasi-War against France erupted in 1798, the Federalists rushed to guard national security. Determined to suppress Republican political dissent, Congress passed the Alien and Sedition Acts. The Acts aimed to prevent espionage, toughen naturalization requirements, and control political speech. Any foreigner who violated the laws could be deported, and U.S. citizens who criticized the government could be imprisoned.

Enraged by the Federalists' attack on civil liberties, Vice President Thomas Jefferson and James Madison secretly authored two treatises on states' rights, which the Kentucky and Virginia legislatures endorsed in 1798. Although Jefferson and Madison directed their protests at the Alien and Sedition Acts, their arguments greatly influenced secessionists in the nineteenth century.

FOCUS QUESTIONS

1. What are the major themes of the Virginia Resolutions?
2. Why is Madison so critical of the Alien and Sedition Acts? How does he propose that states respond to the laws?
3. Do you agree with Madison's views? Explain your answer.

RESOLUTIONS OF VIRGINIA OF DECEMBER 21, 1798

1. Resolved, That the General Assembly of Virginia doth unequivocally express a firm resolution to maintain and defend the Constitution of the United States, and the Constitution of this State, against every aggression either

SOURCE: "Resolutions of Virginia," *The Virginia Report of 1799–1800* (Richmond, 1850), 22–23.

foreign or domestic; and that they will support the Government of the United States in all measures warranted by the former.

2. That this Assembly most solemnly declares a warm attachment to the Union of the States, to maintain which it pledges all its powers; and that, for this end, it is their duty to watch over and oppose every infraction of those principles which constitute the only basis of that Union, because a faithful observance of them can alone secure its existence and the public happiness.

3. That this Assembly doth explicitly and peremptorily declare that it views the powers of the Federal Government as resulting from the compact to which the States are parties, as limited by the plain sense and intention of the instrument constituting that compact; as no further valid than they are authorized by the grants enumerated in that compact; and that, in case of a deliberate, palpable, and dangerous exercise of other powers not granted by the said compact, the States, who are parties thereto, have the right and are in duty bound to interpose for arresting the progress of the evil, and for maintaining within their respective limits the authorities, rights, and liberties appertaining to them.

4. That the General Assembly doth also express its deep regret, that a spirit has in sundry instances been manifested by the Federal Government to enlarge its powers by forced constructions of the constitutional charter which defines them; and that indications have appeared of a design to expound certain general phrases (which, having been copied from the very limited grant of powers in the former Articles of Confederation, were the less liable to be misconstrued) so as to destroy the meaning and effect of the particular enumeration which necessarily explains and limits the general phrases; and so as to consolidate the States by degrees, into one sovereignty, the obvious tendency and inevitable result of which would be to transform the present republican system of the United States into an absolute, or, at best, a mixed monarchy.

5. That the General Assembly doth particularly protest against the palpable and alarming infractions of the Constitution in the two late cases of the "Alien and Sedition Acts," passed at the last session of Congress; the first of which exercises a power nowhere delegated to the Federal Government and which, by uniting legislative and judicial powers to those of [the] executive, subverts the general principles of free government, as well as the particular organization and positive provision of the federal Constitution; and the other of which acts exercises, in like manner, a power not delegated by the Constitution, but, on the contrary, expressly and positively forbidden by one of the amendments thereto,—a power which more than any other, ought to produce universal alarm, because it is leveled against the right of freely examining public characters and measures, and of free communication among the people thereon, which has ever been justly deemed the only effectual guardian of every other right.

6. That this state having by its convention which ratified the federal Constitution expressly declared, "that among other essential rights, the liberty of conscience and of the press cannot be canceled, abridged, restrained, or

modified by any authority of the United States," and from its extreme anxiety to guard these rights from every possible attack of sophistry or ambition, having with other States, recommended an amendment for that purpose, which amendment was in due time annexed to the Constitution,— it would mark a reproachful inconsistency and criminal degeneracy, if an indifference were now shown to the palpable violation of one of the rights thus declared and secured, and to the establishment of a precedent which may be fatal to the other.

7.   That the good people of this commonwealth, having ever felt and continuing to feel the most sincere affection to their brethren of the other States, the truest anxiety for establishing and perpetuating the union of all and the most scrupulous fidelity to that Constitution, which is the pledge of mutual friendship, and the instrument of mutual happiness, the General Assembly doth solemnly appeal to the like dispositions of the other States, in confidence that they will concur with this commonwealth in declaring, as it does hereby declare, that the acts aforesaid are unconstitutional, and that the necessary and proper measure[s] will be taken by each for cooperating with this State, in maintaining unimpaired the authorities, rights, and liberties reserved to the States respectively, or to the people.

8.   That the Governor be desired to transmit a copy of the foregoing resolutions to the Executive authority of each of the other States, with a request that the same may be communicated to the legislature thereof. And that a copy be furnished to each of the Senators and Representatives representing this State in the Congress of the United States.

5

❊

A New Nation

After Thomas Jefferson prevailed in the election of 1800, the nation underwent its first transition of power from one political party to another. The change raised important philosophical and procedural questions about governance. Appealing to members of both parties, Jefferson worked to end the rancorous partisanship of the 1790s. At the same time, he pursued an ambitious political agenda. In order to pay the national debt, he repealed many taxes and drastically cut military expenditures. He resolved a long-standing dispute with pirates off the coast of North Africa. He seized the opportunity to purchase the Louisiana Territory and virtually doubled the geographic area of the United States. These triumphs helped Jefferson easily win reelection in 1804.

But his second term was difficult. Members of his party, the Republicans, fought amongst themselves. Britain and France interfered with U.S. trade and shipping. An embargo designed to resolve these tensions peacefully proved economically disastrous for American merchants and sailors.

James Madison, Jefferson's successor, inherited this delicate situation. After Congress ended the embargo in 1809, a series of weaker measures also failed to persuade the British to respect American neutrality. In 1812, continuing economic problems and intense pressure from fellow Republicans prompted Madison to ask for a declaration of war against Great Britain. Although the nation's military was woefully unprepared, Congress complied with the president's request.

The War of 1812 failed to draw broad popular support. For months, the United States waged poorly conceived and unsuccessful attacks on Canada, the British stronghold in North America. In 1814, after victory over Napoleon allowed them to focus exclusively on the conflict with America, the British went on the offensive and won several battles. But, rather than prolong a minor war, they agreed to begin peace negotiations. The United States neither gained nor lost territory in the subsequent Treaty of Ghent (1814). Nonetheless, the war had significant effects, including the demise of the Federalist Party, a renewed patriotism, and a weakening of many Indian tribes who had resisted white expansion. Now the only significant political party, the Republicans embraced many Federalist ideas.

Throughout the "Era of Good Feelings," the nation scored many achievements. Thousands of traders, explorers, and settlers found opportunities in the West. Eli Whitney's cotton gin and the rise of the British textile industry triggered explosive growth in cotton production. Canals, steamboats, and roads revolutionized transportation and commerce. In international relations, America won territorial concessions and settled diplomatic disputes.

Economic and political crises accompanied these successes. In 1819, the issue of slavery resurfaced when the Missouri territory applied for statehood. Although Congress resolved the crisis, it portended decades of political fighting about servitude and westward expansion. At the same time, risky banking practices and land speculation contributed to a devastating economic depression. Although the Panic of 1819 ended relatively quickly, it fueled demands for political and economic reforms. Within a short time, the birth of a second party system would greatly alter the nation's political landscape.

THEMES TO CONSIDER

- Slaves' resistance
- Partisanship and the transfer of political power from the Federalists to the Republicans
- Territorial expansion and western exploration
- Strict vs. loose interpretations of the Constitution
- The separation of powers and the system of checks and balances
- The role of the judiciary
- The importance of education in shaping American national identity
- Popular depictions of American Indians
- Indians' efforts to resist white encroachment
- The intensification of regional differences
- Efforts to define and defend America's position in international relations
- The complexity and volatility of the early American economy
- Disputes over the fate of slavery in the western territories

5.1

Solomon on Gabriel's Rebellion (1800)

During its early years, the Republic tried to reconcile itself to the contradictions posed by slavery. In the 1790s, most states outlawed the Atlantic slave trade. At the same time, however, most free blacks (eleven percent of the African-American population in 1800) were barred from voting and serving in the military. White reluctance to accept people of color as fellow citizens was also evident in federal legislation. In the Naturalization Act of 1790, Congress declared that only foreign whites could apply for U.S. citizenship. Three years later, the Fugitive Slave law denied accused runaway slaves the right to trial by jury. Slavery received an additional boost when Eli Whitney invented the cotton gin—a mechanism that cleaned short-staple cotton. Once highly labor-intensive, cotton could now be quickly processed for sale to the British textile industry. In a short time, cotton plantations were flourishing throughout the South.

In August 1800, news of a massive slave conspiracy sent shockwaves through the country. Inspired by the 1791 slave revolt in Saint Domingue (Haiti) and republican ideals, Gabriel Prosser (1776–1800) planned an uprising in Richmond, Virginia. Well-educated and a skilled blacksmith, Gabriel was often hired out by his masters, Thomas Prosser and Thomas Henry Prosser. This practice allowed slaves to earn a little money and accorded them some freedom. During these jobs, Gabriel worked and interacted with other hired slaves, free blacks, and white laborers.

In September 1799, Gabriel, his brother Solomon, and another slave named Jupiter were caught stealing a pig. When apprehended by a white overseer, Gabriel wrestled him to the ground and bit off most of his ear. Gabriel was arrested and found guilty of maiming a white man, an offensive punishable by death. However, a legal loophole gave Gabriel a way to save himself. By proving that he could recite a Bible verse, Gabriel was spared death and publicly branded instead. Radicalized by this incident and the egalitarian rhetoric of his fellow workers, Gabriel began formulating a plan to destroy slavery in Virginia.

On August 30, 1800, Gabriel and his men planned to seize Richmond, take Governor James Monroe as a hostage, and proceed to other areas of the state. He had recruited an army of several slaves, free blacks, and a few whites drawn from Richmond and other Virginia communities. They also collected weapons and

SOURCE: H. W. Flournoy, ed., Calendar of Virginia State Papers and Other Manuscripts from January 1, 1799, to December 31, 1807; preserved in the Capitol at Richmond, 11 volumes (Richmond, 1890).

forged swords and bullets. On the night of the scheduled attack, it rained heavily. Postponing the plot to the following night proved a fatal mistake. Unable to take the pressure, two slaves told their masters about Gabriel's conspiracy. Although he eluded capture for three weeks, Gabriel was arrested and imprisoned. He and twenty-five others were executed. Sixty-five additional conspirators were put on trial. In the wake of the rebellion, abolitionist sentiment declined, and Virginia restricted slaves' movement and communication.

In this passage, Solomon confesses to his role in Gabriel's plot. Two court magistrates recorded his testimony. He was found guilty of conspiracy and hanged.

FOCUS QUESTIONS

1. What were the major components of Gabriel's plan? Why did he believe that his plan would work?

2. Why do you think that Gabriel's conspiracy so alarmed whites? Why do you think that whites continued to support slavery despite their commitment to republican ideals?

3. Compared to slave revolts in South America, U.S. slave uprisings were infrequent and much less violent; what might account for these facts?

Communications made to the subscribers by Solomon, the property of Thomas H. Prosser, of Henrico, now under sentence of death for plotting an insurrection.

My brother Gabriel was the person who influenced me to join him and others in order that (as he said) we might conquer the white people and possess ourselves of their property. I enquired how we were to effect it. He said by falling upon them (the whites) in the dead of night, at which time they would be unguarded and unsuspicious. I then enquired who was at the head of the plan. He said Jack, alias Jack Bowler. I asked him if Jack Bowler knew anything about carrying on war. He replied he did not. I then enquired who he was going to employ. He said a man from Caroline who was at the siege of Yorktown, and who was to meet him (Gabriel) at the Brook and to proceed on to Richmond, take, and then fortify it. This man from Caroline was to be commander and manager the first day, and then, after exercising the soldiers, the command was to be resigned to Gabriel. If Richmond was taken without the loss of many men they were to continue there some time, but if they sustained any considerable loss they were to bend their course for Hanover Town or York, they were not decided to which, and continue at that place as long as they found they were able to defend it, but in the event of a defeat or loss at those places they were to endeavor to form a junction with some negroes which, they had understood from Mr. Gregory's overseer, were in rebellion in some quarter of the country. This information which they had gotten from the overseer, made Gabriel anxious, upon which he applied to me to make scythe-swords, which I did to the number of twelve. Every Sunday he came to Richmond to provide ammunition and to find where the military stores were deposited. Gabriel informed me, in case of success that they intended to subdue the whole of the country where slavery was permitted, but no further.

The first places Gabriel intended to attack in Richmond were, the Capitol, the Magazine, the Penitentiary, the Governor's house and his person. The inhabitants were to be massacred, save those who begged for quarter and agreed to serve as soldiers with them. The reason why the insurrection was to be made at this particular time was, the discharge of the number of soldiers, one or two months ago, which induced Gabriel to believe the plan would be more easily executed.

Given under our hands this 5th day of September, 1800.
Gervas Storrs, Joseph Selden.

5.2

Thomas Jefferson, First Inaugural Address (1801)

Given Thomas Jefferson's pronounced hostility to the federal government during the 1790s, Americans did not know what to expect of his presidency. They wondered whether he would dismantle the government institutions created by the Federalists. The fact that the election of 1800 had been very complicated created additional apprehension. When Jefferson and Aaron Burr, both Republicans, each received seventy-three votes, the House of Representatives met in a special session to resolve the impasse. After thirty hours of debate and thirty-five different ballots, Jefferson emerged as president with Burr as his vice president.

Eager to calm the nation, Jefferson used his inauguration as an opportunity to reassure his countrymen and explain his philosophy of government.

SOURCE: Published at the Avalon Project at Yale Law School,
http://www.yale.edu/lawweb/avalon/presiden/inaug/jefinau1.htm.

FOCUS QUESTIONS

1.   What are the major themes of Jefferson's address?
2.   How does he attempt to foster bipartisanship?
3.   What are Jefferson's goals as president?

March 4, 1801

Friends and Fellow-Citizens:

Called upon to undertake the duties of the first executive office of our country, I avail myself of the presence of that portion of my fellow-citizens which is here assembled to express my grateful thanks for the favor with which they have been pleased to look toward me, to declare a sincere consciousness that the task is above my talents, and that I approach it with those anxious and awful presentiments which the greatness of the charge and the weakness of my powers so justly inspire. A rising nation, spread over a wide and fruitful land, traversing all the seas with the rich productions of their industry, engaged in commerce with nations who feel power and forget right, advancing rapidly to destinies beyond the reach of mortal eye—when I contemplate these transcendent objects, and see the honor, the happiness, and the hopes of this beloved country committed to the issue and the auspices of this day, I shrink from the contemplation, and humble myself before the magnitude of the undertaking. Utterly, indeed, should I despair did not the presence of many whom I here see remind me that in the other high authorities provided by our Constitution I shall find resources of wisdom, of virtue, and of zeal on which to rely under all difficulties. To you, then, gentlemen, who are charged with the sovereign functions of legislation, and to those associated with you, I look with encouragement for that guidance and support which may enable us to steer with safety the vessel in which we are all embarked amidst the conflicting elements of a troubled world.

During the contest of opinion through which we have passed the animation of discussions and of exertions has sometimes worn an aspect which might impose on strangers unused to think freely and to speak and to write what they think; but this being now decided by the voice of the nation, announced according to the rules of the Constitution, all will, of course, arrange themselves under the will of the law, and unite in common efforts for the common good. All, too, will bear in mind this sacred principle, that though the will of the majority is in all cases to prevail, that will to be rightful must be reasonable; that the minority possess their equal rights, which equal law must protect, and to violate would be oppression. Let us, then, fellow-citizens, unite with one heart and one mind. Let us restore to social intercourse that harmony and affection without which liberty and even life itself are but dreary things. And let us reflect that, having banished from our land that religious intolerance under which mankind so long bled and suffered, we have yet gained little if we countenance a political intolerance as despotic, as wicked, and capable of as bitter and bloody persecutions. During the throes and convulsions of the ancient world, during the agonizing spasms of infuriated man, seeking through blood and slaughter his long-lost liberty, it was not wonderful that the agitation of the billows should reach even this distant and peaceful shore; that this should be more felt and feared by some and less by others, and should divide opinions as to measures of safety. But every difference of opinion is not a difference of principle. We have called by different names brethren of the same principle. We are all Republicans, we are all Federalists. If there be any among us who would wish to dissolve this Union or to change its republican form, let them stand undisturbed as monuments of the safety with which error of opinion may be tolerated where reason is left free to combat it. I know, indeed, that some honest men fear that a republican government can not be strong, that this Government is not strong enough; but would the honest patriot, in the full tide of successful experiment, abandon a government which has so far kept us free and firm on the theoretic and visionary fear that this Government, the world's best hope, may by possibility want energy to preserve itself? I trust not. I believe this, on the contrary, the strongest Government on earth. I believe it the only one where every man, at the call of the law, would fly to the standard of the law, and would meet invasions of the public order as his own personal concern. Sometimes it is said that man can not be trusted with the government of himself. Can he, then, be trusted with the government of others? Or have we found angels in the forms of kings to govern him? Let history answer this question.

Let us, then, with courage and confidence pursue our own Federal and Republican principles, our attachment to union and representative government. Kindly separated by nature and a wide ocean from the exterminating havoc of one quarter of the globe; too high-minded to endure the degradations of the others; possessing a chosen country, with room enough for our descendants to the thousandth and thousandth generation; entertaining a due sense of our equal right to the use of our own faculties, to the acquisitions of our own industry, to honor and confidence from our fellow-citizens, resulting not from birth, but from our actions and their sense of them; enlightened by a benign religion, professed, indeed, and practiced in various forms, yet all of them inculcating honesty, truth, temperance, gratitude, and the love of man; acknowledging and adoring an overruling Providence, which by all its dispensations proves that it delights in the happiness of man here and his greater happiness hereafter—with all these blessings, what more is necessary to make us a happy and a prosperous people? Still one thing more, fellow-citizens—a wise and frugal Government, which shall restrain men from injuring one another, shall leave them otherwise free to regulate their own pursuits of industry and improvement, and shall not take from the mouth of labor the bread it has earned. This is the sum of good government, and this is necessary to close the circle of our felicities.

About to enter, fellow-citizens, on the exercise of duties which comprehend everything dear and valuable to you, it is proper you should understand what I deem the essential principles of our Government, and consequently those which ought to shape its Administration. I will compress them within the narrowest compass they will bear, stating the general principle, but not all its limitations. Equal and exact justice to all men, of whatever state or persuasion, religious or political; peace, commerce, and honest friendship with all nations, entangling alliances with none; the support of the State governments in all their rights, as the most competent administrations for our domestic concerns and the surest bulwarks against antirepublican tendencies; the preservation of the General Government in its whole constitutional vigor, as the sheet anchor of our peace at home and safety abroad; a jealous care of the right of election by the people—a mild and safe corrective of abuses which are lopped by the sword of revolution where peaceable remedies are unprovided; absolute acquiescence in the decisions of the majority, the vital principle of republics, from which is no appeal but to force, the vital principle and immediate parent of despotism; a well-disciplined militia, our best reliance in peace and for the first moments of war till regulars may relieve them; the supremacy of the civil over the military authority; economy in the public expense, that labor may be lightly burthened; the honest payment of our debts and sacred preservation of the public faith; encouragement of agriculture, and of commerce as its handmaid; the diffusion of information and arraignment of all abuses at the bar of the public reason; freedom of religion; freedom of the press, and freedom of person under the protection of the habeas corpus, and trial by juries impartially selected. These principles form the bright constellation which has gone before us and guided our steps through an age of revolution and reformation. The wisdom of our sages and blood of our heroes have been devoted to their attainment. They should be the creed of our political faith, the text of civic instruction, the touchstone by which to try the services of those we trust; and should we wander from them in moments of error or of alarm, let us hasten to retrace our steps and to regain the road which alone leads to peace, liberty, and safety.

I repair, then, fellow-citizens, to the post you have assigned me. With experience enough in subordinate offices to have seen the difficulties of this the greatest of all, I have learnt to expect that it will rarely fall to the lot of imperfect man to retire from this station with the reputation and the favor which bring him into it. Without pretensions to that high confidence you reposed in our first and greatest revolutionary character, whose preeminent services had entitled him to the first place in his country's love and destined for him the fairest page in the volume of faithful history, I ask so much confidence only as may give firmness and effect to the legal administration of your affairs. I shall often go wrong through defect of judgment. When right, I shall often be thought wrong by those whose positions will not command a view of the whole ground. I ask your indulgence for my own errors, which will never be intentional, and your support against the errors of others, who may condemn what they would not if seen in all its parts. The approbation implied by your suffrage is a great consolation to me for the past, and my future solicitude will be to retain the good opinion of those who have bestowed it in advance, to conciliate that of others by doing them all the good in my power, and to be instrumental to the happiness and freedom of all.

Relying, then, on the patronage of your good will, I advance with obedience to the work, ready to retire from it whenever you become sensible how much better choice it is in your power to make. And may that Infinite Power which rules the destinies of the universe lead our councils to what is best, and give them a favorable issue for your peace and prosperity.

5.3

Thomas Jefferson Instructs Robert Livingston (1802)

The Louisiana Purchase, Jefferson's greatest achievement as president, challenged his political principles. Wary of foreign entanglements, Jefferson was alarmed when Spain signed the Treaty of San Ildefonso (1800), which returned the vast Louisiana Territory to France. While the Spanish empire was rapidly declining, the French dictator Napoleon Bonaparte posed a much bigger threat to the United States. Over the last decade, thousands of Americans had moved westward and become highly reliant on shipping their goods down the Mississippi River to the port of New Orleans. In 1802, when Spain revoked the right to store items bound for export in the city, Jefferson wrongly assumed that France was responsible. Determined to protect U.S. interests, Jefferson dispatched Robert Livingston and James Monroe to negotiate with the French for the purchase of New Orleans and as much of the Floridas as possible.

Jefferson's timing proved fortuitous. Having decided to abandon his efforts to re-create a French empire in the Caribbean, Napoleon wanted to resume war with the British on the European mainland. Desperate for funds, he offered to sell the entire Louisiana Territory. With Jefferson's blessing, the envoys agreed to pay the French government $15 million for the vast territory. At approximately three cents an acre, the deal was a fantastic bargain that nearly doubled the size of the United States. Nonetheless, the agreement gave Jefferson pause. A strict constructionist, he was uncertain that the Constitution gave him the authority to acquire territory. He seriously considered introducing an amendment granting the president such power but rejected the idea in order to avoid a long ratification debate with the Federalists. Recognizing the tremendous value of the Louisiana Purchase, the Senate quickly approved it by a 24-7 vote.

In this letter, Jefferson directs Livingston, then the U.S. minister to France, to approach the French about acquiring New Orleans.

SOURCE: "To the United States Minister to France," *The Works of Thomas Jefferson,* ed. Paul Leicester Ford (New York, 1905), 9:363–368.

FOCUS QUESTIONS

1. Why is Jefferson so concerned about the cession of Louisiana Territory by Spain to France? Why is New Orleans especially important?

2. How did the Louisiana Purchase challenge the principles of governing that Jefferson espoused in his 1801 inaugural address (Document 5.2)?

3. Was Jefferson right to exercise a loose interpretation of the Constitution in pursuing the Louisiana Purchase? Support your answer.

Washington, April 18, 1802

The cession of Louisiana and the Floridas by Spain to France works most sorely on the U.S. On this subject the Secretary of State has written to you fully. Yet I cannot forbear recurring to it personally, so deep is the impression it makes in my mind. It completely reverses all the political relations of the U.S. and will form a new epoch in our political course. Of all nations of any consideration France is the one which hitherto has offered the fewest points on which we could have any conflict of right, and the most points of a communion of interests. From these causes we have ever looked to her as our natural friend, as one with which we never could have an occasion of difference. Her growth therefore we viewed as our own, her misfortunes ours. There is on the globe one single spot, the possessor of which is our natural and habitual enemy. It is New Orleans, through which the produce of three-eighths of our territory must pass to market, and from its fertility it will ere long yield more than half of our whole produce and contain more than half our inhabitants. France placing herself in that door assumes to us the attitude of defiance. Spain might have retained it quietly for years. Her pacific dispositions, her feeble state, would induce her to increase our facilities there, so that her possession of the place would be hardly felt by us, and it would not perhaps be very long before some circumstance might arise which might make the cession of it to us the price of something of more worth to her. Not so can it ever be in the hands of France. The impetuosity of her temper, the energy and restlessness of her character, placed in a point of eternal friction with us, and our character, which though quiet, and loving peace and the pursuit of wealth, is high-minded, despising wealth in competition with insult or injury, enterprising and energetic as any nation on earth, these circumstances render it impossible that France and the U.S. can continue long friends when they meet in so irritable a position. They as well as we must be blind if they do not see this; and we must be very improvident if we do not begin to make arrangements on that hypothesis. The day that France takes possession of N. Orleans fixes the sentence which is to restrain her forever within her low water mark. It seals the union of two nations who in conjunction can maintain exclusive possession of the ocean. From that moment we must marry ourselves to the British fleet and nation. We must turn all our attentions to a maritime force, for which our resources place us on very high grounds: and having formed and cemented together a power which may render reinforcement of her settlements here impossible to France, make the first cannon, which shall be fired in Europe the signal for tearing up any settlement she may have made, and for holding the two continents of America in sequestration for the common purposes of the united British and American nations. This is not a state of things we seek or desire. It is one which this measure, if adopted by France, forces on us, as necessarily as any other cause, by the laws of nature, brings on its necessary effect. It is not from a fear of France that we deprecate this measure proposed by her. For however greater her force is than ours compared in the abstract, it is nothing in comparison of ours when to be exerted on our soil. But it is from a sincere love of peace, and a firm persuasion that bound to France by the interests and the strong sympathies still existing in the minds of our citizens, and holding relative positions which ensure their continuance we are secure of a long course of peace. Whereas the change of friends, which will be rendered necessary if France changes that position, embarks us necessarily as a belligerent power in the first war of Europe....

If France considers Louisiana however as indispensable for her views she might perhaps be willing to look about for arrangements which might reconcile it to our interests. If anything could do this it would be the ceding to us the island of New Orleans and the Floridas. This would certainly in a great degree remove the causes of jarring and irritation between us, and perhaps for such a length of time as might produce other means of making the measure permanently con-ciliatory to our interests and friendships. It would at any rate relieve us from the necessity of taking immediate measures for countervailing such an operation by arrangements in another quarter. Still we should consider N. Orleans and the Floridas as equivalent for the risk of a quarrel with France produced by her vicinage. I have no doubt you have urged these considerations on every proper occasion with the government where you are. They are such as must have effect if you can find the means of producing thorough reflection on them by that government. The idea here is that the troops sent to St. Domingo [modern Haiti and the Dominican Republic], were to proceed to Louisiana after finishing their work in that island. If this were the arrangement, it will give you time to return again and again to the charge, for the conquest of St. Domingo will not be a short work. It will take considerable time to wear down a great number of soldiers. Every eye in the U.S. is now fixed on this affair of Louisiana. Perhaps nothing since the revolutionary war has produced more uneasy sensations through the body of the nation. Notwithstanding temporary bickerings have taken place with France, she has still a strong hold on the affections of our citizens generally. I have thought it not amiss, by way of supplement to the letters of the Secretary of State to write you this private one to impress you with the importance we affix to this transaction.... Accept assurances of my affectionate esteem and high consideration.

5.4

John Marshall, *Marbury*
v. Madison (1803)

Throughout the 1790s, the judiciary was not immune from the partisanship engulfing the nation. While both Republicans and Federalists argued that talent, not party, should determine who received a judicial appointment, realities differed from rhetoric. By 1800, the Federalists had not appointed a single Republican to the federal bench. In February 1801, when the Federalists lost control of the presidency and Congress, they passed the Judiciary Act of 1801 in order to ensure their long-range dominance of the judiciary. The measure created sixteen new federal judgeships, ostensibly so that Supreme Court justices could be relieved of their circuit-riding duties. However, the act also reduced the number of Supreme Court justices from six to five, a move that potentially deprived newly elected president Thomas Jefferson of the opportunity to nominate a justice. Outgoing president John Adams hurriedly announced "midnight appointments" for the new judgeships. His candidates included several unsuccessful candidates from the elections of 1800 as well as members of Chief Justice John Marshall's family. On his last day in office, Adams appointed William Marbury the justice of the peace for the District of Columbia but forgot to deliver Marbury's commission.

Enraged by the Federalists' tactics, the Republicans struck back. When Marbury asked James Madison, the new secretary of state, to deliver his commission, Madison refused. Marbury then asked the Supreme Court for a legal order (a writ of mandamus) compelling Madison to release the commission. In response, Chief Justice Marshall asked Madison to provide just cause for denying Marbury his judgeship. At the same time, Jefferson successfully lobbied Congress to repeal the Judiciary Act of 1801.

In 1803, Marshall issued his eagerly awaited Marbury v. Madison *decision. Born on a Virginia farm, Marshall served in the Revolution and studied law. After the war, he became a noted member of the Virginia state legislature and advocate for strong national government. Recognized as a leader in Virginia's Federalist Party, Marshall rejected several federal appointments. In 1800, he finally agreed to serve as John Adams's secretary of state. A few months later, Adams nominated Marshall to be chief justice of the U.S. Supreme Court.*

SOURCE: Joseph P. Cotton, Jr., ed. *The Constitutional Decisions of John Marshall* (New York, 1905), 1:7–43.

Easily confirmed, Marshall assumed the arduous task of interpreting the U.S. Constitution at a time when the judiciary's role was still evolving. By declaring a law unconstitutional for the first time, the Marbury v. Madison *ruling established the principle of judicial review and demonstrated the independence and vigor of the judicial branch.*

FOCUS QUESTIONS

1. What is Marshall's ruling on William Marbury's appointment?
2. What does Marshall identify as the duties of the Supreme Court? What is the legal basis of his claims?
3. Why is the principle of judicial review so important? What role do the federal courts play in modern American politics?

In the order in which the court has viewed this subject, the following questions have been considered and decided.

1st. Has the applicant a right to the commission he demands?

2d. If he has a right, and that right has been violated, do the laws of his country afford him a remedy?

3d. If they afford him a remedy, is it a mandamus issuing from this court?

The first object of inquiry is,

1st. Has the applicant a right to the commission he demands? . . .

It appears, from the affidavits, that in compliance with this law, a commission for William Marbury, as a justice of the peace for the county of Washington, was signed by John Adams, then President of the United States; after which the seal of the United States was affixed to it; but the commission has never reached the person for whom it was made out. . . .

The commission being signed, the subsequent duty of the secretary of state is prescribed by law, and not to be guided by the will of the president. He is to affix the seal of the United States to the commission, and is to record it.

This is not a proceeding which may be varied if the judgment of the executive shall suggest one more eligible; but is a precise court accurately marked out by law, and is to be strictly pursued. It is the duty of the secretary of state to conform to the law, and in this he is an officer of the United States, bound to obey the laws. . . .

But in all cases of letters patent, certain solemnities are required by law, which solemnities are the evidences of the validity of the instrument. A formal delivery to the person is not among them. In cases of commissions, the sign manual of the President, and the seal of the United States, are those solemnities. This objection, therefore, does not touch the case. . . .

The transmission of the commission is a practice directed by convenience, but not by law. It cannot, therefore, be necessary to constitute the appointment which must precede it, and which is the mere act of the President. . . .

It is, therefore, decidedly the opinion of the court, that when a commission has been signed by the President, the appointment is made; and that the commission is complete when the seal of the United States has been affixed to it by the Secretary of State. . . .

Mr. Marbury, then, since his commission was signed by the President, and sealed by the Secretary of State, was appointed; and as the law creating the office, gave the officer a right to hold for five years, independent of the executive, the appointment was not revocable, but vested in the officer legal rights, which are protected by the laws of his country.

To withhold his commission, therefore, is an act deemed by the court not warranted by law, but violative of a vested legal right.

This brings us to the second inquiry; which is,

2d. If he has a right, and that right has been violated, do the laws of his country afford him a remedy?

The very essence of civil liberty certainly consists in the right of every individual to claim the protection of the laws, whenever he receives an injury. One of the first duties of government is to afford that protection. . . .

By the constitution of the United States, the President is invested with certain important political powers, in the exercise of which he is to use his own discretion, and is accountable only to his country in his political character and to his own conscience. To aid him in the performance of these duties, he is authorized to appoint certain officers, who act by his authority, and in conformity with his orders.

In such cases, their acts are his acts; and whatever opinion may be entertained of the manner in which executive discretion may be used, still there exists, and can exist, no power to control that discretion. The subjects are political. They respect the nation, not individual rights, and being intrusted to the executive, the decision of the executive is conclusive. . . . This officer, as his duties were prescribed by that act, is to conform precisely to the will of the President. He is the mere organ by whom that will is communicated. The acts of such an officer, as an officer, can never be examined by the courts.

But when the legislature proceeds to impose on that officer other duties; when he is directed peremptorily to perform certain acts; when the rights of individuals are dependent on the performance of those acts; he is so far the officer of the law; is amenable to the laws for his conduct; and cannot at his discretion sport away the vested rights of others.

The conclusion from this reasoning is, that where the heads of departments are the political or confidential agents of the executive, merely to execute the will of the President, or rather to act in cases in which the executive possesses a constitutional or legal discretion, nothing can be more perfectly clear than that their acts are only politically examinable. But where a specific duty is assigned by law, and individual rights depend upon the performance of that duty, it seems equally clear that the individual who considers himself injured, has a right to resort to the laws of his country for a remedy.

If this be the rule, let us inquire how it applies to the case under the consideration of the court.

The power of nominating to the senate, and the power of appointing the person nominated, are political powers, to be exercised by the President according to his own discretion. When he has made an appointment, he has exercised his whole power, and his discretion has been completely applied to the case. . . .

The question whether a right has vested or not, is, in its nature, judicial, and must be tried by the judicial authority. . . .

It is, then, the opinion of this Court,

1st. That by signing the commission of Mr. Marbury the President of the United States appointed him a justice of peace for the county of Washington, in the District of Columbia; and that the seal of the United States, affixed thereto by the Secretary of State is conclusive testimony of the verity of the signature, and of the completion of the appointment; and that the appointment conferred on him a legal right to the office for the space of five years.

2d. That, having this legal title to the office he has a consequent right to the commission; a refusal to deliver which is a plain violation of that right, for which the laws of his country afford him a remedy. . . .

This, then, is a plain case for a mandamus, either to deliver the commission, or a copy of it from the record; and it only remains to be inquired, whether it can issue from this court.

The act to establish the judicial courts of the United States authorizes the Supreme court "to issue writs of mandamus in cases warranted by the principles and usages of law, to any courts appointed, or persons holding office, under the authority of the United States."

The Secretary of State, being a person holding an office under the authority of the United States, is precisely within the letter of the description, and if this court is not authorized to issue a writ of mandamus to such an officer, it must be because the law is unconstitutional, and therefore absolutely incapable of conferring the authority and assigning the duties which its words purport to confer and assign.

The constitution vests the whole judicial power of the United States in one Supreme Court, and such inferior as congress shall, from time to time, ordain and establish. This power is expressly extended to all cases arising under the laws of the United States; and, consequently, in some form, may be exercised over the present case; because the right claimed is given by a law of the United States.

In the distribution of this power it is declared that "the Supreme Court shall have original jurisdiction in all cases affecting ambassadors, other public ministers and consuls, and those in which a state shall be a party. In all other cases, the Supreme Court shall have appellate jurisdiction." . . .

To enable this court, then, to issue a mandamus, it must be shown to be an exercise of appellate jurisdiction, or to be necessary to enable them to exercise appellate jurisdiction.

It has been stated at the bar that the appellate jurisdiction may be exercised in a variety of forms, and that if it be the will of the legislature that a mandamus should be used for that purpose, that will must be obeyed. This is true, yet the jurisdiction must be appellate, not original.

It is the essential criterion of appellate jurisdiction, that it revises and corrects the proceedings in a cause already instituted, and does not create that cause. Although, therefore, a mandamus may be directed to courts, yet to issue such a writ to an officer for the delivery of a paper, is in effect the same as to sustain an original action for that paper, and, therefore, seems not to belong to appellate, but to original jurisdiction. Neither is it necessary in such a case as this, to enable the court to exercise its appellate jurisdiction.

The authority, therefore, given to the Supreme court, by the act establishing the judicial courts of the United States [the Judiciary Act of 1801], to issue writs of mandamus to public officers, appears not to be warranted by the constitution; and it becomes necessary to inquire whether a jurisdiction so conferred can be exercised.

The question, whether an act, repugnant to the constitution, can become the law of the land, is a question deeply interesting to the United States; but, happily, not of an intricacy proportioned to its interest. It seems only necessary to recognize certain principles, supposed to have been long and well established, to decide it.

That the people have an original right to establish, for their future government, such principles, as, in their opinion, shall most conduce to their own happiness is the basis on which the whole American fabric has been erected. The exercise of this original right is a very great exertion; nor can it, nor ought it, to be frequently repeated. The principles, therefore, so established, are deemed fundamental. And as the authority from which they proceed is supreme, and can seldom act, they are designed to be permanent.

This original and supreme will organizes the government and assigns to different departments their respective powers. It may either stop here, or establish certain limits not to be transcended by those departments.

The government of the United States is of the latter description. The powers of the legislature are defined and limited; and that those limits may not be mistaken, or forgotten, the constitution is written. To what purpose are powers limited, and to what purpose is that limitation committed to writing, if those limits may, at any time, be passed by those intended to be restrained? The distinction between a government with limited and unlimited powers is abolished, if those limits do not confine the persons on whom they are imposed, and if acts prohibited and acts allowed, are of equal obligation. It is a proposition too plain to be contested, that the constitution controls any legislative act repugnant to it; or, that the legislature may alter the constitution by an ordinary act.

Between these alternatives there is no middle ground. The constitution is either a superior paramount law, unchangeable by ordinary means, or it is on a level with ordinary legislative acts, and, like other acts, is alterable when the legislature shall please to alter it.

If the former part of the alternative be true, then a legislative contrary to the constitution is not law; if the latter part be true, then written constitutions are absurd attempts, on the part of the people, to limit a power in its own nature illimitable.

Certainly all those who have framed written constitutions contemplate them as forming the fundamental and paramount law of the nation, and, consequently, the theory of every such government must be, that an act of the legislature, repugnant to the constitution, is void.

This theory is essentially attached to a written constitution, and, is consequently, to be considered, by this court, as one of the fundamentals of our society. It is not therefore to be lost sight of in the further consideration of this subject. . . .

It is emphatically the province and duty of the judicial department to say what the law is. Those who apply the rule to particular cases, must of necessity expound and interpret that rule. If two laws conflict with each other, the courts must decide on the operation of each.

So if a law in opposition to the constitution; if both the law and the constitution apply to a particular case, so that the court must either decide that case conformably to the law, disregarding the constitution; or conformably to the constitution, disregarding the law; the court must determine which of these conflicting rules governs the case. This is of the very essence of judicial duty.

If, then, the courts are to regard the constitution, and the constitution is superior to any ordinary act of the legislature, the constitution, and not such ordinary act, must govern the case to which they both apply. . . .

Thus, the particular phraseology of the constitution of the United States confirms and strengthens the principle, supposed to be essential to all written constitutions, that a law repugnant to the constitution is void; and that courts, as well as other departments, are bound by that instrument.

The rule must be discharged.

5.5

Lewis and Clark Reach the Pacific Ocean (1805)

Even before the Louisiana Purchase was finalized, Thomas Jefferson dispatched his personal secretary Meriwether Lewis to lead an expedition to the Pacific coast. In order to obtain congressional funding for the journey, Jefferson stressed the commercial potential of the Northwest. But science, not trade, was Jefferson's

SOURCE: *Originals Journals of the Lewis and Clark Expedition, 1804–1806* (New York: Dodd, Mead, 1905), 208–15.

major motivation. He instructed Lewis to obtain knowledge about plant and animal life, geography, American Indians, and weather patterns. Lewis and his second-in-command, William Clark, gathered about fifty men with expertise in various skills, including botany, carpentry, celestial navigation, and canoeing. In May 1804, the party departed from St. Louis and traveled up the Missouri River. They hoped to find the Northwest Passage, a long-sought water route traversing North America.

The journey was challenging. Upon reaching the Dakota territory, they wintered among friendly Mandan Sioux. The next spring, they hired a French-Canadian guide named Touissant Charbonneau. However, Sacagawea, Charbonneau's sixteen-year-old Shoshone wife, proved much more helpful than her husband. While caring for her infant son, she also served as an interpreter, mediated between the expedition and Indians, and identified sources of food in the wild. The group traveled by horseback to the headwaters of the Clearwater River and then canoed down the Clearwater to the Snake River and onto the Columbia River.

After reaching the Pacific Ocean in November 1805, the expedition headed back to St. Louis and arrived in September 1806. Although they encountered accidents, grizzly bears, poisonous snakes, harsh weather, and illness, only one man died en route. Despite its disappointing discovery that the Northwest Passage did not exist, the Lewis and Clark expedition gathered valuable scientific information and spurred popular interest in the West. In this diary excerpt, Lewis and Clark describe the Pacific shoreline.

FOCUS QUESTIONS

1. How do Lewis and Clark describe the geography and people of the Northwest?
2. What are living conditions like on the expedition?
3. Why do you think the Lewis and Clark expedition so intrigued Americans?

November 7th Thursday 1805

A cloudy foggey morning Some rain. We Set out early proceeded under the Star Side under a high rugid hills with Steep assent the Shore boalt and rockey, the fog o thick we could not See across the river, two cano(e)s of Indians met and returned with us to their village which is Situated on the Star Side behind a cluster of Marshey Islands, on a narrow chan of the river through which we passed to the village of 4 Houses, they gave us to eate Some fish, and Sold us, fish . . . roots three *dogs* and 2 otter skins for which we gave fish hooks principally of which they were verry fond. . . .

After delaying at this *village* one hour and a half we Set out piloted by an Indian dressed in a Salors dress, to the Main Chanel from behind those islands, without a pilot, a large marshey Island near the middle of the river near which several Canoes came allong Side with Skins, roots, fish &c. to Sell, and had a temporey residence on this Island, here we see great numbers of water fowls about those Marshey Island; . . .

We proceeded on about 12 miles below the Village under a high mountaneous Countrey on the Star Side, Shore boald and rockey and Encamped under a high hill on the Star Side opposit to a rock Situated half a mile from the shore. . . . We with dificuelty found a place clear of the tide and Sufficiently large to lie on and the only place we could get was on round stones on which we lay our mats rain continu moderately all day. . . .

Great joy in camp we are in view of the Ocian, (*in the morning when fog cleared off just below last village (first on leaving this village)* . . .) this great Pacific Ocean which we been so long anxious to See and the roreing or noise made by the waves brakeing on the rockey Shores (as I suppose) may be heard disti(n)ctly.

We made 34 miles to day as computed.

November 8th Friday 1805

A cloudy morning Some rain, we did not Set out until 9 oClock, having changed our Clothing. Proceeded on close under the star Side, the hills high with steep assent, Shoar boald and rockey . . .

Here we found the Swells or Waves so high that we thought it imprudent to proceed; we landed unloaded and drew up our Canoes. Some rain all day at intervales, we are all wet and disagreeable, as we have been for Several past, and our present Situation a verry disagreeable one in as much, as we have not leavel land Sufficient for an emcampment and for our baggage to lie cleare of the tide, the High hills jutting so close and steep that we cannot retreat back, and the water of the river too Salt to be used, added to the waves are increaseing to Such a hight that we cannot move from this place, in this Situation we are compelled to form our campe between the hite of the Ebb and floor tides, and rase our baggage on logs. . . .

November 10th Sunday 1805

. . . We are all wet the rain having continued all day, our beding and maney other articles, employ our Selves drying our blankets. Northing to eate but dried fish pounded which we brought from the falls. We made 10 miles to day.

5.6

Lessons from a New England Primer (1807)

In the decades immediately following the Revolution, cultural expressions helped Americans develop their national identity. Textbooks using American grammar and spelling began to appear. The works of Noah Webster (1758–1843) provide good examples. In 1783, he published The American Spelling Book, *also known as the "Blue-Backed Speller." Two years later, he produced a reader filled with selections celebrating democracy and morality. In 1807, he started working on a dictionary. First published in 1828,* An American Dictionary of the English Language *contained about 70,000 entries, including many technical and scientific terms.*

Such cultural trends inevitably affected schoolbooks. This alphabet lesson from an 1807 New England primer provides a good example.

FOCUS QUESTIONS

1. What do you think are the educational objectives of this lesson?
2. How does this assignment reflect a growing sense of nationalism among Americans?
3. How would materials like this help children grow up to be good republican citizens?

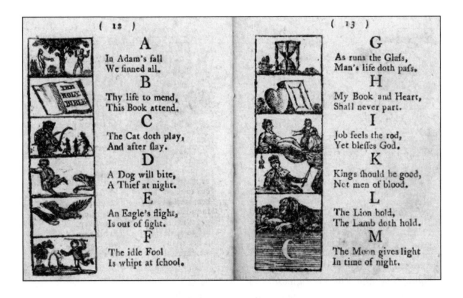

(12)

A
In Adam's fall
We finned all.

B
Thy life to mend,
This Book attend.

C
The Cat doth play,
And after flay.

D
A Dog will bite,
A Thief at night.

E
An Eagle's flight,
Is out of fight.

F
The idle Fool
Is whipt at fchool.

(13)

G
As runs the Glafs,
Man's life doth pafs.

H
My Book and Heart,
Shall never part.

I
Job feels the rod,
Yet bleffes God.

K
Kings fhould be good,
Not men of blood.

L
The Lion bold,
The Lamb doth hold.

M
The Moon gives light
In time of night.

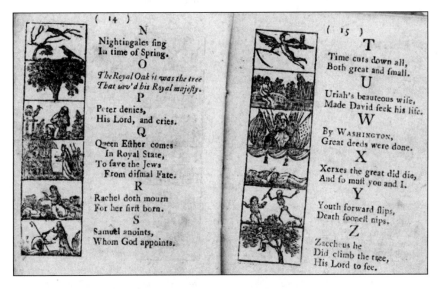

(14)

N
Nightingales fing
In time of Spring.

O
*The Royal Oak it was the tree
That fav'd his Royal majefty.*

P
Peter denies,
His Lord, and cries.

Q
Queen Efther comes
In Royal State,
To fave the Jews
From difmal Fate.

R
Rachel doth mourn
For her firft born.

S
Samuel anoints,
Whom God appoints.

(15)

T
Time cuts down all,
Both great and fmall.

U
Uriah's beauteous wife,
Made David feek his life.

W
By WASHINGTON,
Great deeds were done.

X
Xerxes the great did die,
And fo muft you and I.

Y
Youth forward flips,
Death fooneft nips.

Z
Zaccheus he
Did climb the tree,
His Lord to fee.

The New England Primer Improved, Being an Easy Method to Teach Young Children the English Language (New York: Daniel D. Smith, 1807), 12–15.

5.7

Images of American Indians
(1804, 1821)

*American culture is rife with disparate images of American Indians. Such
depictions offer clues about white societal attitudes toward Indians in different eras.
Whites commonly stereotyped Indians as bloodthirsty killers or "noble savages."*

John Vanderlyn's Murder of Jane McCrea *(1804) is a powerful illustration of the former. Vanderlyn (1776–1852) showed artistic promise as a
young man and won the support of Aaron Burr. Burr sent him to study with
Gilbert Stuart, America's foremost portraitist. In 1796, Vanderlyn traveled to
Paris for additional instruction. When he returned to New York in 1801, he was
largely responsible for introducing the Neoclassical style to the United States.*

The tale of Jane McCrea was well-known to Americans. McCrea
(1752–1777) grew up in New Jersey and was courted by David Jones,
a soldier serving in the British army under General John Borgoyne. In the
summer of 1777, as a large British force neared Fort Edwards, local
residents fled in panic. McCrea, however, had received a letter from Jones
asking her to wait for him. Legend suggests that they were to be married
upon his arrival. On July 27, McCrea and Sarah McNeil left Fort
Edwards and were captured by two Indians working as British scouts.
McNeil escaped, but McCrea was found scalped and riddled with bullet
wounds. Although her captors blamed her death on stray bullets from
nearby American soldiers, most people assumed that the scouts had murdered her. News of her death chilled American and British readers.
Romanticized versions of her story became very popular.

Charles Bird King (1785–1862) depicted Indians more positively. After
studying with Benjamin West in London, King moved to the United States. In
1818, he settled in Washington, D.C., and was hired by the recently formed
Bureau of Indian Affairs. Over a twenty-year period, he produced over 140 portraits
of Indians who came to negotiate with federal authorities. His painting Young
Omahaw, War Eagle, Little Missouri, and Pawnees *features a Pawnee delegation.*

FOCUS QUESTIONS

1. How do these images differ in their depictions of American Indians?
2. What does each suggest about white attitudes?
3. How can art help us to understand an era's history?

John Vanderlyn, *Murder of Jane McCrea*, 1804. Oil on canvas, 32 × 26 in. (81.3 × 67.3 cm) Wadsworth Atheneum, Hartford, Connecticut. Purchased by Wadsworth Atheneum.

Charles Bird King, *Young Omahaw, War Eagle, Little Missouri, and Pawnees*, 1821. Oil on canvas, 36 1/8 × 28 in. (91.7 × 71.1 cm). National Museum of American Art, Smithsonian Institution, Washington, D.C.; gift of Miss Helen Barlow.

5.8

Tecumseh's Plea to the Choctaws and the Chickasaws (1811)

Born in 1768 near modern Springfield, Ohio, Shawnee chief Tecumseh deeply resented white incursions onto Indian lands. Arguing that no single tribe had the right to sell territory to the United States, Tecumseh and his half-brother Tenskwatawa, the Prophet, attempted to build an intertribal confederation. They traveled vast distances urging tribes to unify and to reject white culture.

Their activities infuriated William Henry Harrison, the governor of the Indiana Territory. In 1809, Harrison had purchased huge tracts of land from the Delaware and Miami for only $10,000. In 1811, when the Shawnees rejected the agreement, Harrison led a raid against Tecumseh and the Prophet's settlement. After the Prophet launched a premature attack, Harrison won the Battle of Tippecanoe. Humiliated by the loss, the Prophet fled to Canada. During the War of 1812, Tecumseh became a brigadier general in the British army. After playing a decisive role in several British victories, he was killed in 1813 while fighting in Ontario against American troops commanded by Harrison. His death undermined Indian resistance throughout much of the Midwest.

In this selection, Tecumseh appeals to the Choctaws and the Chickasaws to fight against the United States.

FOCUS QUESTIONS

1. How does Tecumseh describe whites?
2. How does he appeal to the Choctaws and Chickasaws?
3. Could an intertribal confederation have permanently resisted white expansion? Explain your answer.

In view of questions of vast importance, have we met together in solemn council tonight. Nor should we here debate whether we have been wronged or injured, but by what measures we should avenge ourselves; for our merciless oppressors, having long since planned out their proceedings, are not about to make, but have

SOURCE: W. C. Vanderwerth, *Indian Oratory* (Norman: University of Oklahoma Press, 1971)

and are still making attacks upon our race who have as yet come to no resolution. Nor are we ignorant by what steps, and by what gradual advances, the whites break in upon our neighbors. Imagining themselves to be still undiscovered, they show themselves the less audacious because you are insensible. The whites are already nearly a match for us all united, and too strong for any one tribe alone to resist; so that unless we support one another with our collective and united forces; unless every tribe unanimously combines to give check to the ambition and avarice of the whites, they will soon conquer us apart and disunited, and we will be driven away from our native country and scattered as autumn leaves, before the wind. But have we not courage enough remaining to defend our country and maintain our ancient independence? Will we calmly suffer the white intruders and tyrants to enslave us? Shall it be said of our race that we knew not how to extricate ourselves from the three most dreadful calamities—folly, inactivity, and cowardice? But what need is there to speak of the past? It speaks for itself and asks, Where today is the Pequod? Where the Narragansetts, the Mohawks, Pocanokets, and many other once powerful tribes of our race? They have vanished before the avarice and oppression of the white men, as snow before a summer sun. In the vain hope of alone defending their ancient possessions, they have fallen in the wars with the white men. Look abroad over their once beautiful country, and what see you now? Naught but the ravages of the pale face destroyers meet our eyes. So it will be with you Choctaws and Chickasaws! Soon your mighty forest trees, under the shade of whose wide spreading branches you have played in infancy, sported in boyhood, and now rest your wearied limbs after the fatigue of the chase, will be cut down to fence in the land which the white intruders dare to call their own. Soon their broad roads will pass over the grave of your fathers, and the place of their rest will be blotted out forever. The annihilation of our race is at hand unless we unite in one common cause against the common foe. Think not, brave Choctaws and Chickasaws, that you can remain passive and indifferent to the common danger, and thus escape the common fate. Your people, too, will soon be as falling leaves and scattering clouds before their blighting breath. You, too, will be driven away from your native land and ancient domains as leaves are driven before the wintry storms.

Sleep not longer, O Choctaws and Chickasaws, in false security and delusive hopes. Our broad domains are fast escaping from our grasp. Every year our white intruders become more greedy, exacting, oppressive, and overbearing. Every year contentions spring up between them and our people and when blood is shed we have to make atonement whether right or wrong, at the cost of the lives of our greatest chiefs, and the yielding up of large tracts of our lands. Before the pale-faces came among us, we enjoyed the happiness of unbounded freedom, and were acquainted with neither riches, wants, nor oppression. How is it now? Wants and oppression are our lot; for are we not controlled in everything, and dare we move without asking, by your leave? Are we not being stripped day by day of the little that remains of our ancient liberty? Do they not even kick and strike us as they do their black-faces? How long will it be before they tie us to the post and whip us, and make us work for them in their corn fields as they do them? Shall we wait for that moment or shall we die fighting before submitting to such ignominy?

. . . Shall we calmly wait until they become so numerous that we will no longer be able to resist oppression? Will we wait to be destroyed in our turn, without making an effort worthy of our race? Shall we give up our homes, our country, bequeathed to us by the Great Spirit, the graves of our dead, and everything that is dear and sacred to us, without a struggle? I know you will cry with me: Never! Never! Then let us by unity of action destroy them all, which we now can do, or drive them back whence they came. War or extermination is now our only choice. Which do you choose? I know your answer. Therefore, I now call on you, brave Choctaws and Chickasaws, to assist in the just cause of liberating our race from the grasp of our faithless invaders and heartless oppressors. The white usurpation in our common country must be stopped, or we, its rightful owners, be forever destroyed and wiped out as a race of people. I am now at the head of many warriors backed by the strong arm of English soldiers. Choctaws and Chickasaws, you have too long borne with grievous usurpation inflicted by the arrogant Americans. Be no longer their dupes. If there be one here tonight who believes that his rights will not sooner or later be taken from him by the avaricious American pale faces, his ignorance ought to excite pity, for he knows little of the character of our common foe.

And if there be one among you mad enough to undervalue the growing power of the white race among us, let him tremble in considering the fearful woes he will bring down upon our entire race, if by his criminal indifference he assists in the designs of our common enemy against our common country. Then listen to the voice of duty, of honor, of nature, and of your endangered country. Let us form one body, one heart, and defend to the last warrior our country, our homes, our liberty, and the graves of our fathers.

Choctaws and Chickasaws, you are among the few of our race who sit indolently at ease. You have indeed enjoyed the reputation of being brave, but will you be indebted for it more from report than fact? Will you let the whites encroach upon your domains even to your very door before you will assert your rights in resistance? Let no one in their council imagine that I speak more from malice against the pale face Americans than just grounds of complaint. Complaint is just toward friends who have failed in their duty; accusation is against enemies guilty of injustice. And surely, if any people ever had, we have good and just reasons to believe we have ample grounds to accuse the Americans of injustice; especially when such great acts of injustice have been committed by them upon our race, of which they seem to have no manner of regard, or even to reflect. They are a people fond of innovations, quick to contrive, and quick put their schemes into effectual execution no matter how great the wrong and injury to us; while we are content to preserve what we already have. Their designs are to enlarge their possessions by taking yours in turn; and will you, can you longer dally, O Choctaws and Chickasaws?

Do you imagine that the people will not continue longest in the enjoyment of peace who timely prepare to vindicate themselves, and manifest a determined resolution to do themselves right whenever they are wronged? Far otherwise. Then haste to the relief of our common cause, as by consanguinity of blood you are bound; lest the day be not far distant when you will be left single-handed and alone to the cruel mercy of our most inveterate foe.

5.9

The *Niles Weekly Register* Pushes for War (1812)

By 1812, after a long series of disputes over trade, maritime practices, and neutral rights, U.S. relations with Britain were very strained. Angered by British aid to Indians in the western territories and eager to acquire Florida and Canada, many westerners and southerners demanded an aggressive American response. In June 1812, Congress declared war on Great Britain. Although the War of 1812 ended inconclusively, it revitalized American patriotism and lessened U.S. dependence on Europe.

In this reading, a Pennsylvania newspaper makes the case for war against the British.

FOCUS QUESTIONS

1. Why does the author believe that war against Britain is justified?
2. How does he claim that the British can be defeated?
3. What effect does he think that war will have upon the United States? Were his predictions accurate? Explain your answer.

Malvern, PA
Niles Weekly Register, 30 May 1812

Every considerate and unprejudiced man, in every part of the union, freely admits we have just cause for war with both the great belligerents, and especially England; whose maritime depredations are not only far more extensive than those of [other] rivals, but who has superadded thereto the most flagrant violations of the individual, national and territorial rights of the American people; matters of much higher import and consequence. But a state of war is desired by no man. . . . it comes unwished for, excites general apprehension and frequently does partial damage—but it purges the atmosphere, gives a new tone, as it were, to listless nature, and promotes the common good....

It is very certain that no good citizen of the United States would wantonly promote a rupture with Great Britain, or any other country. The American people will never wage offensive war; but every feeling of the heart is interested to preserve the rights our fathers won by countless hardships and innumerable sufferings. Our love of peace is known to the world; nay, so powerful is the desire to preserve it.... Every measure that Forbearance, could devise, has been resorted to—and we have suffered injuries, particularly in the wealth of our citizens, which no independent nation ever submitted to. Embargo was tried: through the timidity of the 10th congress, excited by the insolent clamors of a small, but wicked, portion of the people, aided by the inefficiency of the laws for enforcing it, it failed of its foreign operation. Since that time we have virtually submitted, and thereby only lengthened the chain of encroachment. As has been before observed, we are driven into a corner, and must surrender at the discretion of a wicked and unprincipled enemy, or hew our way out of it—the hazard of life itself is preferable to the certain loss of all that makes it desirable.

... [W]e can do Great Britain more essential injury than another Europe could additionally heap upon her; for we have greater means of annoyance than all that continent possesses in our seamen and shipping...to annihilate her commerce, the very sinews of the existence of her government. Our coasts may be secured, and regular trade be destroyed. But many Paul Jones' will ride and whithersoever a keel can go, just retaliation shall check the enemy's career.... [T]he whole navy of Britain, if applied to no other purpose, will be incompetent to the protection of her vast possessions and commerce. To us she is the most vulnerable of all nations—we can successfully attack her at home and abroad. War will deprive her of an immense stock of raw materials, on the manufacture and application of which so great a portion of her population depends for subsistence; and, in despite of smugglers, the ingress of her manufactures will be denied, for a state of activity and exertion far different from that at present made use of, will be arrayed against them....

The conquest of Canada will be of the highest importance to us in distressing our enemy—in cutting off his supplies of provisions and naval stores for his West India colonies and home demand. There is no place from whence he can supply the mighty void that would be occasioned by the loss of this country, as well in his exports as imports. It would operate upon him with a double force: it would deprive him of a vast quantity of indispensable materials (as well as of food) and close an extensive market for his manufactures. On its retention depends the prosperity of the West India islands.... Canada and Nova Scotia, if not fully conquered immediately, may be rendered useless to him in a few weeks. Without them, and particularly the latter, he cannot maintain those terrible fleets on our coast that we are threatened with, or "bridge" our harbors with frigates, admitting he may have no use for them to defend his own shores; for he will not have a dockyard, fitting the purposes of his navy, within 3,000 miles of us.

"Our red brethren" will soon be taught to wish they had remembered the talks of their "father Jefferson," and of all other persons who advised them to peace.

Upper Canada, at least, would be immediately and completely in our possession. The Pandora boxes at Amherstburg and Malden would be closed, and all the causes of the present murders of the savages would cease; for they make neither guns nor gun-powder, being at this time supplied from the "king's stores" at these places, and urged to the work of death by "his majesty's agents" with liberal rewards and more liberal promises. To our mind there are facts . . . to convince us that all our difficulties with the Indians originated with the British in Canada.

New Orleans, even if it should pass into the hands of the enemy, cannot be held by him. . . . [A] million of persons are immediately interested in the navigation of the Mississippi; and like the torrent of their own mighty river would descend with a force irresistible, sweeping every thing before them. Certain parts of Florida the enemy might take, and perhaps, be permitted to hold; because he would retain them at a greater injury to himself than to us.

The war will not last long. Every scheme of taxation has already been resorted to in Great Britain. Every means have been tried to sustain the credit of her immense paper currency. The notes of the bank of England are 28 percent below their nominal value. A war with the United States will add a third to her present expenditures, at least; and, in a like proportion render her unable to bear them. Her revenue will decrease as her expenses increase; for she will lose all the export and import duties she levied on goods sent to or received from the United States, and all her resources, built upon commerce will be fluctuating and uncertain. She will be assailed on that element she arrogantly assumes as her own, and be perplexed in a thousand new forms, by a people as brave and more enterprising and ingenious than any she can boast of. Her seamen once landed upon our shores, as prisoners or otherwise, will not return to her; and her naval officers will rarely feel themselves safe from mutiny while hovering on our coasts. It is considered lawful in war to encourage such enterprises; and her impressed seamen, sure of our asylum, with "peace, liberty and safety," will retort upon their oppressors some of the pangs they have suffered. Tens of thousands of her former subjects, natives of generous and oppressed Erin [Ireland], will remember the conflagration of their cottages and the murder of their friends, and vie with each other to avenge their wrongs: and Britain, to preserve herself, will be compelled to honest peace.

During the war there will be ample employment for all. Some part of the labor and capital of the United States, at present devoted to commerce, will be directed to objects calculated to seal the independence of the country, in the establishment of a thousand works, needful to the supply of our wants. . . . Some changes in the habits of the people on the seaboard (a small part of our population) may take place; but there will be nothing terrible in them. Our agriculturalists will have a steady and better market at home: of this we are easily assured when we reflect, that all our provisions exported have not produced more than paid for the foreign liquors we consumed. Instead of sending tobacco (the most wretched crop of all others ever raised) to the fluctuating markets of Europe, we will furnish ourselves, and (in a short time) the whole world, with wool; and apply the extra laborers to its manufacture—a state of things that will have a powerful tendency to ameliorate the condition of the unfortunate negro, equally profitable to his master. The bonds which fasten us to Europe will be broken, and our trade and future intercourse with her be materially and beneficially changed.

The political atmosphere being purged, a greater degree of harmony will exist; and the regenerated spirit of freedom will teach us to love, to cherish and support our unparalleled system of government, as with the mind of one man. The hydra party, generated by foreign feelings, will die in agonies. The "new army" will be chiefly employed in the conquered countries, or on the frontiers, and the protection of the states, generally, be confided to the people themselves, who are not "their own worst enemies." Neither the men beyond "the Potomac," nor on this side of that river, are the instigators of the war—the causes for it exist in the conduct of the cabinet of St. James, nourished and cherished by the false hopes they entertain of the strength of "their party" in the United States.

Money will not be wanting. The people will freely supply it when there is need for it. Our country is rich. Our resources are great. Our specie is abundant, and will greatly increase by opening a direct trade with Mexico; and so serve ourselves and the patriots of that country by furnishing them with arms and ammunition and stores, and enable them to drive out their many-headed tyrant. Numerous hardy volunteers, as true as ever pulled a trigger, will flock to their standard, from the western states—and encourage in them an affection for this government and teach them how freemen should fight. . . .

The great body of the people in the "eastern states" prefer their own government to any other—they will be faithful to the constitution. . . . Nor will a conscription be necessary to supply the regular troops or militia. The ranks of the former are filling with great rapidity. . . .

5.10

Report and Resolutions of the Hartford Convention (1815)

Throughout the early 1800s, Federalists opposed Republican policies. The embargo against Britain devastated New England commerce. With the outbreak of hostilities in 1812, many New Englanders were convinced that the nation was being ruled

SOURCE: Published at http://www.nidlink.com/~bobhard/hartford.html.

without regard to their interests. In December 1814, Federalists from five New England states met secretly in Hartford, Connecticut. The delegates approved resolutions calling for dramatic changes in the federal government. News of the Treaty of Ghent and Andrew Jackson's victory in the Battle of New Orleans reached the American public just as the Hartford delegates published their proceedings. This unfortunate coincidence contributed to the demise of the Federalist Party.

FOCUS QUESTIONS

1. What constitutional amendments did the Hartford delegates propose?
2. How would these changes have benefited New England?
3. Why do you think that the Hartford Resolutions turned Americans against the Federalists?

January 5, 1815

That it be and hereby is recommended to the legislatures of the several states represented in this Convention, to adopt all such measures as may be necessary effectually to protect the citizens of said states from the operation and effects of all acts which have been or may be passed by the Congress of the United States, which shall contain provisions, subjecting the militia or other citizens to forcible drafts, conscriptions, or impressments, not authorized by the constitution of the United States.

Resolved, That it be and hereby is recommended to the said Legislatures, to authorize an immediate and earnest application to be made to the government of the United States, requesting their consent to some arrangement, whereby the said states may, separately or in concert, be empowered to assume upon themselves the defense of their territory against the enemy; and a reasonable portion of the taxes, collected within said states, may be paid into the respective treasuries thereof, and appropriated to the payment of the balance due said states, and to the future defense of the same. The amount so paid into the said treasuries to be credited, and the disbursements made as aforesaid to be charged to the United States.

Resolved, That it be, and hereby is, recommended to the legislatures of the aforesaid states, to pass laws (where it has not already been done) authorizing the governors or commanders-in-chief of their militia to make detachments from the same, or to form voluntary corps, as shall be most convenient and conformable to their constitutions, and to cause the same to be well armed, equipped and disciplined, and held in readiness for service; and upon the request of the governor of either of the other states to employ the whole of such detachment or corps, as well as the regular forces of the state, or such part thereof as may be required and can be spared consistently with the safety of the state, in assisting the state, making such request to repel any invasion thereof which shall be made or attempted by the public enemy.

Resolved, That the following amendments of the constitution of the United States be recommended to the states represented as aforesaid, to be proposed by them for adoption by the state legislatures, and in such cases as may be deemed expedient by a convention chosen by the people of each state.

First. Representatives and direct taxes shall be apportioned among the several states which may be included within this Union, according to their respective numbers of free persons, including those bound to serve for a term of years, and excluding Indians not taxed, and all other persons.

Second. No new state shall be admitted into the Union by Congress, in virtue of the power granted by the constitution, without the concurrence of two thirds of both houses.

Third. Congress shall not have power to lay any embargo on the ships or vessels of the citizens of the United States, in the ports or harbors thereof, for more than sixty days.

Fourth. Congress shall not have power, without the concurrence of two thirds of both houses, to interdict the commercial intercourse between the United States and any foreign nation or the dependencies thereof.

Fifth. Congress shall not make or declare war, or authorize acts of hostility against any foreign nation, without the concurrence of two thirds of both houses, except such acts of hostility be in defense of the territories of the United States when actually invaded.

Sixth. No person who shall hereafter be naturalized, shall be eligible as a member of the senate or house of representatives of the United States, nor capable of holding any civil office under the authority of the United States.

Seventh. The same person shall not be elected president of the United States a second time; nor shall the President be elected from the same state two terms in succession.

Resolved, That if the application of these states to the government of the United States, recommended in a foregoing resolution, should be unsuccessful and peace should not be concluded, and the defense of these states should be neglected, as it has been since the commencement of the war, it will, in the opinion of this convention, be expedient for the legislatures of the several states to appoint delegates to another convention, to meet at Boston . . . with such powers and instructions as the exigency of a crisis so momentous may require.

5.11

John Luttig Describes the Western Fur Trade (1812)

Between the 1790s and the 1820s, a thriving trade developed in the American West. Early merchants sailed around South America and built outposts on the Pacific coast. Within a short time, they were exchanging furs, hides, and animal fats (used in making candles and soap) for products sold by New England shippers. Farther inland, commercial networks grew between Santa Fe and St. Louis.

"Mountain men" were crucial to these endeavors. Attracted to the virgin land and plentiful animal life in the Rocky Mountain region, these pioneers explored and hunted in many of North America's most foreboding areas. These trappers interacted closely with Indians, and many adopted Indian customs and clothing. Americans loved reading about the exploits of mountain men like Kit Carson and Jedediah Smith. When permanent settlers began arriving in the West, many mountain men served as guides and interpreters, but their way of life disappeared as the country expanded westward.

In this selection, John Luttig, a clerk for the Missouri Fur Company, describes a trading expedition led by Manuel Lisa on the Upper Missouri River.

FOCUS QUESTIONS

1. How does Luttig describe life in the fur trade?
2. What are some of the difficulties the expedition encounters?
3. What types of people do the trappers encounter? How would you characterize these interactions?
4. Does this reading revise your understanding of America in this era? Explain your answer.

SOURCE: John C. Luttig, *Journal of a fur-trading expedition on the Upper Missouri, 1812–1813* ed. Stella M. Drumm (St. Louis, Missouri Historical Society, 1920).

Friday the 8th of May, I started from St. Louis to Bellefontaine to meet the Boats bound up the Missouri River, arriving there at 1 o'clock P.M., took in Meal and Corn, arranged the Loading, and started at 3 o'clock, went about 4 Miles with a head wind. . . .

Monday the 11th Mr. Manuel Lisa & Choteau came on Board at 9 o'clock A.M. took in some traps, and made the best of our way at 12 o'clock, having a head wind made very little distance.

Tuesday the 12th, head wind and strong Current, made not much Distance.

Wednesday the 13th, the same as yesterday.

Thursday the 14th, the same. . . .

Friday the 15th in the Morning about 8 o'clock—Mr. Majet, Patroon of the large Boat fell over Board on account of a Log slamming against the Rudder, he saved himself by taking hold of the Rudder, and got on Board, both Rudder Irons broke and Lost, were detained to make a steering Oar, head wind all Day, sent some Irons on shore by Mr. Richardson, and camped at Burgois Creek.

Saturday the 16th, detained on Account of the Iron, which however came about 11 o'clock A.M., hard Rain and bad weather, fixed the Rudder and went about 2 Miles distance, Killed 1 Deer.

Sunday the 17th blowing very hard ahead and strong Current we had to stop for several hours, made sail, about 2 P.M., just at starting a Bear crossed the River towards us, Killed him close in shore, and found him very fat.

Monday 18th, still head wind the Rudder Irons of the little Boat broke, and had to lay by all Day. This Day Killed four Deer 2 Turkeys. . . .

Thursday, the 21, arrived at 11 o'clock A.M. at Cote sans Dessin, rested all Day, traded some Beaver, and took LaChapel on Board.

Friday the 22d, started at 6 in the Morning with a favorable breeze, found the River more gentle, had fine weather. . . .

Friday the 29th departed at Day light, opposite the little Osage Island we were obliged to stop on account of head wind and strong Current, arranged a new top Mast, went fishing with the Seine and caught 13 large fish 1 Turtle, the wind having somewhat abated we made way at 2 P.M. but still wind a heads, at the little Osage Prairie we stopped for the little Boat which got around, met a shoal of Cat fish close in shore the Men who were Cordelling [pulling the boat with a tow rope] killed one with a stick which weighed after cleaning 40 lbs, went on a little way and found a small Run full of fish, the other Boat not having come up as yet we took our Seine and caught 161 Bass and other fish, which we salted, camped and killed 2 Deer.

Saturday, the 30th fine weather, but very hard water, swung 3 times at a point of a sandbar, the little Boat broke her Rudder Irons again, repaired at Dinner, Killed 2 Deer 1 Beaver 1 Pelican, made not much Distance. . . .

Monday the 1st of June, hard wind a head with fine weather met 4 Batteaux going to St. Louis, a little above the Prairie du Feu had to stop and make another top mast of Oak, the last one made of Hichberry was crooked and good for nothing, Killed 3 Deer 1 Bear. . . .

Thursday the 4th started after breakfast, about 9 A.M. met several Perogues coming from their Winter quarters, Mess fr Robideau, La Jeuness & others, Louis

Bijou embarked with us, as also two hunters embarked at fort Osage Greenwood & Laurison Immel went back to the fort for his dog and on his Return in formed of the party going to Santa Fe he met this Day at the fort. Strong Current, made 9 Miles Distance....

Friday the 12th, fine weather, made good way cordelling the wind all Day against us, distance 21 Miles camped on a large Sandbar where we found a quantity of turtle Eggs, this Day lost one of our Swivels when swinging round and run against the other Boat, Killed 3 Deer, 2 Turkeys.

Saturday the 13 the fine weather and head wind, this Day had bad luck, crossing for some of our Hunters we came in hard water, and cordelling on a Prairie encountered many Rafts, after having passed we dined 2 Miles above the Prairie. Mr. Manuel L. put our 2 Hogs in the River to wash but they swam off, we were obliged to turn about and followed them several Miles, after two Attempts we caught them, turning a rocky point we had hard work, the little Boat which was a head swung round and went off like lightning, the Cordells broke, and we were obliged to put the hands of both Boats to one to mount distance 12 Miles killed 5 Deer 1 Racoon....

Monday 15th about one o'clock this Morning it began to blow furiously, were obliged to put out our fires, the wind blowing from all quarters, a clear Sky, finished our cooking in the Morning at 6 in the Morning went miles but were stopt by hard head wind and Current crossed the River to find some Hickory for making an Axe handles and Ramrods, but were disappointed, crossed again and stopped till 5 P.M. started about 1 Mile took the Cordell the Boat swung and went down the River like the Wind in full speed, leaving all hands on shore, the few which were on Board landed the Boat opposite to our last nights Lodgings, our hands came on board made a new start, but night overtook us, got on a sandbar and were very near lost running against a Sawyer [a hazard of river navigation, these partially submerged trees could "saw" a boat in half] had to cross again to the North Side, the other Boat came to close swept by the Current we unshipped our Rudder, run against a tree and broke her mast, this ended this dolefull Day camped at 11 o'clock at night distance 1 « Mile, left our hunters on the opposite side Killed 1 Deer, wind N.W. fresh Gales.

Tuesday the 16, hard wind from N.W., went about 1 Mile in the Morning when we had to stop, all hands went out to gather wood for Axe helms, Ramrods and a new Mast, and Game, the first was found but no meat, our hunters on the opposite Side had also been unsuccessful, and crossed the River on a Raft, facing wind and Current about 6 Miles swimming. Killed 1 Deer....

Monday, the 22d, cloudy had now and then some Sailing, the River still rising and strong Currents, at 4 P.M. a thunder storm arose which raged furiously, the hurricane swayed the trees every where luckily we got under some Willows and lay safe, were obliged to Camp, distance 10 Miles, Killed 1 Deer, 1 Turkey....

Saturday the 4th of July, we had ourselves prepared to salute the Day, which gave Birth to the Independence of the United States, but a Salute from Heaven prevented us, a thunder storm arose at 2 in the Morning and the Bank of the River where we camped fell in upon us momentarily. Mr Manuel was nearly drowned in his Bed, and we had run off, rowing and poling all Day, about Sunset a favorable wind sprung up and carried us several Miles, were obliged to leave a large Buck and an Elk which our Hunters had Killed behind, camped at Black Birds Hill, distance 15 Miles. . . .

Monday the 13th, head wind and hard Current, rowed, poled and cordelled all Day, several hunters went out returned at 4 P.M., no game but had seen many fresh track of elk, waited 2 hours for the other Boat at 5 P.M. made Island of Bonhomme and Ponca Country we had flattered ourselves to meet some Indians of Buffaloe but were dissappointed, by this time we had passed the Countries of the following Nations, Little and Big Osage, Mahas, Otoes, Yenctons, & Kanzas, this Morning Immel & Lorimier went a head by land, all hunters went on the Island, Killed but 1 Elk, two of them camped on the N. Side and Boats on the South Side of the Island, distance 18 Miles. . . .

Saturday 18, cloudy about 8 A.M. a fine favorable wind took us and we had good sailing untill 2 o'clock P.M. when we discovered 3 Lodges of Sioux Indians and found Mr. Immel & Lorimier, the Chief of them, LeNez traded with us 32 Beaver 3 otter 2 Robes buffalo 3 Bladders of tallow and upwards of 300 lbs. of dried neat. Camped 1 Mile above them, killed 1 Deer distance 24 Miles.

Sunday the 19th fine Morning about 7 A.M. we took in 2 Sioux who had been hunting, belonging to a band on white River, gave us a buffaloe tounge and stayed on Board all Day, our hunters went in search of Buffaloe but found none, passed Little Cedar Island distance 18 Miles.

Monday the 20, set sail at 4 in the Morning with a fine wind the Indians left us, sailed till 10 A.M. when the wind changed and blew hard a head, at 4 P.M. met with Sioux Chief called the Sleeper and 20 Soldier had some talk and camped with them, distance 15 Miles.

Tuesday the 21, departed at Sunrise as also the Indians we stopped at a small River where 4 Sioux Chiefs came to us, the Black Sky, Black Buffaloe, Big Horse, and Crooked hand we had Counsol and they informed Mr. Manuel Lisa, that at present they had nothing to trade, but would have plenty next fall Immel went with them to their Village, 3 Chiefs and 2 young Man remained to fix on a spot for a trading house they went with us across the River to the Northside 1 Mile below where we camped, laid out the house for Mr. Bijou who was to remain to trade with the Yentonas, Tatons, Shaunee. Mr Manuel present presented the Chief with 10 Carrots of Tobacco and some Powder and Ball they were seemingly well contented, Killed 1 Buffaloe and the Indians brought also some fresh Meat.

Wednesday the 22d rose early, all hands except some lazy Rascals under pretence of being sick went to work—at 3 P.M. Mr. Immel returned with 2 young Indians, the Chief Black Sky had presented him a horse, he reported the Chiefs and warriors would be with us to morrow—he found upwards of 400 Lodges and plenty of Buffaloe in the Morning when he started from there he saw several Buffaloe enter in the Village, this Day raised part of the house, Killed 1 Deer, caught several Catfish and 1 Beaver.

Thursday the 23, early to work, but unfortunately the house fell down when nearly raised, and had to go over the same work, catched 7 fine fish in the forenoon which provided a fine Dinner, at 5 P.M. a party of Indians came opposite which we crossed and found them to be all Boys about 30 in Number they came to give us a Dance, they were all neat and handsome clothed, more so then I saw the Sioux of the Mississippi, in the Evening they danced and we gave them some Biscuit hardtack and 1 Carrot Tobacco they bought plenty Meat with them and gave plenty to the Boats. . . .

Saturday the 25, set sail at 4 in the Morning, fair wind took 6 Indians with us which we landed and stood under sail till 11 A.M. when we took the Cordell for about 1 hour dined, and set sail again, passed white River at 2 P.M. the slakening about 4 P.M. we took the Cordell again, Mr. Manuels Negro Boy Charles went out the Boat to get some grass or grasshoppers for a Prairie Dog which he had caught some days ago, he the Boy went upon the Hills unperceived, they are very high he fell down a precipice overhanging rock, precipice into the River, the Man who was steering the Mackina Boat saw it , and cried out to Mr. Lewis who was walking in the Rear of the Boats to save the Boy but Mr. Lewis unfortunately did not understand the men however saw something strugling in the water, but thought the Boy was a swimming, when the Men came towards him, they went to find the Boy, alas he was gone, he must have been stunned by the fall or otherwise would have saved himself, the River was not 4 feet deep, he drowned at 5 o'clock P.M. we searched for him some time but the Current had swept him off, cordelled a little way, crossed to an Island, set out 3 hunters, at sunset the Wind fair, set sail, took in our hunters, camped on a Sand bar the wind blowing fresh all night distance 30 Miles. . . .

5.12

James Flint Recalls the Panic of 1819 (1822)

In the early nineteenth century, the rise of the market economy transformed U.S. commerce. Americans pursued economic opportunities in national and international markets. Trade connected different regions of the nation. U.S. agriculture exports sharply increased as European demand for American grains expanded.

SOURCE: James Flint, *Letters from America: Observations on the Climate and Agriculture of the Western States, The Manners of the People, The Prospects of Emigrants, &c.* (Edinburgh, W & C Tait, 1822), 198–202.

Southern cotton planters easily sold their crops to the thriving British textile industry and to the emerging textile manufacturers in the Northeast. State banks rapidly issued paper money backed by specie (gold and silver coin), so credit was easy to obtain.

This prosperity diverted attention from risky financial practices. Because commercial farming could be unstable, farmers often borrowed money to cover their expenses, usually in addition to loans already taken to purchase land. A series of flawed federal land policies made it possible for speculators to buy huge tracts of land. These speculators split the land into manageable forty-acre plots and resold it to small farmers sometimes at very high interest rates. While land sold quickly and bank notes circulated freely, the nation's economy appeared to be booming.

Then things imploded. Bumper crops in Europe and a slump in the English economy slowed demand for American agricultural imports. U.S. farm prices plummeted. To redress the crisis, the Bank of the United States, which held scores of state bank notes, demanded payment in specie. In response, state banks called loans held by speculators and farmers—and also demanded payment in coin. These monetary policies sharply contracted credit. Land prices fell from $69 an acre to $2 an acre. Farmers lost their land. Businesses failed. Massive unemployment ensured. Although the Panic of 1819 ended relatively quickly, it left many Americans with a deep hatred of banks, illustrated the need for protective tariffs to shield U.S. factories from foreign competition, and inspired the development of more efficient methods of transportation and commerce.

In this letter, James Flint, a Scotchman who spent several years touring the United States, describes the impact of the Panic of 1819.

FOCUS QUESTIONS

1. What are some of the effects of the Panic of 1819 that Flint observes? Whom does he seem to hold responsible for the economic crisis?

2. What groups of people have been hardest hit by the economic depression?

3. How has the Panic revised Flint's views of the poor?

Jeffersonville, (Indiana) May 4, 1820

The accounts given in my last letter of the depradations committed by bankers, will make you suppose that affairs are much deranged here. Bankruptcy is now a sin prohibited by Law. In the Eastern States, and in Europe, our condition must be viewed as universal insolvency. Who, it may be asked, would give credit to a people whose laws tolerate the violation of contracts? Mutual credit and confidence are almost torn up by the roots. It is said that in China, knaves are openly commended in courts of law for the adroitness of their management. In the interior of the United States, law has removed the necessity of being either acute or honest.

The money in circulation is puzzling to traders, and, more particularly to strangers; for besides the multiplicity of banks, and the diversity in supposed value, fluctuations are so frequent, and so great, that no man who holds it in his possession can be safe for a day. The merchant, when asked the price of an article, instead of making a direct answer, usually puts the question, "What sort of money have you got?" Supposing that a number of bills are shown, and one or more are accepted of, it is not till then, that the price of the goods is declared; and an additional price is laid on, to compensate for the supposed defect in the quality of the money. Trade is stagnated—and produce cheap—and merchants find it difficult to lay in assortments of foreign manufactures. I have lately heard, that if a lady purchases a dress in the city of Cincinnati, she has to call almost all the shops in town, before she can procure trimmings of the suitable colours. . . .

Merchants in Cincinnati, as elsewhere, have got into debt, by buying property, or by building houses, but are now secure in the possession. Such people, notwithstanding, complain of the badness of the times, finding that the trade of buying without paying cannot be continued. Those who have not already secured an independence for life, may soon be willing to have trade and fair dealing as formerly. Property laws deprive creditors of the debts now due to them; but they cannot force them to give credit as they were wont to do.

Agriculture languishes—farmers cannot find profit in hiring labourers. The increase of produce in the United States is greater than any increase of consumption that may be pointed out elsewhere. To increase the quantity of provisions, then, without enlarging the numbers of those who eat them will be only diminishing the price farther. Land in these circumstances can be of no value to the capitalist who would employ his funds in farming. The spare capital of farmers is here chiefly laid out in the purchase of lands.

Labourers and mechanics are in want of employment. I think that I have seen upwards of 1500 men in quest of work within eleven months past, and many of these declared, that they had no money. Newspapers and private letters agree in stating, that wages are so low as eighteen and three-fourth cents (about ten-pence) per day, with board, at Philadelphia and some other places. Great numbers of strangers lately camped in the open near Baltimore, depending on the contributions of the charitable for subsistence.

You have no doubt heard of emigrants returning to Europe without finding the prospect of a livelihood in America. Some who have come out to this of the country do not succeed well. Labourers' wages are at present a dollar and an eighth per day. Board costs them two three-fourths or three dollars per week, and washing three-fourths of a dollar for a dozen pieces. On these terms, it is plain that they cannot live two days by the labour of one, with the other deductions which are to be taken from their wages. Clothing, for example, will cost about three times its price in Britain and the poor labourer is almost certain of being paid in depreciated money; perhaps from thirty to fifty percent, under par. I have seen several men turned out of boarding houses, where their money would not be taken. They had no other resource left but to lodge in the woods, without any covering except their clothes. They set fire to a decayed log, spread some boards alongside of it for a bed, laid a block of timber across for a pillow, and pursued their labour by day as usual. A still greater misfortune than being paid with bad money is to be guarded against, namely, that of not being paid at all. . . .

You have often heard that extreme poverty does not exist in the United States. For some time after my arrival in the country supposed to be exempt from abject misery; I never heard the term poor, (a word, by the by, not often used,) without imagining that it applied to a class in moderate circumstances, who had it not in their power to live in fine houses, indulge in foreign luxuries, and wear expensive clothing; and on seeing a person whose external appearance would have denoted a beggar in Britain, I concluded that the unfortunate must have been improvident or dissipated, or perhaps possessed of both qualities. My conjectures may have on two or three occasions been just, as people of a depressed appearance are very rarely to be seen, but I now see the propriety of divesting myself of such a hasty and ungenerous opinion. . . .

5.13

James Tallmadge Denounces Slavery in Missouri (1819)

In 1819, after simmering beneath the surface for decades, slavery exploded onto the national political stage. Thomas Jefferson compared the ensuing controversy to "a fire bell in the night" warning of impending catastrophe. With the nation divided into eleven free states and eleven slave states, Congress faced a delicate question when Missouri, a slave territory, applied for statehood. James Tallmadge, a Republican congressman from New York, complicated matters by offering an amendment that prohibited the further introduction of slaves into Missouri and emancipated, at age twenty-five, all slaves already living there. The House of Representatives, dominated by the more populous North, passed Tallmadge's amendment. The Senate, however, defeated the measure.

When Congress reconvened in December 1819, Maine, a free territory, had also applied for statehood. Henry Clay, a Republican from Kentucky, began orchestrating a series of compromises. In March 1820, Congress voted to admit Maine as a free state and Missouri as a slave state, and to ban slavery in the

SOURCE: *Annals of Congress, Fifteenth Congress Second Session,* V.I. (1819). (Washington, D.C.: Government Printing Office, 1855), 1203–1205.

remainder of the Louisiana Purchase north of latitude 36° 30'. In 1821, Missouri's attempt to bar free blacks and mulattos nearly unraveled the compromise. Henry Clay again interceded and Congress passed the Second Missouri Compromise stipulating that Missouri could not join the Union if it curtailed the rights of U.S. citizens. Missouri agreed and became a state in August 1821.

The Missouri Crisis highlighted many of the issues that consumed national politics in the following four decades. The affair exposed deep sectional differences on the question of slavery and its fate in the western territories. Northerners and Southerners accused one another of attempting to destroy the Union. The inability to resolve these differences would plunge the country into civil war.

In this speech, James Tallmadge urges the House of Representatives to end slavery in Missouri.

FOCUS QUESTIONS

1. Why has Tallmadge limited his efforts to end slavery to the Missouri Territory?

2. How have other congressmen criticized Tallmadge's proposal? How does he respond to these attacks?

3. Was the Missouri Compromise a good solution to the problems posed by westward expansion and slavery? Support your answer.

When I had the honor to submit to this House the amendment now under consideration, I accompanied it with a declaration, that it was intended to confine its operation to the newly acquired territory across the Mississippi; and I then expressly declared that I would in no manner intermeddle with the slaveholding States, nor attempt manumission in any one of the original States in the Union. Sir, I even went further, and stated that I was aware of the delicacy of the subject and that I had learned from Southern gentlemen the difficulties and the dangers of having free blacks intermingling with slaves; and on that account, and with a view to the safety of the white population of the adjoining States, I would not even advocate the prohibition of slavery in the Alabama Territory; because, surrounded as it was by slaveholding States, and with only imaginary lines of division, the intercourse between slaves and free blacks could not be prevented and a *servile* war might be the result. While we deprecate and mourn over the evil of slavery, humanity and good morals require us to wish its abolition, under circumstances consistent with the safety of the white population. Willingly, therefore, will I submit to an evil which we cannot safely remedy. I admitted all that had been said of the danger of having free blacks visible to slaves, and therefore did not hesitate to pledge myself that I would neither advise nor attempt to coercive manumission. But, sir, all these reasons cease when we cross the banks of the Mississippi, a newly acquired territory, never contemplated in the formation of our Government, not included within the compromise or mutual pledge in the adoption of our Constitution, a new territory acquired by our common fund, and ought justly to be subject to our common legislation.

Sir, when I submitted the amendment now under consideration, accompanied with these explanations, and with these avowals of my intentions and of my motives, I did expect that gentlemen who might differ from me in my opinion would appreciate the liberality of my views, and would meet me with moderation, as upon a fair subject for legislation. Sir, I did expect at least that the frank declaration of my views would protect me from harsh expressions, and from the unfriendly imputations which have been cast out on this occasion. But, sir, such has been the character and the violence of this debate, and expressions of so much intemperance, and of an aspect so threatening have been used, that continued silence on my part would ill become me, who had submitted to this House the original proposition. . . .

Sir, the honorable gentleman from Missouri, (Mr. Scott,) who has just resumed his seat, has told us the *Ides of March*, and has cautioned us to "*beware of the fate of Caesar and of Rome.*" Another gentleman, (Mr. Coss) from Georgia, in addition to other expressions of great warmth, has said, "that, if we persist, the Union will be dissolved:" and with a look fixed on me, has told us, "we have kindled a fire which all the waters of the ocean cannot put out, which seas of blood can only distinguish."

Sir, language of this sort has no effect on me; my purpose is fixed, it is interwoven with my existence, its durability is limited with my life, it is a great and glorious cause, setting bounds to a slavery the most cruel and debasing the world ever witnessed; it is freedom of man; it is the cause of unredeemed and unregenerated human beings.

Sir, if dissolution of the Union must take place, let it be so! If civil war, which gentlemen so much threaten must come, I can only say, let it come! My hold on life is probably as frail as that of any man who now hears me; but while the hold lasts, it shall be devoted to the service of my country—to the freedom of man. If blood is necessary to extinguish any fire which I have assisted to kindle, I can assure you, gentlemen, while I regret the necessity, I shall not forbear to continue my mite. Sir, the violence to which gentlemen have resorted on this subject will not move my purpose, nor drive me from my stand here as the representative of freemen, who possess intelligence to know their rights, who have the spirit to maintain them. Whatever might be my own private sentiments on this subject, standing here as the representative of others, no choice is left me. I know the will of my constituents, and regardless of consequences, I will avow it; as their representative, I will proclaim their hatred to slavery in every shape; as their representative, here I will hold my stand, until this floor, with the Constitution of my country which supports it, shall sink beneath me. If I am doomed to fall, I shall at least have the painful consolation to believe that I fall, as a fragment, in the ruins of my country.

5.14

The Monroe Doctrine (1823)

On December 2, 1823, President James Monroe addressed Congress on the American role in international affairs. Concerned that European powers might attempt to restore Spain's newly independent colonies in Latin America, British foreign minister George Canning had suggested that the United States and Great Britain issue a joint declaration opposing future colonization efforts in the Western Hemisphere. Although the nation lacked the military power to enforce such a policy on its own, Secretary of State John Quincy Adams persuaded Monroe to issue an exclusively American proclamation. As the United States became a global power, it zealously enforced the Monroe Doctrine.

FOCUS QUESTIONS

1. What are the major components of the Monroe Doctrine?
2. Does the Monroe Doctrine still affect U.S. foreign policy? Explain your answer.

... [T]he occasion has been judged proper for asserting, as a principle in which the rights and interests of the United States are involved, that the American continents, by the free and independent condition which they have assumed and maintain, are henceforth not to be considered as subjects for future colonization by any European powers....

The citizens of the United States cherish sentiments the most friendly in favor of the liberty and happiness of their fellow-men on that side of the Atlantic. In the wars of the European powers in matters relating to themselves we have never taken any part, nor does it comport with our policy to do so. It is only when our rights are invaded or seriously menaced that we resent injuries or make preparation for our defense. With the movements in this hemisphere we are of necessity more immediately connected, and by causes which must be obvious to all enlightened and impartial observers. The political system of the allied powers is essentially different in this respect from that of America.... We

SOURCE: Published by the Avalon Project at the Yale University Law School,
http://www.yale.edu/lawweb/avalon/monroe.htm

owe it, therefore, to candor and to the amicable relations existing between the United States and those powers to declare that we should consider any attempt on their part to extend their system to any portion of this hemisphere as dangerous to our peace and safety. With the existing colonies or dependencies of any European power we have not interfered and shall not interfere. But with the Governments who have declared their independence and maintain it, and whose independence we have, on great consideration and on just principles, acknowledged, we could not view any interposition for the purpose of oppressing them, or controlling in any other manner their destiny, by any European power in any other light than as the manifestation of an unfriendly disposition toward the United States. In the war between those new Governments and Spain we declared our neutrality at the time of their recognition, and to this we have adhered, and shall continue to adhere, provided no change shall occur which, in the judgment of the competent authorities of this Government, shall make a corresponding change on the part of the United States indispensable to their security. . . .

The late events in Spain and Portugal show that Europe is still unsettled. . . . Our policy in regard to Europe, which was adopted at an early stage of the wars which have so long agitated that quarter of the globe, nevertheless remains the same, which is, not to interfere in the internal concerns of any of its powers; to consider the government *de facto* as the legitimate government for us; to cultivate friendly relations with it, and to preserve those relations by a frank, firm, and manly policy, meeting in all instances the just claims of every power, submitting to injuries from none. But in regard to those continents circumstances are eminently and conspicuously different.

It is impossible that the allied powers should extend their political system to any portion of either continent without endangering our peace and happiness; nor can anyone believe that our southern brethren, if left to themselves, would adopt it of their own accord. It is equally impossible, therefore, that we should behold such interposition in any form with indifference. If we look to the comparative strength and resources of Spain and those new Governments, and their distance from each other, it must be obvious that she can never subdue them. It is still the true policy of the United States to leave the parties to themselves, in hope that other powers will pursue the same course. . . .

5.15

Henry Clay Calls for Economic Development (1824)

As the market economy grew, politicians explored several ways to foster national prosperity. Henry Clay (1777–1852) was one of the nineteenth century's political giants. Born in Virginia, Clay studied law and moved to Kentucky. Armed with a sharp intellect and a gift for oratory, Clay entered state politics. In 1811, he won election to the U.S. House of Representatives as a Republican. He immediately became one of the "War Hawks" who pushed the country into the War of 1812. In 1814, he served as one of the peace commissioners who drafted the Treaty of Ghent, ending the conflict. Throughout his illustrious political career in the House and later the U.S. Senate, Clay earned the nickname "The Great Compromiser" for his uncanny ability to craft agreements on thorny issues.

Clay was one of the nation's staunchest advocates of economic development. His calls for an "American System" based on publicly funded internal improvements, a protective tariff, a national bank, manufacturing, and land distribution won Clay powerful allies—and enemies. In the 1824 presidential election, his decision to throw his support behind John Quincy Adams enraged Andrew Jackson. When Adams appointed Clay secretary of state shortly thereafter, Jackson's men accused the duo of striking a "corrupt bargain." After briefly retiring from public life, Clay won a seat in the U.S. Senate in 1831. The following year, he ran unsuccessfully as the Republican candidate for president. A passionate opponent of Jacksonian policies, Clay became a leader in the Whig Party.

In this speech to the House of Representatives, Clay proposes federal support for an ambitious program of internal improvements.

FOCUS QUESTIONS

1. Why does Clay believe that the federal government has the constitutional power to fund internal improvements? How does he respond to critics of these views?

SOURCE: "On Internal Improvement," In the House of Representatives, January 16, 1824, *Life and Speeches of Henry Clay* (New York: James B. Swain, 1842), I:179–184.

2. Which region does Clay believe will benefit most from his program? Why does he think that developing this region will benefit the nation as a whole?

3. Was Clay correct in asserting that the federal government should promote commerce and internal improvements? Why do you think many Americans opposed Clay's economic plan? Support your answers.

January 16, 1824

Of all the powers bestowed on this government, none are more clearly vested, than that to regulate the distribution of the intelligence, private and official, of the country; to regulate the distribution of commerce; and to regulate the distribution of the physical force of the Union. In the execution of the high and solemn trust which these beneficial powers imply, we must look to the great ends which the framers of our admirable constitution had, in view. We must reject, as wholly incompatible with their enlightened and beneficent intentions, that construction of these powers which would resuscitate all the debility and inefficiency of the ancient confederacy. In the vicissitudes of human affairs, who can foresee all the possible cases, in which it may be necessary to apply the public force, within or without the Union? This government is charged with the use of it, to repel invasions, to suppress insurrections, to enforce the laws of the Union; in short, for all the unknown and undefinable purposes of war, foreign or intestine, wherever and however it may rage. During its existence, may not government, for its effectual prosecution, order a road to be made, or a canal to be cut, to relieve, for example, an exposed point of the Union? If, when the emergency comes, there is a power to provide for it, that power must exist in the constitution, and not in the emergency. A wise, precautionary, and parental policy, anticipating danger, will beforehand provide for the hour of need. Roads and canals are in the nature of fortifications, since, if not the deposits of military resources, they enable you to bring into rapid action the military resources of the country, whatever they may be. They are better than any fortifications, because they serve the double purposes of peace and of war. . . .

I was much surprised at one argument of the honorable gentleman [Virginia representative Barbour]. He told the House, that the constitution had carefully guarded against inequality, among the several States, in the public burdens, by certain restrictions upon taxation; that the effect of the adoption of a system of internal improvements would be to draw the resources from one part of the Union, and to expend them in the improvements of another; and that the spirit, at least, of the constitutional equality would be thus violated. From the nature of things, the constitution could not specify the theatre of the expenditure of the public treasure. That expenditure, guided by and looking to the public good, must be made, necessarily, where it will most subserve the interests of the whole Union. The argument is, that the *locale* of the collection of the public contributions, and the *locale* of their disbursement, should be the same. Now, sir, let us carry this argument out. . . .

The locale of the collection of the public revenue is the pocket of the citizen; and, to abstain from the violation of the principle of equality adverted to by the gentleman, we should restore back into each man's pocket precisely what was taken from it. If the principle contended for be true, we are habitually violating it. We raise about twenty millions of dollars, a very large revenue, considering the actual distresses of the country. And, sir, notwithstanding all the puffing, flourishing statements of its prosperity, emanating from printers who are fed upon the pap of the public treasury, the whole country is in a condition of very great distress. Where is this vast revenue expended? Boston, New York, the great capitals of the north, are the theatres of its disbursement. There the interest upon the public debt is paid. There the expenditure in the building, equipment, and repair of the national vessels takes place. There all the great expenditures of the government necessarily concentrate. This is no cause of just complaint. It is inevitable, resulting from the accumulation of capital, the state of the arts, and other circumstances belonging to our great cities. . . . Internal improvements of that general, federative character, for which we contend, would also be for the interest of the whole. . . .

But, Mr. Chairman, if there be any part of this Union more likely than all others to be benefited by the adoption of the gentleman's principle, regulating the public expenditure, it is the west. There is a perpetual drain, from that embarrassed and highly distressed portion of our country, of its circulating medium to the east. There, but few and inconsiderable expenditures of the public money take place. There we have none of those public works, no magnificent edifices, forts, armories, arsenals, dockyards, &c., which, more or less, are to be found in every Atlantic State. In at least seven States beyond the Alleghany, not one solitary public work of this government is to be found. If, by one of those awful and terrible dispensations of Providence which sometimes occur, this government should be annihilated, everywhere on the seaboard traces of its former existence would be found; whilst we should not have, in the west, a single monument remaining, on which to pour out our affections and our regrets. Yet, sir, we do not complain. No portion of your population is more loyal to the Union, than the hardy freemen of the west. Nothing can weaken or eradicate their ardent desire for its lasting preservation. None are more prompt to vindicate the interests and rights of the nation from all foreign aggression. Need I remind you of the glorious scenes in which they participated during the late war—a war in which they had no peculiar or direct interest, waged for no commerce, no seamen of theirs. But it was enough for them that it was a war demanded by the character and the honor of the nation. They did not stop to calculate its cost of blood or of treasure. They flew to arms; they rushed down the valley of the Mississippi, with all the impetuosity of that noble river. They sought the enemy. They found him at the beach. They fought; they bled; they covered themselves and their country with immortal glory. They enthusiastically shared in all the transports occasioned by our victories, whether won on the ocean or on the land. They felt, with the keenest distress, whatever disaster befell us. No, sir, I repeat its neglect, injury itself, cannot alienate the affections of the west from this government. They cling to it, as to their best, their greatest, their last hope. You may impoverish them, reduce them to ruin by the mistakes of your policy, and you cannot drive them from you. They do not complain of the expenditure of the public money where the public exigencies require its disbursement. But, I put it to your candor, if you ought not, by a generous and national policy, to mitigate, if not prevent, the evils resulting from the perpetual transfer of the circulating medium from the west to the east. One million and a half of dollars annually is transferred for the public lands alone; and almost every dollar goes, like him who goes to death—to a bourne from which no traveller returns. In ten years it will amount to fifteen millions; in twenty, to—but I will not pursue the appalling results of arithmetic.

Gentlemen who believe that these vast sums are supplied by emigrants from the east, labor under great error. There was a time when the tide of emigration from the east bore along with it the means to effect the purchase of the public domain. But that tide has, in a great measure, now stopped. And, as population advances farther and farther west; it will entirely cease. The greatest migrating States in the Union, at this time, are Kentucky first, Ohio next, and Tennessee. The emigrants from those States carry with them, to the States and Territories lying beyond them, the circulating medium, which, being invested in the purchase of the public land, is transmitted to the points where the wants of government require it. If this debilitating and exhausting process were inevitable, it must be borne with manly fortitude. But we think that a fit exertion of the powers of this government would mitigate the evil. We believe that the government incontestably possesses the constitutional power to execute such internal improvements as are called for by the good of the whole. And we appeal to your equity, to your parental regard, to your enlightened policy, to perform the high and beneficial trust thus sacredly reposed. . . .

But, sir, the bill on your table is no western bill. It is emphatically a national bill, comprehending all, looking to the interests of the whole. The people of the west never thought of, never desired, never asked for, a system exclusively for their benefit. The system contemplated by this bill looks to great national objects, and proposes the ultimate application to their accomplishment of the only means by which they can be effected, the means of the nation—means which, if they be withheld from such objects, the Union, I do most solemnly believe, of these now happy and promising States, may, at some distant (I trust a far, far distant) day, be endangered and shaken at its centre.

6

✳

Antebellum Politics and Reform

The years between 1820 and 1850 marked sweeping changes in virtually every aspect of American life. Western expansion, industry, agriculture, and transportation fueled spectacular economic growth. But the nation's financial success also brought new problems. The gap between rich and poor expanded. Unsound financial practices created devastating depressions. White demands for Indian lands intensified. Sectional disputes over slavery and the role of the federal government deepened.

Americans searched for ways to adapt to these events. As people challenged traditional authorities and established new social organizations, politics became more inclusive. With the rise of universal white male suffrage, politicians had to court potential supporters through campaigns, rallies, and speeches. A second American party system emerged with the Whigs and Democrats replacing the Federalists and Republicans. Despite these changes, the political system still excluded large numbers of people. Women and free blacks could not vote. Parties avoided difficult issues such as slavery and women's rights.

Reformers hoped to ameliorate social and economic inequities. Usually inspired by religious convictions, reformers worked on causes ranging from temperance to abolition. Their efforts to build a more just nation created new arenas for people to develop leadership skills and forced political officials to address controversial subjects. While the reformers were occasionally self-righteous, they also aided many of the nation's disadvantaged.

THEMES TO CONSIDER

- The elements, limitations, and implications of the rise of democracy
- The professionalization of American political parties and the onset of political campaigning
- The significance of and contradictions within Andrew Jackson's presidency
- The intensification of and resistance to white encroachment upon Indian lands
- Debates over the proper scope of federal authority
- The origins and aims of antebellum reform movements
- The changes workers faced in an industrializing society
- The intensification of challenges to slavery, racism, and gender inequality

6.1

Margaret Bayard Smith on Andrew Jackson's Inaugural (1829)

Throughout the 1820s, many states extended suffrage to all white men. The resulting democratization greatly aided the political career of Andrew Jackson. Born to a poor family in South Carolina, Jackson studied law and moved to Nashville. Extremely successful in forging alliances with wealthy landowners, Jackson helped draft the Tennessee constitution and later represented the state in the U.S. Congress. During the War of 1812, Jackson's defeat of the Creek Indians and his triumph in the Battle of New Orleans made him a national hero.

In 1824, Jackson ran for the presidency against William Crawford, John Quincy Adams, and Henry Clay. Although Jackson received the most electoral votes, he did not have a majority, and it fell to the House of Representatives to determine the victor. After Clay threw his support behind Adams, Jackson lost. Adams became president and made Clay his secretary

SOURCE: Margaret Bayard Smith, *The First Forty Years of Washington Society*, ed. Gaillard Hunt (New York, 1906), 290–298.

of state. Jackson's supporters derided the "corrupt bargain" and clamored for Jackson to run again.

The Election of 1828 was vicious. Adams's supporters called Jackson a murderer, an adulterer, and illiterate. Jackson's camp retorted by deriding Adams as an aristocrat who wore silk underwear. They presented Jackson as a man of the common people. Despite Jackson's wealth and ties to Tennessee elites, the tactic worked, and Jackson won handily, especially among Southern and Western voters.

In this passage, Margaret Bayard Smith, wife of U.S. senator Samuel Smith, describes Jackson's inauguration.

FOCUS QUESTIONS

1. How does Smith describe Washington, D.C., during the inauguration?
2. What does Jackson do after taking the oath of office?
3. How do these events reflect changes in American politics?

I left the rest of this sheet for an account of the inauguration.... Thousands and thousands of people, without distinction of rank, collected in an immense mass round the Capitol, silent, orderly and tranquil, with their eyes fixed on the front of that edifice, waiting the appearance of the President in the portico. The door from the Rotunda opens, preceded by the marshals, surrounded by the Judges of the Supreme Court, the old man with his grey locks, that crown of glory, advances, bows to the people, who greet him with a shout that rends the air, the Cannons, from the heights around, from Alexandria and Fort Warburton proclaim the oath he has taken and all the hills, reverberate the sound. It was grand,—it was sublime! An almost breathless silence, succeeded and the multitude was still,—listening to catch the sound of his voice, tho' it was so low, as to be heard only by those nearest to him. After reading his speech, the oath was administered to him by the Chief Justice. The Marshal presented the Bible. The President took it from his hands, pressed his lips to it, laid it reverently down, then bowed again to the people—Yes, to the people in all their majesty, rising to sublimity, and far surpassing the majesty of Kings and Princes, surrounded with armies and glittering in gold. I will not anticipate, but will give you an account of the inauguration in mere detail. The whole of the proceeding day, immense crowds were coming into the city from all parts, lodgings could not be obtained, and the newcomers had to go to George Town, which soon overflowed and others had to go to Alexandria. I was told the Avenue and adjoining streets were so crowded on Tuesday afternoon that it was difficult to pass....

By ten o'clock the Avenue was crowded with carriages of every description, from the splendid Barronet and coach, down to wagons and carts, filled with women and children, some in finery and some in rags, for it was the people's President, and all would see him; the men all walked. . . .

At last he enters the gate at the foot of the hill and turns to the road that leads round to the front of the Capitol. In a moment every one who until then had stood like statues gazing on the scene below them, rushed onward, to right, to left, to be ready to receive him in the front. . . . The Capitol in all its grandeur and beauty. The Portico and grand steps leading to it, were filled with ladies. Scarlet, purple, blue, yellow, white draperies and waving plumes of every kind and color, among the white marble pillars, had a fine effect. In the center of the portico was a table covered with scarlet, behind it the closed door leading into the rotunda, below the Capitol and all around, a mass of living beings, not a ragged mob, but well dressed and well behaved respectable and worthy citizens.

6.2

Davy Crockett, Advice to Politicians (1833)

As the American political system became more democratic, politicians appealed to potential voters. With the help of their party organizations, candidates hosted barbeques, rallies, and picnics to gain audiences for political speeches. Frequent elections ensured that politicians molded their positions to popular opinion.

Like Andrew Jackson, Davy Crockett was a frontier hero who became a politician. Born in Tennessee, Crockett had little formal education. Earning notoriety in the Creek War (1813–1815), Crockett was elected to the Tennessee legislature in 1821. Between 1825 and 1835, he won and lost several campaigns for the U.S. House of Representatives. Lacing his speeches with stories of hunting and Indian fighting, Crockett adopted a folksy political style. After losing his congressional seat in 1835, he headed to Texas. He died in the Battle of the Alamo the following year.

In this reading, Crockett dispenses advice for politicians in Jacksonian America.

SOURCE: David Crockett, *Exploits and Adventures in Texas* (1836), 56–59.

FOCUS QUESTIONS

1. What suggestions does Crockett make for winning political office?
2. What does Crockett say politicians should do once they are elected?
3. What does his advice indicate about politics of the day? Do you see any similarities to our current political candidates and campaigns? Explain your answer.

"Attend all public meetings," says I, "and get some friend to move that you take the chair. If you fail in this attempt, make a push to be appointed secretary. The proceeding of course will be published, and your name is introduced to the public. But should you fail in both undertakings, get two or three acquaintances, over a bottle of whisky, to pass some resolutions, no matter on what subject. Publish them, even if you pay the printer. It will answer the purpose of breaking the ice, which is the main point in these matters."

"Intrigue until you are elected an officer of the militia. This is the second step toward promotion, and can be accomplished with ease, as I know an instance of an election being advertised, and no one attending, the innkeeper at whose house it was to be held, having a military turn, elected himself colonel of his regiment." Says I, "You may not accomplish your ends with as little difficulty, but do not be discouraged—Rome wasn't built in a day."

"If your ambition or circumstances compel you to serve your country and earn three dollars a day, by becoming a member of the legislature, you must first publicly avow that the constitution of the state is a shackle upon free and liberal legislation, and is, therefore, of as little use in the present enlightened age as an old almanac of the year in which the instrument was framed. There is policy in this measure, for by making the constitution a mere dead letter, your headlong proceedings will be attributed to a bold and unshackled mind; whereas, it might otherwise be thought they arose from sheer mulish ignorance. 'The Government' has set the example in his [Jackson's] attack upon the Constitution of the United States, and who should fear to follow where 'the Government' leads?"

"When the day of election approaches, visit your constituents far and wide. Treat liberally, and drink freely, in order to rise in their estimation, though you fall in your own. True, you may be called a drunken dog by some of the clean-shirt and silk-stocking gentry, but the real roughnecks will style you a jovial fellow. Their votes are certain, and frequently count double."

"Do all you can to appear to advantage in the eyes of the women. That's easily done. You have but to kiss and slabber [slobber over] their children, wipe their noses, and pat them on the head. This cannot fail to please their mothers, and you may rely on your business being done in that quarter."

"Promise all that is asked," said I, "and more if you can think of anything. Offer to build a bridge or a church, to divide a county, create a batch of new offices, make a turnpike, or anything they like. Promises cost nothing; therefore, deny nobody who has a vote or sufficient influence to obtain one."

"Get up on all occasions, and sometimes on no occasion at all, and make long-winded speeches, though composed of nothing else than wind. Talk of your devotion to your country, your modesty and disinterestedness, or on any such fanciful subject. Rail against taxes of all kinds, officeholders, and bad harvest weather; and wind up with a flourish about the heroes who fought and bled for our liberties in the times that tried men's souls. To be sure, you run the risk of being considered a bladder of wind, or an empty barrel. But never mind that; you will find enough of the same fraternity to keep you in countenance."

"If any charity be going forward, be at the top of it, provided it is to be advertised publicly. If not, it isn't worth your while. None but a fool would place his candle under a bushel on such an occasion."

"These few directions," said I, "if properly attended to, will do your business. And when once elected—why, a fig for the dirty children, the promises, the bridges, the churches, the taxes, the offices, and the subscriptions. For it is absolutely necessary to forget all these before you can become a thoroughgoing politician, and a patriot of the first water."

6.3

George Caleb Bingham, *County Election* (1852)

The democratization of American politics necessitated changes in politicians' styles and attitudes. Where they had formerly viewed themselves as gentlemen acting on behalf of the common people, politicians now responded directly to popular demand. The expansion of voting rights, the adoption of written ballots, and an increase in the number of elected offices required political figures to interact closely with potential supporters.

Many of the paintings of George Caleb Bingham (1811–1879) demonstrate this transformation. Raised in Missouri, Bingham was a largely self-taught artist captivated by the frontier. Works such as Jolly Flatboatman in Port *(1857) and*

SOURCE: George Caleb Bingham, *County Election*, d. 1852. Oil on canvas, 38" x 52." Saint Louis Art Museum, gift of Bank of America.

Fur Traders Descending the Missouri *(circa 1845) vividly portray river life in the Midwest. His fascination with politics is evident in* Canvassing for a Vote *(1852) and* Stump Speaking *(1852). Bingham's technical prowess, composition, and lyricism made him one of the leading painters of antebellum America. In the late 1850s, Bingham studied in Germany with masters of the Düsseldorf school. Emulating their attention to detail and sentimentality, Bingham adopted a drier and less critically acclaimed style. After returning to Missouri, he entered state politics, serving as treasurer in 1862 and as adjutant general in 1875. He spent the remainder of his life as a professor of art at the University of Missouri.*

FOCUS QUESTIONS

1. How does this painting reflect political life in antebellum America?
2. What is striking about the individuals depicted here? Who is not represented?
3. How would an image of a modern political rally compare to Bingham's?

6.4

The Cherokees Resist Removal (1830)

By the 1820s, white demands for Indian lands had reached fever pitch. They rejected the federal government's "civilization" policy that permitted Indians who embraced white culture to retain their lands. Andrew Jackson, a notorious Indian hater, argued that the government was not obliged to honor its treaties with Indian nations. His position was very popular among the Southerners and Westerners who helped him win the presidency in 1828.

Determined to honor this political debt, President Jackson implemented a coercive removal policy in 1829. In 1830, Jackson persuaded Congress to pass the Indian Removal Act, granting the president authority to remove Indians forcibly if necessary. At the same time, Southern states moved against local tribes. After the discovery of gold on Cherokee property, the Georgia legislature attempted to invalidate Cherokee laws and to confiscate tribal lands.

These developments infuriated the Cherokee. Having adopted white culture more than any other tribe, the Cherokee farmed, owned slaves, had a written language and legal code, and embraced evangelical Christianity. They appealed to the U.S. Supreme Court to stop Georgia's actions. In Worcester v. Georgia (1832), the Court ruled on behalf of the Cherokee, claiming that no state had the right to invalidate a federal treaty made with a "domestic dependent nation." Jackson ignored the ruling. In 1835, federal officials negotiated the Treaty of New Echota with a small group of Cherokee. The treaty ceded all Cherokee lands east of the Mississippi in exchange for $5.6 million and relocation. Other Cherokees later murdered those who signed the agreement. Between 1835 and 1838, approximately 15,000 Cherokee were moved westward to the Indian Territory. About 4,000 died on the so-called Trail of Tears.

In this selection, the Cherokees protest the state of Georgia's attempts to relocate them.

FOCUS QUESTIONS

1. Why do the Cherokees reject the removal policy? Give several examples.

2. Compare the Cherokees' arguments to those made by Andrew Jackson (Document 6.5). Whose position do you find most persuasive? Explain your answer.

SOURCE: "Memorial of the Cherokee Nation," *Niles Weekly Register*, Vol. 38 (August 21, 1830), pp. 454–457.

We are aware, that some persons suppose it will be for our advantage to remove beyond the Mississippi. We think otherwise. Our people universally think otherwise. Thinking that it would be fatal to their interests, they have almost to a man sent their memorial to congress, deprecating the necessity of a removal. This question was distinctly before their minds when they signed their memorial. Not an adult person can be found, who has not an opinion on the subject, and if the people were to understand distinctly, that they could be protected against the laws of the neighboring states, there is probably not an adult person in the nation, who would think it best to remove; though possibly a few might emigrate individually. There are doubtless many, who would flee to an unknown country, however beset with dangers, privations and sufferings, rather than be sentenced to spend six years in a Georgia prison for advising one of their neighbors not to betray his country. And there are others who could not think of living as outlaws in their native land, exposed to numberless vexations, and excluded from being parties or witnesses in a court of justice. It is incredible that Georgia should ever have enacted the oppressive laws to which reference is here made, unless she had supposed that something extremely terrific in its character was necessary in order to make the Cherokees willing to remove. We are not willing to remove; and if we could be brought to this extremity, it would be not by argument, not because our judgment was satisfied, not because our condition will be improved; but only because we cannot endure to be deprived of our national and individual rights and subjected to a process of intolerable oppression.

We wish to remain on the land of our fathers. We have a perfect and original right to remain without interruption or molestation. The treaties with us, and laws of the United States made in pursuance of treaties, guarantee our residence and our privileges, and secure us against intruders. Our only request is, that these treaties may be fulfilled, and these laws executed. . . .

The removal of families to a new country, even under the most favorable auspices, and when the spirits are sustained by pleasing visions of the future, is attended with much depression of mind and sinking of heart. This is the case, when the removal is a matter of decided preference, and when the persons concerned are in early youth or vigorous manhood. Judge, then, what must be the circumstances of a removal, when a whole community, embracing persons of all classes and every description, from the infant to the man of extreme old age, the sick, the blind, the lame, the improvident, the reckless, the desperate, as well as the prudent, the considerate, the industrious, are compelled to remove by odious and intolerable vexations and persecutions, brought upon them in the forms of law, when all will agree only in this, that they have been cruelly robbed of their country, in violation of the most solemn compacts, which it is possible for communities to form with each other; and that, if they should make themselves comfortable in their new residence, they have nothing to expect hereafter but to be the victims of a future legalized robbery!

Such we deem, and are absolutely certain, will be the feeling of the whole Cherokee people, if they are forcibly compelled, by the laws of Georgia, to remove; and with these feelings, how is it possible that we should pursue our present course of improvement, or avoid sinking in to utter despondency? We have been called a poor, ignorant, and degraded people. We certainly are not rich; nor have we ever boasted of our knowledge, or our moral or intellectual elevation. But there is not a man within our limits so ignorant as not to know that he has a right to live on the land of his fathers, in the possession of his immemorial privileges, and that this right has been acknowledged and guaranteed by the United States; nor is there a man so degraded as not to feel a keen sense of injury, on being deprived of this right and driven into exile.

6.5

Andrew Jackson's Second Annual Message to Congress (1830)

Andrew Jackson's actions toward American Indians were among the most controversial features of his presidency. Making no secret of his disdain for Indians, Jackson instituted a relocation policy guaranteed to please his Southern and Western constituents. Despite his vigorous defense of federal authority in the nullification crisis, Jackson deferred to the states on Indian issues. When the Supreme Court ruled for the Cherokees in Worcester v. Georgia *(1832), Jackson allegedly declared "[Chief Justice] John Marshall has made his decision, now let him enforce it!" Jackson's racist attitudes and failure to abide the Court's ruling drew widespread criticism, particularly among Northern missionaries and philanthropists who supported the Cherokees.*

In this excerpt, Jackson explains his policy on Indian removal.

FOCUS QUESTIONS

1. Why does Jackson support Indian relocation?
2. How does he view the Indians?

SOURCE: Andrew Jackson, Second Annual Message, December 6, 1830, in James
D. Richardson, ed. *A Compilation of the Messages and Papers of the Presidents, 1789–1897*
(Washington, D.C.: Government Printing Office, 1896), Vol. 2, pp. 519–523.

3. Compare Jackson's arguments to those made by the Cherokees (Document 6.4). Whose position do you find most persuasive? Explain your answer.

It gives me pleasure to announce to Congress that the benevolent policy of the Government, steadily pursued for nearly thirty years, in relation to the removal of the Indians beyond the white settlements is approaching...a happy consummation. Two important tribes, [the Choctaws and the Chickasaws], have accepted the provision made for their removal at the last session of Congress, and it [is] believed that their example will induce the remaining tribes also to see the same obvious advantages.

The consequences of a speedy removal will be important to the United States, to individual States, and to the Indians themselves. The pecuniary advantages which it promises to the Government are the least of its recommendations. It puts an end to all possible danger of collision between the authorities of the General and State Governments on account of the Indians. It will place a dense and civilized population in large tracts of country now occupied by a few savage hunters. By opening the whole territory between Tennessee on the north and Louisiana on the south to the settlement of the whites it will incalculably strengthen the southwestern frontier and render the adjacent States strong enough to repel future invasions without remote aid. It will relieve the whole State of Mississippi and the western part of Alabama of Indian occupancy, and enable those States to advance rapidly in population, wealth, and power. It will separate the Indians from immediate contact with settlements of whites; free them from the power of the States; enable them to pursue happiness in their own way and under their own rude institutions; will retard the progress of decay, which is lessening their numbers, and perhaps cause them gradually, under the protection of the Government and through the influence of good counsels, to cast off their savage habits and become an interesting, civilized, and Christian community....

It is...a duty which this Government owes to the new States to extinguish as soon as possible the Indian title to all lands which Congress themselves have included within their limits. When this is done the duties of the General Government in relation to the States and the Indians within their limits are at an end. The Indians may leave the State or not, as they choose. The purchase of their lands does not alter in the least their personal relations with the State government. No act of the General Government has ever been deemed necessary to give the States jurisdiction over the persons of the Indians. That they possess by virtue of their sovereign power within their own limits in as full a manner before as after the purchase of the Indian lands; nor can this Government add to or diminish it.

6.6

John C. Calhoun, *South Carolina Exposition and Protest* (1828)

In 1828, Congress passed a high protective tariff that benefited Western farmers and Northern manufacturers. Angered by increased prices of manufactured goods and fearful of retaliatory tariffs on cotton exports, Southerners denounced the "Tariff of Abominations." Convinced that tariffs harmed his native state South Carolina, Vice President John C. Calhoun (1782–1850) was one of the tariff's most acerbic critics. He and other Southerners claimed that federal intervention on tariffs could lead to interference with slavery.

In 1828, Calhoun anonymously authored South Carolina Exposition and Protest, *outlining his theory of nullification. Three years later, Calhoun openly recommended that South Carolina not enforce the Tariff of 1828. His remarks and presidential ambitions exacerbated a political feud with President Andrew Jackson. The ensuing nullification crisis was resolved when Congress lowered tariffs and authorized the president to use force to collect customs duties in South Carolina. Although South Carolina did not renounce the doctrine of nullification, it accepted the compromise tariff and avoided a showdown with the federal government. In 1832, Calhoun resigned the vice presidency and represented South Carolina in the U.S. Senate until his death.*

FOCUS QUESTIONS

1. Why is South Carolina so opposed to the Tariff of 1828?

2. What does Calhoun believe is the proper response to the tariff? On what legal basis does he make this recommendation?

3. How do Calhoun's views compare to those of Daniel Webster (Document 6.7)? With whom do you most agree? Explain your answer.

SOURCE: "S.C. Protest: Committee Version," *The Papers of John C. Calhoun*, Vol. 10, *1825–1829*, eds. Clyde N. Wilson and W. Edwin Hemphill (Columbia, CS, 1977), 535–539. Reprinted with permission of the University of South Carolina Press.

December 19, 1828

The Senate and House of Representatives of South Carolina, now met and sitting in General Assembly ... do, in the name and on behalf of the good people of the said Commonwealth, solemnly protest against the system of protecting duties lately adopted by the Federal Government, for the following reasons:

1. Because the good people of this Commonwealth believe that the powers of Congress were delegated to it in trust for the accomplishment of certain specified objects which limit and control them, and that every exercise of them for any other purposes is a violation of the Constitution as unwarrantable as the undisguised assumption of substantive independent powers not granted or expressly withheld.

2. Because the power to lay duties on imports is, and in its nature can only be, only a means of effecting objects specified by the Constitution; since, no free government, and least of all a government of enumerated powers, can of right impose any tax (any more than a penalty,) which is not at once justified by public necessity, and clearly within the scope and purview of the social compact, and since the right of confining appropriations of the public money to such legitimate and constitutional objects, is as essential to the liberties of the people, as their unquestionable privilege to be taxed only by their own consent.

3. Because they believe that the Tariff Law, passed by Congress at its last session, and all other acts of which the principal object is the protection of manufacturers, or any other branch or domestic industry ... is a violation of these fundamental principles, a breach of a well defined trust and a perversion of the high powers vested in the Federal Government for Federal purposes only.

4. Because such acts considered in the lights of a regulation of commerce are equally liable to objection ... since the encouragement of domestic industry implies an absolute control over all the interests, resources and pursuits of a people, and is inconsistent with the idea of any other than a simple consolidated government.

5. Because from the contemporaneous exposition of the Constitution, in the numbers of the Federalist, (which is cited only because the Supreme Court has recognized its authority,) it is clear that the power to regulate commerce was considered by the convention as only incidentally connected with the encouragement of agriculture and manufactures; and because the power of laying imposts and duties on imports, was not understood to justify in any case a prohibition of foreign commodities, except as a means of extending commerce by coercing foreign nations to a fair reciprocity in their intercourse with us, or for some bona fide commercial purpose.

6. Because that whilst the power to protect manufactures is no where expressly granted to Congress, nor can be considered as necessary and proper to carry

into effect any specified power, it seems to be expressly reserved to the States by the tenth section of the first article of the Constitution.

7. Because even admitting Congress to have a constitutional right to protect manufactures by the imposition of the duties or by regulations of commerce, . . . yet a Tariff of which the operation is grossly unequal and oppressive, is such an abuse of power, as is incompatible with the principles of a free government and the great ends of civil society, justice and equality of rights and protection.

8. Finally, because South Carolina, from her climate, situation, and peculiar institutions, is, and must ever continue to be, wholly dependent upon agriculture and commerce, not only for her prosperity, but for her very existence as a state—because the valuable products of her soil—the blessings by which Divine Providence seems to have designed to compensate for the great disadvantages under which she suffers in other respects—are among the very few that can be cultivated with any profit by slave labor—and if by the loss of her foreign commerce, these products should be confined to an inadequate market, the fate of the fertile State would be poverty and utter desolation—her citizens in despair would emigrate to more fortunate regions, and the whole frame and constitution of her civil polity be impaired and deranged, if not dissolved entirely.

Deeply impressed with these considerations, the Representatives of the good people of this Commonwealth, anxiously desiring to live in peace with their fellow citizens, and to do all that in them lies to preserve and perpetuate the union of the States and the liberties of which it is the surest pledge—but feeling it to be their duty to expose and to resist all encroachments upon the true spirit of the Constitution, lest an apparent acquiescence in the system of protecting duties should be drawn into precedent, do, in the name of the Commonwealth of South Carolina, claim to enter upon the journals of the [U.S.] Senate, their protest against it as unconstitutional, oppressive, and unjust.

6.7

Daniel Webster's Second Reply to Robert Y. Hayne (1830)

The publication of John C. Calhoun's South Carolina Exposition and Protest *sparked national discussion on the appropriate limits of federal authority. In 1829, a congressional debate over western land sales illustrated differing views on states' rights. The most famous exchanges were between South Carolina senator Robert Y. Hayne and Massachusetts senator Daniel Webster. A gifted orator, Webster was a famous lawyer noted for his advocacy of business interests. He later emerged as a leader in the Whig Party and served as secretary of state.*

In this extract, Webster reacts to Haynes's views on states' rights.

FOCUS QUESTIONS

1. What is Webster's position on states' rights?
2. What does he believe are the advantages of the national government?
3. Compare Webster's views to those of John C. Calhoun (Document 6.6). With whom do you most agree? Explain your answer.

I profess, Sir, in my career hitherto, to have kept steadily in view the prosperity and honor of the whole country, and the preservation of our Federal Union. It is to that Union we owe our safety at home, and our consideration and dignity abroad. It is to that Union that we are chiefly indebted for whatever makes us most proud of our country. That Union we reached only by the discipline of our virtues in the severe school of adversity. It has its origin in the necessities of disordered finance, prostrate commerce, and ruined credit. Under its benign influences, these great interests immediately awoke, as from the dead, and sprang forth with newness of life. Every year of its duration has teemed with fresh proofs of its utility and its blessings; and although our territory has stretched out wider

SOURCE: "Second Speech on Foot's Resolution," *The Writings and Speeches of Daniel Webster* (Boston, 1903), 6:74–75.

and wider, and our population spread farther and farther, they have not outrun its protection or its benefits. It has been to us all a copious fountain of national, social, and personal happiness.

I have not allowed myself, Sir, to look beyond the Union, to see what might lie hidden in the dark recess behind. I have not coolly weighed the chances of preserving liberty when the bonds that unite us together shall be broken asunder. I have not accustomed myself to hang over the precipice of disunion, to see whether, with my short sight, I can fathom the depth of the abyss below; nor could I regard him as a safe counselor in the affairs of this government, whose thoughts should be mainly bent on considering, not how the Union may be best preserved, but how tolerable might be the condition of the people when it should be broken up and destroyed. While the Union lasts we have high, exciting, gratifying, prospects spread out before us, for us and our children. Beyond that I seek not to penetrate the veil. God grant that in my day, at least, that curtain may not rise! God grant that on my vision never may be opened what lies behind! When my eyes shall be turned to behold for the last time the sun in heaven, may I not see him shining on the broken and dishonored fragments of a once glorious Union; on States dissevered, discordant, belligerent; on a land rent with civil feuds, or drenched, it may be, in fraternal blood! Let their last feeble and lingering glance rather behold the gorgeous ensign of the republic, now known and honored throughout the earth, still full high advanced, its arms and trophies streaming in their original luster, not a stripe erased or polluted, nor a single star obscured, bearing for its motto, no such miserable interrogatory as "What is all this worth?" nor those words of delusion and folly, "Liberty first and Union afterwards"; but everywhere, spread all over in characters of living lights, blazing on all its ample folds, as they float over the sea and over the land, and in every wind under the whole heavens, that other sentiment, dear to every true American heart,—Liberty and Union, now and for ever, one and inseparable!

6.8

Bishop McIlvaine Decries the Curse of Intemperance (Undated)

In the early nineteenth century, many Americans consumed alcohol throughout the day. Per capita consumption averaged seven gallons annually—nearly three times higher than modern levels. Convinced that alcohol contributed to domestic violence and poverty, temperance advocates urged either moderate alcohol use or complete abstinence from alcoholic beverages. The nation's first temperance societies appeared in the northeast. By 1833, there were about 6,000 local temperance organizations across the United States. Many temperance activists were evangelical Protestants who denounced the "evils" of alcohol. Several factory owners also advocated temperance in the hopes of improving worker efficiency. At first, many workers were reluctant to abandon their drinking rituals. The Panic of 1837, however, convinced laborers that the economic crisis made temperance a good idea. By the 1840s, many individuals curbed their use of alcohol, and consumption rates declined by over 50 percent from the 1820s' levels.

In this reading, a Protestant minister urges temperance.

FOCUS QUESTIONS

1. How does McIlvaine view alcohol?
2. What recommendations does he make?
3. How might McIlvaine's class status and religious beliefs have affected his views?
4. Would you have joined the temperance movement? Explain your answer.

It cannot be denied that our country is most horribly scourged by intemperance. In the strong language of Scripture: "it groaneth and travaileth in pain to be delivered from the bondage of this corruption." ... [I]t cannot be denied that our country is enslaved [by intemperance]. Yes, we are groaning under a most desolating bondage. The land is trodden down under its polluting foot. Our

SOURCE: Charles P. McIlvaine, *Tracts of the American Tract Society*, General Series, (n.d.), Vol. 7, No. 244, pp. 1–23.

families are continually dishonored, ravaged, and bereaved; thousands annually slain and hundreds of thousands carried away into a loathsome slavery, to be ground to powder under its burdens or broken upon the wheel of its tortures. . . .

Another assertion is equally unquestionable. *The time has come when a great effort must be made to exterminate this unequaled destroyer.* It was high time this was done when the first drunkard entered eternity to receive the award of Him who has declared that no drunkard shall enter the kingdom of God. The demand for this effort has been growing in the peremptory tone of its call, as "the overflowing scourge" has passed with constantly extending sweep through the land. But a strange apathy has prevailed among us. As if the whole nation had been drinking the cup of delusion, we saw the enemy coming in like a flood and we lifted up scarcely a straw against him. . . .

There is but one possible answer. *Persuade people to use none at all. Total abstinence* is the only plan on which reformation can be hoped for. We are shut up to this. We have tried the consequences of encouraging people to venture but moderately into the atmosphere of infection; and we are now convinced that it was the very plan to feed its strength and extend its ravages. We are forced to the conclusion that to arrest the pestilence, we must starve it. All the healthy must abstain from its neighborhood. All those who are not temperate must give up the use of the means of intemperance. The deliverance of this land from its present degradation and from the increasing woes attendant on this vice depends altogether upon the extent to which the principle of total abstinence shall be adopted by our citizens. . . .

In order to exert ourselves with the best effect in the promotion of the several objects in this great cause to which young men should apply themselves, let us associate ourselves into *temperance societies.* We know the importance of associated exertions. We have often seen how a few instruments, severally weak, have become mighty when united. Every work, whether for evil or benevolent purposes, has felt the life, and spur, and power of cooperation. The whole progress of temperance reformation, thus far, is owing to the influence of *societies*; to the coming together of the temperate and the union of their resolutions, examples, and exertions under the articles of temperance societies.

6.9

Dorothea Dix Calls for Humane Treatment of the Mentally Ill (1843)

Many of the antebellum reformers were devoted to fighting crime and poverty. Rejecting previous notions that crime stemmed from innate evilness, they stressed the importance of environmental factors and parenting in causing deviant behavior. They created highly regimented penitentiaries and reformatories designed to make criminals embrace morality and responsibility.

The era also saw changes in perceptions of the mentally ill. The insane and mentally unbalanced were incarcerated in prisons and workhouses, regardless of age or sex. Dorothea Dix (1802–1887), a Unitarian schoolteacher, brought these conditions to the nation's attention. Appalled by her discovery of mentally ill people locked in an unheated room in a Massachusetts prison, she spent two years investigating jails across the state. In 1843, she presented her findings to the Massachusetts legislature. Her remarks are excerpted below. Despite poor health, she spent the next four decades working for humane treatment of the mentally ill. By 1860, she inspired twenty-eight states and the federal government to build mental hospitals.

FOCUS QUESTIONS

1. How does Dix appear to feel about addressing the legislators? What might explain her attitude?
2. What has Dix discovered in her investigation?
3. What suggestions does she offer?
4. How do modern attitudes toward and treatment of the mentally ill differ from the antebellum era?

Gentlemen,—I respectfully ask to present this report, believing that the *cause*, which actuates to and sanctions so unusual a movement, presents no equivocal claim to public consideration and sympathy. Surrendering to calm and deep

SOURCE: Dorothea Dix, "Memorial to the Legislature of Massachusetts," in *Old South Leaflets* (Boston: Directors of the Old South Work, 1902), Vol. 6, No. 148, pp.1–3.

convictions of duty my habitual views of what is womanly and becoming, I proceed briefly to explain what has conducted me before you unsolicited and unsustained, trusting, while I do so, that the reporter will be speedily forgotten in the report....

I come to present the strong claims of suffering humanity. I come to place before the Legislature of Massachusetts the condition of the miserable, the desolate, the outcast. I come as the advocate of helpless, forgotten, insane, and idiotic men and women; of beings sunk to a condition from which the most unconcerned would start with real horror; of being wretched in our prisons, and more wretched in our almshouses. And I cannot suppose it needful to employ earnest persuasion, or stubborn argument, in order to arrest and fix attention upon a subject only the more strongly pressing in its claims because it is revolting and disgusting in its details.

I must confine myself to few examples, but am ready to furnish other and more complete details, if required. If my pictures are displeasing, coarse, and severe, my subjects, it must be recollected, offer no tranquil, refined, or composing features. The condition of human beings, reduced to the extremist states of degradation and misery, cannot be exhibited in softened language, or adorn a polished page.

I proceed, gentlemen, briefly to call your attention to the *present* state of insane persons confined within this Commonwealth, in *cages, closets, cellars, stalls, pens! Chained, naked, beaten with rods*, and *lashed* into obedience.

As I state cold, severe *facts*, I feel obliged to refer to persons, and definitely to indicate localities. But it is upon my subject, not upon localities or individuals, I desire to fix attention and I would speak as kindly as possible of all wardens, keepers, and other responsible officers, believing that *most* of these have erred not through hardness of heart and willful cruelty so much as want of skill and knowledge, and want of consideration. Familiarity with suffering, it is said, blunts the sensibilities, and where neglect once finds a footing other injuries are multiplied. This is not all, for it may justly and strongly be added that, from the deficiency of adequate means to meet the wants of these cases, it has been an absolute impossibility to do justice in this matter. Prisons are not constructed in view of being converted into county hospitals, and almshouses are not founded as receptacles for the insane. And yet, in the face of justice and common sense, wardens are by law compelled to receive, and the masters of almshouses not to refuse, insane and idiotic subjects in all stages of mental disease and privation.

It is the Commonwealth, not its integral parts, that is accountable for most of the abuses which have lately and do still exist. I repeat it, it is defective legislation which perpetuates and multiplies these abuses.

6.10

Horace Mann on Educational Reform (1840)

Convinced education was necessary for creating productive workers and patriotic citizens, reformers worked to improve public schools. Like temperance activists, school reformers stressed middle-class values. Set class times encouraged punctuality. Placement of students in grades according to age and academic performance generated competition. Schoolbooks like the enormously influential McGuffey readers emphasized honesty, frugality, and hard work. All of these values, reformers believed, were essential in an industrializing society.

But reformers also saw schools as a way to preserve a certain vision of American society as the nation grew increasingly diverse. Many texts contained anti-Irish and anti-Catholic epithets. Public schools were racially segregated. Mandatory attendance rules upset families who depended on their children's contributions to household income. Despite these limitations, public schools drew wide support from urban residents, businessmen, and women.

Horace Mann (1796–1859) was the country's most noted education activist. Despite erratic childhood schooling, Mann performed brilliantly at Brown University. He studied law and then served in the Massachusetts state legislature. No issue stirred him more than public education. Accordingly, he gave up a promising political career to become the first secretary of the new Massachusetts Board of Education in 1837.

Mann strongly believed that public schools should be free, nonsectarian, and professional. Targeting poorly funded and disorganized local schools, Mann implemented state educational funding, mandatory attendance, standardized curricula, and teaching training. While some religious groups and poor people objected to these measures, Mann's reforms were emulated throughout the country. In 1848, Mann resigned his post to serve in the U.S. House of Representatives. After losing a bid for Massachusetts governor in 1852, he became president of Antioch College, an Ohio institution devoted to coeducation, integration, and nonsectarian education.

Mann included the following letter in his 1839 annual report to the state legislature.

SOURCE: Horace Mann, "Report of 1839," *Annual Reports on Education* (Boston, 1868), 8–10.

FOCUS QUESTIONS

1. What benefits of public education does the author identify?
2. What moral values does the author promote? Why might someone have objected to his assertions?
3. Do public schools still perform the functions described here? What should the role of public schools be? Explain your answers.

Extracts from a Letter of Jonathan Crane, Esquire, for several years a large Contractor on the Railroads in Massachusetts.

My principal business, for about ten years past, has been grading railroads. During that time, the number of men employed has varied from fifty to three hundred and fifty, nearly all Irishmen, with the exception of superintendents. Some facts have been so apparent, that my superintendents and myself could not but notice them: these I will freely give you. I should say that not less than three thousand different men have been, more or less, in my employment during the before-mentioned period, and that the number that could read and write intelligibly was about one to eight. Independently of their natural endowments, those who could read and write, and had some knowledge of the first principles of arithmetic, have almost invariably manifested a readiness to apprehend what was required of them, and skill in performing it, and have more readily and frequently devised new modes by which the same amount of work could be better done. Some of these men we have selected for super-intendents, and they are now contractors. With regard to the morals of the two classes, we have seen very little difference; but the better-educated class are more cleanly in their persons and their households, and generally discover more refinement in their manners, and practice a more economical mode in their living. Their families are better brought up, and they are more anxious to send their children to school. In regard to their standing and respectability among co-laborers, neighbors, and fellow-citizens, the more educated are much more respected; and in settling minor controversies, they are more commonly applied to as arbitrators. With regard to the morals of the two classes before mentioned, permit me to remark, that it furnishes an illustration of the truth of a common saying, that merely cultivating the understanding, without improving the heart, does not make a man better. The more extensively knowledge and virtue prevail in our country, the greater security have we that our institutions will not be overthrown. Our common-school system, connected as it is, or ought to be, with the inculcation of sound and practical morality, is the most vigilant and efficient police for the protection of persons, property, and character, that could be devised; and is it not gratifying that men of wealth are beginning to see, that, if they would protect their property and persons, a portion of that property should be expended for the education of the poorer classes? Merely selfish considerations would lead any man of wealth to do this, if he would only view the subject in its true light. Nowhere is this subject better understood than in Massachusetts; and the free discussions which have of late been held, in county and town meetings, have had the effect to call the attention of the public to it; and I trust the time is not far distant, when, at least in Massachusetts, the common-school system will accomplish all the good which it is capable of producing. Why do we not in these United States have a revolution, almost annually, as in the republics of South America? Ignorance and vice always have invited, and always will invite, such characters as Shakespeare's Jack Cade★ to rule over them. And may we not feel an assurance, that in proportion as the nation shall recover from the baneful influence of intemperance, so will its attention be directed pre-eminently to the promotion of virtue and knowledge, and nowhere in our country will an incompetent or intemperate common-school teacher be entrusted with the education of our children?

★ Jack Cade, leader of a band of rebels, appears in William Shakespeare's *Henry VI*, pt. II.

6.11

Women Workers Protest "Lowell Wage Slavery" (1847)

Blessed with rivers ideal for powering mills, New England became the nation's first industrial region. Because many young men had migrated westward in pursuit of better economic opportunities, factory owners relied on young women for cheap industrial labor. Textile companies were the first industrial employers. Small textile mills appeared in the 1790s. In 1813, the establishment of the Boston Manufacturing Company sparked dramatic industrial growth. The company built two textile complexes in the Massachusetts towns of Lowell and Waltham. By 1836, more than 6,000 people, mostly women, worked in these factories.

SOURCE: "Factory Life-Romance and Reality," *Voice of Industry* (Boston), 3 December 1847, 2.

In contrast to early mills which hired entire families, the Lowell and Waltham factories relied on unmarried women between fifteen and thirty years old. To attract workers, mill owners offered educational, religious, and moral instruction. Workers lived in company boarding houses under strict supervision. But this cheerful portrait of factory life was belied by poor working conditions. During the 1830s, as competition increased and the economy slowed, mill owners cut wages and instituted speed-ups. In 1834 and 1836, workers went on strike to protest these changes. Despite these demonstrations, the Massachusetts state legislature did not regulate industry for several more decades.

FOCUS QUESTIONS

1. How does the author contrast visitors' impressions of factory life to the realities of workers' lives?

2. Does the author believe that the educational and religious opportunities at the mill are valuable? Explain your answer.

3. What does the author claim happens to long-term factory workers?

Aristocratic strangers, in broad cloths and skills, with their imaginations excited by the wonderful stories—romances of Factory Life—which they have heard, have paid hasty visits to Lowell, or Manchester, and have gone away to praise, in prose and verse, the beauty of our "Factory Queens," and the comfort, elegance, and almost perfection, of the arrangements by which the very fatherly care of Agents, Superintendents, Overseers, &c., has surrounded them. To these nice visitors everything in and around a Lowell Cotton Mill is bathed in an atmosphere of rose-colored light. . . .

These lovers of the Romance of Labor—they don't like the reality very well—see not the pale and emaciated ones. They see not those who wear Consumption's hectic flush. They think little of the weariness and pain of these fair forms, as they stand there, at the loom and spindle, thirteen long hours, each day! They know not how long these hours of toil seem to them, as they look out upon the fields, and hills, and woods, which lie beyond the Merrimack, steeped in golden sunlight and radiant with beauty. . . . Six days shalt thou labor and do all thy work, and on the seventh thou shalt go to church, is the Commandment as improved by the mammon worshiping Christianity of modern Civilization. The factory girl is required to go to meeting on Sunday, where long, and too often unmeaning, word-prayers are repeated, and dull prosey sermons "delivered," and where God is worshiped, according to the law, by pious Agents and Overseers, while the poor Irishman is blasting rocks for them in the Corporation's canal, that the mills may not be stopped on Monday. . . . There are lectures of various kinds, some of them free, and others requiring only a trifling fee to secure admission, to which all can have access.

Those who recollect the fable of *Tantalus* in the old Mythology, will be able to appreciate the position of a large portion of the population with respect to these exalted privileges.... The unremitted toil of thirteen long hours, drains off the vital energy and unfits for study or reflection. They need amusement, relaxation, rest, and not mental exertion of any kind. A really sound and instructive lecture cannot, under such circumstances, be appreciated, and the lecturer fails, to a great extent, in making an impression.—"Jim Crow" performances are much better patronized than scientific lectures, and the trashy, milk-and-water sentimentalities of the *Lady's Book* and *Olive Branch*, are more read than the works of Gibbon, or Goldsmith, or Bancroft.

If each factory girl could suspend her labors in the Mill for a few months each year, for the purpose of availing herself of the advantages for intellectual culture by which she is surrounded, much good might be derived.... But day by day they feel their over-tasked systems give way.—A dizziness in the head or a pain in the side, or the shoulders or the back, admonishes them to return to their country homes before it is too late. But too often these friendly monitions are unheeded. They resolve to toil a little longer.—But nature cannot be cheated, and the poor victim of a false system of Industrial Oppression is carried home—to die!... There are now in our very midst hundreds of these loving, self-sacrificing martyr-spirits. They will die unhonored and unsung, but not unwept; for the poor factory girl has a home and loved one, and dark will be that home, and sad those loved ones when the light of her smile shines on them no more.

6.12

David Walker, *Appeal to the Coloured Citizens of the World* (1829)

After many Northern states abolished slavery following the Revolution, the antislavery movement declined. At the same time, cotton production made slavery more profitable than ever. Explosive slave revolts in the Caribbean and the South attested to continuing slave resistance. In 1817, the American Colonization Society advocated gradual emancipation, compensation for owners, and settlement of freed slaves in Africa as humane ways to end slavery.

SOURCE: David Walker, *Walker's Appeal in Four Articles: Together with a Preamble to the Coloured Citizens of the World* (Boston, 1830), 11–87.

Such solutions did not satisfy David Walker (1785–1830). Born in North Carolina to a slave father and a free mother, Walker lived as a free man. After attaining an education and traveling widely, he settled in Boston and opened a clothing store. Enduring harassment from white clothing dealers and local police, Walker became involved with the black community and joined the abolitionist movement. He was enraged by the views on race expressed in Thomas Jefferson's Notes on the State of Virginia (included in Chapter Four). In response, he wrote a seventy-six page pamphlet known as Walker's Appeal to the Coloured Citizens of the World (1829), attacking myths about slavery and urging African Americans to resist. Free black sailors smuggled the Appeal into slave-holding regions.

Deeply alarmed, the South responded intensely. Rewards were offered for Walker's capture or murder. New laws outlawed abolitionist literature and teaching slaves to read and write. After Walker died suddenly in 1830, many people suspected that he had been poisoned. His writings foreshadowed a more militant phase of the antislavery movement.

FOCUS QUESTIONS

1. How does Walker debunk common racial stereotypes?
2. How would you describe Walker's tone?
3. How does Walker believe that slavery and racism should be challenged?
4. Was the Southern response to the *Appeal* justified? Explain your answer.

All the inhabitants of the earth, (except, however, the sons of Africa) are called men, and of course are, and ought to be free. But we, (colored people) and our children are brutes!! And of course are, and ought to be SLAVES to the American people and their children forever!! To dig their mines and work their farms; and thus go on enriching them, from one generation to another with our blood and our tears!!!!

... We, (colored people of these United States of America) are the most wretched, degraded and abject set of beings that ever lived since the world began, and that the white Americans having reduced us to the wretched state of slavery, treat us in that condition more cruel (they being an enlightened and Christian people,) than any heathen nation did any people whom it had reduced to our condition. These affirmations are so well confirmed in the minds of all unprejudiced men, who have taken the trouble to read histories, that they need no elucidation from me. . . .

Do they not institute laws to prohibit us from marrying among the whites? I would wish, candidly, however, before the Lord, to be understood, that I would not give a pinch of snuff to be married to any white person I ever saw in all the days of my life. And I do say it, that the black man, or man of color, who will leave his own color (provided he can get one, who is good for any thing) and marry a white woman, to be a double slave to her, just because she is white, ought to be treated by her as he surely will be. . . .

. . . Show me a page of history, either sacred or profane, on which a verse can be found, which maintains, that the Egyptians heaped the unsupportable insult upon the children of Israel, by telling them that they were not of the human family. Can the whites deny the charge? Have they not, after having reduced us to the deplorable condition of slaves under their feet, held us as descending originally from the tribes of Monkeys and Orangutans? . . . So far, my brethren, were the Egyptians from heaping those insults upon their slaves, that the Pharaoh's daughter took Moses, a son of Israel for her own. . . .

They think because they hold us in their infernal chains of slavery, that we wish to be white, or of their color—but they are dreadfully deceived—we wish to be just as it pleased our Creator to have made us, and no avaricious and unmerciful wretches, have any business to make slave of, or hold us in slavery. How would they like for us to make slave of, and hold them in cruel slavery, and murder them as they do to us? . . .

Fear not the number and education of our enemies, against whom we shall have to contend for our lawful light; guaranteed to us by our Maker; for why should we be afraid, when God is, and will continue, (if we continue humble) to be on our side?

The man who would not fight under our Lord and Master Jesus Christ, in the Glorious and heavenly cause of freedom and of God—to be delivered from the most wretched, abject and servile slavery, that ever a people was afflicted with since the foundation of the world, to the present day—ought to be kept with all of his children or family, in slavery, or in chains, to be butchered by his *cruel enemies*. . . .

I have been for years troubling the pages of historians, to find out what our fathers have done to the white Christians of America, to merit such condign punishment as they have inflicted upon them, and do continue to inflict upon us their children. But I must aver, that my researches have hitherto been to no effect. I have therefore, come to the immovable conclusion, that they (Americans) have, and do continue to punish us for nothing else, but for enriching them and their country. For I cannot conceive of anything else. Nor will I ever believe otherwise, until the Lord shall convince me. . . .

We, and the world wish to see the charges of Mr. Jefferson refuted by the blacks themselves, . . . I know well, that there are some talents and learning among the colored people of this country. Which we have not a chance to develop, in consequence of oppression; but our oppression ought not to hinder us from acquiring all we can. For we will have a chance to develop them by and by. God will not suffer us, always to be oppressed. Our sufferings will come to an end, in spite of all the Americans this side of eternity. Then we will want all the learning and talents among ourselves, and perhaps more, to govern ourselves.—"Every dog must have its day," the American's is coming to an end. . . .

. . . Are we MEN!!—I ask you, O my brethren! are we Men? Did our creator make us to be slaves to dust and ashes like ourselves? Are they not dying worms as well as we? Have they not to make their appearance before the tribunal of Heaven, to answer for the deeds done in the body, as well as we? Have we any other Master but Jesus Christ alone? Is he not their Master as well as ours?—What right then, have we to obey and call any other Master, but Himself? How we could be so submissive to a gang of men, whom we cannot tell whether they are as good as ourselves or not, I never could conceive. However, this is shut up with the Lord, and we cannot precisely tell—but I declare, we judge men by their works.

The whites have always been an unjust, jealous, unmerciful, avaricious, and blood-thirsty set of beings, always seeking after power and authority....

6.13

William Lloyd Garrison on Slavery (1831)

William Lloyd Garrison (1805–1879) was one of the most famous abolitionists. Born in Massachusetts, Garrison worked as a printer. In 1828, he moved to Baltimore and worked as an editorial assistant to Benjamin Lundy, a Quaker who published the antislavery newspaper Genius of Universal Emancipation. *Philosophical differences with Lundy convinced Garrison to start his own paper. The following passage is from Garrison's first issue of* The Liberator, *published in January 1831. The paper was a sensation. While African Americans were the majority of the subscribers, many whites bitterly denounced Garrison. In 1835, he narrowly escaped lynching by a Boston mob.*

Garrison helped to found the New England Anti-Slavery Society in 1833. As antislavery groups spread throughout the North, they flooded Congress with abolitionist petitions. Between 1836 and 1845, outraged Southern congressmen enforced a "gag rule" prohibiting the introduction of antislavery petitions and discussion of slavery in the House of Representatives. At the same time, abolitionists split over whether to found their own political party and the appropriate role of women in the movement. Embracing the strategy of non-violence, Garrison urged activists not to vote, hold public office, or pay taxes to a government that condoned slavery. A true radical, he also advocated racial and gender equality.

SOURCE: "To the Public," *The Liberator* (Boston), 1 January 1831, 1.

FOCUS QUESTIONS

1. What does Garrison advocate?
2. Compare Garrison's tone to that of David Walker (Document 6.12).
3. Why do you think people reacted so strongly to Garrison's writings?
4. Do you think that the abolitionists helped the slaves? Explain your answer.

During my recent tour for the purpose of exciting the minds of the people by a series of discourses on the subject of slavery, every place that I visited gave fresh evidence of the fact that a greater revolution in public sentiment was to be effected in the free states—and particularly in New England—than at the south. I found contempt more bitter, opposition more active, detraction more relentless, prejudice more stubborn, and apathy more frozen, than among slave owners themselves. Of course, there were individual exceptions to the contrary. This state of things afflicted, but did not dishearten me. I determined, at every hazard, to lift up the standard of emancipation in the eyes of the nation, within sight of Bunker Hill and in the birthplace of liberty. That standard is now unfurled; and long may it float, unhurt by the spoliations of time of the missiles of a desperate foe—yea, till every chain be broken, and every bondman set free! Let southern oppressors tremble —let their secret abettors tremble—let their northern apologists tremble—let all the enemies of the persecuted blacks tremble.

...Assenting to the "self-evident truth" maintained in the American Declaration of Independence, "that all men are created equal, and endowed by their Creator with certain inalienable rights—among which are life, liberty, and the pursuit of happiness," I shall strenuously contend for the immediate enfranchisement of our slave population....

I am aware that many object to the severity of my language; but is there not cause for severity? I will be as harsh as truth, and as uncompromising as justice. On this subject, I do not wish to think, or speak, or write, with moderation. No! No! Tell a man whose house is on fire, to give a moderate alarm; tell him to moderately rescue his wife from the hands of the ravisher; tell the mother to gradually extricate her babe from the fire into which it has fallen;—but urge me not to use moderation in a cause like the present. I am in earnest—I will not equivocate—I will not excuse—I will not retreat a single inch—AND I WILL BE HEARD. The apathy of the people is enough to make every statue leap from its pedestal, and to hasten the resurrection of the dead.

It is pretended, that I am retarding the cause of emancipation by the coarseness of my invective, and the precipitancy of my measure. The charge is not true. On this question my influence,—humble as it is,—is felt at this moment to a considerable extent, and shall be felt in the coming years—not perniciously, but beneficially—not as a curse, but as a blessing; and posterity will bear testimony that I was right....

6.14

Elizabeth Cady Stanton, *Declaration of Sentiments* (1848)

Elizabeth Cady Stanton (1815–1902) ranks among the most important women in U.S. history. After an exceptional education, Stanton graduated from Emma Willard's Troy Female Seminary in 1832. In a telling incident, she once tore out pages containing laws that discriminated against women from the books of her father, U.S. congressman Daniel Cady. Demanding that the word "obey" be omitted from the wedding vows, she married Henry Brewster Stanton, an abolitionist and attorney. The couple spent their honeymoon attending the 1840 World antislavery Convention in London. When women attendees were forced to sit behind a curtain, Stanton was outraged. She and Lucretia Mott vowed to hold a separate meeting on women's rights. When Stanton returned to America, her women's rights activism contributed to New York's adoption of a law protecting married women's property.

In July 1848, Stanton and over 300 delegates met in Seneca Falls, New York, for the long-awaited women's rights convention. Stanton introduced her Declaration of Sentiments, *most of which received quick approval. Although Stanton's demand for women's suffrage ignited heated debate, it also passed narrowly. For the next fifty years, Stanton worked tirelessly for women's rights. Her extraordinary partnership with Susan B. Anthony merged Stanton's writing skills with Anthony's organizing talents.*

FOCUS QUESTIONS

1. Why do you think that Stanton modeled her *Declaration* on the Declaration of Independence?

2. What are the major demands of the *Declaration of Sentiments*?

3. Why do you think that many abolitionists also supported the women's rights movement? How might working in the antislavery movement have aided women's rights advocates?

SOURCE: "Declaration of Sentiments," *History of Women Suffrage*, eds. Susan B. Anthony, Elizabeth Cady Stanton, and Matilda Joslyn Gage (New York, 1881), 1:70–73.

4. Do modern women face problems like those described by Stanton? What has changed? What remains the same?

When, in the course of human events, it becomes necessary for one portion of the family of man to assume among the people of the earth a position different from that which they have hitherto occupied, but one to which the laws of nature and of nature's God entitle them, a decent respect to the opinions of mankind requires that they should declare the causes that impel them to such a course.

We hold these truths to be self-evident: that all men and woman are created equal; that they are endowed by their Creator with certain inalienable rights; that among these are life, liberty and the pursuit of happiness; that to secure these rights governments are instituted, deriving their powers from the consent of the governed. Whenever any form of government becomes destructive of these ends, it is the right of those who suffer from it to refuse allegiance to it, and to insist upon the institution of a new government, laying its foundation on such principles, and organizing its powers in such form, as to them shall seem most likely to effect their safety and happiness. Prudence, indeed, will dictate that governments long established should not be changed for light and transient causes; and accordingly all experience has shown that mankind are more disposed to suffer, while evils are sufferable, than to right themselves by abolishing the forms to which they are accustomed. But when a long train of abuses and usurpations, pursuing invariably the same object, evinces a design to reduce them under absolute despotism, it is their duty to throw off such government, and to provide new guards for their future security. Such has been the patient sufferance of the women under this government, and such is now the necessity which constrains them to demand the equal station to which they are entitled.

The history of mankind is a history of repeated injuries and usurpations on the part of man toward woman, having in direct object the establishment of an absolute tyranny over her. To prove this, let facts be submitted to a candid word.

He has never permitted her to exercise her inalienable right to the elective franchise.

He has compelled her to submit to laws, in the formation of which she had no voice.

He has withheld from her rights which are given to the most ignorant and degraded men—both natives and foreigners.

Having deprived her of this first right of a citizen, the elective franchise, thereby leaving her without representation in the halls of legislation, he has oppressed her on all sides.

He has made her, if married, in the eye of the law, civilly dead.

He has taken from her all right in property, even to the wages she earns.

He has made her, morally, an irresponsible being, as she can commit many crimes with impunity, provided they be done in the presence of her husband. In the covenant of marriage, she is compelled to promise obedience to her husband, he becoming, to all intents and purposes, her master, the law giving him power to deprive her of her liberty, and to administer chastisement.

He has so framed the laws of divorce, as to what shall be the proper causes, and in case of separation, to whom the guardianship of the children shall be given, as to be wholly regardless of the happiness of women—the law, in all cases, going upon a false supposition of the supremacy of man, and giving all power into his hands.

After depriving her of all rights as a married woman, if single, and the owner of property, he has taxed her to support a government which recognizes her only when her property can be made profitable to it.

He has monopolized nearly all the profitable employments, and from those she is permitted to follow, she receives but a scanty remuneration. He closes against her all the avenues to wealth and distinction which he considers most honorable to himself. As a teacher of theology, medicine, or law, she is not known. He has denied her the facilities for obtaining a thorough education, all colleges being closed against her.

He allows her in Church, as well as in State, but a subordinate position, claiming Apostolic authority for her exclusion from the ministry, and, with some exceptions, from any public participation in the affairs of the Church.

He has created a false public sentiment by giving to the world a different code of morals for men and women, by which the moral delinquencies which exclude women from society are not only tolerated, but deemed of little account in man.

He has usurped the prerogative of Jehovah himself, claiming it as his right to assign for her a sphere of action, when that belongs to her conscience and to her God.

He has endeavored, in every way he could, to destroy her confidence in her own powers, to lessen her self-respect, and to make her willing to lead a dependent and abject life.

Now, in the view of this entire disfranchisement of one-half of the people of this country, their social and religious degradation, in view of the unjust laws above mentioned, and because women do feel themselves aggrieved, oppressed, and fraudulently deprived of their most sacred rights, we insist that they have immediate admission to all the rights and privileges which belong to them as citizens of the United States.

In entering upon the great work before us, we anticipate no small amount of misconception, misrepresentation, and ridicule; but we shall use every instrumentality within our power to effect our object. We shall employ agents, circulate tracts, petition the State and National legislatures, and endeavor to enlist the pulpit and the press on our behalf. We hope this Convention will be followed by a series of Conventions embracing every part of the country.

7

※

Social and Cultural Change, 1820–1865

Sweeping social and cultural changes accompanied the rise of democracy. Americans questioned all forms of traditional authority and celebrated individualism. Children challenged parental authority. Marriages became more egalitarian. People sought spiritual fulfillment in new faiths and religious revivals. Capitalizing on improvements in technology and transportation, many Americans eagerly pursued commercial success. Others experimented with new health movements and communal living arrangements. Throughout the era, artists and writers created distinctly American forms of popular and high culture.

THEMES TO CONSIDER

- Shifts in marriage and family life during the antebellum era
- The concept of separate spheres and changes in gender relations
- Religious trends and revivals
- Foreign views of Americans
- Americans' experimentation with new ideas and living arrangements
- Utopian communities and their critiques of mainstream values
- The democratization of American culture

7.1

Joshua and Sally Wilson, Letters to George Wilson (1823)

As Americans questioned traditional forms of authority, family relationships changed dramatically. Where most colonial families worked collectively to ensure economic survival, antebellum families were more independent. Many young people left their families in pursuit of better employment. A growing number of husbands began working outside the home. Many affluent families embraced the doctrine of separate spheres in which men earned the family income while women exerted moral influence on family members. The traditional view that women were subordinate in all ways yielded to a belief that men and women were separate but equal. Men ruled in the public world of commerce and politics. Women reigned in the private, domestic sphere. Primary responsibility for child rearing shifted from fathers to mothers.

These events greatly affected courtship and marriage patterns. No longer dependent on parents for land, young people demanded more autonomy in choosing spouses. They expected to marry for love, not duty. Long engagements became popular as women attempted to prolong their independence. Additionally, a significant number of people elected not to marry. The following letters from Joshua and Sally Wilson to their son, George Wilson, reflect these changes. Joshua Wilson (1774–1846) served as minister of Cincinnati's First Presbyterian Church.

FOCUS QUESTIONS

1. Why have Joshua and Sally Wilson written these letters?
2. How do the letters of Joshua and Sally differ?
3. What do these letters reveal about gender roles and courtship rituals in antebellum America?

SOURCE: The Wilson Family Letters, Durratt Collection, Joseph Regenstein Library, University of Chicago.

November 23, 1823

We presume you are already informed that your letter of the 28th was duly received. The delicate and important subject suggested for our consideration forms a sufficient reason for some delay that we might not give advice in a matter of such moment without meditation, prayer, and serious conference. It would be very unreasonable for us to attempt to restrain the lawful and laudable desires of our children, all we ought to do is to endeavor to direct and regulate their innocent wishes and curb and conquer those which are vicious. Nor are we ignorant of the great advantages which frequently result from virtuous love and honorable wedlock. But there is a time for all things, and such are the fixed laws of nature that things are only beautiful and useful when they occupy their own time and place. Premature love and marriage are often blighted by the frosts of adversity and satiety leaving hasty lovers to droop in the meridian of life and drag out a miserable existence under the withering influence of disappointment and disgust. . . . We do not say you have been hasty but we wish you to reflect seriously upon this question. Is not the whole affair premature? We know from experience and observation that schemes which appear reasonable and desirable at the age of twenty wear a very different aspect at twenty-five. We think it probable that greater maturity, more experience in business, and larger acquaintance with the world might change your views and feelings. Besides we are not sure that you have sufficiently considered the weighty responsibility. We feel no disposition to place any insuperable barrier in your way. Our advice is that you give the subject that consideration which its importance demands, that you unite with us in praying for divine direction, that every thing be done deliberately, decently, orderly, honorably, and devoutly.

[Joshua Wilson]

December 9, 1823

Your letter of Nov 18 has been duly received. On its contents we have meditated with deep solicitude. . . . You seem confident that your decision is not premature or hasty. Here we feel compelled to demur and beg you to weigh the matter again. You express a hope that before great length of time we shall have an opportunity of receiving Miss B much to our satisfaction. Dear George, it will not be any satisfaction to us to see you place a lady in a more precarious condition than you found her and this we are sure would be the case if marriage with this young lady should take place shortly. We must remind you of a pledge given in your former letter and insist upon its obligation, that you marry no woman without the prospect of supporting her in a suitable manner. Think of the circumstances in which she has been educated, of the circle of society in which she has been accustomed to move, of her delicate constitution and refined sensibility and then imagine to yourself her disappointment upon entering a poor dependent family occupying an indifferent tenement without the means of affording a comfortable lodging or decently accommodating her friends. She has been accustomed to see you in the agreeable aspect of the scholar and a gentleman and she has seen your father also in flattering circumstances.... We do not say things to discourage you but to show you the necessity of prudence in your plans, diligence in your studies and such application to business as will afford you a reasonable prospect of success before you become head of a family.

[Sally Wilson]

7.2

Catharine Beecher on Domestic Economy (1841)

The rise of an industrial economy greatly altered gender roles. No longer content with unquestioned male authority, couples tried to build more equal relationships. The rise of the doctrine of separate spheres reflected these changes. Where men ruled the public sphere of governance and business, women controlled the private sphere of domestic life. Home and family became refuges from a disorderly society. Although women still faced significant economic and political obstacles, they exercised greater influence over children.

Catharine Beecher (1800–1878) helped to popularize the ideal of separate spheres. A member of one of the most renowned families in nineteenth-century America, Beecher gained notoriety as an advocate for women's education. Her writings inspired the creation of several women's colleges and schools. Although childless and unmarried, Beecher extolled domesticity and family life as women's most important roles. An opponent of legal equality between the sexes, Beecher often clashed with women's rights activists.

This reading is an excerpt from Beecher's A Treatise on Domestic Economy for the Use of Young Ladies at Home and at School. *Published in 1841, it was widely reprinted and won Beecher national recognition. Covering topics ranging from child care to plumbing, the manual celebrated and defined the middle-class home.*

SOURCE: Catharine Beecher, *A Treatise on Domestic Economy for the Use of Young Ladies at Home and at School* (Boston: Marsh, Capen, Lyon, and Webb, 1841), pp. 1–14, 142–154, *passim.*

FOCUS QUESTIONS

1. What does Beecher believe is the proper role for women in a democratic society?
2. Why does she consider women's education so important?
3. How do Beecher's ideas illustrate the concept of separate spheres? What traits does she seem to value in women?
4. What suggestions does Beecher offer for improving women's daily lives? Were her recommendations realistic for all women? Explain your answer.

The tendencies of democratic institutions, in reference to the rights and interests of the female sex, have been fully developed in the United States; and it is in this aspect, that the subject is one of peculiar interest to American women. In this Country, it is established, both by opinion and by practice, that woman has an equal interest in all social and civil concerns; and that no domestic, civil, or political institution, is right, which sacrifices her interest to promote that of the other sex. But in order to secure her the more firmly in all these privileges, it is decided, that, in the domestic relation, she take a subordinate station, and that, in civil and political concerns, her interests be entrusted to the other sex, without her taking any part in voting, or in making and administering laws. . . .

The success of democratic institutions, as is conceded by all, depends upon the intellectual and moral character of the mass of the people. If they are intelligent and virtuous, democracy is a blessing; but if they are ignorant and wicked, it is only a curse and as such more dreadful than any other form of civil government as a thousand tyrants are more to be dreaded than one. It is equally conceded, that the formation of the moral and intellectual character of the young is committed mainly to the female hand. The mother forms the character of the future man; the sister bends the fibers that are hereafter to be the forest tree; the wife sways the heart, whose energies may turn for good or for evil the destinies of a nation. Let the women of a country be made virtuous and intelligent, and the men will certainly be the same. The proper education of a man decides the welfare of an individual; but educate a woman, and the interests of a whole family are secured. . . .

The woman who is rearing a family of children; the woman who labors in the schoolroom; the woman who, in her retired chamber, earns, with her needle, the mite to contribute for the intellectual and moral elevation of her Country; even the humble domestic, whose example and influence may be moulding and forming young minds, while her faithful services sustain a prosperous domestic state;—each and all may be animated by the consciousness that they are agents in accomplishing the greatest work that ever was committed to human responsibility. . . .

The discussion of the question of the equality of the sexes, in intellectual capacity, seems both frivolous and useless, not only because it can never be decided, but because there would be no possible advantage in this decision. But one topic, which is often drawn into this discussion, is of far more consequence and that is, the relative importance and difficulty of the duties a woman is called to perform. . . .

There is no one thing more necessary to a housekeeper, in performing her varied duties, than *a habit of system and order*, and yet the peculiarly desultory nature of women's pursuits, and the embarrassments resulting from the state of domestic service in this Country, render it very difficult to form such a habit. But it is sometimes the case, that women, who could and would carry forward a systematic plan of domestic economy, do not accept it, simply from a want of knowledge of the various modes of introducing it. It is with reference to such, that various modes of securing system and order, which the Writer has seen adopted, will be pointed out.

A wise economy is nothing more conspicuous, than in the right *apportionment of time* to different pursuits. There are duties of a religious, intellectual, social, and domestic nature, each having different relative claims on attention. Unless a person has some general plan of apportioning these claims, some will intrench on others, and some, it is probable, will be entirely excluded. . . .

Instead of attempting some such systematic employment of time, and carrying it out so far as they can control circumstances, most women are rather driven along by the daily occurrences of life, so that, instead of being the intelligent regulators of their own time, they are the mere sport of circumstances. There is nothing which so distinctly marks the difference between weak and strong minds, as the fact, whether they control circumstances, or circumstances control them. . . .

In regard to the minutiae of domestic arrangements, the Writer has known the following methods adopted. *Monday*, with some of the best housekeepers, is devoted to preparing the labors of the week. Any extra cooking, the purchasing of articles to be used during the week, and the assorting of clothes for the wash, and mending such as would be injured without—these and similar items belong to this day. *Tuesday* is devoted to washing, and *Wednesday* to ironing. On *Thursday*, the ironing is finished off, the clothes folded and put away, and all articles which need mending put in the mending basket, and attended to. *Friday* is devoted to sweeping and housecleaning. On *Saturday*, and especially the last Saturday of every month, every department is put in order; the castors and table furniture are regulated, the pantry and cellar inspected, the trunks, drawers, and closets arranged, and every thing about the house put in order for *Sunday*. All the cooking is also prepared. By this regular recurrence of a particular time for inspecting every thing, nothing is forgotten till ruined by neglect.

Another mode of systematizing, relates to providing proper supplies of conveniences, and proper places in which to keep them. Thus, some ladies keep a large closet, in which are placed the tubs, pails, dippers, soap-dishes, starch, bluing, clothes-line and every other article used in washing; and in the same or another place are kept every convenience for ironing. In the sewing department, a trunk, with suitable partitions, is provided, in which are placed, each in its proper place, white thread of all sizes, colored thread, yarns for mending, colored and black sewing-silks and twist, tapes and bobbins of all sizes, white and colored welting-cords, silk braids and cords, needles of all sizes, papers of pins, remnants of linen and colored cambric, a supply of all kinds of buttons used in the family, black and white hooks and eyes, a yard measure, and all the patterns used in cutting and fitting. These are done up in separate parcels and labeled. . . .

The full supply of all conveniences in the kitchen and cellar, and a place appointed for each article, very much facilitates domestic labor. . . .

Another important item, in systematic economy, is the apportioning of *regular* employment to the various members of the family. If a housekeeper can secure the cooperation of *all* her family, she will find that "many hands make light work." There is no greater mistake, than in bringing up children to feel that they must be taken care of, and waited on, by others, without any corresponding obligations on their part. The extent to which young children can be made useful in a family, would seem surprising to those who have seen a *systematic* and *regular* plan for securing their services. The Writer has been in a family, where a little girl of eight or nine washed and dressed herself and little brother, and made their little beds before breakfast, set and cleared all the tables at meals, with a little help from a grown person in moving tables and spreading cloths, while all the dusting of parlors and chambers was also neatly performed by her. A little brother of ten, brought in and piled all the wood used in the kitchen and parlor, brushed the boots and shoes neatly, went on errands and took care of the poultry. They were children whose parents could afford to hire this service, but who chose to have their children grow up healthy and industrious. . . .

It is impossible for a conscientious woman to secure all that peaceful mind and cheerful enjoyment of life, which all should seek, who is constantly finding her duties jarring with each other, and much remaining undone, which she feels that she ought to do. . . .

And here the Writer would urge upon young ladies the importance of forming habits of system, while unembarrassed with multiplied cares which will make the task so much more difficult and hopeless. Every young lady can systematize her pursuits, to a certain extent. She can have a particular day for mending her wardrobe, and for arranging her trunks, closets, and drawers. She can keep her workbasket, her desk at school, and all her conveniences in proper places and regular order. She can have regular periods for reading, walking, visiting, study, and domestic pursuits. And by following this method, in youth, she will form a taste for regularity, and a habit of system, which will prove a blessing to her through life.

7.3

Henry Clarke Wright on Marriage and Parentage (1858)

The doctrine of separate spheres gave many women more control in child rearing and family planning. In 1800, the U.S. birthrate was quite high with an average of seven pregnancies per woman. Large families were essential on labor-intensive farms. With the rise of the industrial economy, couples, especially those living in urban areas, began having fewer children. By 1900, the birthrate declined to approximately four children per woman. Families remained larger among those in rural areas, immigrants, and racial minorities.

Abstinence, coitus interruptus (premature withdrawal), condoms, dia-phragms, and abortion were the most commonly used birth-control methods. Prior to the point of quickening (when a woman can feel her child move—usually in the fifth or sixth month of pregnancy), abortion was not illegal. Women used herbs like savin or pennyroyal to induce miscarriages. Magazines featured subtly worded advertisements for products to cure "female irregularity" or "female maladies."

Henry Clarke Wright was a noted advocate for family planning and women's rights. In this passage, he advises men on sex in marriage.

FOCUS QUESTIONS

1. What are the major themes of this reading?
2. How does Clark contrast male and female sexuality?
3. What does this passage suggest about family life in antebellum America? How does it support the concept of separate spheres?
4. Compare Wright's claims to modern notions of sex and reproduction.

A man has no right to compel his wife to lie or murder. He has no more right to compel her to yield to his passion, and thus to lie against the instincts of her nature, and kill the yearnings of her soul for true companionship, by urging upon her a passion which swallows up all other forces of her nature. No matter whether the violence that

SOURCE: Henry C. Wright, *Marriage and Parentage* or *The Reproductive Element in Men, as Means to His Elevation and Happiness* (Boston: Bela Marsh. 1858), 252–53, 301–02.

enables the man, under the name of husband, to enforce upon her the conditions of maternity, be in his own superior muscular energy, or in the shape of civil law or social and ecclesiastical sanction, the outrage upon her person is the same. . . .

Man can perpetuate no deeper wrong to himself, to his wife and child and to his domestic peace, than to urge upon his wife maternity, when he knows her nature rebels against it. Nor can woman commit a greater crime against herself and her child, than to consent to become a mother, when her nature not only does not call for it, but actively repels it.

Let the wife say to the husband, "Show me thy love in some gentler way, let my head repose upon thee as upon a rock of trust, let me feel thine arms around me, to defend me from all harm, not to bring it to me."... Who but a ruffian would disregard such a request? Who but a being less than a man would say, "No matter how *you* feel, *I* wish to be gratified." The wife should be the regulator of *this* marriage relation, for only in obedience to the laws of her nature can she hope to continue to be the loving, healthful, happy wife. . . .

The man who regards the presence of the reproductive element in himself as a means of sensuous gratification, and marriage as a licensed mode of expending that element and of obtaining that gratification, can never hope to make for himself a pure and happy home. . . . By a constant expenditure of the vital element of his manhood, he enfeebles his reason, his conscience, his affection, and his power to love and appreciate his wife and child. He becomes repulsive, and incapable of forming true family relations. On our knowledge of the natural laws which should govern the expenditure of the reproductive element, and on our obedience to them, depend the question of a happy home.

7.4

Reverend Peter Cartwright, "A Muscular Christian" (1830)

From the 1790s to 1840s, America was engulfed by a second wave of religious revivalism. Particularly strong in New England and on the frontier, the Second Great Awakening reflected the democratization of American society and culture.

SOURCE: Peter Cartwright, *Autobiography* (edited by W. P. Strickland, New York, etc., 1856), 312–19, *passim*.

Ministers used everyday language and emotion to appeal to the masses. Abandoning notions of predestination based on a negative view of human nature, preachers offered inspirational messages about human perfectibility and a loving God. Thousands flocked to camp meetings that often lasted for days and sent converts into ecstatic fits.

The Methodists were the most successful in drawing new members on the frontier. By 1844, the church became the nation's largest Protestant denomination with over a million congregants. Stressing emotion over intellect, Methodist circuit riders traveled widely. They criticized drunkenness, violence, gossip, fornication, materialism, and virtually all other denominations.

Peter Cartwright was the most famous Methodist circuit rider. After converting in the great 1801 revival in Cane Ridge, Kentucky, he was licensed by the Methodist Episcopal Church and began preaching in dozens of frontier towns. An opponent of slavery, Cartwright moved to the free soil of Illinois in 1824. He was later elected to the Illinois state assembly but lost an 1846 race for the U.S. House of Representatives to Abraham Lincoln.

This excerpt from Cartwright's autobiography demonstrates his energetic preaching and religious zeal.

FOCUS QUESTIONS

1. How did people react to Cartwright's exhortations? What do the varying responses suggest about the Second Great Awakening?

2. How might the Second Great Awakening have contributed to the reform movements of the antebellum era (See Chapter 6)?

3. Do we have anything similar to these camp meetings in modern America? Why do you think someone might attend a religious revival? Explain your answers.

There was a great and good work going on in our congregation from time to time; and on Sunday there were a great many from Springfield, and all the surrounding country. A great many professors of religion in other Churches professed to wish their children converted, but still they could not trust them at a Methodist meeting, especially a camp meeting. A great many of these young people attended the camp-meetings, and on Sunday the awful displays of Divine power were felt to the utmost verge of the congregation. When I closed my sermon, I invited mourners to the altar, and there was a mighty shaking among the dry bones; many came forward, and among the rest there were many young ladies whose parents were members of a sister Church; two in particular of these young ladies came into the altar. Their mother was present; and when she heard her daughters were kneeling at the altar of God, praying for mercy, she sent an elder of her Church to bring them out. When he came to tell them their mother had sent for them, they refused to go. He then took hold of them, and said they must go. I then took hold of him, and told him they should not go, and if that was his business, I wanted him to leave the altar instantly. He left, and reported to their mother; and while we were kneeling all round the altar, and praying for the mourners, the mother in a great rage rushed in. When she came, all were kneeling around, and there was no place for her to get in to her daughters. As I knelt and was stooping down, talking, and encouraging the mourners, this lady stepped on my shoulders, and rushed right over my head. As, in a fearful rage, she took hold of her daughters to take them out by force. I took hold of her arm, and tried to reason with her, but I might as well have reasoned with a whirlwind. She said she would have them out at the risk of her life.

"They are my daughters," said she, "and they shall come out."

Said I to her, "This is my altar and my meeting, and I say, these girls shall not be taken out."

She seized hold of them again. I took hold of her, and put her out of the altar, and kept her out. Both of these young ladies professed religion, but they were prevented by their mother from joining the Methodists. She compelled them to join her Church, solely against their will. They married in their mother's Church, but I fear they were hindered for life, if not finally lost. . . .

We had a camp-meeting in Morgan County, Sangamon District. While I was on this district the following remarkable providence occurred: There were large congregations from time to time, many awakened and converted to God, fifty joined the Church. G.W. Teas, now a traveling preacher in the Iowa Conference, made the fiftieth person that joined the Church. We had worship for several days and nights. On Monday, just after we dismissed for dinner, there was a very large limb of a tree that stood on the side of the ground allotted for the ladies, which, without wind or any other visible cause, broke loose and fell, with a mighty crash, right in among the ladies' seats; but as the Lord would direct it, there was not a woman or child there when the limb fell. If it had fallen at any time while the congregation was collected, it must have killed more than a dozen persons. Just in the south of Morgan, near Lynnville, we had another camp-meeting, perhaps the same summer. In the afternoon, at three o'clock, I put a very good local preacher to preach. He was not as interesting as some, and the congregation became restless, especially the rowdies. I went out among them, and told them they ought to hear the preacher.

"O," said they, "if it was you we would gladly hear you."

"Boys," said I, "do you really want to hear me?"

"Yes, we do," said they.

"Well," said I, "if you do, go and gather all those inattentive groups, and come down in the grove, two hundred yards south, and I will preach to you."

They collected two or three hundred. I mounted an old log; they all seated themselves in the shade. I preached to them about an hour, and not a soul moved or misbehaved. In this way I matched the rowdies for once.

7.5

Joseph Smith, The Wentworth Letter (1842)

While growing up in upstate New York during the Second Great Awakening, Joseph Smith (1805–1844) was perplexed by differences among Protestant faiths. At age fourteen, Smith had a divine revelation that clarified his religious views. He claimed that an angel had directed him to a buried set of golden plates. Aided by special stones, Smith translated the tablets into The Book of Mormon. *The book described a Hebrew prophet whose descendants migrated to America and built a civilization. After some tribesmen departed from God's ways, the Lord cursed them with dark skin. These defectors were the American Indians.*

The Mormon community proved very attractive to those disillusioned with rising individualism and materialism. But many Americans objected to Mormon practices such as plural marriage (polygamy), block voting, and community ownership. Plagued by religious prosecution, the Mormons moved from New York to Ohio and then to Missouri. In 1839, the Mormons arrived in Illinois and established the city Nauvoo. But the Mormons' commercial success and growing political power generated new controversies. In 1844, Smith's suppression of dissidents who objected to polygamy led to his arrest and imprisonment. A mob stormed the jail and murdered Smith and his brother Hiram. The majority of Mormons soon followed Brigham Young to Utah while a smaller faction moved to Independence, Missouri.

In this passage, Smith describes the history of the Mormons to John Wentworth, a newspaper editor seeking information about the church.

FOCUS QUESTIONS

1. How does Smith describe the early history of the Mormon church?
2. Why do you think people joined the Mormons?
3. What does this reading suggest about religious life in antebellum America?

SOURCE: *Messages of the First Presidency*, Vol. 1, p.136–142. Copyright © Deseret Book.
Published at All About Mormons, http://www.mormons.org/daily/history/people/joseph_smith/wentworth.htm.

March 1, 1842

At the request of Mr. John Wentworth, Editor and Proprietor of the Chicago Democrat. I have written the following sketch of the rise, progress, persecution, and faith of the Latter-day Saints, of which I have the honor, under God, of being the founder. Mr. Wentworth says that he wishes to furnish Mr. Bastow, a friend of his, who is writing the history of New Hampshire, with this document. As Mr. Bastow has taken the proper steps to obtain correct information, all that I shall ask at his hands, is, that he publish the account entire, ungarnished, and without misrepresentation. . . .

On the 6th of April 1830, the "Church of Jesus Christ of Latter-day Saints" was first organized in the town of Fayette, Seneca county, state of New York. Some few were called and ordained by the Spirit of revelation and prophecy, and began to preach as the Spirit gave them utterance, and though weak, yet were they strengthened by the power of God, and many were brought to repentance, were immersed in the water, and were filled with the Holy Ghost by the laying on of hands. They saw visions and prophesied, devils were cast out, and the sick healed by the laying on of hands. From that time the work rolled forth with astonishing rapidity, and churches were formed in the states of New York, Pennsylvania, Ohio, Indiana, Illinois, and Missouri; in the last named state a considerable settlement was formed in Jackson county: numbers joined the Church and we were increasing rapidly; we made large purchases of land, our farms teemed with plenty, and peace and happiness were enjoyed in our domestic circle, and throughout our neighborhood; but as we could not associate with our neighbors (who were, many of them, of the basest of men, and had fled from the face of civilized society, to the frontier country to escape the hand of justice,) in their midnight revels, their Sabbath breaking, horse racing and gambling; they commenced at first to ridicule, then to persecute, and finally an organized mob assembled and burned our houses, tarred and feathered and whipped many of our brethren, and finally, contrary to law, justice and humanity, drove them from their habitations; who, houseless and homeless, had to wander on the bleak prairies till the children left the tracks of their blood on the prairie. This took place in the month of November, and they had no other covering but the canopy of heaven, in this inclement season of the year; this proceeding was winked at by the government, and although we had warrantee deeds for our land, and had violated no law, we could obtain no redress.

There were many sick, who were thus inhumanly driven from their houses, and had to endure all this abuse and to seek homes where they could be found. The result was, that a great many of them being deprived of the comforts of life, and the necessary attendances, died; many children were left orphans, wives, widows and husbands, widowers; our farms were taken possession of by the mob, many thousands of cattle, sheep, horses and hogs were taken, and our household goods, store goods, and printing press and type were broken, taken, or otherwise destroyed.

Many of our brethren removed to Clay county, where they continued until 1836, three years; there was no violence offered, but there were threatenings of violence. But in the summer of 1836 these threatenings began to assume a more serious form, from threats, public meetings were called, resolutions were passed, vengeance and destruction were threatened, and affairs again assumed a fearful attitude, Jackson county was a sufficient precedent, and as the authorities in that county did not interfere they boasted that they would not in this; which on application to the authorities we found to be too true, and after much privation and loss of property, we were again driven from our homes.

We next settled in Caldwell and Daviess counties, where we made large and extensive settlements, thinking to free ourselves from the power of oppression, by settling in new counties, with very few inhabitants in them; but here we were not allowed to live in peace, but in 1838 we were again attacked by mobs, an exterminating order was issued by Governor Boggs, and under the sanction of law, an organized banditti ranged through the country, robbed us of our cattle, sheep, hogs, &c., many of our people were murdered in cold blood, the chastity of our women was violated, and we were forced to sign away our property at the point of the sword; and after enduring every indignity that could be heaped upon us by an inhuman, ungodly band of marauders, from twelve to fifteen thousand souls, men, women, and children were driven from their own firesides, and from lands to which they had warrantee deeds, houseless, friendless, and homeless (in the depths of winter) to wander as exiles on the earth, or to seek an asylum in a more genial clime, and among a less barbarous people. Many sickened and died in consequence of the cold and hardships they had to endure; many wives were left widows, and children, orphans, and destitute. It would take more time than is allotted me here to describe the injustice, the wrongs, the murders the bloodshed, the theft, misery and woe that have been caused by the barbarous, inhuman, and lawless proceedings of the state of Missouri.

In the situation before alluded to, we arrived in the state of Illinois in 1839, where we found a hospitable people and a friendly home: a people who were willing to be governed by the principles of law and humanity. We have commenced to build a city called "Nauvoo," in Hancock county. We number from six to eight thousand here, besides vast numbers in the county around, and in almost every county of the state. We have a city charter granted us, and charter for a Legion, the troops of which now number 1,500. We have also a charter for a University, for an Agricultural and Manufacturing Society, have our own laws and administrators, and possess all the privileges that other free and enlightened citizens enjoy.

Persecution has not stopped the progress of truth, but has only added fuel to the flame, it has spread with increasing rapidity. Proud of the cause which they have espoused, and conscious of our innocence, and of the truth of their system, 'midst calumny and reproach, have the Elders of this Church gone forth, and planted the Gospel in almost every state in the Union; it has penetrated our cities, it has spread over our villages, and has caused thousands of our intelligent, noble, and patriotic citizens to obey its divine mandates, and be governed by its sacred truths. It has also spread into England, Ireland, Scotland, and Wales, where, in the year 1840, a few of our missionaries were sent, and over five thousand joined the Standard of Truth; there are numbers now joining in every land.

Our missionaries are going forth to different nations, and in Germany, Palestine, New Holland, Australia, the East Indies, and other places, the Standard of Truth has been erected; no unhallowed hand can stop the work from progressing; persecutions may rage, mobs may combine, armies may assemble, calumny may defame, but the truth of God will go forth boldly, nobly, and independent, till it has penetrated every continent, visited every clime, swept every country, and sounded in every ear, till the purposes of God shall be accomplished, and the Great Jehovah shall say the work is done. . . .

Respectfully, &c.,
JOSEPH SMITH.

7.6

Frances Trollope, *Domestic Manners of the Americans* (1831)

Although many foreign visitors wrote about antebellum America, Frances Trollope was among the most critical. The novelist toured the United States from 1827 to 1831, spending most of her time in Cincinnati. After a failed attempt to start her own business, Trollope returned to Great Britain and penned a book on American society. While Domestic Manners of the Americans *(1831) was a resounding success in England, its American reception was decidedly cooler.*

In this excerpt, Trollope describes her arrival in and first impressions of Cincinnati.

FOCUS QUESTIONS

1. How does Trollope describe the residents of Cincinnati?
2. Why do you think many Americans disliked Trollope's book?
3. Do any of Trollope's stereotypes of Americans still endure? Give examples.

SOURCE: Frances Trollope, *Domestic Manners of the Americans* (London, 1832), 48–188, *passim.*

The "simple" manner of living in Western America was more distasteful to me from its levelling effects on the manners of the people, than from the personal privations that it rendered necessary; and yet, till I was without them, I was in no degree aware of the many pleasurable sensations derived from the little elegancies and refinements enjoyed by the middle classes in Europe. There were many circumstances, too trifling even for my gossiping pages, which pressed themselves daily and hourly upon us, and which forced us to remember painfully that we were not at home. It requires an abler pen than mine to trace the connection which I am persuaded exists between these deficiencies and the minds and manners of the people. All animal wants are supplied profusely at Cincinnati, and at a very easy rate; but, alas! these go but a little way in the history of a day's enjoyment. The total and universal want of manners, both in males and females, is so remarkable, that I was constantly endeavouring to account for it. It certainly does not proceed from want of intellect. I have listened to much dull and heavy conversation in America, but rarely to any that I could strictly call silly (if I except the every where privileged class of very young ladies). They appear to me to have clear heads and active intellects; are more ignorant on subjects that are only of conventional value, than on such as are of intrinsic importance; but there is no charm, no grace in their conversation. I very seldom, during my whole stay in the country, heard a sentence elegantly turned, and correctly pronounced from the lips of an American. There is always something either in the expression or the accent that jars the feelings and shocks the taste. . . .

Had I passed as many evenings in company in any other town that I ever visited as I did in Cincinnati, I should have been able to give some little account of the conversations I had listened to; but, upon reading over my notes, and then taxing my memory to the utmost to supply the deficiency, I can scarcely find a trace of any thing that deserves the name. Such as I have, shall be given in their place. But, whatever may be the talents of the persons who meet together in society, the very shape, form, and arrangement of the meeting is sufficient to paralyze conversation. The women invariably herd together at one part of the room, and the men at the other; but, in justice to Cincinnati, I must acknowledge that this arrangement is by no means peculiar to that city, or to the western side of the Alleghenies. Sometimes a small attempt at music produces a partial reunion; a few of the most daring youths, animated by the consciousness of curled hair and smart waistcoats, approach the piano–forte, and begin to mutter a little to the half-grown pretty things, who are comparing with one another "how many quarters' music they have had." Where the mansion is of sufficient dignity to have two drawing-rooms, the piano, the little ladies, and the slender gentlemen are left to themselves, and on such occasions the sound of laughter is often heard to issue from among them. But the fate of the more dignified personages, who are left in the other room, is extremely dismal. The gentlemen spit, talk of elections and the price of produce and spit again. The ladies look at each other's dresses till they know every pin by heart; talk of Parson Somebody's last sermon on the day of judgment, on Dr. Totherbody's new pills for dyspepsia, till the "tea" is announced, when they all console themselves together for whatever they may have suffered in keeping awake, by taking more tea, coffee, hot cake and custard, hoe cake, johnny cake, waffle cake, and dodger cake, pickled peaches, and preserved cucumbers, ham, turkey, hung beef, apple sauce, and pickled oysters, than ever were prepared in any other country of the known world. After this massive meal is over, they return to the drawing room, and it always appeared to me that they remained together as long as they could bear it, and then they rise en masse, cloak, bonnet, shawl, and exit. . . .

The theatre was really not a bad one, though the very poor receipts rendered it impossible to keep it in high order; but an annoyance infinitely greater than decorations indifferently clean, was the style and manner of the audience. Men came into the lower tier of boxes without their coats; and I have seen shirt sleeves tucked up to the shoulder; the spitting was incessant, and the mixed smell of onions and whiskey was enough to make one feel even the Drakes' acting dearly bought by the obligation of enduring its accompaniments. The bearing and attitudes of the men are perfectly indescribable; the heels thrown higher than the head, the entire rear of the person presented to the audience, the whole length supported on the benches, are among the varieties that these exquisite posture-masters exhibit. The noises, too, were perpetual, and of the most unpleasant kind; the applause is expressed by cries and thumping with the feet, instead of clapping; and when a patriotic fit seized them, and "Yankee Doodle" was called for, every man seemed to think his reputation as a citizen depended on the noise he made.

7.7

Alexis de Tocqueville, *Democracy in America* (1835)

The French aristocrat Alexis de Tocqueville (1805–1859) was one of the most astute foreign observers of antebellum America. A political scientist, historian, and politician, Tocqueville and his colleague Gustave de Beaumont spent two years investigating American prison reforms. They traveled widely and met many notable Americans. When they returned to France in 1832, Tocqueville began writing his four-volume

SOURCE: Alexis de Tocqueville, *Democracy in America* (London, 1875), II, 137–43, *passim.*

Democracy in America *(1835–1840). He characterized America as a religious, vibrant, and egalitarian nation.* Democracy in America *was an international success and remains an insightful treatise on American politics and society.*

FOCUS QUESTIONS

1. What does Tocqueville identify as the defining characteristics of Americans?
2. Compare Tocqueville's observations to those made by Frances Trollope (Document 7.6). With whose appraisal do you most agree? Explain your answer.
3. What do you think a foreign observer would find most distinctive about American society today?

Among a democratic people, where there is no hereditary wealth, every man works to earn a living, or has worked, or is born of parents who have worked. The notion of labor is therefore presented to the mind, on every side, as the necessary, natural, and honest condition of human existence. Not only is labor not dishonorable among such a people, but it is held in honor; the prejudice is not against it, but in its favor. In the United States a wealthy man thinks that he owes it to public opinion to devote his leisure to some kind of industrial or commercial pursuit or to public business. He would think himself in bad repute if he employed his life solely in living. It is for the purpose of escaping this obligation to work that so many rich Americans come to Europe, where they find some scattered remains of aristocratic society, among whom idleness is still held in honor.

Equality of conditions not only ennobles the notion of labor, but raises the notion of labor as a source of profit. . . . No profession exists in which men do not work for money; and the remuneration that is common to them all gives them all an air of resemblance. This serves to explain the opinions that the Americans entertain with respect to different callings. In America no one is degraded because he works, for everyone about him works also; nor is anyone humiliated by the notion of receiving pay, for the President of the United States also works for pay. He is paid for commanding, other men for obeying orders. In the United States professions are more or less laborious, more or less profitable; but they are never either high or low: every honest calling is honorable. . . .

The United States of America has only been emancipated for half a century from the state of colonial dependence in which it stood to Great Britain; the number of large fortunes there is small and capital is still scarce. Yet no people in the world have made such rapid progress in trade and manufactures as the Americans; they constitute at the present day the second maritime nation in the world, and although their manufactures have to struggle with almost insurmountable natural impediments, they are not prevented from making great and daily advances.

In the United States the greatest undertakings and speculations are executed without difficulty, because the whole population are engaged in productive industry, and because the poorest as well as the most opulent members of the commonwealth are ready to combine their efforts for these purposes. The consequence is that a stranger is constantly amazed by the immense public works executed by a nation which contains, so to speak, no rich men. The Americans arrived but as yesterday on the territory which they inhabit, and they have already changed the whole order of nature for their own advantage. They have joined the Hudson to the Mississippi and made the Atlantic Ocean communicate with the Gulf of Mexico, across a continent of more than five hundred leagues in extent which separates the two seas. The longest railroads that have been constructed up to the present time are in America.

But what most astonishes me in the United States is not so much the marvelous grandeur of some undertakings as the innumerable multitude of small ones. Almost all the farmers of the United States combine some trade with agriculture; most of them make agriculture itself a trade. It seldom happens that an American farmer settles for good upon the land which he occupies; especially in the districts of the Far West, he brings land into tillage in order to sell it again, and not to farm it: he builds a farmhouse on the speculation that, as the state of the country will soon be changed by the increase of population, a good price may be obtained for it.

Every year a swarm of people from the North arrive in the Southern states and settle in the parts where the cotton plant and the sugar-cane grow. These men cultivate the soil in order to make it produce in a few years enough to enrich them; and they already look forward to the time when they may return home to enjoy the competency thus acquired. Thus the Americans carry their businesslike qualities into agriculture, and their trading passions are displayed in that as in their other pursuits.

The Americans make immense progress in productive industry, because they all devote themselves to it at once; and for this same reason they are exposed to unexpected and formidable embarrassments. As they are all engaged in commerce, their commercial affairs are affected by such various and complex causes that it is impossible to foresee what difficulties may arise. As they are all more or less engaged in productive industry, at the least shock given to business all private fortunes are put in jeopardy at the same time, and the state is shaken. I believe that the return of these commercial panics is an endemic disease of the democratic nations of our age. It may be rendered less dangerous, but it cannot be cured, because it does not originate in accidental circumstances, but in the temperament of these nations.

7.8

The Wonders of Phrenology Revealed (1841)

In an age where epidemics were common and misunderstood, many Americans distrusted doctors and turned to alternative medicines. During the antebellum era, "water cures," dietary changes, and restricted sexual activity were popular therapies. Phrenology was the most popular health fad. Created by Viennese physician Franz-Joseph Gall, phrenology interprets skull shapes in order to assess mental faculties and character traits. In the 1840s, brothers Orson and Lorenzo Fowler popularized phrenology in the United States. Although it appealed to Americans' desire for simple and expedient medical information, it has been wholly discredited by modern science.

FOCUS QUESTIONS

1. What does the author claim can be learned from a person's head?
2. Give examples of Americans' continuing interest in health fads.

Between eminently intellectual individuals and idiots the difference is similar to that which obtains between man and mammalia. Men of large heads ... have capacious minds; whereas in idiots ... the brain is small, the convolutions few and shallow, and the anterior lobes but little developed. If, indeed, we extend the comparison through all the intermediate gradations of intellect, we shall be astonished to find a corresponding agreement. "The mind of the Negro and the Hottentot, of the Calmuck and the Carib, is inferior to that of the European, and their organization is less perfect"—"the intellectual characters are reduced, the animal features enlarged and exaggerated." Even hatters have ascertained that servants and Negroes have smaller heads than others. Women are as unlike men in the form of their heads as in the qualities of their minds. In men of commanding talents the greater quantity of cerebral matter is anterior to the ear; but in heads which are truncated before, and largely developed in the opposite direction, the passions will be found to be stronger than the understanding. The higher

SOURCE: "The Wonders of Phrenology Revealed," *American Phrenological Journal*, Vol. 3 (July 1841).

sentiments elevate the *calvaria* or top of the head; it is accordingly observed, that from men whose heads are flattened, as in quadrupeds, "Conscience, virtue, honor, are exiled."

7.9

Nathaniel Hawthorne,
A Letter from Brook Farm (1841)

During the antebellum period, unprecedented numbers of Americans worked to improve society. The reformers' pursuit of human perfection took its most radical form in the utopian communities. Founded by intellectuals hoping to free expression and spirituality from the material world, the utopians experimented with group living and collective work. They hoped to inspire others to abandon economic competition. In 1825, the industrialist Robert Owen founded New Harmony, the first U.S. planned community. Owen believed that social problems would vanish if individuals lived in a cooperative environment. Although Owen's experiment failed, similar communities sprang up across the country.

Brook Farm is a good example. The transcendentalists George Ripley and Bronson Alcott founded Brook Farm as a refuge from nearby Boston. In 1841, the novelist Nathaniel Hawthorne, most noted for The Scarlet Letter, *arrived in the community. Although he later satirized Brook Farm in* The Blithedale Romance *(1852), this letter to his fiancée indicates his more sympathetic first impressions.*

FOCUS QUESTIONS

1. What does Hawthorne do at Brook Farm?
2. What is his opinion of his experiences there?
3. What elements of mainstream society were the residents of Brook Farm rejecting? Why would someone want to live in a utopian community?

SOURCE: *Voices from America's Past*, Richard B. Morris and James Woodress (New York: E. P. Dutton & Co., 1961, 1962, 1963), 2:46–47.

As the weather precludes all possibility of ploughing, hoeing, sowing and other such operations, I bethink me that you may have no objection to hear something of my whereabout and whatabout. You are to know then, that I took up my abode here on the 12th ultimo, in the midst of a snowstorm, which kept us all idle for a day or two. At the first glimpse of fair weather, Mr. Ripley summoned us into the cowyard and introduced me to an instrument with four prongs, commonly called a dung-fork. With this tool, I have already assisted to load twenty or thirty carts of manure, and shall take part in loading nearly three hundred more. Besides, I have planted potatoes and peas, cut straw and hay for the cattle, and done various other mighty works. This very morning, I milked three cows; and I milk two or three every night and morning. The weather has been so unfavorable, that we have worked comparatively little in the fields; but, nevertheless, I have gained strength wonderfully—grown quite a giant, in fact— and can do a day's work without the slightest inconvenience. In short, I am transformed into a complete farmer.

This is one of the most beautiful places I ever saw in my life, and as secluded as if it were a hundred miles from any city or village. There are woods, in which we can ramble all day, without meeting anybody, or scarcely seeing a house. Our house stands apart from the main road; so that we are not troubled even with passengers looking at us. Once in a while, we have a transcendental visitor, such as Mr. [Bronson] Alcott; but, generally, we pass whole days without seeing a single face, save those of the brethren. At this present time, our effective force consists of Mr. Ripley, Mr. Farley (a farmer from the far west), Rev. Warren Burton (author of various celebrated works), three young men and boys, who are under Mr. Ripley's care, and William Allen, his hired man, who has the chief direction of our agricultural labors. In the female part of the establishment there is Mrs. Ripley and two women folks. The whole fraternity eat together; and such a delectable way of life has never been seen on earth, since the days of the early Christians. We get up at half-past four, breakfast at half-past six, dine at half-past twelve, and go to bed at nine.

The thin frock, which you made for me, is considered a most splendid article; and I should not wonder if it were to become the summer uniform of the community. I have a thick frock, likewise; but it is rather deficient in grace, though extremely warm and comfortable. I wear a tremendous pair of cow-hide boots, with soles two inches thick. Of course, when I come to see you, I shall wear my farmer's dress.

We shall be very much occupied during most of this month, ploughing and planting; so that I doubt whether you will see me for two or three weeks. You have the portrait by this time, I suppose; so you can very well dispense with the original. When you write to me (which I beg you will do soon) direct your letter to West Roxbury, as there are two post offices in the town. I would write more; but William Allen is going to the village, and must have this letter; so good-bye.

Nath Hawthorne
Ploughman

7.10

John Humphrey Noyes on Free Love at Oneida (1865)

The most controversial utopian experiment was the Oneida Community in New York. Founded in 1848 by John Humphrey Noyes (1811–1886), Oneida challenged traditional conceptions of religion, marriage, sex, gender, and parenting. After making a religious conversion in 1831, Noyes decided to become a minister. While at Yale Divinity School, he challenged religious orthodoxy by declaring that humans could attain perfection through conversion and willpower. He was denied a preaching license and forced to leave the seminary.

In 1836, Noyes and fellow "Bible Communists" congregated in Putney, Vermont. In 1846, the group adopted Noyes's system of "complex marriage." Under this agreement, all of the women were wives of all of the men, and all men were husbands of all of the women. A committee led by Noyes approved all couplings. To control pregnancies, men practiced premature withdrawal or "continence." All children over the age of four were placed in a group nursery. After Noyes was arrested for adultery, he fled to New York and founded the Oneida Community. While other communes failed, Oneida flourished because of success in trap-making, silk embroidery, and canning. By 1875, about 300 people had joined Noyes. When the community began to disintegrate, he fled to Canada. In 1880, the residents of Oneida abandoned complex marriage and organized a joint-stock company manufacturing silver flatware.

FOCUS QUESTIONS

1. How does Noyes explain marriage and family life at Oneida?

2. How do these ideas represent a critique of marriage and gender roles in nineteenth-century America? What types of people do you think lived in Oneida?

3. What is your opinion of Noyes? Would you want to live in a community like Oneida? Explain your answers.

SOURCE: *Circular*, February 6, 1865.

The obvious and essential difference between marriage and whoredom may be stated thus:

Marriage is a permanent union. Whoredom is a temporary flirtation.

In Marriage, communism of property goes with communism of persons. In Whoredom, love is paid for by the job.

Marriage makes the man responsible for the consequences of his acts of love to a woman. In whoredom a man imposes on a woman the heavy burdens of maternity, ruining perhaps her reputation and her health, and then goes on his way without responsibility.

Marriage provides for the maintenance and education of children. Whoredom ignores children as nuisances, and leaves them to chance.

Now in respect to every one of these points of difference between marriage and whoredom, *we stand with marriage*. Free love with us does not mean freedom of love today and leave tomorrow; or freedom to take a woman's person and keep our property to ourselves; or freedom to freight a woman with our offspring and send her downstream without care or help; or freedom to beget children and leave them to the street and the poorhouse.

Our Communities are *families*, as distinctly bounded and separated from promiscuous society as ordinary households. The tie that binds us together is as permanent and sacred, to say the least, as that of marriage, for it is our religion. We receive no members (except by deception and mistake), who do not give heart and hand to the family interest for life and forever. Community of property extends just as far as freedom of love. Every man's care and every dollar of the common property is pledged for the maintenance and protection of the women and the education of the children and of the Community. Bastardy, in any disastrous sense of the word, is simply impossible in such a social state. Whoever will take the trouble to follow our track from the beginning will find no forsaken women or children by the way. In this respect we claim to be a little ahead of marriage in common civilization.

7.11

"Jim Crow," A Minstrel Song (undated)

Throughout much of the nineteenth century to the early 1900s, minstrel shows were one of the most popular forms of entertainment in the United States. The shows likely began after Thomas Dartmouth "Daddy" Rice, a struggling actor, blackened his face, donned shabby clothes, and performed an elaborate dance to a tune called "Jump Jim Crow." Allegedly modeled on the actions of an elderly African-American man whom Rice encountered in a city street, the dance was wildly popular. Minstrel troupes such as Dan Emmett's Virginia Minstrels and Christy's Minstrels became internationally famous. In these shows, white men, mostly Irish immigrants, blackened their faces with burnt cork and performed songs and skits that demeaned blacks and idealized slavery.

Although the shows drew upon African-American culture, whites wrote most of the music. Stephen Foster's "Camptown Races," "My Old Kentucky Home," and "O Susanna" are only a few of the songs popularized by minstrelsy. Many whites viewed these performances as authentic reflections of black culture, not racist caricatures. Catering to the prejudices of their mostly white and working-class audiences, minstrels portrayed African Americans as lazy and stupid. At a time of intensifying social and political tensions over race and slavery, many whites were receptive to such images.

These are the lyrics of a popular minstrel song. Its composer and date of origin are unknown.

FOCUS QUESTIONS

1. How do these lyrics portray African Americans? How might these images have affected the lives of African Americans?

2. Why do you think whites found the minstrel shows so appealing?

3. Do we have anything similar to minstrelsy in modern American culture? Explain your answer.

SOURCE: "Jim Crow Complete in 150 Verses," Library of Congress, Rare Book and Special Collections Division, America Singing: Nineteenth-Century Song Sheets.

One ting tickle me,
To see both brack and white,
For ebery little jig a ma gee,
Dey get a patent right.
So I wheel about.
I turn about,
A I do just so,
And ebery time I wheel about,
I jump Jim Crow.
In dis here city,
Soon as de day do peep,
You nebber cotch a wink ob sleep,
For de damn patent sweep.
So I wheel, etc. . . .
Here am I from ole Kentuck,
As I hab yon all to know,
I's come to learn de Yorkers,
De style to jump Jim Crow;
Oh dat is de place for niggars,
Dey fatten dem on mush,
But if dey go de hul figur,
Dey make dem cry, OH HUSH? . . .
Ice cream is bery good,
And so is lemonade.
But I likes better dan dese,
To kiss de pretty maid.
Cuff hoe de bacco,
Sambo drive de plongh.
Nobody plays to day,
But our ole sow.
Damn ole sow,
She grunt all de day,
An upset de swill tub,
When massa gone away . . .
Massa sent me to buy oyster.
Now warnt I deep,
I gutted dem on road,
For fear dey would'nt keep. . . .
But I don't admire de liquor,
It bery good for some,
But we gentlemen ob color,
Always prefer de niggar rum. . . .
Now my verses are de best kind,
And dis I'm sure's no bore,
For ebery time I dance and sing,
De people cry encore. . . .

I hab a gal in dis city
She's as quick as a trigger,
And she nebber looks so handsome,
As when kissed by a nigger.
A white kiss is good enuff
But it dont sound so keen
As when giben by a brack man,
Wid a great broad grin.
When I do kiss de lubly creatures,
I screw my mouth jist so,
For it makes me feel so bery good,
Dat I don't know what to do.
But I nebber kissed a white gal
And I hope I neber will,
For you hab to be so delicate,
You cannot get your fill. . . .

7.12

Walt Whitman, "Song of Myself" (1855)

While sentimental novels and minstrel shows became mainstays of antebellum popular culture, many Americans were producing serious creative expressions of individualism and democracy. Breaking free of European artistic and literary conventions, they shaped a uniquely American high culture.

Walt Whitman (1819–1892) was one of the great artistic spirits of nineteenth-century America. A poet, journalist, and essayist, he celebrated ordinary people. He spent countless days wandering the streets of New York and totally immersed himself in the city's cultural diversity. After several publishers rejected his poetry, Whitman sold his house to finance the printing of Leaves of Grass. *Originally published in 1855,* Leaves of Grass *was praised by Ralph Waldo Emerson as a poetic masterpiece but initially generated little public interest. Undeterred, Whitman revised and reorganized* Leaves of Grass *several times. As it gained attention, some critics lambasted Whitman's "indecency" and crude verse.* Leaves of Grass *is now considered a landmark in American literature.*

This is an excerpt from Whitman's poem, "Song of Myself."

SOURCE: *Leaves of Grass* (1855 edition).

FOCUS QUESTIONS

1. What types of images does Whitman's poem convey?
2. Why do you think some people found *Leaves of Grass* shocking?
3. How does Whitman's poetry reflect the rise of American democracy?

The pure contralto sings in the organ loft,
The carpenter dresses his plank, the tongue of his
foreplane whistles its wild ascending lisp,
The married and unmarried children ride home to their
Thanksgiving dinner,
The pilot seizes the king-pin, he heaves down with a strong arm,
The mate stands braced in the whale-boat, lance and harpoon
are ready,
The duck-shooter walks by silent and cautious stretches,
The deacons are ordained with crossed hands at the altar,
The spinning-girl retreats and advances to the hum of the
big wheel,
The farmer stops by the bars as he walks on a First-day loafe
and looks at the oats and rye,
The lunatic is carried at last to the asylum a confirmed case,
(He will never sleep any more as he did in the cot in his
mother's bedroom;)
The jour printer with gray head and gaunt jaws works at his case,
He turns his quid of tobacco while his eyes get blurred with the manuscript;
The malformed limbs are tied to the surgeon's table,
What is removed drops horribly in a pail;
The quadroon girl is sold at the auction-stand, the drunkard nods
by the bar-room stove,
The machinist rolls up his sleeves, the policeman travels his beat,
the gatekeeper marks who pass,
The young fellow drives the express-wagon, (I love him, though
I do not know him;)
The half-breed straps on his light boots to compete in the race,
The western turkey-shooting draws old and young,
some lean on their rifles, some sit on logs,
Out from the crowd steps the marksman,
takes his position, levels his piece;
The groups of newly-come immigrants cover the wharf or levee,
As the woolly-pates hoe in the sugar-field, the overseer views them
from his saddle,
The bugle calls in the ball room, the gentlemen run for their
partners, the dancers bow to each other,

The youth lies awake in the cedar-roofed garret and harks to the
musical rain,
The Wolverine sets traps on the creek that helps fill the Huron,
The squaw wrapt in her yellow-hemmed cloth is offering
moccasins and bead-bags for sale,
The connoisseur peers along the exhibition-gallery with half-shut
eyes bent sideways,
The deck-hands make fast the steamboat, the plank is thrown
for the shore-going passengers,
The young sister holds out the skein while the elder sister winds
it off in a ball, and stops now and then for the knots,
The one-year wife is recovering and happy, a week ago
she bore her first child,
The clean-haired Yankee girl works with her sewing-machine or in
the factory or mill,
The paving-man leans on his two-handed rammer, the reporter's
lead flies swiftly over the notebook, the
sign-painter is lettering with blue and gold,
The canal boy trots on the towpath, the bookkeeper counts
at his desk, the shoemaker waxes his thread,
The conductor beats time for the band and all the performers
follow him,
The child is baptized, the convert is making his first professions,
The regatta is spread on the bay, the race is begun,
(how the white sails sparkle!)
The drover watching his drove sings out to them that would stray,
The peddler sweats with his pack on his back,
(the purchaser higgling about the odd cent;)
The bride unrumples her white dress, the minute-hand of the
clock moves slowly,
The opium-eater reclines with rigid head and just-opened lips,
The prostitute draggles her shawl, her bonnet bobs on her
tipsy and pimpled neck,
The crowd laugh at her blackguard oaths, the men jeer and
wink to each other,
(Miserable! I do not laugh at your oaths nor jeer you;)
The President holding a cabinet council is surrounded by the
great Secretaries,
On the piazza walk three matrons stately and friendly with twined arms,
The crew of the fish-smack pack repeated-layers of halibut in the hold,
The Missourian crosses the plains toting his wares and his cattle,
As the fare-collector goes through the train he gives notice by the
jingling of loose change,
The floor-men are laying the floor, the tinners are tinning the
roof, the masons are calling for mortar,
In single file each shouldering his hod pass onward the laborers;

Seasons pursuing each other the indescribable crowd is gathered,
it is the Fourth of July (what salutes of cannon and small arms!)
Seasons pursuing each other the plougher ploughs, the mower
mows, and the winter-grain falls in the ground;
Off on the lakes the pike-fisher watches and waits by the hole in
the frozen surface,
The stumps stand thick round the clearing, the squatter strikes
deep with his axe,
The Flatboatmen make fast towards dusk near the cotton-wood or
pecan-trees,
The Coon seekers go through the regions of the Red river or through
those drained by the Tennessee, or through those of the Arkansas,
Torches shine in the dark that hangs on the Chattahooche or Altamahaw,
Patriarchs sit at supper with sons and grandsons and great-
grandsons around them,
In walls of adobe, in canvas tents, rest hunters and trappers
after their day's sport,
The city sleeps and the country sleeps,
The living sleep for their time, the dead sleep for their time,
The old husband sleeps by his wife and the young husband sleeps
by his wife;
And these tend inward to me, and I tend outward to them,
And such as it is to be of these more or less I am,
And of these one and all I weave the song of myself.

7.13

John Neagle, *Pat Lyon at the Forge* (1826–1827)

Much of the art of the nineteenth century celebrated ordinary Americans and the American nation. This portrait is a great example. John Neagle (1796–1865) lived most of his life in Philadelphia where he studied painting. Bass Otis, one of his teachers, introduced him to Thomas Sully, the city's leading portraitist. Neagle married Sully's stepdaughter. Sully and Gilbert Stuart, the most cele-brated portraitist of the era, greatly influenced Neagle's artistic style.

Pat Lyon at the Forge is Neagle's masterpiece. Patrick Lyon, a successful Irish-American engineer, was close to retirement. He commissioned Neagle to paint him as the blacksmith he was as a young man, not as the rich businessman he had become. Falsely accused of bank robbery, the young Lyon had been briefly imprisoned. Note the image of Philadelphia's Walnut Street jail in the painting's upper left corner. By glorifying Lyon's humble origins, the portrait reflects the democratic spirit of the age. It also gave Lyon a chance to taunt the social elites of Philadelphia.

FOCUS QUESTIONS

1. What does this painting and the story of its creation suggest about American democracy?

2. Why was the appearance of artistic depictions of ordinary people culturally significant?

John Neagle, American, 1796–1896. *Pat Lyon at the Forge*, 1826–1827. Oil on canvas, 238.1 × 172.7 cm (93 3/4 × 68 in). Museum of Fine Arts, Boston: Henry M. and Zoë Oliver Sherman Fund. 1975 1975.806. Photograph © 2002 Museum of Fine Arts, Boston.

8

✳

Slavery and the Old South

The antebellum South was a dynamic and complicated place. While cotton production dominated the Southern economy, other crops, textiles, and iron were also important in the region's commerce. It is erroneous to assume that the Old South was economically backward and exclusively rural.

The role of slavery in Southern society also defies simple characterization. In the 1830s, after the North and the British Empire banned slavery, Southerners faced increasing criticism of their way of life. Although most Southern whites did not own slaves, they responded with a strident celebration of the South's virtues. A common racial identity bonded the non-slaveholding majority to the slave-holding elites.

While whites defended their social order, slaves attempted to preserve their dignity under intensely difficult circumstances. Family life, religion, and culture helped the slaves survive. They also resisted their masters in both direct and indirect ways.

THEMES TO CONSIDER

- The diversity and complexity of the antebellum South
- Master-slave relations
- The impact of enslavement on individuals
- Southern nationalism and the defense of slavery
- Slaves' resistance

8.1

Anne Newport Royall Describes the Alabama Frontier (1821)

In 1790, the Southern economy was stagnant. Tobacco, once the region's most lucrative crop, was losing its value. Unsound farming practices had eroded formerly rich farmlands. Only 25 percent of Southerners lived away from the Atlantic seaboard.

The introduction of the cotton gin in 1793 drastically changed Southern history. Once quite labor-intensive, cotton could now be inexpensively and easily produced. Huge demand for cotton by British textile mills convinced thousands to move to the "Cotton Kingdom," the fertile lands in South Carolina, Georgia, Florida, Alabama, Tennessee, Mississippi, Arkansas, and Texas. Planters began relying heavily on slaves to work their lucrative cotton plantations. Settlers built frontier towns virtually overnight.

Anne Newport Royall (1769–1854) describes these events in much of her work. Left financially strapped after the death of her husband, Royall moved to the new state of Alabama in 1819. Over the next four years, she traveled widely and wrote many letters to her lawyer and friend, Matthew Dunbar. Despite her rather atrocious spelling and grammar, she decided to publish her correspondence. After leaving Alabama, she wrote a series of travel books noted for their vivid depictions of locales and people. She also published two newspapers dedicated to exposing political and religious corruption. In this letter, Royall describes the thriving community of Florence, Alabama.

FOCUS QUESTIONS

1. How does Royall describe Florence?
2. What types of people are moving to Florence?
3. How does Royall's depiction of Florence challenge your notions of the Old South? Explain your answer.

SOURCE: Anne Newport Royall to Matthew Dunbar, 10 July 1821, Letter 45, *Letters from Alabama on Various Subjects* (Washington: DC, 1830), 144–146.

Florence, July 10th, 1821.

Florence is one of the new towns of this beautiful and rapid rising state. It is happily situated for commerce at the head of steamboat navigation, on the north side of Tennessee river, in the county of Lauderdale, five miles below the port of the Muscle Shoals, and ten miles from the line of the state of Tennessee.

Florence is to be the great emporium of the northern part of this state I do not see why it should not; it has a great capital and is patronized by the wealthiest gentlemen in the state. It has a great state at its back; another in front, and a noble river on all sides, the steamboats pouring every necessary and every luxury into its lap. Its citizens, bold, enterprising, and industrious—much more so than any I have seen in the state.

Many large and elegant brick buildings are already built here, (although it was sold out, but two years since,) and frame houses are putting up daily. It is not uncommon to see a framed building begun in the morning and finished by night.

Several respectable mercantile houses are established here, and much business is done on commission also. The site of the town is beautifully situated on an eminence, commanding an extensive view of the surrounding country, and Tennessee river, from which it is three quarters of a mile distant.—It has two springs of excellent and never failing water. Florence has communication by water with *Mississippi, Missouri, Louisiana, Indiana, Illinois, Ohio, Kentucky, West Pennsylvania, West Virginia*, and *East Tennessee*, and very shortly will communicate with the Eastern States, through the great canal! The great Military road that leads from Nashville to New Orleans, by way of Lake Ponchartrain, passes through this town, and the number of people who travel through it, and the numerous droves of horses for the lower country, for market, are incredible. Florence contains one printing press, and publishes a paper weekly called the Florence Gazette; it is ably patronized, and edited by one of our first men, and said to be the best paper in the state. Florence is inhabited by people from almost all parts of Europe and the United States; here are English, Irish, Welch, Scotch, French, Dutch, Germans, and *Grecians*. The first Greek I ever saw was in this town. I conversed with him on the subject of his country, but found him grossly ignorant. He butchers for the town, and has taken to his arms a mulatto woman for a wife. He very often takes an airing on horseback of a Sunday afternoon, with his wife riding by his side, and both arrayed in shining costume.

The river at Florence is upwards of five-hundred yards wide; it is ferried in a large boat worked by four horses, and crosses in a few minutes.

There are two large and well kept Taverns in Florence, and several *Doggeries*. A Doggery is a place where spirituous liquors are sold; and where men get drunk, quarrel, and fight, as often as they choose, but where there is nothing to eat for man or beast. Did you ever hear any thing better named? "I sware!" said a Yankee pedlar, one day, with both his eyes bunged up, "that are Doggery, be rightly named. Never seed the like on't. If I get to hum agin it 'il be a nice man 'il catch me in these here parts. Awfullest place one could beat." It appeared the inmates of the Doggery enticed him under pretence of buying his wares, and forced him to drink; and then forced him to fight; but the poor little Yankee was sadly beaten. Not content with blacking up his eyes, they overturned his tin—cart, and scattered his tins to the four winds; frightened his horse, and tormented his very soul out about *lasses*, &c: He was a laughable object—but to hear his dialect in laying off the law, was a complete farce, particularly when Pat came to invite him into the same Doggery to drink friends—"I bent a dog to go into that are dog house."

The people, you see, *know a thing* or two, here; they call things by their right names. But to proceed—there may be about one hundred dwelling houses and stores, a court house, and several ware houses in Florence. The latter are however on the river. One of the longest buildings I ever saw, is in Florence. It was built by a company of gentlemen, and is said to have cost $90,000, and is not yet finished. The proprietors, being of this place, are men of immense wealth, and are pushing their capital with great foresight and activity. For industry and activity, Florence outstrips all the northern towns in the state. More people travel this road than all our western roads put together. . . .

Yours, &c.

8.2

Life in the Pine Woods (1831)

Approximately 10 percent of Southern whites squatted on land in "pine barrens." After haphazardly clearing some land, they planted corn between tree stumps and let their hogs and cattle roam in the woods. While this lifestyle appeared disorganized and lazy to outsiders, piney woods residents prized their independence and sustained themselves economically. This newspaper story gives a glimpse of this world.

FOCUS QUESTIONS

1. How does the author describe the residents of the pine barrens?
2. What effect has illness had upon this area?
3. What might explain the residents' attitudes toward medicine?

SOURCE: Augusta (Ga.) *Constitutionalist*, Oct. 18, 1831.

4. How do the lives of the pine barren folk compare to those living in Florence, Alabama (Document 8.1)?

Augusta (Ga.) Constitutionalist, Oct. 8, 1831

The inhabitants of our city are scarcely aware that exists within one hundred miles of them a people peculiar in habits, pursuits and manners, and among whom the absence of refinement and luxury is compensated by a republican simplicity—native vigor of intellect and kindness of heart. We allude particularly to the counties of Emanuel and Tattnall, where although wealth and polish do not abound—the inhabitants are perhaps as happy and comfortable as those who breathe the air of our towns and reside in more populous and flourishing regions. Trained to labor from their youth, they shrink from no toil or hardship—and content with little, their ideas do not stray beyond the farms where grow their cotton, and corn and sugar cane, and the pine woods where their flocks feed upon the luxuriant wild-oats. The country is wild, sparsely settled, full of game, and if we except one or two highways leading to Savannah, almost without roads, the paths dignified by the name of roads being almost overgrown by grass, and so dim and blind that the traveler almost unconsciously wanders from them into the forest.

Health is the inheritance of sire and son, although it must be confessed that in this sickly 1831, it has not been so generally enjoyed as of yore. The ague [a fever accompanied by chills and sweating] has made its appearance in several places and bilious fever [a gastric disorder] have in one or two cases astounded the inhabitants by their ravages. In the county of Emanuel no physician resides—he could not make his bread– and in Tattnall, the ailments of the people, usually slight, are ministered unto by an amiable gentleman who has some skill in medicine but who never listened to a lecture or witnessed a dissection, and perhaps his patients like him the better for it. The aid of this kind amateur, however, is not always invoked in time of need—some of the good people have a horror of doctors and their means, an instance of which occurred but recently. An excellent old man, a Methodist preacher, died, full of years and ripe for future happiness, for he was followed to the grave by the blessings and lamentations of all who knew him. In a year or two afterwards a daughter followed him, and disease, a bilious fever, by which they had been taken away, still remained to afflict two brothers of the family. They were visited by some intelligent gentlemen, who learned with surprise that medical assistance had not been called in. There sat the wretched mother watching the progress of that malady which had already deprived her of the most cherished of her heart, and there lay the brothers; the abated fever, of the one inspiring hope that strength of constitution would finally o come his complaint—the parched and yellow skin torpid condition of the other foreboding the speedy close of his worldly cares. Anxiously did the visitors recommend immediate application to a physician earnestly did they describe the fatal consequences neglect and delay—one of them offered his own services and his purse to procure a medical attendant—in vain, the mother trusted in "the good one above," and would on no account allow a doctor of medicine to approach her family. One of the visitors proposed to prescribe, he suggested calomel, he might as well have recommended arsenic; the mother was sure that calomel and death were synonymous. Our gentlemen departed with such feelings as humane men must experience when they perceive an ill within the reach of a remedy which ignorance and prejudice, courting destruction, reject.

8.3

Managing the Butler Estate (1828)

By 1830, almost two million slaves worth over $1 billion lived in the South. While many successful planters lived modestly, others built lavish homes and hosted elaborate parties. But plantation life was not always easy or predictable. Masters and their overseers set work schedules, ordered equipment and supplies, and maintained family members and slaves. Price fluctuations and uncertain market conditions kept many planters mired in debt.

Slaves were vital to the success of large plantations. Although only 12 percent of slaveholders owned more than twenty slaves, all slaveowners carefully regulated slaves' lives. Most slaves spent about fourteen hours a day in backbreaking farm work supervised by black drivers and white overseers. On rice plantations, the task system sometimes left slaves time to tend their own gardens. Other slaves worked as skilled artisans such as blacksmiths, coopers, and ironworkers. House slaves cooked, cleaned, and tended the master's children. Virtually all slaves lived in crowded, unsanitary conditions and suffered from malnutrition. High rates of infant mortality and low life expectancy attested to the physical rigors of slavery.

Many slaveholders downplayed or ignored these wretched conditions. Combining religion, history, and racism into justifications for slavery, some masters claimed that slaves were intellectually and emotionally unable to appreciate their plight. Others owners viewed themselves as gentle patriarchs responsible for the material and spiritual needs of their slave "children."

Such attitudes are evident in this selection. In it, Roswell King, Jr., a slave overseer, describes how he and his father manage the Georgia estate of Pierce Butler. With over 700 slaves, the Butler plantation was one of the country's largest.

SOURCE: *Southern Agriculturalist,* December 1828, South Carolina Historical Society.
Reprinted with permission.

FOCUS QUESTIONS

1. Why does King believe the Butler plantation is so efficient?
2. What does King believe slave management requires? What are his attitudes toward the slaves?
3. What are some of the punishments and incentives that King uses?
4. How does King describe the diet of slaves?
5. What special provisions does King make for female slaves?
6. Compare King's description of the Butler estate to that of Fanny Kemble (Document 8.4). How do their accounts differ? Whose account do you think was more accurate? Why?

The reputed good condition of the Butler Estate, has been the work of time, and a diligent attention to the interest of said estate, and the comfort and happiness of the slaves on it.

To Mr. R. King, sen'r. more is due than to myself. In 1802, he assumed the management. The gang was a fine one, but was very disorderly, which invariably is the case when there is a frequent change of managers. Rules and regulations were established, (I may say laws,) a few forcible examples made, after a regular trial, in which every degree of justice was exhibited, was the first step. But the grand point was to suppress the brutality and licentiousness practiced by the principal men on it; (say the drivers and tradesmen.) More punishment is inflicted on every plantation by the men in power, from private pique, than from a neglect of duty. This I assert as a fact; I have detected it often. No person of my age, knows more the nature of these persons than myself; since childhood I have been on this place, and from the age of eighteen to this time, have had the active management; therefore I speak with confidence. They have a perfect knowledge of right and wrong. When an equitable distribution of rewards and punishments is observed, in a short time they will conform to almost every rule that is laid down.

The owner or overseer knows, that with a given number of hands, such a portion of work is to be done. The driver, to screen favorites, or apply their time to his own purposes, imposes a heavy task on some. Should they murmur, and opportunity is taken, months after, to punish those unfortunate fellows for not doing their own and others tasks. Should they not come at the immediate offenders, it will descend on the nearest kindred. As an evidence of the various opportunities that a burial driver has to gratify his revenge, (the predominant principle of the human race,) let any planter go into his field, and in any Negro's task, he can find apparently just grounds for punishment. To prevent this abuse, no driver in the field is allowed to inflict punishment, until after a regular trial. When I pass sentence myself, various modes of punishment are adopted; the lash, least of all—Digging stumps, or clearing away trash about the settlements, in their own time; but the most severe is, confinement at home six months to twelve months, or longer. No intercourse is allowed with other plantations. A certain number are allowed to go to town on Sundays, to dispose of eggs, poultry, coopers' ware, canoes, &c. but must be home by 12 o'clock, unless by special permit. Any one returning intoxicated, (a rare instance) goes into stocks, and not allowed to leave home for twelve months.

An order from a driver is to be as implicitly obeyed as if it came from myself, nor do I counteract the execution, (unless directly injurious,) but direct his immediate attention to it. It would be endless for me to superintend the drivers and field hands too, and would of course make them useless. The lash is, unfortunately, too much used; every mode of punishment should be devised in preference to that, and when used, never to lacerate—all young persons will offend. A Negro at twenty-five years old, who finds he has the marks of a rogue inflicted when a boy, (even if disposed to be orderly) has very little or no inducement to be otherwise. Every means are used to encourage them, and impress on their minds the advantage of holding property, and the disgrace attached to idleness. Surely, if industrious for themselves, they will be so for their masters, and no Negro, with a well stocked poultry house, a small crop advancing, a canoe partly finished, or a few tubs unsold, all of which he calculates soon to enjoy, will ever run away. In ten years I have lost, by absconding, forty-seven days, out of nearly six hundred Negroes. Any Negro leaving the plantation, field, to complain to me, is registered and treated as such. Many may think that they lose time, when Negroes can work for themselves; it is the reverse on all plantations under good regulations—time is absolutely gained to the master.

An indolent Negro is most always sick, and unless he is well enough to work for his master, he cannot work for himself, and when the master's task is done, he is in mischief, unless occupied for himself. And another evidence arising from the encouragement of industry, I make on this estate as good crops as most of my neighbors; plant as much to the hand, do as much plantation work, and very often get clear of a crop earlier than many where these encouragements are not held out. I have no before-day work, only as punishments; every hand must be at work by daylight. The tasks given are calculated to require so much labour. It is as easy to cut three tasks of Rice, as it is to bind two, or to bring two home. It is easier to ditch eight hundred cubic feet of marsh, than four hundred feet of rooty river swamp. There are many regulations on a plantation that must be left discretionary with the manager. In harvesting a crop of Rice, some acres are heavier, or further off than others, some hands quicker, or more able than others all these, considered, make a wide difference—by giving a far and a near task to bring in, or putting them in gangs, the burthen is borne equally, and all come home at once. Frequently (always I can say) by Friday night, I have nearly as much Rice in, as if the regular task during the week, had been given....

By this mode I not only gain time, but afford them some also. A man, white or black, that knows such will be the result, will seldom deviate from the right course. All these things are not to be slipped into at once; it has been the work of nearly twenty-seven years, and I find many things yet to correct. With regard to feeding, they have plenty of the best Corn, well ground, by water and animal power, with a portion of Fish, (No. 3, Mackerel,) Beef, Pork, and Molasses, and when much exposed, a little Rum. To each gang there is a cook, who carefully prepares two meals per day. The very grinding and cooking for them affords the time that they apply to their own purposes; if their provisions was given underground, many would trade it off, or be too lazy to cook it. Any one that has spent a night on a plantation where the Negroes grind their own Corn, must recollect the horrible sound of a *hand mill, all night*. It is this that wears them down. He goes to the mill—it is occupied—he must wait until the first has done, and so on; some are at it all night—their natural rest is destroyed. Many masters think they give provision and clothing in abundance, but unless they use means to have these properly prepared, half the benefit is lost. Another great advantage in grinding and cooking for them is, that the little Negroes are sure to get enough to eat. On this estate, there are two hundred and thirty-eight Negroes from fifteen years down, and every one knows that they do not increase in proportion in a large gang, as in a small one, with the same attention. I cannot exemplify in too strong terms, the great advantage resulting from properly preparing the food for Negroes.—They will object to it at first, but no people are more easily convinced of any thing tending to their comfort, than they are. In fact, a master does not discharge his duty to himself, unless he will adopt every means to promote his interest and their welfare. Again, many will say it takes too many to wait on the others. An old woman for a cook, who will raise one little Negro extra, which will certainly pay her wages, besides the very great comfort it will afford the others; a machine that will not cost in twenty years, more than $15 per annum; a little boy to drive an old horse two days in the week, and an old man, (or even the overseer on a place of thirty hands,) to act as a commissary in issuing the provisions, I am sure, well regulated, will add 25 per cent to the owner, including gain in Negroes, comfort to them, and to their master's feelings. During the summer, little Negroes should have an extra mess. I find at Butler's Island, where there are about one hundred and fourteen little Negroes, that it costs less than two cents each per week, in giving them a feed of Okra soup, with Pork, or a little Molasses or Hominy, or Small Rice. The great advantage is, that there is not a *dirt-eater* among them—an incurable propensity produced from a morbid state of the stomach, arising from the want of a proper quantity of wholesome food, and at a proper time.

I have invariably found that women, that had been accustomed to waiting in the houses of white persons, have the largest and finest families of children, even after going into the field. I believe it arises from this circumstance, that they had contracted a habit of cleanliness, and of preparing their food properly. You, on looking round, will find this the case. An hospital should be on each plantation, with proper nurses and apartments for lying-in women, for the men, and for a nursery; when any enter, not to leave the house until discharged. I have found physicians of little service, except in surgical cases. An intelligent woman will in a short time learn the use of medicine. The labour of pregnant women is reduced one half, and they are put to work in dry situations.

It is a great point in having the principal drivers men that can support their dignity; a condescension to familiarity should be prohibited. Young Negroes are put to work early, twelve to fourteen years old; four, five, or six, rated a hand. It keeps them out of mischief, and by giving light tasks, thirty to forty rows, they acquire habits of perseverance and industry....

8.4

Fanny Kemble Describes Plantation Slavery (1863)

Due to the enormous popularity of the film and novel Gone with the Wind, *many people believe that white women of the antebellum South enjoyed carefree lives of barbeques, balls, and romance. The reality is considerably less glamorous. Most Southern white women completed grueling household and farming chores without slaves. They were less likely to be literate and more likely to die young than their Northern counterparts. Even the wives of large slaveholders, who comprised less than 5 percent of Southern women, worked long hours supervising plantation accounts, ensuring family health, distributing meals, and performing other chores.*

While rural life could be lonely and isolating for all Southerners, slave-holding women faced unique challenges. Many filled their diaries with rage and anguish at the sexual relationships between white men and slave women. Children produced by such liaisons were painful reminders of masters' sexual abuse of slave women. Nonetheless, most planters' wives also recognized the economic and social status that slavery accorded them and rarely opposed the institution.

Fanny Kemble (1809–1893) proved a notable exception. One of England's most famous actresses, she began an American tour in 1832. Two years later, she married Pierce Butler, a wealthy Georgia planter. After marrying Butler in Philadelphia, she retired from the stage and accompanied him to his estate, the same plantation described by Roswell King in Document 8.3. During her four-month stay, she wrote about her horror at the realities of slavery. Although Butler's infidelity led to a scandalous divorce, Kemble did not publish her writings for several years. In 1846, she returned to Britain and resumed her acting career. Butler, meanwhile, squandered his considerable fortune through actions like losing $24,000 in a single hand of cards. In 1857, he attempted to pay his debts by selling his slaves in the largest slave auction in the nation's history. While the event netted Butler over $300,000, it devastated slave families whose members were dispersed all over the South.

SOURCE: Frances Anne Kemble, *Journal of a Residence on a Georgian Plantation in 1838–1839* (New York: Harper & Brothers Publishers, 1863), 189–91.

When the Civil War erupted in 1861, Kemble was afraid that the British might officially recognize the Confederacy. Hoping to sway popular opinion against the South, she published her accounts of life on the Butler estate in 1838 and 1839. Her Journal of a Residence on a Georgian Plantation *(1863) proved instrumental in mobilizing English support for the Union and the Emancipation Proclamation. In this excerpt, Kemble describes some of her interactions with female slaves.*

FOCUS QUESTIONS

1. What requests do these female slaves make? What do their situations suggest about slavery's impact on women?

2. How does Kemble respond to the women's pleas? Do you think her attitude toward her slaves was common? Explain your answer.

3. Compare Roswell King's description of the Butler estate (Document 8.3) to that of Fanny Kemble. How do their accounts differ? Whose account do you think was more accurate? Why?

Before closing this letter, I have a mind to transcribe to you the entries for today recorded in a sort of daybook, where I put down very succinctly the number of people who visit me, their petitions and ailments, and also such special particulars concerning them as seem to me worth recording. You will see how miserable the physical condition of many of these poor creatures is; and their physical condition, it is insisted by those who uphold this evil system, is the only part of it which is prosperous, happy, and compares well with that of Northern laborers. Judge from the details I now send you; and never forget, while reading them, that the people on this plantation are well off, and consider themselves well off, in comparison with the slaves on some of the neighboring estates.

Fanny has had six children; all dead but one. She came to beg to have her work in the field lightened.

Nanny has had three children; two of them are dead. She came to implore that the rule of sending them into the field three weeks after their confinement might be altered.

Leah, Caesar's wife, has had six children; three are dead.

Sophy, Lewis's wife, came to beg for some old linen. She is suffering fearfully; has had ten children; five of them are dead. The principal favor she asked was a piece of meat, which I gave her.

Sally, Scipio's wife, has had two miscarriages and three children born, one of whom is dead. She came complaining of incessant pain and weakness in her back. This woman was a mulatto daughter of a slave called Sophy, by a white man of the name of Walker, who visited the plantation.

Charlotte, Renty's wife, had had two miscarriages, and was with child again. She was almost crippled with rheumatism, and showed me a pair of poor swollen knees that made my heart ache. I have promised her a pair of flannel trousers, which I must forthwith set about making.

Sarah, Stephen's wife: this woman's case and history were alike deplorable. She had had four miscarriages, had brought seven children into the world, five of whom were dead, and was again with child. She complained of dreadful pains in the back, and an internal tumor which swells with the exertion of working in the fields; probably, I think, she is ruptured. She told me she had once been mad and had run into the woods, where she contrived to elude discovery for some time, but was at last tracked and brought back, when she was tied up by the arms, and heavy logs fastened to her feet, and was severely flogged. After this she contrived to escape again, and lived for some time skulking in the woods, and she supposes mad, for when she was taken again she was entirely naked. She subsequently recovered from this derangement, and seems now just like all the other poor creatures who come to me for help and pity. I suppose her constant childbearing and hard labor in the fields at the same time have produced the temporary insanity. . . .

This is only the entry for today, in my diary, of the people's complaints and visits. Can you conceive a more wretched picture than that which it exhibits of the conditions under which these women live? Their cases are in no respect singular, and though they come with pitiful entreaties that I will help them with some alleviation of their pressing physical distresses, it seems to me marvelous with what desperate patience (I write it advisedly, patience of utter despair) they endure their sorrow-laden existence. . . .

8.5

Religion as Social Control: A Catechism for Slaves (1854)

After the Nat Turner rebellion in 1831, white Southerners' defense of slavery grew much more defiant. Relying on Christian theology and ancient history, they defined themselves as civilized and enlightened. The rise of the proslavery argument greatly affected Southern religious life. Invoking St. Paul's edict

SOURCE: "Frederick Douglass' Paper," June 2, 1854, from *The Southern Episcopalian* (Charleston: S.C., April 1854).

"servants obey your masters" and references to slavery in the Old Testament, many whites used the Bible to justify slavery. By the 1830s, many Protestant ministers argued that slavery was not inconsistent with Christianity. Whites, they claimed, had a Christian duty to take care for their "inferiors" and to ensure that African Americans embraced religious virtues like submission and humility. By 1845, differences over slavery split the Methodist Episcopal Church and Baptist Church into separate Southern and Northern wings. The following reading offers an example of religious instruction directed at slaves. In such lessons, slaves answered questions asked by their masters.

FOCUS QUESTIONS

1. What are the central themes of this passage?
2. How would religious instruction like this reinforce slavery?

Q: Who keeps the snakes and all bad things from hurting you?

A: God does.

Q: Who gave you a master and a mistress?

A: God gave them to me.

Q: Who says that you must obey them?

A: God says I must.

Q: What book tells you these things?

A: The Bible.

Q: How does God do all his work?

A: He always does it right.

Q: Does God love to work?

A: Yes, God is always at work.

Q: Do the angels work?

A: Yes, they do what God tells them.

Q: Do they love to work?

A: Yes, they love to please God.

Q: What does God say about your work?

A: That they who will not work shall not eat.

Q: Did Adam and Eve have to work?

A: Yes, they had to keep the garden.

Q: Was it hard to keep the garden?

A: No, it was very easy.

Q: What makes the crops so hard to grow now?

A: Sin makes it.

Q: What makes you lazy?

A: My wicked heart.

Q: How do you know your heart is wicked?

A: I feel it every day.

Q: Who teaches you so many wicked things?

A: The Devil.

Q: Must you let the Devil teach you?

A: No, I must not.

8.6

George Fitzhugh Defends Southern Society (1854)

Simmering sectional disputes exploded in the 1850s. As Southerners grew more determined to protect their way of life, Northerners became more alarmed. Increasing numbers of Northerners embraced free soil—the belief that slavery should be banned from the territories. Southerners feared such views could jeopardize their social and economic investment in slavery. Bitter disagreements over property rights, race, and labor led to outbursts of violence and moral outrage. By decade's end, the nation's fragmented political system could no longer prevent secession.

George Fitzhugh (1806–1881) was one of the most effective defenders of antebellum Southern society. He practiced law and struggled as a small planter but won national attention for his two books on slavery, Sociology for the South *(1854) and* Cannibals All! Slaves without Masters *(1857). Fitzhugh advanced proslavery arguments based on his personal travels and study of political*

SOURCE: George Fitzhugh, *The Sociology for the South; Or, The Failure of Free Society* (Richmond: VA, 1854), 253–55.

economy. In this passage, Fitzhugh draws sharp distinctions between the Northern and Southern ways of life.

FOCUS QUESTIONS

1. How does Fitzhugh compare the North and the South? Why does he believe that the South is the superior society?

2. What is your opinion of Fitzhugh's claims? Is his portrait of the white antebellum South accurate? Explain your answers.

3. Would you have preferred to live in the antebellum North or South? Explain your answer.

At the slaveholding South, all is peace, quiet, plenty, and contentment. We have no mobs, no trades unions, no strikes for higher wages, no armed resistance to the law, but little jealousy of the rich by the poor. We have but few in our jails, and fewer in our poor houses. We produce enough of the comforts and necessaries of life for a population three or four times as numerous as ours. We are wholly exempt from the torrent of pauperism, crime, agrarianism, and infidelity which Europe is pouring from her jails and alms houses on the already crowded North. Population increases slowly, and wealth rapidly. In the tidewater region of Eastern Virginia, as far as our experience extends, the crops have doubled in fifteen yards, whilst the population has been almost stationary. In the same period in the lands, owing to improvements of the soil and the many fine houses erected in the country, have nearly doubled in value. This ratio of improvements has been approximated or exceeded wherever in the South slaves are numerous. We have enough for the present, and no Malthusian spectres frightening us for the future.

Wealth is more equally distributed than at the North, where a few millionaires own most of the property of the country. (These millionaires are men of cold hearts and weak minds; they know how to make money, but not how to use it, either for the benefit of themselves or of others.) High intellectual and moral attainments, refinement of head and heart, give standing to a man in the South, however poor he may be. Money is, with few exceptions, the only thing that ennobles at the North. We have poor among us, but none who are overworked or under-fed. We do not crowd cities because lands are abundant and their owners kind, merciful and hospitable. The poor are as hospitable as the rich, the negro as the white man. Nobody dreams of turning a friend, a relative, or a stranger from his door. The very negro who deems it no crime to steal, would scorn to sell his hospitality. We have no loafers, because the poor relative or friend who borrows our horse, or spends a week under our rood, is a welcome guest. The loose economy, the wasteful mode of living at the South, is a blessing when rightly considered; it keeps want, scarcity and famine at a distance, because it leaves no room to retrenchment. The nice, accurate economy of France, England, and New

England, keeps society, always on the verge of famine, because it leaves no room to retrench, that is to live on a part only of what they now consume.

Our society exhibits no appearance of precocity, no symptoms of decay. A long course of continuing improvement is in prospect before us, with no limits which human foresight can decry. Actual liberty and equality with our white population has been approached much nearer than in the free States. Few of our white population ever work as day laborers, none as cooks, scullions, ostlers [someone who tends horses], body servants, or in other menial capacities. One free citizen does not lord it over another; hence that pride of character, that self-respect, that give us ascendance when we come in contact with Northerners. It is a distinction to be a Southerner, as it once was to be a Roman citizen. . . .

8.7

Daniel Hundley, The Southern Yeoman (1860)

Although many people still associate the Old South with plantations and slaves, the majority of white Southerners were nonslaveholding family farmers (yeomen). Only 12 percent of slaveholders owned more than twenty slaves and a mere 1 percent owned more than 100 slaves. Large portions of the South were ill-suited for plantation agriculture or cotton production. Yeomen usually grew foodstuffs and a few cash crops in pursuit of economic self-sufficiency. Despite the class differences among whites, racial ties and resentment of Northern criticism of the South drew slaveholders and nonslaveholders together. While planters dominated Southern politics, they needed the votes of yeomen to remain in power. Accordingly, slaveholding politicians could not afford to ignore the demands of nonslaveholders.

SOURCE: Daniel R. Hundley, *Social Relations in Our Southern States* (New York, 1860), 192–198.

In Social Relations in Our Southern States, *Daniel R. Hundley tried to counter common stereotypes about Southern society. Born on an Alabama plantation, Hundley received a law degree from Harvard in 1853. He moved to Chicago and pursued a variety of business interests. Despite living in the North, Hundley visited the South often. In the following selection, Hundley explains the role yeomen played in the antebellum South.*

FOCUS QUESTIONS

1. How does Hundley describe the white social structure in the South?
2. How does Hundley characterize the relationship between yeomen and slaves?
3. What does Hundley identify as the yeoman's "greatest ambition"? Why would the yeomen aspire to such a goal?

For while princes, presidents, and governors may boast of their castles and lands, their silken gowns and robes of ceremony—all which can be made the sport of fortune, and do often vanish away in a moment, leaving their sometime owners poor indeed—the COMMON PEOPLE, as the masses are called, possess in and of themselves a far richer inheritance, which is the ability and the will to earn an honest livelihood (not by the tricks of trade and the lying spirit of barter, nor yet by trampling on any man's right, but) by the toilsome sweat of their own brows, delving patiently and trustingly in old mother earth, who under the blessing of God, never deceives or disappoints those who put their trust in her generous bosom. And of all the hardy sons of toil, in all free lands the Yeomen are most deserving of our esteem....

But you have no Yeomen in the South, my dear Sir? Beg your pardon, our dear Sir, but we have hosts of them. I thought you had only poor White Trash?...

Know, then, that the Poor Whites of the South constitute a separate class to themselves; the Southern Yeomen are as distinct from them as the Southern Gentlemen is from the Cotton Snob. Certainly the Southern Yeomen are nearly always poor, at least so far as this world's goods are to be taken into account. As a general thing they own no slaves; and even in case they do, the wealthiest of them rarely possess more than from ten to fifteen. But even when they are slaveholders, they seem to exercise but few of the rights of ownership over their human chattels, making so little distinction between master and man, that their negroes invariably become spoiled, like so many frequently see black and white, slave and freeman, camping out together, living sometimes in the same tent or temporary pine-pole cabin; drinking... out of the same tin dipper or long-handled gourd their home distilled brandy; dining on the same homely but substantial fare, and sharing one bed in common, the cabin floor.

Again should you go among the hardy yeomanry of Tennessee, Kentucky, or Missouri, whenever or wherever they own slaves (which in these States is not often the case) you will invariably see the negroes and their masters ploughing side by side in the fields; or bared to the waists, and with old-fashioned scythe vying with one another who can cut down the broadest swath of yellow wheat, or of the waving timothy; or bearing the tall stalks of maize and packing them into the stout built barn, with ear and fodder on, ready for the winter's husking. . . .

And yet, notwithstanding the Southern Yeoman allows his slaves so much freedom of speech and action, is not offended when they call him familiarly by his Christian name, and hardly makes them work enough to earn their salt, still he is very proud to be a slaveholder; and when he is not such, his greatest ambition is to make money enough to buy a negro. . . .

8.8

Nat Turner's "Confession" (1831)

The threat of slave insurrections plagued the Old South. In swampy areas, slaves often outnumbered whites. Whites suspected free blacks of inspiring slave revolts. Cognizant of the massive slave rebellion that ended French rule in Santo Domingo (Haiti), masters imposed strict controls on slaves.

Although there were dozens of unplanned slave uprisings, most were quickly suppressed. Slaves who planned rebellions were often betrayed by other slaves who feared white reprisals and/or identified with their masters. In 1800, slaves reported Gabriel Prosser's plans to lead a slave revolt in Richmond, Virginia. Prosser and his coconspirators were hanged. In 1822, Denmark Vesey, a free black artisan, devised plans for arming hundreds of slaves near Charleston, South Carolina. After slaves reported Vesey's plans, 139 blacks were arrested. Vesey and thirty-six others were executed.

Nat Turner (1800–1831) led the most successful slave insurrection. Born a slave on an isolated Virginia plantation, Turner abhorred slavery. As a child, Turner was taught to read by one of his master's sons and immersed himself in religious writings. He became a mesmerizing preacher who described himself as a prophet destined to lead his people out of servitude. In August 1831, Turner

SOURCE: Thomas R. Gray, *The Confessions of Nat Turner* (Baltimore: Lucas & Dearer, 1831).

decided it was time to act. He and a few slaves began marauding through Southampton, Virginia. As they moved from plantation to plantation, they murdered fifty-five whites and inspired dozens of slaves to join them. Within three days, militia and volunteers crushed the rebellion. After eluding his pursuers for six weeks, Turner was captured, tried, and hanged. His insurrection sent shock waves through the South and prompted many states to adopt repressive laws regulating both free blacks and slaves.

While imprisoned, Turner was interviewed by Thomas R. Gray, a doctor. This excerpt is drawn from Gray's account of this conversation, The Confessions of Nat Turner *(1831).*

FOCUS QUESTIONS

1. How does Turner describe his boyhood?
2. What inspired Turner to lead the insurrection?
3. How does Turner describe the insurrection? Does he seem remorseful?
4. Why were white Southerners so alarmed by the Nat Turner revolt? How did they react?

The Confession Agreeable to his own appointment, on the evening he was committed to prison, with permission of the jailer, I visited NAT on Tuesday the 1st November, when, without being questioned at all, he commenced his narrative in the following words:

SIR,—You have asked me to give a history of the motives which induced me to undertake the late insurrection, as you call it—To do so I must go back to the days of my infancy, and even before I was born. I was thirty-one years of age the 2nd of October last, and born the property of Benj. Tuner, of this county. In my childhood a circumstance occurred which made an indelible impression on my mind, and laid the ground work of that enthusiasm, which has terminated so fatally to many, both white and black, and for which I am about to atone at the gallows. It is here necessary to relate this circumstance—trifling as it may seem, it was the commencement of that belief which has grown with time, and even now, sir, in this dungeon, helpless and forsaken as I am, I cannot divest myself of. Being at play with other children, when three or four years old, I was telling them something, which my mother overhearing, said it had happened before I was born—I stuck to my story, however, and related some thing's which went, in her opinion, to confirm it—others being called on were greatly astonished, knowing that these things had happened, and caused them to say in my hearing, I surely would be a prophet, as the Lord had shewn me things that had happened before my birth. And my father and mother strengthened me in this my first impression, saying in my presence, I was intended for some great purpose, which they had always thought from certain marks on my head and breast. . . .

My grandmother, who was very religious, and to whom I was much attached—my master, who belonged to the church, and other religious persons who visited the house, and whom I often saw at prayers, noticing the singularity of my manners, I suppose, and my uncommon intelligence for a child, remarked I had too much sense to be raised, and if I was, I would never be of any service to any one as a slave—To a mind like mine, restless, inquisitive and observant of every thing that was passing, it is easy to suppose that religion was the subject to which it would be directed, and although this subject principally occupied my thoughts—there was nothing that I saw or heard of to which my attention was not directed—The manner in which I learned to read and write, not only had great influence on my own mind, as I acquired it with the most perfect ease, so much so, that I have no recollection whatever of learning the alphabet—but to the astonishment of the family, one day when a book was shewn to me to keep me from crying, I began spelling the names of different objects—this was a source of wonder to all in the neighborhood, particularly the blacks—and this learning was constantly improved at all opportunities. . . .

Having soon discovered to be great, I must appear so, and therefore studiously avoided mixing in society, and wrapped myself in mystery, devoting my time to fasting and prayer—By this time having arrived to man's estate, and hearing the scriptures commented on at meetings, I was struck with that particular passage which says: "Seek ye the kingdom of Heaven and all things shall be added unto you." I reflected much on this passage, and prayed daily for light on this subject—As I was praying one day at my plough, the spirit spoke to me, saying "Seek ye the kingdom of Heaven and all things shall be added unto you."

Question—what do you mean by the Spirit.

Answer. The Spirit that spoke to the prophets in former days—and I was greatly astonished, and for two years prayed continually, whenever my duty would permit—and then again I had the same revelation, which fully confirmed me in the impression that I was ordained for some great purpose in the hands of the Almighty. Several years rolled round, in which many events occurred to strengthen me in this my belief. At this time I reverted in my mind to the remarks made of me in my childhood, and the things that had been shewn me—and as it had been said of me in my childhood by those by whom I had been taught to pray, both white and black, and in whom I had the greatest confidence, that I had too much sense to be raised, and if I was, I would never be of any use to any one as a slave. Now finding I had arrived to man's estate, and was a slave, and these revelations being made known to me, I began to direct my attention to this great object, to fulfill the purpose for which, by this time, I felt assured I was intended. Knowing the influence I had obtained over the minds of my fellow servants, (not by the means of conjuring and such like tricks—for to them I always spoke of such things with contempt) but by the communion of the Spirit whose revelations I often communicated to them, and they believed and said my wisdom came from God. I now began to prepare them for my purpose, by telling them something was about to happen that would terminate in fulfilling the great promise that had been made to me. . . .

And about this time I had a vision—and I saw white spirits and black spirits engaged in battle, and the sun was darkened—the thunder rolled in the Heavens, and blood flowed in streams and I heard a voice saying, "Such is your luck, such you are called to see, and let it come rough or smooth, you must surely bare it." I now withdrew myself as much as my situation would permit, from the intercourse of my fellow servants, for the avowed purpose of serving the Spirit more fully—and it appeared to me, and reminded me of the things it had already shown me, and that it would then reveal to me the knowledge of the elements, the revolution of the planets, the operation of tides, and changes of the seasons. After this revelation in the year of 1825, and the knowledge of the elements being made known to me, I sought more than ever to obtain true holiness before the great day of judgment should appear, and then I began to receive the true knowledge of faith. . . .

And by signs in the heavens that it would make known to me when I should commence the great work—and until the first sign appeared, I should conceal it from the knowledge of men—And on the appearance of the sign, (the eclipse of the sun last February) I should arise and prepare myself, and slay my enemies with their own weapons. And immediately on the sign appearing in the heavens, the seal was removed from my lips, and I communicated the great work laid out for me to do, to four in whom I had the greatest confidence, (Henry, Hark, Nelson, and Sam)—It was intended by us to have begun the work of death on the 4th of July last—Many were the plans formed and rejected by us, and it affected my mind to such degree, that I fell sick, and the time passed without our coming to any determination how to commence—Still forming new schemes and rejecting them, when the sign appeared again, which determined me not to wait longer.

Since the commencement of 1830, I had been living with Mr. Joseph Travis, who was to me a kind master, and placed the greatest confidence in me; in fact, I had no cause to complain of his treatment to me. On Saturday evening, the 20th of August, it was agreed between Henry, Hark, and myself, to prepare a dinner the next day for the men we expected, and then to concert a plan, as we had not yet determined on any. Hark, on the following morning, brought a pig, and Henry brandy, and being joined by Sam, Nelson, Will and Jack, they prepared in the woods a dinner, where, about three o'clock, I joined them. . . .

I saluted them on coming up, and asked Will how came he there, he answered, his life was worth no more than others, and his liberty as dear to him. I asked him if he thought to obtain it? He said he would, or lose his life. This was enough to put him in full confidence. Jack, I knew, was only a tool in the hands of Hark, it was quickly agreed we should commence at home (Mr. J. Travis') on that night, and until we had armed and equipped ourselves, and gathered sufficient force, neither age nor sex was to be spared, (which was invariably adhered to). We remained at the feast, until about two hours in the night, when we went to the house and found Austin; they all went to the cider press and drank, except myself. On returning to the house, Hark went to the door with an axe, for the purpose of breaking it open, as we knew we were strong enough to murder the family, if they were awaked by the noise; but reflecting that it might create an alarm in the neighborhood, we determined to enter the house secretly, and murder them whilst sleeping. Hark got a ladder and set it against the chimney, on which I ascended, and hoisting a window, entered and came down stairs, unbarred the door, and removed the guns from their places. It was then observed that I must spill the first blood. On which, armed with a hatchet, and accompanied by Will, I entered my master's chamber, it being dark, I could not give a death blow, the hatchet glanced from his head, he sprang from the bed and called his wife, it was his last word, Will laid him dead, with a blow of his axe, and Mrs. Travis shared the same fate, as she lay in bed. The murder of this family, five in number, was the work of a moment, not one of them awoke; there was a little infant sleeping in a cradle, that was forgotten, until we had left the house and gone some distance, when Henry and Will returned and killed it; we got here, four guns that would shoot, and several old muskets, with a pound or two of powder. We remained some time at the barn, where we paraded; I formed them in a line as soldiers, and after carrying them through all the maneuvers I was master of marched them off to Mr. Salathul Francis', about six hundred yards distant. Sam and Will went to the door and knocked. Mr. Francis asked who was there, Sam replied it was him, and he had a letter for him, on which he got up and came to the door; they immediately seized him, and dragging him out a little from the door, he was dispatched by repeated blows on the head; there was no other white person in the family. We started from there for Mrs. Reese's, Maintaining the most perfect silence on our march, where finding the door unlocked, we entered, and murdered Mrs. Reese in her bed, while sleeping; her son awoke, but it was only to sleep the sleep of death, he had only time to say who is that, and he was no more. From Mrs. Reese's we went to Mrs. Turner's, a mile distant, which we reached about sunrise, on Monday morning. Henry, Austin, and Sam, went to the still, where, finding Mr. Peeples, Austin shot him, and the rest of us went to the house; as we approached, the family discovered us, and shut the door. Vain hope! Will, with one stroke of his axe, opened it, and we entered and found Mrs. Turner and Mrs. Newsome in the middle of a room, almost frightened to death. Will immediately killed Mrs. Turner, with one blow of his axe. I took Mrs. Newsome by the hand, and with the sword I had when I was apprehended, I struck her several blows over the head, but not being able to kill her, as the sword was dull. Will turning around and discovering it, dispatched her also. A general destruction of property and search for money and ammunition, always succeeded the murders. . . .

I ordered them to mount and march instantly, this was about nine or ten o'clock, Monday morning. I proceeded to Mr. Levi Waller's, two or three miles distant. I took my station in the rear, and as it was my object to carry terror and devastation wherever we went, I placed fifteen or twenty of the best armed and most relied on, in front, who generally approached the houses as fast as their horses could run; this was for two purposes, to prevent escape and strike terror to the inhabitants—on this account I never got to the houses, after leaving Mrs. Whitehead's, until the murders were committed, except in one case. I sometimes got in sight in time to see the work of death completed, viewed the mangled bodies as they lay, in silent satisfaction, and immediately started in quest of other victims. . . .

8.9

Frederick Douglass on Slavery (1845)

Of the many African Americans in the abolitionist movement, Frederick Douglass (1817–1895) was the most famous. Born to a slave mother and a white father whom he never met, Douglass lived in Maryland. When he was a child, the wife of his master violated state law and taught Douglass to read. When his master ordered his wife to stop the instruction, Douglass secretly continued his learning with the help of local white children. In 1838, he successfully escaped slavery. At a Massachusetts antislavery meeting in 1841, Douglass extemporaneously described his experience as a slave. His eloquence and brilliance soon made him one of the leading human rights advocates of the nineteenth century. His writings and speeches gained attention throughout the United States and Europe. Following the Civil War, he became the first African American to hold high posts in the U.S. government.

In this excerpt from Douglass's classic autobiography, he describes the psychological effects of enslavement.

FOCUS QUESTIONS

1. How does Douglass describe his life as a slave? What does he seem to find most objectionable about slavery?

2. Why do you think Douglass was such an effective antislavery activist?

I have met many religious colored people, at the south, who are under the delusion that God requited them to submit to slavery, and to wear their chains with meekness and humility. I could entertain no such nonsense as this; and I almost lost my patience when I found any colored man weak enough to believe such stuff. Nevertheless, the increase of knowledge was attended with bitter as well as sweet results. The more I read, the more I was led to abhor and detest slavery, and my enslavers.... Knowledge had come; light had penetrated the moral dungeon where I dwelt; and, behold! there lay the bloody whip, for my back, and here was the iron chain; and my good, *kind master*, he was the author of my situation. The revelation haunted me, stung me, and made me gloomy and

SOURCE: Frederick Douglass, *My Bondage and My Freedom* (New York: Miller, Orton and Co., 1857), pp. 159–161, 218–219, 278–279.

miserable. As I writhed under the sting and torment of this knowledge, I almost envied my fellow slaves their stupid contentment.... It was this everlasting thinking which distressed and tormented me; and yet there was no getting rid of the subject of my thoughts. All nature was redolent of it. Once awakened by the silver trump of knowledge, my spirit was roused to eternal wakefulness. Liberty! the inestimable birthright of every man, had, for me, converted every object into an asserter of this great right....

My feelings were not the result of any marked cruelty in the treatment I received; they sprung from the consideration of my being a slave at all. It was slavery—not its mere *incidents*—that I hated. I had been cheated. I saw through the attempt to keep me in ignorance; I saw that slaveholders would have gladly made me believe that they were merely acting under the authority of God, in making a slave of me, and in making slaves of others; and I treated them as robbers and deceivers. The feeding and clothing me well, could not atone for taking my liberty from me.... [P]ious as Mr. Covey was, he proved himself to be as unscrupulous and base as the worst of his neighbors. In the beginning, he was only able—as he said—"to buy one slave"; and scandalous and shocking as is the fact, he boasted that he bought her simply "*as a breeder.*" But the worst is not told in this naked statement. This young woman (Caroline was her name) was virtuously compelled by Mr. Covey to abandon herself to the object for which he had purchased her; and the result was, the birth of twins at the end of the year. At this addition to his human stock, both Edward Covey and his wife, Susan, were ecstatic with joy. No one dreamed of reproaching the woman, or of finding fault with the hired man—Bill Smith—the father of the two children, for Mr. Covey himself had locked the two up together every night, thus inviting the result.

But I will pursue this revolting subject no further. No better illustration of the unchaste and demoralizing character of slavery can be found, than is furnished in the fact that this professedly Christian slaveholder, admist all his prayers and hymns, was shamelessly and boastfully encouraging, and actually compelling, in his own house, undisguised and unmitigated fornication, as a means of increasing his human stock. I may remark here, that, while this fact will be read with disgust and shame at the north, it will be *laughed at*, as smart and praiseworthy in Mr. Covey, at the south; for a man is no more condemned there for buying a woman and devoting her to this life of dishonor, than for buying a cow, and raising stock from her. The same rules are observed, with a view to increasing the number of quality of the former, as of the latter....

[A]s I now look back, I can see that we [slaves] did many silly things, very well calculated to awaken suspicion. We were, at times, remarkably buoyant, singing hymns and making joyous exclamations, almost as triumphant in their tone as if we had reached a land of freedom and safety. A keen observer might have detected in our repeated singing of "O Canaan, sweet Canaan, I am bound for a land of Canaan," something more than a hope of reaching heaven. We meant to reach the north—and the north was our Canaan.

8.10

Uncle Ben on the Punishment of Slaves (1910)

Slavery is perhaps the most controversial topic in American history. While some historians describe mutually beneficial relationships between slaves and masters, others emphasize the brutal treatment of many slaves. Neither side fully depicts the complexities of slave society. In reality, a slave's experience varied according to his or her owner, location, and era. While some masters treated their slaves kindly, others were sadistic. While some slaves felt genuine affection for their owners, others despised them. In either instance, slavery stripped African Americans of the ability to control their lives.

In this passage, a former slave recounts work and discipline on a Southern plantation.

FOCUS QUESTIONS

1. How does Uncle Ben describe his experience as a slave?
2. What are some of the methods of discipline Uncle Ben's masters used?
3. What do you think would have been the worst part of being a slave?

Interviewed, 1910, Alabama, by Mary White Ovington
Enslaved: Alabama, Texas, N.C.

Yes, we was worked hard in those days, we sure was. You think, maybe, people done have a rest on Sunday? I done never see it. Half-time work on Sunday pullin' fodder in the field for the mules an' cows. Then Sunday mornin' we'd build fences for the cattle, old fashion' bridge fences, we calls 'em. The women too was worked terrible. You see the railroad yonder? Women helped grade that railroad. Other times they's plow in the field an' when night come they mus' spin two cuts o'cotton. Don't matter how tired they might be, they mus' spin their two cuts or in the morning they'd be whipt. That's what I's tellin' you.

SOURCE: *Independent,* 48 (May 26, 1910), pp. 1131–36.

There were terrible persecution then. I's seen men with fly blows. You don't know what that mean, perhaps? Fly blows is what we calls the meat when it turns to maggots. They'd whip a man until he's so warm the blood creep thru' his shirt, an' the flies 'ud come. Workin' out in the fiel' all the time, bendin' over the hoe, an' the flies suckin' the blood. Some men wouldn't stan' it. They'd take to the woods, an' then the dogs 'ud ketch 'em. After that they'd be chained, an' you'd hear rattling like they was chained logs. When night comes, there by deir bed there'd be a staple. The overseer'd come along an' lock the chain to the staple so they couldn't get away. In the mornin' the overseer let 'em out. They done put 'em, too, in screw boxes, what you call presses. When they put down the foller-block, then the nigger was tight. It was out-o-doors an' he was like to freeze. They chain him in the graveyard, too, keep him there all the night to skeer him. Oh, I knows what I's talking about, yes ma'am. Now an' den you can ketch some ole person who knows, who bear witness like hallelujah meeting, to what I say. . . .

8.11

Slave Music and Resistance

Most slaves endured long workdays, harsh discipline, and horrible living conditions. Malnutrition, overwork, and disease contributed to very high mortality rates. But slaves' experiences varied. While the majority were agricultural laborers, others worked as artisans, house servants, and other roles. Although laws did not recognize slave marriages, slaves forged lifelong partnerships and close-knit families despite the threats of sexual exploitation and sale of loved ones.

To preserve their dignity, slaves resisted their masters in a host of ways. While organized insurrections like the Nat Turner rebellion were rare, slaves undermined their masters' authority with work stoppages, arson, poisoning, infanticide, and theft. They also created a vibrant culture that melded African and white traditions. The following two songs provide examples of slaves' cultural resistance.

SOURCE: "Go Down, Moses" and "I Thank God I'm Free at Last" in Thomas R. Frazier, ed. *Afro-American History: Primary Sources* (New York: Harcourt Brace, & World, 1970), pp. 92, 95.

FOCUS QUESTIONS

1. What are the major themes of these songs? How do they contradict the messages found in "Religion as Social Control: A Catechism for Slaves" (Document 8.5)?

2. Why do you think slaves found songs like these inspirational? How did singing such songs represent a form of resistance against slavery?

GO DOWN, MOSES

Go down, Moses,
'Way down in Egypt land,
Tell ole Pharaoh,
To let my people go.
Go down, Moses,
'Way down in Egypt land,
Tell old Pharaoh,
To let my people go.
When Israel was in Egypt land,
Let my people go,
Oppressed so hard they could not stand,
Let my people go,
Thus spoke the Lord, bold Moses said,
Let my people go,
If not I'll smite your first-born dead,
Let my people go.
Go down, Moses,
'Way down in Egypt land,
Tell ole Pharaoh,
To let my people go.

I THANK GOD

Free at last, free at last,
I thank God I'm free at last.
Free at last, free at last,
I thank God I'm free at last.
Way down yonder in the graveyard walk,
I thank God I'm free at last,
Me and my Jesus gonna meet an' talk,
I thank God I'm free at last.

On-a my knees when the light pass by,
I thank God I'm free at last,
Thought my soul would rise an' fly,
I thank God I'm free at last.
One o' these mornin's bright an' fair,
I thank God I'm free at last,
Gonna meet my Jesus in the middle o' the air,
I thank God I'm free at last.
Free at last, free at last,
I thank God I'm free at last,
Free at last, free at last,
I thank God I'm free at last.

8.12

Benjamin Drew, Narratives of Escaped Slaves (1855)

The stories of escaped slaves provided powerful ammunition for the antislavery cause. While many slaves were able to flee for short periods, relatively few escaped permanently. Male runaways greatly outnumbered female escapees. Those who succeeded often did so by borrowing, stealing, or forging papers that classified them as free. Lighter-skinned runaways sometimes passed as white. Occasionally, slaves reached freedom with the help of the former slaves and abolitionists who ran the "Underground Railroad." In these readings, abolitionist Benjamin Drew records the stories of two former slaves who escaped to Canada.

FOCUS QUESTIONS

1. How do these women depict their lives as slaves?

2. How did each woman escape? Why do you think female slaves ran away less often than male slaves did?

SOURCE: *From a Northside View of Slavery: The Refuge, or The Narratives of Fugitive Slaves in Canada, Related by Themselves,* ed. Benjamin Drew (Boston: John P. Jowett, 1856), 41–43, 50–51, 138, 140–141, 224–227.

3. Do you see any differences in the treatment of male and female slaves? Explain your answer.

[Mrs. James Steward]

The slaves want to get away bad enough. They are not contented with their situation. I am from the eastern shore of Maryland. I never belonged but to one master; he was very bad indeed. I was never sent to school, nor allowed to go to church. They were afraid we would have more sense than they. I have a father there, three sisters, and a brother. My father is quite an old man, and he is used very badly. Many a time he has been kept at work a whole long summer day without sufficient food. A sister of mine has been punished by his taking away her clothes and locking them up, because she used to run when master whipped her. He kept her at work with only what she could pick up to tie on her for decency. He took away her child which had just begun to walk, and gave it to another woman—but she went and got it afterward. He had a large farm eight miles from home. Four servants were kept at the house. My master could not manage to whip my sister when she was strong. He waited until she was confined, and the second week after her confinement he said, "Now I can handle you, now you are weak." She ran from him, however, and had to go through water, and was sick in consequence.

I was beaten at one time over the head by my master, until the blood ran from my mouth and nose: then he tied me up in the garret, with my hands over my head—then he brought me down and put me in a little cupboard, where I had to sit cramped up, part of the evening, all night, and until between four and five o'clock, next day, without any food. The cupboard was near a fire, and I thought I should suffocate.

My brother was whipped on one occasion until his back was as raw as a piece of beef, and before it got well, master whipped him again. His back was an awful sight.

We were all afraid of master: when I saw him coming, my heart would jump up into my mouth, as if I had seen a serpent.

I have been wanting to come away for eight years back. I waited for Jim Seward to get ready. Jim had promised to take me away and marry me. Our master would allow no marriages on the farm. When Jim had got ready, he let me know—he brought to me two suits of clothes—men's clothes—which he had bought on purpose for me. I put on both suits to keep me warm. We eluded pursuit and reached Canada in safety.

[Mrs. Nancy Howard]

I was born in Anne Arundel County, Maryland—was brought up in Baltimore. After my escape, I lived in Lynn, Mass., seven years, but I left there through fear of being carried back, owing to the fugitive slave law. I have lived in St. Catherines [Ontario, Canada] less than a year.

The way I got away was—my mistress was sick, and went into the country for her health. I went to stay with her cousin. After a month, my mistress was sent back to the city to her cousin's, and I waited on her. My daughter had been off three years. A friend said to me—"Now is your chance to get off." At last I concluded to go—the friend supplying me with money. I was asked no questions on the way north.

My idea of slavery is, that it is one of the blackest, the wickedest things everywhere in the world. When you tell them the truth, they whip you to make you lie. I have taken more lashes for this, than for any other thing, because I would not lie.

One day I set the table, and forgot to put on the carving-fork—the knife was there. I went to the table to put it on a plate. My master said,—"Where is the fork?" I told him "I forgot it." He says,—"You d − − d black b − −, I'll forget you!"—at the same time hitting me on the head with the carving knife. The blood spurted out— you can see. (Here the woman removed her turban and showed a circular cicatrices denuded of hair, about an inch in diameter, on the top of her head.) My mistress took me into the kitchen and put on camphor, but she could not stop the bleeding. A doctor was sent for. He came but asked no questions. I was frequently punished with raw hides—was hit with tongs and poker and anything. I used when I went out, to look up at the sky, and say, "Blessed Lord, oh, do take me out of this!" It seemed to me I could not bear another lick. I can't forget it. I sometimes dream that I am pursued, and when I wake, I am scared almost to death.

8.13

Images of Slavery

Although we know little about the individuals featured here, these images convey the diversity of slaves' experiences. They offer glimpses of the working and living conditions that challenged slaves and their families. They illustrate some of the complexities of master-slave relations. When analyzing these pictures, be sure to consider information gleaned from the preceding readings on slavery.

FOCUS QUESTIONS

1. What do these images suggest about the impact of slavery on slave families?
2. How would you characterize the relationships between whites and slaves shown here?
3. Do you see any evidence of slaves' resistance in these pictures?

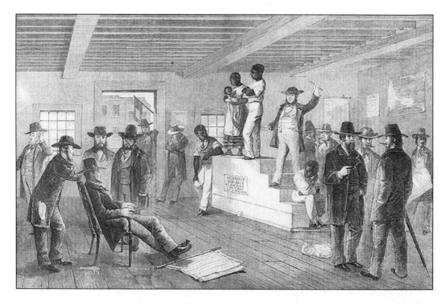

A Slave Auction in Virginia (1861). Wood Engraving. *The Illustrated London News*, February 16, 1861, p. 139. Schomburg Center for Reseach in Black Culture, Photographs and Prints Division.

Five Generations on Smith's Plantation, Beaufort, South Carolina (1862). Civil War Photograph Collection, Library of Congress Prints and Photographs Division.

Household Servant with Child, circa 1860. Tintype from Persistence of the Spirit, Arkansas Territorial Restoration.

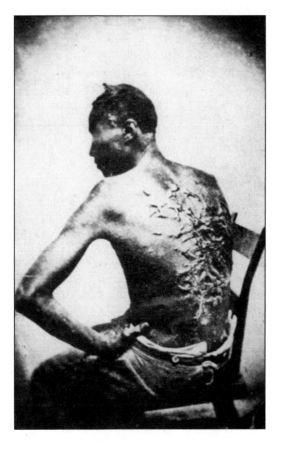

"'Overseer Artayou Carrier whipped me. I was two months in bed sore from the whipping. My master came after I was whipped; he discharged the overseer.' The very words of poor Peter, taken as he sat for his picture." From description on untitled photograph, Baton Rouge, LA, April 2, 1863. National Archives and Records Administration.

9

⁂

Moving Westward

During the 1840s, tens of thousands of Americans began the process of settling the far reaches of the West. In pursuit of fertile lands and economic opportunities, whites encountered Indians and Mexicans who had lived in the region for hundreds of years and who had established their own distinctive ways of life. But most Americans believed that "manifest destiny" and white supremacy accorded them a God-given right to impose their civilization on "inferior" people of color. While westward migration benefited many pioneers, the drive for expansion also created new problems. Contentious debates over the annexation of Texas and the Mexican-American War destabilized the country's political system and intensified sectional disputes. By 1850, slavery, states' rights, and expansion were tearing at the fabric of national unity.

THEMES TO CONSIDER

- Indian resistance and accommodation
- The diversity of the West
- Racial and cultural clashes accompanying white settlement
- The origins and impact of the Mexican American War
- The meanings and effects of Manifest Destiny
- Individual experiences of Western migrants

9.1

Sharitarish on Indian Life (1822)

In the early nineteenth century, a wave of American migration greatly affected American Indians, especially in the South and the Great Plains. The Pawnee are a good example. They had long lived in the valley of the Platte River, in what is now Nebraska. They likely encountered Shoshones, Athabascas, and Sioux. In the seventeenth and eighteenth centuries, Pawnee villages were in areas far from territories contested by the French and Spanish. But by the late 1700s, increasing contact with whites and disease were eroding tribal power. In 1803, the Louisiana Purchase put Pawnee territory under U.S. control. When the War of 1812 ended alliances with the British and the Adams-Onís Treaty removed Spanish protection, many tribes found themselves increasingly vulnerable. Calling for Indians to "civilize" themselves, Quaker missionaries urged Indians to stop hunting and to become farmers despite the fact that several tribes, including the Pawnee, already possessed great skill in agriculture.

Hoping to convince the Great Plains tribes not to oppose white settlement, the Monroe administration invited a delegation of sixteen Pawnee, Omaha, Oto, Missouri, and Kansa Indians on a lavish tour of eastern cities and forts. Major Benjamin O'Fallon, the federal Indian agent for the Upper Missouri, chaperoned the group. On February 4, 1822, President James Monroe formally received them at the White House. Through a translator, Monroe urged them to accept Christianity, peace, and farming. Pawnee chief Sharitarish's response to Monroe follows.

FOCUS QUESTIONS

1. How would you characterize the tone of Sharitarish's speech?
2. What differences does Sharitarish identify between white and Indian life?
3. How is white migration changing Sharitarish's tribe?
4. What does Sharitarish propose in order to foster good relations between whites and Indians? Would his suggestions have worked? Explain your answers.

SOURCE: Jedediah Morse, *A Report to the Secretary of War of the United States on Indian Affairs* (New Haven, CT: S. Converse, 1822), 242–45.

My Great Father.—I have travelled a great distance to see you. I have seen you, and my heart rejoices; I have heard your words; they have entered one ear, and shall not escape the other; and I will carry them to my people as pure, as they came from your mouth.

My Great Father.—I am going to speak the truth. The Great Spirit looks down upon us, and I call Him to witness all that may pass between us on this occasion. If I am here now, and have seen your people, your houses, your vessels on the big lake, and a great many wonderful things, far beyond my comprehension, which appear to have been made by the Great Spirit, and placed in your hands, I am indebted to my father here, [O'Fallon] who invited me from home, under whose wings I have been protected. Yes, my Great Father, I have travelled with your chief. I have followed him, and trod in his tracks; but there is still another Great Father, to whom I am much indebted—it is the Father of us all. Him who made us and placed us on this earth. . . . The Great Spirit made us all—he made my skin red, and yours white. He placed us on this earth, and intended that we should live differently from each other. He made the whites to cultivate the earth, and feed on domestic animals; but he made us red skins, to rove through the uncultivated woods and plains, to feed on wild animals, and to dress in their skins. He also intended that we should go to war to take scalps—steal horses, and triumph over our enemies—cultivate peace at home, and promote the happiness of each other. I believe there are no people, of any color, on this earth, who do not believe in the Great Spirit—in rewards and in punishments. We worship him, but we worship him not as you do. We differ from you in appearance and manners, as well as in our customs; and we differ from you in our religion. . . .

My Great Father.—Some of your good chiefs, or, as they are called, *Missionaries*, have proposed to send of their good people among us to change our habits, to make us work, and live like the white people. I will not tell a lie, I am going to tell the truth. You love your country; you love your people; you love the manner in which they live, and you think your people brave. I am like you, my Great Father, I love my country; I love my people; I love the manner in which we live, and think myself and warriors brave; spare me then, my Father, let me enjoy my country, and pursue the buffalo, and the beaver, and the other wild animals of our wilderness, and I will trade the skins with your people. I have grown up and lived thus long without work; I am in hopes you will suffer me to die without it. We have yet plenty of buffalo, beaver, deer, and other wild animals; we have also an abundance of horses. We have every thing we want. We have plenty of land, *if you will keep your people off of it.* . . .

You have already sent us a father [O'Fallon]; it is enough, he knows us, and we know him. We have confidence in him. We keep our eye constantly upon him, and since we have heard your words, we will listen more attentively to his.

It is too soon, my Great Father, to send those good men among us. We are not starving yet. We wish you to permit us to enjoy the chase, until the game of our country is exhausted; until the wild animals become extinct. Let us exhaust our present resources, before you make us toil, and interrupt our happiness. Let me continue to live as I have done, and after I have passed to the Good or Evil Spirit from the wilderness of my present life, the subsistence of *my children* may become so precious, as to need and embrace the offered assistance of those good people.

There was a time when we did not know the whites. Our wants were then fewer than they are now. They were always within our control. We had then seen nothing which we could not get. But since our intercourse with the whites, who have caused such a destruction of our game, our situation is changed. We could lie down to sleep, and when we awoke, we found the buffalo feeding around our camp; but now we are killing them for their skins, and feeding the wolves with their flesh, to make our children cry over their bones.

Here my Great Father, is a pipe which I present you, as I am accustomed to present pipes to all red skins in peace with us. It is filled with such tobacco as we were accustomed to smoke, before we knew the white people. I know that the robes, leggings, moccasins, bear's claws &c. are of little value to you, but we wish you to have them deposited and preserved in some conspicuous part of your lodge, so that when we are gone, and the sod turned over our bones, if our children should visit this place, as we do now, they may see and recognize with pleasure the deposits of their fathers, and reflect on the ties that are past.

9.2

George Catlin on Pigeon's Egg Head (1837–1839, 1842)

George Catlin (1796–1872) was the first and perhaps the most important painter of American Indians. At a time when many whites believed the savage depictions of Indians often found in captivity narratives and popular culture (Documents 2.6 and 5.7), Catlin accepted Native Americans on their own terms. His attitude was even more remarkable given the fact that his mother had been temporarily kidnapped by Indians.

A self-trained artist, Catlin abandoned a career in law in order to focus on his painting. He became a celebrated portraitist and miniaturist. In 1824, his encounter with an Indian delegation passing through Philadelphia en route to Washington, D.C., inspired him to devote himself to studying and painting Native Americans in their tribal environments. In 1830, Catlin traveled to

SOURCE: George Catlin, *Letters and Notes on the Manners, Customs, and Condition of the North American Indians*, vol. II (London: Tilt and Bogue, 1842), 194–200.

*St. Louis and befriended U.S. Superintendent of Indian Affairs William Clark,
famed for his 1804 western expedition with Meriwether Lewis (Document 5.5).
General Clark took Catlin to an Indian encampment along the Mississippi
River. Over the next eight years, Catlin journeyed throughout the frontier living
among forty-eight Plains tribes and producing over 500 portraits. In 1838,
after Congress refused to purchase his "Indian Gallery," Catlin staged
wildly successful exhibitions in Washington, D.C., Philadelphia, New York,
London, and Paris. Four years later, he published* Letters and Notes on the
Manners, Customs, and Condition of the North American Indians.
*Never able to persuade the U.S. government to buy his work, Catlin went
bankrupt in 1852. A Philadelphia businessman paid Catlin's debts and
acquired the Indian Gallery. Shortly after the artist's death, the collection
was donated to the Smithsonian.*

*In the following painting and excerpt, Catlin records his impressions of
Pigeon's Egg Head (The Light) [Wee-jun-jon].*

FOCUS QUESTIONS

1. Who was Pigeon's Egg Head (The Light) [Wee-jun-jon]? What happens to him?

2. What are Catlin's first impressions of Pigeon's Egg Head (The Light) [Wee-jin-jon]? How and why do Catlin's views change?

3. In evaluating this painting and story, what can we infer about Catlin's opinion of the clash between Indians and whites? Do you think his attitudes were common? Why or why not?

Now you shall hear the Story of the Pigeon's Egg Head. [Beloved ones, sweetheart]

The Indian name of this man (being its literal translation into the Assinneboin language) was Wi-jun-jon. . . .

Wi-jun-jon (the Pigeon's Egg Head) was a brave and a warrior of the Assinneboins: young, proud, handsome, valiant, and graceful. He had fought many a battle, and won many a laurel. The numerous scalps from his enemies' heads adorned his dress, and his claims were fair and just for the highest honours that his country could bestow upon him; for his father was chief of the nation. . . .

Well, this young Assinneboin, the Pigeon's Egg Head, was selected by Major Sanford, the Indian Agent, to represent his tribe in a delegation which visited Washington city under his charge in the winter of 1832. With this gentleman, the Assinneboin, together with representatives from several others of those North Western tribes, descended the Missouri river, several thousand miles, on their way to Washington.

Pigeon's Egg Head (The Light) Going to and Returning from Washington, 1837–39. Assiniboine/Nakoda. Oil, 29 x 24 in. Smithsonian American Art Museum Washington, DC/Art Resource, NY. Smithsonian American Art Museum, Washington DC, U.S.A., gift of Mrs. Joseph Harrison, Jr.

While descending the river in a Mackinaw boat, from the mouth of Yellow Stone [the Yellow Stone River], Wi-jun-jon and another of his tribe who was with him, at the first approach to the civilized settlements, commenced a register of the white men's houses (or cabins), by cutting a notch for each on the side of a pipe stem, in order to be able to show when they got home, how many white men's houses they saw on their journey. At first the cabins were scarce; but continually as they advanced down the river, more and more rapidly increased in numbers; and they soon found their pipe-stem filled with marks, and they determined to put the rest of them on the handle of a war-club, which they soon got marked all over likewise, and at length, while the boat was moored at the shore for the purpose of cooking the dinner of the party, Wi-jun-jon and his companion stepped into the bushes, and cut a long stick, from which they peeled the bark; and when the boat was again underweigh, they sat down, and with much labour, copied the notches on to it from the pipe-stem and club; and also kept adding a notch for every house they passed. This stick was soon filled; and in a day or two several others; when, at last, they seemed much at a loss to know what to do with their troublesome records, until they came in sight of St. Louis, which is a town of 10,000 inhabitants; upon which, after consulting a little, they pitched their sticks overboard into the river!

I was in St. Louis at the time of their arrival, and painted their portraits while they rested in that place. Wi-jun-jon was the first, who reluctantly yielded to the solicitations of the Indian agent and myself, and appeared as sullen as death in my painting-room, with eyes fixed like those of a statue upon me, though his pride had plumed and tinted him in all the freshness and brilliancy of an Indian's toilet [make-up]. In his nature's uncowering pride he stood a perfect model; but superstition had hung a lingering curve upon his lip, and pride had stiffened it into contempt. He had been urged into a measure, against which his fears had pleaded; yet he stood unmoved and unflinching amid the struggles of mysteries that were hovering about him, foreboding ills of every kind, and misfortunes that were to happen to him in consequence of this operation.

He was dressed in his native costume, which was classic and exceedingly beautiful; his leggings and shirt were of the mountain goat skin, richly garnished with quills of the porcupine, and fringed with locks of scalps, taken from his enemies' heads. Over these floated his long hair in plaits, that fell nearly to the ground; his head was decked with the war-eagle's plumes—his robe was of the skin of the young buffalo bull, richly garnished and emblazoned with the battles of his life; his quiver and bow were slung, and his shield, of the skin of the bull's neck.

I painted him in this beautiful dress, and so also the others who were with him; and after I had done, Major Sanford went on to Washington with them, where they spent the winter.

Wi-jun-jon was the foremost on all occasions—the first to enter the levee— the first to shake the President's hand, and make his speech to him—the last to extend the hand to them, but the first to catch the smiles and admiration of the gentler sex. He travelled the giddy maze, and beheld amid the buzzing din of civil life, their tricks of art, their handiworks, and their finery; he visited their principal cities—he saw their forts, their ships, their great guns, steamboats, balloons, &c. &c; and in the spring returned to St. Louis, where I joined him and his companions on their way back to their own country.

Through the politeness of Mr. Chouteau, of the American Fur Company, I was admitted (the only passenger except Major Sanford and his Indians) to a passage in their steamboat, on her first trip to the Yellow Stone; and when I had embarked, and the boat was about to depart, Wi-jun-jon made his appearance on deck, in a full suit of regimentals! He had in Washington exchanged his beautifully garnished and classic costume, for a full dress "en militaire." It was, perhaps, presented to him by the President. It was broadcloth, of the finest blue, trimmed with lace of gold; on his shoulders were mounted two immense epaulettes; his neck was strangled with a shining black stock, and his feet were pinioned in a pair of waterproof boots, with high heels, which made him "step like a yoked hog."

On his head was a high-crowned beaver hat, with a broad silver lace band, surmounted by a huge red feather, some two feet high; his coat collar stiff with lace, came higher up than his ears, and over it flowed, down towards his haunches—his long Indian locks, stuck up in rolls and plaits, with red paint.

A large silver medal was suspended from his neck by a blue ribbon—and across his right shoulder passed a wide belt, supporting by his side a broad sword.

On his hands he had drawn a pair of white kid gloves, and in them held, a blue umbrella in one, and a large fan in the other. In this fashion was poor Wi-jun-jon metamorphosed, on his return from Washington; and, in this plight was he strutting and whistling Yankee Doodle, about the deck of the steamer that was wending its way up the mighty Missouri, and taking him to his native-land again; where he was soon to light his pipe, and cheer the wigwam fire-side with tales of novelty and wonder.

. . . I travelled with this new-fangled gentleman until he reached his home, two thousand miles above St. Louis, and I could never look upon him for a moment without excessive laughter, at the ridiculous figure he cut—the strides, the angles, the stiffness of this travelling beau! . . .

After Wijunjon had got home, and passed the usual salutations among his friends, he commenced the simple narration of scenes he had passed through, and of things he had beheld among the whites; which appeared to them so much like fiction, that it was impossible to believe them, and they set him down as an impostor. "He has been, (they said,) among the whites, who are great liars, and all he has learned is to come home and tell lies." He sank rapidly into disgrace in his tribe; his high claims to political eminence all vanished; he was reputed worthless—the greatest liar of his nation; the chiefs shunned him and passed him by as one of the tribe who was lost; yet the ears of the gossiping portion of the tribe were open, and the campfire circle and the wigwam fireside, gave silent audience to the whispered narratives of the "Travelled Indian."

The next day after he had arrived among his friends, the superfluous part of his coat, (which was a laced frock), was converted into a pair of leggings for his wife; and his hat-band of silver lace furnished her a magnificent pair of garters. The remainder of the coat, curtailed of its original length was seen buttoned upon the shoulders of his brother, over and above a pair of leggings of buckskin; and Wi-jun-jon was parading about among his gaping friends, with a bow and quiver slung over his shoulders, which, sans coat, exhibited a fine linen shirt with studs and sleeve buttons. His broad-sword kept its place, but about noon, his boots gave way to a pair of garnished moccasins; and in such plight he gossiped away the day among his; friends, while his heart spoke so freely and so effectually from the bung-hole of a little keg of whiskey, which he had brought the whole way, (as one of the choicest presents made him at Washington), that his tongue became silent. . . .

Two days' revel of this kind had drawn from his keg all its charms; and in the mellowness of his heart, all his finery had vanished, and all of its appendages except his umbrella, to which his heart's strongest affections still clung, and with it, and under it, in rude dress of buckskin, he was afterwards to be seen, in all sorts of weather, acting the fop and the beau as well as he could, with his limited means. In this plight, and in this dress, with his umbrella always in his hand, (as the only remaining evidence of his quondam greatness,) he began in his sober moments, to entertain and instruct his people by honest and simple narratives of things and scenes he had beheld during his tour to the East; but which (unfortunately for him), were to them too marvellous and improbable to be believed. He told the gaping multitude that were constantly gathering about him, of the distance he had travelled, of the astonishing number of houses he had seen—of the towns and cities, with all their wealth and splendour—of travelling on steamboats, in stages and on railroads. He described our forts, and seventy-four gun ships, which he had visited—their big guns—our great bridges—our great council-house at Washington, and its doings—the curious and wonderful machines in the patent office, (which he pronounced the greatest medicine place he had seen); he described the great war parade, which he saw in the city of New

York—the ascent of the balloon from Castle Garden—the numbers of the white people, the beauty of the white squaws; their red cheeks, and many thousands of other things, all of which were so much beyond their comprehension, that they "could not be true," and "he must be the very greatest liar in the whole world."

But he was beginning to acquire a reputation of a different kind. He was denominated a medicine-man, and one too of the most extraordinary character; for they deemed him far above the ordinary sort of human beings, whose mind could invent and conjure up for their amusement, such an ingenious fabrication of novelty and wonder. He steadily and unostentatiously persisted, however, in this way of entertaining his friends and his people, though he knew his standing was affected by it. He had an exhaustless theme to descant upon through the remainder of his life; and he seemed satisfied to lecture all his life, for the pleasure which it gave him.

So great was his medicine, however, that they began, chiefs and all, to look upon him as a most extraordinary being, and the customary honours and forms began to be applied to him, and the respect shewn him, that belongs to all men in the Indian country, who are distinguished for their medicine or mysteries. In short, when all became familiar with the astonishing representations that he made, and with the wonderful alacrity with which he created them, he was denominated the very greatest of medicine; and not only that, but the "lying medicine." That he should be the greatest of medicine, and that for lying, merely, rendered him a prodigy in mysteries that commanded not only respect, but at length, (when he was more maturely heard and listened to) admiration, awe, and at last dread and terror; which altogether must needs conspire to rid the world of a monster, whose more than human talents must be cut down, to less than human measurement. . . .

One of the young men of the tribe took the duty upon himself, and after much perplexity, hit upon the following plan, to-wit:—he had fully resolved, in conjunction with others who were in the conspiracy, that the medicine of Wi-jun-jon was too great for the ordinary mode, and that he was so great a liar that a rifle bullet would not kill him; while the young man was in this distressing dilemma, which lasted for some weeks, he had a dream one night, which solved all difficulties; and in consequence of which, he loitered about the store in the Fort, at the mouth of the Yellow Stone, until he could procure, by stealth, (according to the injunction of his dream,) the handle of an iron pot, which he supposed to possess the requisite virtue, and taking it into the woods, he there spent a whole day in straightening and filing it, to fit it into the barrel of his gun; after which, he made his appearance again in the Fort, with his gun under his robe, charged with the pot handle, and getting behind poor Wi-jun-jon, whilst he was talking with the Trader, placed the muzzle behind his head and blew out his brains! . . .

9.3

Richard Henry Dana on the Coast of California (1835)

Beginning in the 1790s, a network of Russian, British, American, and Mexican traders sprang up along the Pacific coast. Americans and Mexicans forged other trading partnerships in Santa Fe, Colorado, and Utah. They exchanged furs, tallow, cattle, and other goods. While clashes between Americans and Mexicans occasionally erupted, most interchanges were mutually beneficial and peaceful.

In 1821, Mexico won its independence from Spain and gained control of vast territories spanning from Texas to California. In order to protect its empire and to spread Catholicism, Spain had erected twenty-one missions throughout California. By 1823, approximately 20,000 Indians lived among the Franciscan priests who ran the missions. After secularizing the mission system, the Mexican government distributed the mission lands to government officials and private ranchers. In the ensuing chaos, some of the Indians were enslaved while others joined tribes who opposed the Mexicans. The corrupt and inefficient Mexican Army proved unable to protect residents from Indian raids. Not surprisingly, the Mexican territory remained underpopulated.

Richard Henry Dana (1815–1882) was one of the few Americans who traveled to California before the Gold Rush. After measles forced his withdrawal from Harvard College, Dana became a sailor to improve his health. In 1840, he published Two Years before the Mast, *a popular book about his experiences at sea. He later worked as a lawyer and served as U.S. minister to Great Britain during the Grant administration. In this excerpt, Dana describes his impressions of California.*

FOCUS QUESTIONS

1. What observations does Dana make about Californians? Are his assessments generally negative or positive? Explain your answer.

2. How do you think a Californian might have responded to Dana's conclusions?

SOURCE: Richard Henry Dana, *Two Years before the Mast* (New York, 1840), 87–212, *passim.*

3. How do accounts like Dana's reflect the racial and cultural clashes that accompanied white settlement of the West?

The bay of Monterey is very wide at the entrance, being about twenty-four miles between the two points. Año Nuevo at the north, and Pinos at the south, but narrows gradually as you approach the town. . . . We came to anchor within two cable lengths of the shore, and the town lay directly before us, making a very pretty appearance; its houses being plastered, which gives a much better effect than those of Santa Barbara, which are of a mud-color. The red tiles, too, on the roofs, contrasted well with the white plastered sides, and with the extreme greenness of the lawn upon which the houses—about a hundred in number—were dotted about, here and there, irregularly. . . .

. . . The next day we were "turned-to" early, and began taking off the hatches, overhauling the cargo, and getting everything ready for inspection. At eight, the officers of the customs, five in number, came on board, and began overhauling the cargo, manifest, etc. The Mexican revenue laws are very strict, and require the whole cargo to be landed, examined, and taken on board again; but our agent, Mr. R – – – , had succeeded in compounding with them for the last two vessels, and saving the trouble of taking the cargo ashore.

The officers were dressed in the costume which we found prevailed through the country. A broad-brimmed hat, usually black or dark-brown color, with a gilt or figured band round the crown, and lined inside with silk; a short jacket of silk or figured calico, (the European skirted body-coat is never worn;) the shirt open in the neck; rich waistcoat, if any; pantaloons wide, straight, and long, usually of velvet, velveteen, or broadcloth; or else short breeches and white stockings. They wear the dear-skin shoe, which is of a dark-brown color, and, (being made by Indians,) usually a good deal ornamented. They have no suspenders, but always wear a sash round the waist, which is generally red, and varying in quality with the means of the wearer. Add to this the never-failing cloak, and you have the dress of a Californian.

This last garment, the cloak, is always a mark of the rank and wealth of the owner. The "*gente de razón*," or aristocracy, wear cloaks of black or dark blue broadcloth, with as much velvet and trimmings as may be; and from this they go down to the blanket of the Indian; the middle classes wearing something like a large table-cloth, with a hole in the middle for the head to go through. This is often as coarse as a blanket, but being beautifully woven with various colors is quite a show at a distance.

Among the Spaniards there is no working class; (the Indians being slaves and doing all the hard work;) and every rich man looks like a grandee, and very poor scamp like a broken-down gentleman. I have often seen a man with a fine figure, and courteous manners, dressed in broadcloth and velvet, with a noble horse completely covered with trappings; without a *real* in his pockets, and absolutely suffering for something to eat. . . .

The Californians are an idle, thriftless people, and can make nothing for themselves. The country abounds in grapes, yet they buy bad wine made in

Boston and brought round by us, at an immense price, and retail it among themselves. . . . Things sell, on average, at an advance of nearly three hundred percent upon the Boston prices. This is partly owing to the heavy duties which the government, in their wisdom, with the intent, no doubt, of keeping silver in the country, has laid upon imports. These duties, and the enormous expenses of so long a voyage, keep all the merchants, but those of heavy capital, from engaging in the trade. . . .

. . . Generally speaking, each person's caste is decided by the quality of the blood, which shows itself, too plainly to be concealed, at first sight. Yet the least drop of Spanish blood, if it be only of quatroon or octoon, is sufficient to raise them from the rank of slaves, and entitle them to a suit of clothes—boots, hat, cloak, spurs, long knife, and all complete, though coarse and dirty as may be,—and to call themselves Españolos, and to hold property, if they can get any. . . .

Another thing that surprised me was the quantity of silver that was in circulation. I certainly never saw so much silver at one time in my life, as during the week that we were in Monterey. The truth is, they have no credit system, no banks, and no way of investing money but in cattle. They have no circulating medium but silver and hides—which the sailors call "California bank notes." Everything that they buy they must pay for in one of the other of these things . . .

Monterey, as far as my observation goes, is decidedly the pleasantest and most civilized-looking place in California. In the center of it is an open square, surrounded by four lines of one-story plastered buildings with half a dozen cannon in the center; some mounted, and others not. This is the "Presidio," or fort. Every town has a presidio in its center; or rather, every presidio has a town built around it; for the forts were first built by the Mexican government, and then the people built near them for protection. The presidio here was entirely open and unfortified. There were several officers with long titles, and about eighty soldiers, but they were poorly paid, fed, clothed, and disciplined. The governor-general, or as he is commonly called, the "general," lives here; which makes it the seat of government. He is appointed by the central government of Mexico, and is the chief civil and military officer. In addition to him, each town has a commandant, who is the chief military officer, and has charge of the fort, and of all transactions with foreigners and foreign vessels; and two or three *alcaldis* and *corregidores*, elected by the inhabitants, who are the civil officers.

Courts and jurisprudence they have no knowledge of. . . . No Protestant has any civil rights; nor can he hold any property, or indeed, remain more than few weeks on shore, unless he belongs to some vessel. Consequently, the Americans and English who intend to reside here become Catholics, to a man. . . .

In Monterey there are a number of English and Americans (English or "Ingles" all are called who speak the English language) who have married Californians, become united to the Catholic church, and acquired considerable property. Having more industry, frugality, and enterprise than the natives, they soon get nearly all the trade into their hands. . . . The people are naturally suspicious of foreigners, and they would not be allowed to remain, were it not that they become good Catholics, and by marrying natives, and bringing up their children as Catholics and Spaniards, and not teaching them the English language, they quiet suspicion, and even become popular and leading men. The chief *alcaldis* in Monterey and Santa Barbara were both Yankees by birth....

On the expulsion of the Jesuits from the Spanish dominions, the missions passed into the hands of the Franciscans, though without any essential change in their management. Ever since the independence of Mexico, the missions have been going down; until, at last, a law was passed, stripping them of all their possessions, and confining the priests to their spiritual duties; and at the same time declaring all the Indians free and independent *Rancheros*. The change in the condition of the Indians was, as may be supposed only nominal: they are virtually slaves, as much as they ever were. But in the missions, the change was complete. The priests have now no power, except in their religious character, and the great possessions of the missions are given over to be preyed upon by the harpies of civil power, who are sent there in the capacity of *administradores*, to settle up the concerns; and who usually end, in a few years, by making themselves fortunes, and leaving their stewardships worse than they found them.... The change had been made but a few years before our arrival upon the coast, yet, in that short time, the trade was much diminished, credit impaired, and the venerable missions going rapidly to decay.

9.4

General Manuel de Mier y Terán on Texas (1828)

In 1821, hoping to foster trade and to populate its territories, the Mexican government invited Americans to settle in Texas (Tejas). The government awarded generous land grants to agents (empresarios) charged with luring Americans to new Texas colonies. By 1825, Stephen F. Austin, the most successful empresario, had persuaded 300 families to move to his settlements. Within five years, almost 7,000 Americans lived in Texas. These changes generated tensions. Although they were nominally Mexican citizens and adopted Roman Catholicism, Americans complained about the inefficiency of the Mexican

SOURCE: *Texas by Terán: The Diary Kept by General Manuel de Mier y Terán on His 1828 Inspection of Texas*, edited by Jack Johnson, translated by John Wheat, 96–101. Copyright © 2000. By permission of the University of Texas Press.

legal system. At the same time, native-born Mexicans (tejanos) worried about the growing influence and size of the American population. Indians who had come to Texas to escape U.S. relocation policies were also alarmed.

General Manuel de Mier y Terán (1789–1832) witnessed this discontent during an 1828 expedition. Born in Mexico City, Terán studied mathematics, mining, and engineering. After distinguished military service in the Mexican revolt against Spain, he served as a congressman and as minister of war. In 1827, the Mexican government sent him to Texas to assess its military, commercial, and agricultural potential.

Throughout his mission, Terán warned that Mexico was losing control over Texas. In response, the government limited immigration and barred the importation of additional slaves. Appointed commandant general for the northeast states and federal commissioner of colonization, Terán improved defenses, instituted new taxes, and tried to offset Anglo dominance of Texas. When these efforts failed and political instability rocked Mexico, a despondent Terán committed suicide. Four years later, Texas won its independence from Mexico. It joined the United States of America in 1845.

In this 1828 letter to President Guadalupe Victoria, Terán appraises the American colonies in Texas and offers possible solutions for the deepening crisis.

FOCUS QUESTIONS

1. What types of problems does Terán identify in Texas?
2. How does he describe the local people?
3. How is slavery complicating matters in Texas?
4. What solutions does Terán propose?
5. Could Mexico have avoided the Texas Revolution? If so, how? Explain your answers.

Nacodoches, June 30, 1828.

...As one covers the distance from Béjar to this town, he will note that Mexican influence diminishes, so much so that it becomes clear that in this town that influence is almost nonexistent. But where could such influence come from? Not from the population, because the ratio of the Mexican population is precisely the contrary: the Mexicans of this town consist of what people everywhere call the abject class, the poorest and most ignorant. The North Americans residing in the town run an English school, and send their children north for their education. The poor Mexicans neither have the resources to create schools, nor is there anyone to think about improving their institutions and abject condition.

Authorities and magistrates are also lacking.... [W]e have in the most important post on our frontier ... grave incidents of a political and judicial nature are taking place. Therefore, Señor President, I must disturb you in the same way I was disturbed to see the foreign colonists' attitude toward our nation. Most of them, with the exception of a few who have traveled to our capital—knowing no Mexicans other than those who live here and lacking the authorities that are necessary in every society—think that [Mexico] consists of nothing more than blacks and Indians, all of them ignorant. In some homes, where they have done me the favor of considering me an educated man, they have told me to my face that it could not be so unless I were French or Spanish.

From this state of affairs an antipathy has emerged between Mexicans and foreigners that is not the least of the volatile elements I have found to make me tell you that, if timely measures are not taken, Tejas will pull down the entire federation. The foreigners grumble about the political disorganization on the frontier, and the Mexicans complain about the advantages and better education that the former [enjoy]. The foreigners find it intolerable to have to travel 200 leagues to complain about the petty vexations that a corrupt and ignorant *alcalde* [a mayor having judicial powers] causes them, and the Mexicans—who, having no notion of the laws of their country or even of the laws of colonization, feel themselves pushed aside for the foreigners—create complications on their part in order to deprive [the foreigners] of the right to vote and to exclude them from the *ayuntamiento* [town hall or municipal government]. Meanwhile, the new settlers continue to arrive. The first news we have of them is through the discovery of an already cultivated property where they have been settled for months. The older inhabitants claim the land, based on a duly issued title from the Spanish government—of doubtful authenticity, since the archives have disappeared—and litigation arises wherein the *alcalde* has occasion to demand money [in fees]. Thus it is that this town without magistrates is where the most lawsuits abound. This should be understood for Nacodoches and its environs, because with regard to more distant lands, especially those belonging to the national government, it is known that the natural order continues its course; that is, that the lands are being settled with anyone's knowledge.

In addition to the small number of North Americans who settled during the Spanish regime, there are two classes of settlers—one consists of fugitives from the neighboring republic, many of them branded on the face with the mark they use there for thieves and scoundrels. These people locate between Nacodoches and the Sabine River, ready to cross the river whenever they have just committed a crime. Some of them have reserved and spend their lives working the land. The other class is that of poor laborers [*jornaleros*] who did not have four or five thousand pesos to purchase plots of land in the north and who wished to become landowners, which is one of the virtues of our neighbors who have come to Tejas. The latter, who compose the colony of Austin, are generally industrious and honorable and respect the country. Most of them have at least one or two slaves.

Unfortunately, it is difficult for the latter to emigrate, because they lack means of transportation. In order to achieve this we need what has not existed up to now, which is *empresarios* with capital to advance [the colonists] what they need in order to settle. Prosperous North Americans in Louisiana and other western states wish to acquire lands in Tejas for large-scale speculation, but they are restricted by the laws prohibiting slavery. If these laws were rescinded (may God forbid), in just a few years Tejas would be a powerful state that would rival Louisiana in production and wealth.

The rescinding of those [antislavery] laws is the object toward which the colonists direct their efforts. . . .

What I perceive in all this is that certainly in Nacodoches, at least, more government action is needed in the town, since it is a frontier [outpost] with which the Republic should maintain closer contact. By law, the general government possesses vast tracts of land in this country, and in order to distribute them wisely, it is necessary to pay attention to the economy no less than to politics and national security. The total population is a mixture of such strange or incoherent elements that no other like it exists in our entire federation: tribes of savages, numerous and peaceful but armed and always ready for war, whose progress toward civilization surely will be achieved through close vigilance by a zealous and well-educated political authority, and colonists who have come from another, more advanced, society, better educated but also more malicious and mistrustful than are the Mexicans. Among the foreigners there are all kinds: fugitive criminals, honorable farmers, vagabonds and ne'er-do-wells, laborers, etc. They all go about with their constitution in their pocket, demanding their rights and the authorities and functionaries that [their constitution] provides. Most of them hold slaves who, now having perceived the favorable intent of Mexican law with regard to their tragic state, are becoming restless to throw off their yoke, while their masters believe they can keep them by making [the yoke] heavier. They commit the barbarities on their on their slaves that are so common where men live in a relationship contradictory to their nature: they pull their teeth, they set dogs upon them until they tear them apart, and the mildest of them will whip the slaves until they are flayed.

Thus, the growth of the population, its extraordinary nature, and the interests and security of the nation to my mind call for us to put here a political chief. . . and a tribunal or counselor. . . .

Then we could proceed to create prosperity for the colonists, many of whom—who are not prosperous because of their situation—lean toward rebellion and troublemaking. . . .

9.5

John O'Sullivan on Annexation (1845)

Like their colonial forebears, nineteenth-century Americans cherished the opportunity to acquire land. The Panic of 1837 sparked popular demands for more markets, especially in Oregon and California. Expansionists argued that "manifest destiny" compelled Americans to spread democracy, freedom, and Protestantism to "uncivilized" peoples. The expansion issue split the two parties. Democrats claimed that territorial acquisition would preserve the nation's agricultural character and benefit the working poor. In contrast, Whigs believed that the lofty rhetoric of the expansionists cloaked an evil conspiracy to spread slavery. After Democrat James K. Polk won the election of 1844, the annexation of Texas ignited a heated national debate on expansion.

In this selection, Democrat and New York-based journalist John L. O'Sullivan defines "manifest destiny."

FOCUS QUESTIONS

1. What is O'Sullivan's position on the annexation of Texas?

2. What are the major components of "manifest destiny"?

3. What does O'Sullivan identify as the benefits of American expansion? How does he view the people already living in the West?

4. Who might have objected to O'Sullivan's views? Why?

It is time now for opposition to the annexation of Texas to cease.... Texas is now ours. Already, before these words are written, her convention has undoubtedly ratified the acceptance, by her congress, of our proffered invitation into the Union; and made the requisite changes in her already republican form of constitution to adapt it to its future federal relations. Her star and her stripe may already be said to have taken their place in the glorious blazon of our common nationality; and the sweep of our eagle's wing already includes within its circuit the wide extent of her fair and fertile land....

SOURCE: John O'Sullivan, "Annexation," *United States Magazine and Democratic Review* (July 1845); 5–10.

Why, were other reasoning wanting, in favor of now elevating this question of the reception of Texas into the Union, out of the lower region of our past party dissensions, up to its proper level of a high and broad nationality, it surely is to be found, found abundantly, in the manner in which other nations have undertaken to intrude themselves into it, between us and the proper parties to the case, in a spirit of hostile interference against us, for the avowed object of thwarting our policy and hampering our power, limiting our greatness and checking the fulfillment of our manifest destiny to overspread the continent allotted by Providence for the free development of our yearly multiplying millions....

The independence of Texas was complete and absolute. It was an independence, not only in fact, but of right. No obligation of duty toward Mexico tended in the least degree to restrain our right to effect the desired recovery of the fair province.... If Texas became peopled with an American population, it was by no contrivance of our government, but on the express invitation of that of Mexico herself; accompanied with such guaranties of state independence, and the maintenance of a federal system analogous to our own, as constituted a compact fully justifying the strongest measures of redress on the part of those afterward deceived in this guaranty, and sought to be enslaved under the yoke imposed by its violation.

She was released, rightfully and absolutely released, from all Mexican allegiance, or duty of cohesion to the Mexican political body, by the acts and fault of Mexico herself, and Mexico alone. There never was a clearer case. It was not revolution; it was resistance to revolution....

Nor is there any just foundation for the charge that annexation is a great proslavery measure—calculated to increase and perpetuate that institution. Slavery had nothing to do with it. Opinions were and are greatly divided, both at the North and South, as to the influence to be exerted by it on slavery and on the slave states. That it will tend to facilitate and hasten the disappearance of slavery from all the northern tier of the present slave states, cannot surely admit of serious question. The greater value in Texas of the slave labor now employed in those states, must soon produce the effect of draining off the labor southwardly, by the same unvarying law that bids water descend the slope that invites it....

The Spanish-Indian-American population of Mexico, Central America, and South America, afford the only receptacle capable of absorbing that race whenever we shall be prepared to slough it off—to emancipate it from slavery, and (simultaneously necessary) to remove it from the midst of our own. Themselves already of mixed and confused blood, and free from the "prejudices" which among us so insuperably forbid the social amalgamation which can alone elevate the Negro race out of a virtually servile degradation....

California will, probably, next fall away from the loose adhesion which, in such a country as Mexico, holds a remote province in a slight equivocal kind of dependence on the metropolis. Imbecile and distracted, Mexico never can exert any real government authority over such a country....

The Anglo-Saxon foot is already on its borders. Already the advance guard of the irresistible army of Anglo-Saxon emigration has begun to pour down upon it, armed with the plough and the rifle, and marking its trail with schools and colleges, courts and representative halls, mills and meetinghouses. A population will soon be in actual occupation of California, over which it will be idle for Mexico to dream of dominion. They will necessarily become independent. . . .

Their right to independence will be the natural right of self-government belonging to any community strong enough to maintain—distinct in position, origin and character, and free from any mutual obligations of memberships of a common political body, binding it to others by the duty of loyalty and compact of public faith. This will be their title to independence; and by this title, there can be no doubt that the population now fast streaming down upon California will both assert and maintain that independence.

Whether they will then attach themselves to our Union or not, is not to be predicted with any certainty. Unless the projected railroad across the continent to the Pacific be carried into effect, perhaps they may not; though even in that case, the day is not distant when the empires of the Atlantic and Pacific would again flow together into one, as soon as their inland border should approach each other. But that great work, colossal as appears the plan on its first suggestions, cannot remain long unbuilt.

Its necessity for this very purpose of binding and holding together in its iron clasp our fast-settling Pacific region with that of the Mississippi Valley. . . . these considerations give assurance that the day cannot be distant which shall witness the conveyance of the representatives from Oregon and California to Washington within less time than a few years ago was devoted to a similar journey by those from Ohio; while the magnetic telegraph will enable the editors of the *San Francisco Union*, the *Astoria Evening Post*, or the *Nootka Morning News*, to set up in type the first half of the President's inaugural before the echoes of the latter half shall have died away beneath the lofty porch of the Capitol, as spoken from his lips. . . .

9.6

Thomas Corwin Opposes the Mexican War (1847)

The Mexican War (1846–1848) was extremely controversial. Provoked by an aggressive U.S. attempt to redraw the southern border of Texas, the war

SOURCE: Published in *The American Reader: Words That Moved a Nation*, ed. Diane Ravitch (New York: HarperCollins, 1991), 77–79.

intensified sectional conflict and political partisanship. Despite their differences on the expansion issue, racism and arrogance convinced most Americans that the Mexicans would be easily defeated. In reality, the Mexicans resisted coura- geously—if unsuccessfully—against a foe with superior weapons and organiza- tion. In February 1848, Mexico signed the Treaty of Guadalupe-Hidalgo and ceded 500,000 square miles spanning from the Rio Grande River to the Pacific Ocean. California, New Mexico, Nevada, Utah, most of Arizona, and parts of Wyoming and Colorado sprang from the enormous territory. In exchange, the United States assumed American claims against Mexico and paid $15 million.

While patriotic press coverage initially created widespread popular support for the conflict, fierce opposition to the war soon emerged. Many Whigs denounced the conflict as naked aggression against a weak neighbor. Abolitionists viewed the war as an immoral attempt to spread slavery. The bitter disputes over expansion and slavery destroyed the nation's political stability.

In this reading, Thomas Corwin, a Whig senator from Ohio, criticizes the Democrats and the Mexican War.

FOCUS QUESTIONS

1. Why is Corwin so opposed to the war against Mexico?
2. How does Corwin view the Mexicans?
3. Compare Corwin's assertions to those of John O'Sullivan (Document 9.5). How do their remarks demonstrate differences between the Whig and Democratic parties?

What is the territory, Mr. President, which you propose to wrest from Mexico? It is consecrated to the heart of the Mexican by many a well-fought battle with his old Castilian master. His Bunker Hills, and Saratogas, and Yorktowns are there! The Mexican can say, "There I bled for liberty! And shall I surrender that consecrated home of my affections to the Anglo-Saxon invaders? What do they want with it? They have Texas already. They have possessed themselves of the territory between the Nueces and the Rio Grande. What else do they want? To what shall I point my children as memorials of that independence which I bequeath to them, when those battlefields shall have passed from my possession?"

Sir, had one come and demanded Bunker Hill of the people of Massachu- setts, had England's lion ever showed himself there, is there a man over thirteen and under ninety who would not have been ready to meet him? Is there a river on this continent that would not have run red with blood? Is there a field but would have been piled high with the unburied bones of slaughtered Americans before these consecrated battlefields of liberty should have been wrested from us? But this same American goes into a sister republic, and says to poor, weak Mexico, "Give up your territory, you are unworthy to possess it; I have got one half already, and all I ask of you is to give up the other!" . . .

Sir, look at this pretense of want of room. With twenty millions of people, you have about one thousand millions of acres of land, inviting settlement by every conceivable argument, bringing them down to a quarter of a dollar an acre, and allowing every man to squat where he pleases. . . .

There is one topic connected with this subject which I tremble when I approach, and yet I cannot forbear to notice it. It meets you in every step you take; it threatens you which way soever you go in the prosecution of this war. I allude to the question of slavery. Opposition to its further extension, it must be obvious to everyone, is a deeply rooted determination with men of all parties in what we call the nonslave-holding states. New York, Pennsylvania, and Ohio, three of the most powerful, have already sent their legislative instructions here. So it will be, I doubt not, in all the rest. It is vain now to speculate about the reasons for this. Gentlemen of the South may call it prejudice, passion, hypocrisy, fanaticism. I shall not dispute with them now on that point. You and I cannot alter or change this opinion, if we would. These people only say we will not, cannot consent that you shall carry slavery where it does not already exist. They do not seek to disturb you in that institution as it exists in your states. Enjoy it if you will and as you will. This is their language; this their determination. How is it in the South? Can it be expected that they should expend in common their blood and their treasure in the acquisition of immense territory, and then willingly forgo the right to carry thither their slaves, and inhabit the conquered country if they please to do so? Sir, I know the feelings and opinions of the South too well to calculate on this. Nay, I believe they would even contend to any extremity for the mere right, had they no wish to exert it. I believe (and I confess I tremble when the conviction presses upon me) that there is equal obstinacy on both sides of this fearful question. . . .

Should we prosecute this war another moment, or expend one dollar in the purchase or conquest of a single acre of Mexican land, the North and the South are brought into collision on a point where neither will yield. Who can foresee or foretell the result! Who so bold or reckless as to look such a conflict in the face unmoved! I do not envy the heart of him who can realize the possibility of such a conflict without emotions too painful to be endured. Why, then, shall we, the representatives of the sovereign states of the Union—the chosen guardians of this confederated Republic, why should we precipitate this fearful struggle, by continuing a war the result of which must be to force us at once upon a civil conflict? Sir, rightly considered, this is treason, treason to the Union, treason to the dearest interests, the loftiest aspirations, the most cherished hopes of our constituents. It is a crime to risk the possibility of such a contest. It is a crime of such infernal hue that every other in the catalogue of iniquity, when compared with it, whitens into virtue. . . .

Let us abandon all idea of acquiring further territory and by consequence cease at once to prosecute this war. Let us call home our armies, and bring them at once within our own acknowledged limits. Show Mexico that you are sincere when you say you desire nothing by conquest. She has learned that she cannot encounter you in war, and if she had not, she is too weak to disturb you here. Tender her peace, and, my life on it, she will then accept it. But whether she shall or not, you will have peace without her consent. It is your invasion that has made war; your retreat will restore peace. Let us then close forever the approaches of internal feud, and so return to the ancient concord and the old ways of national prosperity and permanent glory. Let us here, in this temple consecrated to the Union, perform a solemn lustration; let us wash Mexican blood from our hands, and on these altars, and in the presence of that image of the Father of his Country that looks down upon us, swear to preserve honorable peace with all the world and eternal brotherhood with each other.

9.7

José Fernando Ramírez Describes the U.S. Occupation of Mexico City (1847)

During the Mexican War, U.S. forces mounted naval and ground attacks across the vast Mexican territory. In March 1847, General Winfield Scott began the war's final and most decisive campaign. After a successful amphibious landing at Vera Cruz, Scott's troops captured the city and headed inland. Superior artillery and logistics helped the Americans outmaneuver a larger Mexican army. On September 13, 1847, U.S. forces captured and occupied Mexico City.

José Fernando Ramírez (1805–1871) documented Mexico's history during these tumultuous years. Born in Chihuahua, Ramírez earned acclaim for his legal expertise and writings in history, literature, and archeology. In the 1830s and 1840s, he held several government positions and headed the national law school. When war with the United States erupted, Ramírez orchestrated efforts to hide historic records in private homes. In this letter, he describes the American occupation of Mexico City.

FOCUS QUESTIONS

1. How does Ramírez characterize life in Mexico City?
2. How are local residents responding to U.S. troops?

SOURCE: José Fernando Ramírez, *Mexico During the War with the United States* edited by Walter V. Scholes, translated by Elliott B. Scherr, 160–62. By permission of the University of Missouri Press. Copyright © 1970 by the Curators of the University of Missouri.

3. What is Ramírez's opinion of the American occupation forces?
4. Whom does Ramírez blame for Mexico's defeat?

Mexico City, September 30, 1847

My dear friend:

I have not received any word from you to which I can reply, because, since the unfortunate inhabitants of this city are being treated as enemies, there has been no opportunity to get mail in from the outside. Where it is being held heaven only knows. We have hopes that the mail will eventually be permitted to come in, and then I shall know what I have to reply to.

What shall I tell you? Well, to be frank, nothing because this city is no longer the center of political life. According to reports, the center has been transferred to many other centers that will exhaust whatever political life is left to us by our enemy who is oppressing and humiliating us. How I would like to bring home this lesson to certain politicians who have talked incessantly about despotism, etc! Here they would see and get a taste of what it means to live without guarantees! It is all so frightful. I must say that those who have conquered us, brutally savage as they are, have conducted themselves in a manner different from that of European armies belonging to nations that bear the standard of civilization. This does not mean that they do not commit countless excesses every day. But we have here a phenomenon consisting of mingled barbarism and restraint. This has been the situation for several days, and there is no way to account for it.

Open fighting ceased the third day after the city was occupied; but the undercover struggle goes on, and it is assuming a fearful aspect. The enemy's forces are growing weaker day by day because of assassinations, and it is impossible to discover who the assassins are. Anyone who takes a walk through the streets or goes a short distance away from the center of the city is a dead man. I have been told that a small cemetery has been found in a pulque [a fermented milky drink made from certain varieties of agave] tavern where deadly liquor was dispensed for the purpose of assuring an increasing number of victims. Seven corpses were discovered inside the establishment, but the tavern keeper could not be found. I am also told that the number of those who have been taken off this way amounts to 300, without counting those dying of sickness and wounds. Five days ago a funeral cortege with the bodies of four officers passed by my residence. The plague has begun to show its signs, and the monuments that those filthy soldiers have scattered along the streets of their quarters unmistakably testify to the fact that dysentery is destroying them. I have never before seen such sodden drunkenness, nor any more scandalous or impudent than the drunkenness that holds these men in its grip. Nor have I ever seen more unrestrained appetites. Every hour of the day, except during the evenings, when they are all drunk, one can find them eating everything they see.

The Palace and almost all public buildings have been savagely ransacked and destroyed. I think it only right to say, however, that our disgraceful rabble were the ones who began it all. When the enemy's troops entered the Palace, the doors had already been broken down and the building had been plundered. Three days later the embroidered velvet canopy was sold for four pesos at the Palace entrance. The Government records and other items were sold for two reales. The infamous and eternally accursed Santa Anna abandoned us all, both individuals and property, to the mercy of the enemy and did not leave even one sentinel to defend us.

In Durango you probably know more of what is going on than I do, and you no doubt can see how horrible our future is. I am forwarding to you some documents, two of which I want you to keep as testimony of the iniquitous and shameful rule that the Americans have imposed upon us. The sad thing about all this is that the punishment has been deserved.

Forward the enclosed letters and tell the members of my family that we are all in good health. Do not forget your friend, who holds you in great esteem.

9.8

Henry David Thoreau, "Civil Disobedience" (1849)

Henry David Thoreau (1817–1862) was one of the most prominent opponents of the Mexican War. A Transcendentalist, Thoreau celebrated individuality, emotion, and nature in his poetry and essays. From 1845 to 1847, his quest for spiritual enlightenment and rejection of materialism led him to adopt a semiisolated existence at Walden Pond near Concord, Massachusetts. But the outbreak of the Mexican War disrupted Thoreau's simple life. In July 1846, Thoreau refused to pay his poll tax as a protest against slavery and the war. After spending a night in jail, Thoreau began producing several essays on individual rights and social justice. While these writings drew little attention in Thoreau's day, they have profoundly influenced modern human rights advocates, including Mahatma Gandhi, Martin Luther King, Jr., and Nelson Mandela.

SOURCE: *The Writings of Henry David Thoreau*, Vol. 4, Cape Cod and Miscellanies (New York, 1968; reprint of 1906 edition), 356–387.

FOCUS QUESTIONS

1. What are the major themes of Thoreau's "Civil Disobedience"?
2. What are Thoreau's views on wealth and government?
3. What type of life does Thoreau advocate?
4. Do you find Thoreau's suggestions persuasive? Explain your answer.

Under a government which imprisons any unjustly, the true place for a just man is also a prison. The proper place today, the only place which Massachusetts has provided for her freer and less desponding spirits, is in her prisons, to be put out and locked out of the State by her own act, as they have already put themselves out by their principles. It is there that the fugitive slave, and the Mexican prisoner on parole, and the Indian come to plead the wrongs of his race should find them; on that separate, but more free and honorable, ground where the State in which a free man can abide with honor. If any think that their influence would be lost there, and their voices no longer afflict the ear of the State, that they would not be as an enemy within its walls, they do not know by how much truth is stronger than error, nor how much more eloquently and effectively he can combat injustice who has experienced a little in his own person. Cast your whole vote, not a strip of paper merely, but your whole influence. A minority is powerless while it conforms to the majority; it is not even a minority then; but it is irresistible when it clogs by its whole weight. If the alternative is to keep all just men in prison, or give up war and slavery, the State will not hesitate which to choose. If a thousand men were not to pay their tax-bills this year, that would not be a violent and bloody measure, as it would be to pay them, and enable the State to commit violence and shed innocent blood. This is, in fact, the definition of a peaceable revolution, if any such is possible. If the tax-gatherer, or any other public officer, asks me, as one has done, "But what shall I do?" my answer is, "If you really wish to do anything, resign your office." When the subject has refused allegiance, and the officer has resigned his office, then the revolution is accomplished. But even suppose blood should flow. Is there not a sort of bloodshed when the conscience is wounded? Through this would a man's real manhood and immortality flow out, and he bleeds to an everlasting death. I see this blood flowing now.

I have contemplated the imprisonment of the offender, rather than the seizure of his goods,—though both will serve the same purpose,—because they who assert the purest right, and consequently are most dangerous to a corrupt State, commonly have not spent much time in accumulating property. To such the State renders comparatively small service, and a slight tax is wont to appear exorbitant, particularly if they are obliged to earn it by special labor with their hands. If there were one who lived wholly without the use of money, the State itself would hesitate to demand it of him. But the rich man—not to make any invidious comparison—is always sold to the institution which makes him rich.

Absolutely speaking, the more money, the less virtue; for money comes between a man and his objects, and obtains them for him; and it was certainly no great virtue to obtain it. It puts to rest many questions which he would otherwise be taxed to answer; while the only new question which it puts is the hard but superfluous one, how to spend it. Thus his moral ground is taken from under his feet. The opportunities of living are diminished in proportion as what are called the "means" are increased. The best thing a man can do for his culture when he is rich is to endeavor to carry out those schemes which he entertained when he was poor. Christ answered the Herodians according to their condition. "Show me the tribute-money," said he;—and one took a penny out of his pocket;—if you use money which has the image of Caesar on it, and which he has made current and valuable, that is, if you are men of the State, and gladly enjoy the advantages of Caesar's government, then pay him back some of his own when he demands it. "Render therefore to Caesar that which is Caesar's, and to God those things which are God's,"—leaving them no wiser than before as to which was which; for they did not wish to know.

When I converse with the freest of my neighbors, I perceive that, whatever they may say about the magnitude and seriousness of the question, and their regard for the public tranquility, the long and the short of the matter is, that they cannot spare the protection of the existing government, and they dread the consequences to their property and families of disobedience to it. For my own part, I should not like to think that I ever rely on the protection of the State. But, if I deny the authority of the State when it presents its taxbill, it will soon take and waste all my property, and so harass me and my children without end. This is hard. This makes it impossible for a man to live honestly, and at the same time comfortably, in outward respects. It will not be worth the while to accumulate property; that would be sure to go again. You must hire or squat somewhere, and raise but a small crop, and eat that soon. You must live within yourself, and depend upon yourself always tucked up and ready for a start, and not have many affairs. . . .

9.9

Elizabeth Dixon Smith Greer Describes Life on the Frontier (1847–1850)

During the 1840s, thousands of Americans headed for Oregon and California. Facing four months of arduous travel on the Overland Trail, most settlers joined carefully organized wagon trains. While hostile encounters with Indians were rare, pioneers encountered other hardships, including illness, injury, bad weather, and shortages. In 1846, the Donner party lost several weeks following an incorrect guidebook. Trapped by frigid winter weather, members resorted to cannibalism in order to survive.

Such horrors did not deter people from seeking prosperity in the West. Between 1840 and 1848, almost 12,000 Americans moved to Oregon while another 2,700 ventured to California. By 1860, 340,000 people had traversed the Oregon Trail. Over 34,000 died of exposure and disease while about 400 perished in Indian attacks. Many women found life on the trail quite difficult because it exaggerated their dependence on men and added to their already considerable daily workloads. In these journal entries, a pioneer woman recounts her experiences on the frontier.

FOCUS QUESTIONS

1. Why does Greer keep this journal?
2. How does she describe life on the trail? How do the experiences of men and women differ?
3. What impact does moving west have on Greer's family?
4. Would you have wanted to be a pioneer? Explain your answer.

Dear Friends—By your request I have endeavored to keep a record of our journey from "the States" to Oregon, though it is poorly done, owing to my having a young babe and besides a large family to do for; and, worst of all, my education is very limited.

SOURCE: *The Thirty-Fifth Transactions of the Oregon Pioneer Association* (1907), 153, 171–78.

April 21, 1847—Commenced our journey from La Porte, Indiana, to Oregon; made fourteen miles. . . .

[After six months of hard travel, the party reaches the Columbia River in Oregon.]

November 9—Finds us still in trouble. Waves dashing over our raft and we already stinting ourselves in provisions. My husband started this morning to hunt provisions. Left no man with us except our oldest boy. It is very cold. The icicles are hanging from our wagon beds to the water. Tonight about dusk Adam Polk expired. No one with him but his wife and myself. We sat up all night with him while the waves was dashing below. . . .

November 12—Ferried our cattle over the river and buried Mr. Polk. Rain all day. We are living entirely on beef.

November 18—My husband is sick. It rains and snows. We start this morning around the falls with our wagons. We have 5 miles to go. I carry my babe and lead, or rather carry, another through snow, mud and water, almost to my knees. It is the worst road that a team could possibly travel. I went ahead with my children, and I was afraid to look behind me for fear of seeing the wagons turn over into the mud and water with everything in them. My children gave out with cold and fatigue and could not travel, and the boys had to unhitch the oxen and bring them and carry the children on to camp. I was so cold and numb that I could not tell by the feeling that I had any feet at all. We started this morning at sunrise and did not get to camp until after dark, and there was not one dry thread on one of us—not even my babe. I had carried my babe and I was so fatigued that I could scarcely speak or step. When I got here I found my husband lying in Welch's wagon, very sick. He had brought Mrs. Polk down the day before and was taken sick here. We had to stay up all night, for our wagons are left halfway back. I have not told half we suffered. I am not adequate to the task. Here were some hundreds camped, waiting for boats to come and take them down the Columbia to Vancouver or Portland or Oregon City.

November 19—My husband is sick and can have but little care. Rain all day.

November 20—Rain all day. It is almost an impossibility to cook, and quite so to keep warm or dry. I froze or chilled my feet so that I cannot wear a shoe, so I have to go around in the cold water barefooted.

November 21—Rain all day. The whole care of everything falls upon my shoulders. I cannot write any more at present.

November 27—Embarked once more on the Columbia on a flatboat. Rain all day, though the waves threatened hard to sink us. Passed Fort Vancouver in the night. Landed a mile below. My husband never left his bed since he was taken sick.

November 28—Still moving on the water.

November 29—Landed at Portland on the Willamette, 12 miles above the mouth, at 11 o'clock at night.

November 30—Raining. This morning I ran about trying to get a house to get into with my sick husband. At last I found a small, leaky concern, with two families already in it. Mrs. Polk had got down before us. She and another widow was in this house. My family and Welch's went in with them, and you could have stirred us with a stick. Welch and my oldest boy was driving the cattle around. My children and I carried up a bed. The distance was nearly a quarter of a mile.

Made it down on the floor in the mud. I got some men to carry my husband up through the rain and lay him on it, and he never was out of that shed until he was carried out in his coffin. Here lay five of us bedfast at one time . . . and we had no money, and what few things we had left that would bring money, I had to sell. I had to give 10 cents a pound for fresh pork, 75 cents per bushel for potatoes, 4 cents a pound for fish. There are so many of us sick that I cannot write any more at present. I have not time to write much, but I thought it would be interesting to know what kind of weather we have in the winter.

1848—January 14—Rain this morning. Warm weather. We suppose it has rained half of the time that I have neglected writing.

January 15—My husband is still alive, but very sick. There is no medicine here except at Fort Vancouver, and the people there will not sell one bit—not even a bottle of wine.

February 1—Rain all day. This day my dear husband, my last remaining friend, died.

February 2—Today we buried my earthly companion. Now I know what none but widows know; that is, how comfortless is a widow's life, especially when left in a strange land, without money or friends, and the care of seven children. Cloudy. . . .

[September 2, 1850—] Well, after the boys were gone, it is true I had plenty of cows and hogs and plenty of wheat to feed them on and to make my bread. Indeed, I was well off if I had only known it; but I lived in a remote place where my strength was of little use to me. I could get nothing to do, and you know I could not live without work. I employed myself in teaching my children: yet that did not fully occupy my mind. I became as poor as a snake, yet I was in good health, and never was so nimble since I was a child. I could run a half a mile without stopping to breathe. Well, I thought perhaps I had better try my fortunes again; so on the 24th of June, 1849, I was married to a Mr. Joseph Greer, a man 14 years older than myself, though young enough for me. He is the father of ten children. They are all married, but two boys and two girls. He is a Yankee from Connecticut and he is a Yankee in every sense of the word, as I told you he would be if it proved my lot to marry him. . . .

[W]e are all well but Perley. I cannot answer for him; he has gone to the Umpqua for some money due him. The other two are working for four dollars a day. The two oldest boys have got three town lots in quite a stirring place called Lafayette in Yamhill County. Perley has four horses. A good Indian horse is worth one hundred dollars. A good American cow is worth sixty dollars. My boys live about 25 miles from me, so that I cannot act in the capacity of a mother to them; so you will guess it is not all sunshine with me, for you know my boys are not old enough to do without a mother. Russell Welch done very well in the mines. He made about twenty hundred dollars. He lives 30 miles below me in a little town called Portland on the Willamette River. Sarah has got her third son. It has been one year since I saw her. Adam Polk's two youngest boys live about wherever they see fit. The oldest, if he is alive, is in California. There is some ague [a fever characterized by sweating fits, chills, and aches] in this country this season, but neither I nor my children, except those that went to California, have had a day's sickness since we came to Oregon.

9.10

Alonzo Delano, A Forty-Niner (1849–1850)

In 1848, the discovery of gold in California shattered the popular belief that the West was an arid wasteland. As news of the first gold strike on Sutter's Mill near the Sacramento River filtered out, thousands of people from all over the world descended on the gold fields. Almost overnight, California was transformed from a sleepy backwater to an ethically diverse, violent boomtown. Within a year, approximately 80,000 "forty-niners" arrived. By 1853, the number hit 250,000. Tensions between miners often exploded. Free men refused to compete with slaves. Some whites pushed Mexicans, Chinese immigrants, and African Americans out of the best mining areas. Others shot local Indians for sport. Such violence prompted calls for law enforcement and centralized government. Within months, large mining companies with capital and machinery controlled the most lucrative mines. Nonetheless, many individuals considered the gold rush a great adventure.

In this excerpt, Alonzo Delano, who arrived in California in 1849, describes the gold rush.

FOCUS QUESTIONS

1. How are people affected by rumors of gold strikes?
2. How does Delano describe the lives of the miners? How do conditions in his camp change over time?
3. Would you have joined the gold rush? Explain your answer.

In May 1850, a report reached the settlements that a wonderful lake had been discovered, a hundred miles back among the mountains, towards the head of the Middle Fork of Feather River, the shores of which abounded with gold, and to such an extent that it lay like pebbles on the beach. An extraordinary ferment among the people ensued, a grand rush was made from the towns, in search of this splendid El Dorado. Stores were left to take care of themselves, business of all kinds was dropped, mules were suddenly bought up at exorbitant prices, and crowds started off to search for the golden lake.

SOURCE: A[lonzo] Delano, *Life on the Plains among the Diggings* (Auburn, etc., 1854), 14–351, *passim.*

Days passed away, when at length the adventurers began to return, with disappointed looks, and their worn out and dilapidated garments showed that they had "seen some service," and it proved that, though several lakes had been discovered, the Gold Lake *par excellence* was not found. The mountains swarmed with men, exhausted and worn out with toil and hunger; mules were starved, or killed from falling from precipices. Still the search was continued over snow forty or fifty feet deep, till the highest ridge of the Sierra was passed, when the disappointed crowds began to return without getting a glimpse of the grand *desideratum*, having had their labor for their pains.

Yet this sally was not without some practical and beneficial results. The country was perfectly explored, some rich diggings were found, and, as usual, a few among the many were benefited. A new field for enterprise was opened, and within a month, roads were made and traversed by wagons, trading posts were established, and a new mining country was opened, which really proved in the main to be rich, and had it not been for the gold-lake fever, it might have remained many months undiscovered and unoccupied. . . .

From the mouth of Nelson's Creek to its source, men were at work in digging. Sometimes the stream was turned from its bed, and the channel worked; in other places, wing dams were thrown out, and the bed partially worked; while in some, the banks only were dug. Some of these, as is the case everywhere in the mines, paid well, some, fair wages, while many were failures. One evening, while waiting for my second supply of goods, I strolled by a deserted camp. I was attracted to the ruins of a shanty, by observing the effigy of a man standing upright in an old torn shirt, a pair of ragged pantaloons, and boots which looked as if they had been clambering over rocks since they were made—in short, the image represented a lean, meager, worn-out, and woe-begone miner, such as might daily be seen at almost every point in the upper mines. On the shirt was inscribed, in a good business hand, "My claim failed—will you pay the taxes?" (an allusion to the tax on foreigners.) Appended to the figure was a paper, bearing the following words: "Californians—Oh, Californians, look at me! Once fat and saucy as a privateersman, but now—look ye—a miserable skeleton. In a word, I am a used up man. . . ."

Ludicrous as it may appear, it was a truthful commentary on the efforts of hundreds of poor fellows in the "golden land." This company had penetrated the mountain snows with infinite labor, in the early part of the season, enduring hardships of no ordinary character—had patiently toiled for weeks, living on the coarsest fare; had spent time and money in building a dam and digging a race through the rocks to drain off the water; endured wet and cold, in the chilling atmosphere of the country, and when the last stone was turned, at the very close of all this labor, they did not find a single cent to reward them for their toil and privations, and what was still more aggravating, a small wing dam, on the very claim below them, yielded several thousand dollars. Having paid out their money, and lost their labor, they were compelled to abandon the claim, and search other diggings, where the result might be precisely the same. . . .

The population of Independence represented almost every State in the Union, while France, England, Ireland, Germany, and even Bohemia had their delegates.

As soon as breakfast was dispatched, all hands were engaged in digging and washing gold in the banks, or in the bed of the stream. When evening came, large fires were built, around which the miners congregated, some engrossed with thoughts of home and friends, some to talk of new discoveries, and richer diggings somewhere else; or, sometimes a subject of debate was started, and the evening was whiled away in pleasant, and often instructive, discussion, while many, for whom this kind of recreation had not excitement enough, resorted to dealing monte [gambling game played with a 40-card deck], on a small scale, thus either exciting or keeping up a passion for play. Some weeks were passed in this way under the clear blue sky of the mountains, and many had made respectable piles. I highly enjoyed the wild scenery, and quite as well, the wild life we were leading, for there were many accomplished and intelligent men; and a subject for amusement or debate was rarely wanting. As for ceremony of dress, it gave us no trouble: we were all alike.... At length a monte dealer arrived, with a respectable bank.

A change had been gradually coming over many of our people, and for three or four days several industrious men had commenced drinking, and after the monte bank was set up, it seemed as if the long smothered fire burst forth into flame. Labor, with few exceptions, seemed suspended, and a great many miners spent their time in riot and debauchery.... The monte dealer, who, in his way was a gentleman, and honorable according to the notions of that class of men, won in two nights three thousand dollars! When he had collected his taxes on our bar, he went to Onion Valley, six miles distant, and lost in one night four thousand, exemplifying the fact, that a gambler may be rich today and a beggar tomorrow....

10

✳

A House Divided

When the Mexican War ended in 1848, the United States was comprised of fifteen free and fifteen slave states. Debates over the territories recently won from Mexico soon jeopardized this equilibrium. The question of whether and how slavery would spread to the West consumed American political life throughout the 1850s. As a series of proposed solutions of the slave expansion issue failed, sectional tensions exploded.

Profoundly different views of slavery permeated these disputes. Where Southerners claimed slavery was humane and essential to white economic prosperity, Northerners embraced free-soil ideology—the belief that slavery threatened the economic independence of free white men and therefore could not be permitted to expand into the western territories. Although many free-soil advocates explicitly rejected abolitionism and accepted Southern slavery, an increasing number of Southerners became convinced that secession (withdrawal from the United States) was the only way to protect their way of life.

The conflicts over slavery destroyed the second party system pitting Whigs against Democrats. As regional differences on slavery and states' rights killed the Whig Party, new parties emerged. Fusing free-soil beliefs, anti-Catholicism, and opposition to immigrants, the American or Know-Nothing Party quickly rose—and then collapsed. These events greatly benefited the Republican Party, a new sectional party advocating free-soil doctrine, protective tariffs, and federally supported internal improvements—positions opposed by most Southerners. When the Democrats proved unable to reconcile their Southern and Northern members, Southerners feared that Republican rule would bring them abolition, race war, and financial ruin. When Republican Abraham Lincoln won the 1860 presidential election with virtually no Southern support, the nation's shattered political system could not avert secession.

THEMES TO CONSIDER

- Proposed solutions for the debate on the westward expansion of slavery
- Intensification of sectional tensions
- Differing opinions on the morality of slavery and racial equality
- The collapse of the Second Party System and the appearance of new sectional parties
- Political debates on immigration and Catholicism
- The eruption of violence in disputes between proslavery and antislavery forces
- The failure of political and legal means to resolve the issues of slavery and westward expansion of slavery
- Rebuttals to proslavery arguments

10.1

John C. Calhoun, Proposal to Preserve the Union (1850)

Following the U.S. victory in the Mexican War, contentious disputes arose on the fate of slavery in the Mexican cession, the territories acquired from Mexico. Proposed solutions included a free-soil doctrine of no slavery, an extension of the Missouri Compromise line, or popular sovereignty—allowing the residents of a territory to choose whether or not to permit slavery.

Events in the West gave these debates added urgency. Utah and California, both acquired in the Mexican cession, requested admission to the Union as free states. Texas, a slave state since 1845, claimed the eastern portion of New Mexico.

SOURCE: John C. Calhoun's speech to the United States Senate against the Compromise of 1850, 4 March 1850, Library of Congress, Manuscript Division, John C. Calhoun Papers.

Other complicated issues got entangled in these territorial questions. Increasingly embarrassed by the presence of slavery in the nation's capital, Northerners called for abolition in the District of Columbia. At the same time, Southerners, displeased with the poorly enforced Fugitive Slave Act of 1793, sought stronger measures to retrieve runaway slaves.

In an attempt to resolve these problems simultaneously, Senator Henry Clay, renowned as "The Great Compromiser," proposed an "omnibus" bill with several major components. Clay's legislation called for the admission of California as free state; the organization of New Mexico and Utah with the slavery question to be resolved by popular sovereignty; an end of the slave trade, but not slavery itself, in the District of Columbia; and a more rigorous national fugitive slave law.

The subsequent congressional debates featured the last major speeches by Clay, Daniel Webster, and John C. Calhoun, all icons in nineteenth-century American politics. Just a month before his death, Calhoun offered this impassioned defense of the South—which a colleague read while the ailing Calhoun listened. In September 1850, Stephen A. Douglas (D-IL) split Clay's bill into separate parts and gained passage for each measure.

FOCUS QUESTIONS

1. Why does Calhoun believe that the Union is in danger?
2. What does Calhoun say about the North? Do you think his views were justified? Explain your answer.
3. How does Calhoun think the Union can be preserved?
4. Would Calhoun's proposal have prevented secession? Explain your answer.

I have, Senators, believed from the first that the agitation of the subject of slavery would, if not prevented by some timely and effective measure, end in disunion. . . . The agitation has been permitted to proceed, with almost no attempt to resist it, until it has reached a period when it can no longer be disguised or denied that the Union is in danger. You have thus had forced upon you the greatest and the gravest question that can ever come under your consideration: How can the Union be preserved?

. . . The first question, then, presented for consideration, in the investigation I propose to make, in order to obtain such knowledge, is: What is it that has endangered the Union?

To this question there can be but one answer: That the immediate cause is the almost universal discontent which pervades all the States composing the southern section of the Union. . . .

It is a great mistake to suppose, as is by some, that it originated with demagogues. . . . No; some cause, far deeper and more powerful than the one supposed must exist to account for discontent so wide and deep. The question, then, recurs: What is the cause of this discontent? It will be found in the belief of the people of the southern States, as prevalent as the discontent itself, that they cannot remain, as things now are, consistently with honor and safety, in the Union. The next question to be considered is: What has caused this belief?

One of the causes is, undoubtedly, to be traced to the long-continued agitation of the slave question on the part of the North, and the many aggressions which they have made on the rights of the South during the time. . . .

There is another, lying back of it, with which this is intimately connected, that may be regarded as the great and primary cause. That is to be found in the fact that the equilibrium between the two sections in the Government, as it stood when the Constitution was ratified and the Government put in action has been destroyed. At that time there was nearly a perfect equilibrium between the two, which afforded ample means to each to protect itself against the aggression of the other; but, as it now stands, one section has the exclusive power of controlling the Government, which leaves the other without any adequate means of protecting itself against its encroachment and oppression. . . .

[The] great increase of Senators, added to the great increase of the House of Representatives and the electoral college on the part of the North, which must take place under the next decade, will effectually and irretrievably destroy the equilibrium which existed when the Government commenced. . . .

What was once a constitutional federal republic is now converted, in reality, into one as absolute as that of the Autocrat of Russia, and as despotic in its tendency as any absolute Government that ever existed.

As, then, the North has the absolute control over the Government, it is manifest that on all questions between it and the South, where there is a diversity of interests, the interests of the latter will be sacrificed to the former, however oppressive the effects may be. . . . But if there was no question of vital importance to the South, in reference to which there was a diversity of views between the two sections, this state of things might be endured without the hazard of destruction to the South. But such is not the fact. . . .

I refer to the relation between the two races in the southern section, which constitutes a vital portion of her social organization. Every portion of the North entertains views and feelings more or less hostile to it. . . .

If the agitation goes on, the same force, acting with increased intensity, as has been shown, will finally snap every cord, when nothing will be left to bind the States together except force. . . .

How can the Union be saved? To this I answer, there is but one way by which it can be, and that is by adopting such measures as will satisfy the States belonging to the southern section that they can remain in the Union consistently with their honor and their safety.

10.2

William H. Seward, "Higher Law" Speech (1850)

Throughout early 1850, the Senate vigorously debated Henry Clay's "omnibus" bill. While Clay, Daniel Webster, and John C. Calhoun offered compromises to resolve the divisive question of slave expansion in the Mexican cession, William H. Seward (1801–1872) was much less conciliatory. An antislavery activist in the Whig Party, Seward enraged Southerners with the speech featured here.

When the Whigs collapsed in the mid-1850s, Seward became a leader in the newly formed Republican Party. Although he never received the party's presidential nomination, he served as secretary of state under Abraham Lincoln and Andrew Johnson. He is perhaps best known for negotiating the U.S. purchase of Alaska from Russia in 1867.

FOCUS QUESTIONS

1. What is Seward's view of the concept of slave and free states?
2. What is Seward's opinion of slavery? On what does he base his assertions? Explain your answers.
3. Why is Seward so opposed to Henry Clay's omnibus bill?
4. Compare William Seward's remarks to those of John C. Calhoun (Document 10.1). How do their speeches reflect growing sectional disputes in American politics?

... The proposition of an established classification of states as *slave states* and *free states*, as insisted on by some, and into *northern* and *southern*, as maintained by others, seems to me purely imaginary, and of course the supposed equilibrium of those classes a mere conceit. This must be so, because, when the Constitution was adopted, twelve of the thirteen states were slave states, and so there was no equilibrium. And so as to the classification of states as northern states and southern states. It is the maintenance of slavery by law in a state, not parallels of

SOURCE: George E. Baker, ed., *The Works of William H. Seward* (New York: Redfield, 1853), vol. I, pp. 70–93.

latitude, that makes it a southern state; and the absence of this, that makes it a northern state. And so all the states, save one, were southern states, and there was no equilibrium. But the Constitution was made not only for southern and northern states, but for states neither northern nor southern, namely, the western states, their coming in being foreseen and provided for. . . .

There is another aspect of the principle of compromise which deserves consideration. It assumes that slavery, if not the only institution in a slave state, is at least a ruling institution, and that this characteristic is recognized by the Constitution. But *slavery* is only *one* of many institutions there. Freedom is equally an institution there. Slavery is only a temporary, accidental, partial, and incongruous one. Freedom on the contrary, is a perpetual, organic, universal one, in harmony with the Constitution of the United States. The slaveholder himself stands under the protection of the latter, in common with all the free citizens of the state. But it is, moreover, an indispensable institution. You may separate slavery from South Carolina, and the state will still remain; but if you subvert freedom there, the state will cease to exist. But the principle of this compromise gives complete ascendancy in the slave states, and in the Constitution of the United States, to the subordinate, accidental, and incongruous institution, over its paramount antagonist. To reduce this claim of slavery to an absurdity, it is only necessary to add that there are only two states in which slaves are a majority, and not one in which the slaveholders are not a very disproportionate minority.

But there is yet another aspect in which this principle must be examined. It regards the domain only as a possession, to be enjoyed either in common or by partition by the citizens of the old states. It is true, indeed, that the national domain is ours. It is true it was acquired by the valor and with the wealth of the whole nation. But we hold, nevertheless, no arbitrary power over it. We hold no arbitrary authority over anything, whether acquired lawfully or seized by usurpation. The Congress regulates our stewardship; the Constitution devotes the domain to union, to justice, to defense, to welfare, and to liberty.

But there is a higher law than the Constitution, which regulates our authority over the domain, and devotes it to the same noble purposes. The territory is a part, no inconsiderable part, of the common heritage of mankind, bestowed upon them by the Creator of the universe. We are his stewards, and must so discharge our trust as to secure in the highest attainable degree their happiness. How momentous that trust is. . . .

And now the simple, bold, and even awful question which presents itself to us is this: Shall we, who are founding institutions, social and political, for countless millions; shall we, who know by experience the wise and the just, and are free to choose them, and to reject the erroneous and the unjust; shall we establish human bondage, or permit it by our sufferance to be established? Sir, our forefathers would not have hesitated an hour. They found slavery existing here, and they left it only because they could not remove it. There is not only no free state which would now establish it, but there is no slave state, which, if it had had the free alternative as we now have, would have founded slavery. Indeed, our revolutionary predecessors had precisely the same question before them in establishing an organic law under which the states of Ohio, Indiana, Michigan,

Illinois, and Wisconsin, have since come into the Union, and they solemnly repudiated and excluded slavery from those states forever. I confess that the most alarming evidence of our degeneracy which has yet been given is found in the fact that we even debate such a question.

Sir, there is no Christian nation, thus free to choose as we are, which would establish slavery. I speak on due consideration because Britain, France, and Mexico, have abolished slavery, and all other European states are preparing to abolish it as speedily as they can. We cannot establish slavery, because there are certain elements of the security, welfare, and greatness of nations, which we all admit, or ought to admit, and recognize as essential; and these are the security of natural rights, the diffusion of knowledge, and the freedom of industry. Slavery is incompatible with all of these; and, just in proportion to the extent that it prevails and controls in any republican state, just to that extent it subverts the principle of democracy, and converts the state into an aristocracy or a despotism. . . .

I cannot stop to debate long with those who maintain that slavery itself is practically economical and humane. I might be content with saying that there are some axioms in political science that a statesman or a founder of states may adopt, especially in the Congress of the United States, and that among those axioms are these: That all men are created equal, and have inalienable rights of life, liberty, and the choice of pursuits of happiness; that knowledge promotes virtue, and right-eousness exalteth a nation; that freedom is preferable to slavery, and that democratic governments, where they can be maintained by acquiescence, without force, are preferable to institutions exercising arbitrary and irresponsible power.

It remains only to remark that our own experience has proved the dangerous influence and tendency of slavery. All our apprehensions of dangers, present and future, begin and end with slavery. If slavery, limited as it yet is, now threatens to subvert the Constitution, how can we as wise and prudent statesmen, enlarge its boundaries and increase its influence, and thus increase already impending dangers? Whether, then, I regard merely the welfare of the future inhabitants of the new territories, or the security and welfare of the whole people of the United States, or the welfare of the whole family of mankind, I cannot consent to introduce slavery into any part of this continent which is now exempt from what seems to me so great an evil. These are my reasons for declining to compromise the question relating to slavery as a condition of the admission of California. . . .

Let, then, those who distrust the Union make compromises to save it. I shall not impeach their wisdom, as I certainly cannot their patriotism; but, indulging no such apprehensions myself, I shall vote for the admission of California directly, without conditions, without qualifications, and without compromise.

For the vindication of that vote, I look not to the verdict of the passing hour, disturbed as the public mind now is by conflicting interests and passions, but to that period, happily not far distant, when the vast regions over which we are now legislating shall have received their destined inhabitants.

While looking forward to that day, its countless generations seem to me to be rising up and passing in dim and shadowy review before us; and a voice comes forth from their serried ranks, saying: "Waste your treasures and your armies, if you will; raze your fortifications to the ground; sink your navies into the sea;

transmit to us even a dishonored name, if you must; but the soil you hold in trust for us—give it to us free. You found it free, and conquered it to extend a better and surer freedom over it. Whatever choice you have made for yourselves, let us have no partial freedom; let us all be free; let the reversion of your broad domain descend to us unencumbered, and free from the calamities and from the sorrows of human bondage."

10.3

Harriet Beecher Stowe, *Uncle Tom's Cabin* (1852)

After months of discussions on his "omnibus" bill left Henry Clay exhausted, Stephen A. Douglas, a Democrat from Illinois, began shepherding the stalled legislation. Cognizant that different constituencies supported its various elements, Douglas broke the bill into separate measures. By September 1850, the Senate had passed each part, and the Compromise of 1850 was in place.

One component, the Fugitive Slave Act, proved enormously controversial. Denying accused runaways the right of trial by jury, the law made fugitives subject to commissioners given financial incentives to rule against them. The act put all blacks, whether runaway slaves or not, at risk of enslavement. It also required Northerners not to interfere with the detention of accused fugitives. The measure generated a furor in the North. In many places, people helped endangered blacks escape to Canada and/or thwarted enforcement of the law.

Harriet Beecher Stowe (1811–1896) was among the thousands of Northerners outraged by the Fugitive Slave Act. The daughter of noted Congregationalist minister Lyman Beecher, Stowe came from one of the most accomplished families in nineteenth-century America. While living in Cincinnati for eighteen years, she observed slave auctions across the Ohio River in Kentucky. In 1852, she penned Uncle Tom's Cabin; or Life Among the Lowly *to denounce slavery. Within a year, the book sold 1.2 million copies and was dramatized in theaters across the country. While Southerners vilified* Uncle Tom's Cabin, *it persuaded millions to contemplate life under slavery.*

SOURCE: Harriet Beecher Stowe, *Uncle Tom's Cabin* (Boston: J.P. Jewett and Co., 1852), pp. 419–423.

FOCUS QUESTIONS

1. How does *Uncle Tom's Cabin* portray slavery?
2. How does Stowe's portrait of Tom contradict the era's racial stereotypes?
3. Why do you think Southerners objected to Stowe's novel?

"And now," said Legree, "come here, you Tom. You see I telled ye I didn't buy ye jest for the common work; I mean to promote ye and make a driver of ye; and tonight ye may jest as well begin to get yer hand in. Now, ye jest take this yer gal and flog her; ye've seen enough on't to know how."

"I beg Mas'r's pardon," said Tom, "hopes Mas'r won't set me at that. It's what I an't used to—never did—and can't do, no way possible."

"Ye'll larn a pretty smart chance of things ye never did know before i've done with ye!" said Legree, taking up a cowhides and striking Tom a heavy blow across the cheek, and following up the infliction by a shower of blows.

"There!" he said, as he stopped to rest, "now will ye tell me ye can't do it?"

"Yes, Mas'r," said Tom, putting up his hand to wipe the blood that trickled down his face. "I'm willin' to work night and day, and work while there's life and breath in me, but this yer thing I can't feel it right to do; and, Mas'r, I *never* shall do it—*never!*"

Tom had a remarkably smooth, soft voice, and a habitually respectful manner that had given Legree an idea that he would be cowardly and easily subdued. When he spoke these last words, a thrill of amazement went through everyone; the poor woman clasped her hands and said, "O Lord!" And everyone involuntarily looked at each other and drew in their breath, as if to prepare for the storm that was about to burst.

Legree looked stupefied and confounded; but at last burst forth—

"What! Ye blasted black beast! Tell *me* you don't think it *right* to do what I tell! What have any of you cussed cattle to do with thinking what's right? I'll put a stop to it! Why, what do you think ye are? May be ye think ye're a gentleman, master Tom, to be a telling your master what's right and what an't! So you pretend it's wrong to flog the gal!"

"I think so, Mas'r," said Tom, "the poor critur's sick and feeble; 't would be downright cruel and it's what I never will do, not begin to. Mas'r, if you mean to kill me, kill me; but as to my raising my hand agin anyone here, I never shall—I'll die first!"

Tom spoke in a mild voice but with a decision that could not be mistaken. Legree shook with anger; his greenish eyes glared fiercely and his very whiskers seemed to curl with passion; but, like some ferocious beast that plays with its victim before he devours it, he kept back his strong impulse to proceed to immediate violence and broke out into bitter raillery.

"Well, here's a pious dog, at last, let down among us sinners!—a saint, a gentleman, and no less, to talk to us sinners about our sins! Powerful, holy critur, he must be! Here, you rascal, you make believe to be so pious—didn't you never hear out of yer Bible, 'Servants, obey yer masters'? An't I yer master? Didn't I pay down $1,200 cash for all there is inside yer old cussed black shell? An't yer mine, now, body and soul?" he said, giving Tom a violent kick with his heavy boot. "Tell me!"

In the very depth of physical suffering, bowed by brutal oppression, this question shot a gleam of joy and triumph through Tom's soul. He suddenly stretched himself up, and, looking earnestly to heaven, while the tears and blood that flowed down his face mingled, he exclaimed—

"No! No! No! My soul ain't yours, Mas'r! You haven't bought it—ye can't buy it! It's been bought and paid for by one that is able to keep it—no matter, no matter, you can't harm me!"

"I can't!" Said Legree, with a sneer, "we'll see—we'll see! Here, Sambo, Quimbo, give this dog such a breakin' in as he won't get over this month!"

The two gigantic Negroes that now laid hold of Tom, with fiendish exultation in their faces, might have formed no unapt personification of the powers of darkness. The poor woman screamed with apprehension and all arose as by a general impulse while they dragged him unresisting from the place....

10.4

The Know-Nothing Party Platform

Between 1840 and 1860, 4.2 million European immigrants arrived in the United States. Three-quarters of the emigrants were Irish or German, and many were also Catholic. Their arrival sparked a wave of nativism (anti-immigrant sentiment) and anti-Catholicism throughout the country. Many Protestant Americans believed that the immigrants posed a threat to their economic security and religious beliefs. In 1849, a secret nativist group called the Order of the Star-Spangled Banner formed in New York City and soon spread throughout New England. When members were asked about its activities, they replied, "I know nothing." As the organization grew more powerful and less clandestine, it evolved into the American Party, also known as the Know-Nothing Party. The party endorsed limits on immigration, restriction of voting and political offices to native-

SOURCE: Published at http://scriptorium.lib.duke.edu/americavotes/know-nothing-letter.jpeg Copyright held by The Digital Scriptorium, Rare Book, Manuscript, and Special Collections Library, Duke University, http://scriptorium.lib.duke.edu/.

*born Americans, and a twenty-one-year residency requirement for naturalized
citizenship. By 1855, Know-Nothings had gained scores of adherents and
controlled several political offices but broke apart the following year.*

FOCUS QUESTIONS

1. What are the major goals of the Know-Nothing Party? Why would someone find these demands attractive?

2. What does the rapid rise and fall of the Know-Nothings suggest about politics in the 1850s?

3. If the Know-Nothings existed today, do you think that they would have many supporters? Explain your answer.

THE KNOW-NOTHING PARTY PLATFORM

1. Repeal of all Naturalization laws.

2. None but native Americans for office.

3. A pure American Common School system.

4. War to the hilt, on political Romanism.

5. Opposition to the formation of Military Companies, comprised of Foreigners.

6. The advocacy of a sound, healthy and safe Nationality.

7. Hostility to all Papal influences, when brought to bear against the Republic.

8. American Institutions and American Sentiments.

9. More stringent and effective Emigration Laws.

10. The amplest protection to Protestant Interests.

11. The doctrines of the revered Washington....

12. Formation of societies to protect American Interests.

13. Eternal enmity to all who attempt to carry out the principles of a foreign Church or State.

14. Our Country, our whole country, and nothing but our Country....

10.5

Charles Sumner on
"Bleeding Kansas" (1856)

The passage of the Kansas-Nebraska Act in May 1854 dealt another blow to an already faltering political system. Despite the racism and disdain for abolitionists shared by most of its new inhabitants, Kansas became ground zero in the battle between proslavery and antislavery forces. In 1855, massive electoral fraud gave slavery advocates control of the territorial government. A series of violent incidents soon plunged Kansas into a small civil war.

Charles Sumner, a Republican senator from Massachusetts and a zealous opponent of slavery, delivered the blistering "Crime against Kansas" speech excerpted here. Sumner's attack on Senator Pierce Butler enraged Congressman Preston Brooks, Butler's nephew. Two days later, Brooks strolled into the nearly empty Senate chamber and thrashed Sumner with a cane. It took Sumner three years to recover. While the "Crime against Kansas" sold a million copies in the North, Brooks received dozens of canes from admiring Southerners. Although Southern representatives blocked an attempt to expel Brooks from the House, Congress did adopt new rules barring firearms and knives from its chambers.

FOCUS QUESTIONS

1. How does Sumner criticize the South and slavery? Why does he target Senator Pierce Butler?

2. Why do you think Sumner's remarks infuriated Preston Brooks and other Southerners?

3. What does the Sumner-Brooks episode suggest about relations between the North and South in the 1850s?

Before entering upon the argument, I must say something of a general character, particularly in response to what has fallen from senators who have raised themselves to eminence on this floor in the championship of human wrong; I mean

SOURCE: "Speech on Kansas," *Memoirs and Letters of Charles Sumner*, ed. Edward L. Pierce (London, 1893), 3: 446–452.

the senator from South Carolina [Mr. Butler] and the senator from Illinois [Mr. Douglas], who though unlike as Don Quixote and Sancho Panza, yet, like this couple, sally forth together in the same adventure, I regret much to miss the elder senator from his seat; but the cause against which he has run a tilt, with such ebullition of animosity, demands that the opportunity of exposing him should not be lost; and it is for the cause that I speak. The senator from South Carolina has read many books of chivalry and believed himself a chivalrous knight, with sentiments of honor and courage. Of course he has chosen a mistress to whom he has made his vows and who, though ugly to others, is always lovely to him; though polluted in the sight of the world, is chaste in his sight. I mean the harlot Slavery. To her his tongue is always profuse in words. Let her be impeached in character, or any proposition to be made from the extension of her wantonness, and no extravagance of manner or hardihood of assertion is then too great for this senator. The frenzy of Don Quixote in behalf of his wench ... is all surpassed. The asserted rights of slavery which shock equality of all kinds, are cloaked by a fantastic claim of equality. If the slave States cannot enjoy what, in mockery of the great fathers of the republic, he misnames equality under the Constitution,— in other words the full power in the national territories to compel fellow-men to unpaid toil, separate husband and wife, and to sell little children at the auction-block, then, sir, the chivalric senator will conduct the State of South Carolina out of the Union! Heroic knight! Exalted senator! A second Moses come for the second exodus!

Not content with this poor menace, ... the senator, in the unrestrained chivalry of his nature, has undertaken to apply opprobrious words to those who differ from him. . . . He calls them "sectional and fanatical;" and resistance to the usurpation of Kansas he denounces as "an uncalculating fanaticism." To be sure, these charges lack all grace of originality and all sentiment of truth; but the adventurous senator does not hesitate. He is the uncompromising, unblushing representative on this floor of a flagrant sectionalism now domineering over the republic; and yet with a ludicrous ignorance of his own position, unable to see himself as others see him, or with an effrontery which even his white head ought not to protect from rebuke, he applies to those here who resist her sectionalism the very epithet which designates himself. The men who strive to bring back the government to its original policy when freedom and not slavery was national, while slavery and not freedom was sectional, he arraigns as sectional. This will not do; it involves too great a perversion of terms. I tell that senator that it is to himself, and to the "organization" of which he is the "committed advocate," that this epithet belongs. I now fasten it upon them. For myself, ... I affirm that the Republican party of the Union is in no just sense sectional, but, more than any other party, national; and that it now goes forth to dislodge from the high places that tyrannical sectionalism of which the senator from South Carolina is one of the maddest zealots.

. . . The senator from South Carolina [Mr. Butler], who, omnipresent in this debate, overflows with rage at the simple suggestion that Kansas has applied for admission as a State, and with incoherent phrase discharges the loose expectoration of his speech, now upon her representative, and then upon her people. . . .

The senator touches nothing which he does not disfigure with error,—sometimes of principle, sometimes of fact. He shows an incapacity of accuracy, whether in stating the Constitution or in stating the law, whether in details of statistics or diversions of scholarship. He cannot open his mouth but out here flies another blunder. . . .

But it is against the people of Kansas that the sensibilities of the senator are particularly aroused. Coming, as he announces, "from a State,"—ay, sir, from South Carolina,—he turns his lordly disgust from this newly formed community, which he will not recognize even as "a member of the body politic." Pray, sir, by what title does he indulge in this egotism? Has he read the history of the "State" which he represents? . . . He cannot forget its wretched persistence in the slave trade, as the very apple of its eye, and the condition of its participation in the Union. He cannot forget its constitution, which is republican only in name, confirming power in the hands of the few, . . . Were the whole history of South Carolina blotted out of existence, . . . civilization might lose—I do not say how little, but surely less than it has already gained by the example of Kansas in that valiant struggle against oppression. . . .

The contest which, beginning in Kansas, reaches us, will be transferred soon from Congress to that broader stage, where every citizen is not only spectator but actor; and to their judgment I confidently turn. To the people about to exercise the electoral franchise in choosing a chief magistrate of the republic, I appeal to vindicate the electoral franchise in Kansas. Let the ballot-box of the Union with multidinous might protect the ballot-box in that Territory. Let the voters everywhere, while rejoicing in their own rights, help guard the equal rights of distant fellow-citizens, that the shrines of popular institutions now desecrated may be sanctified anew; . . . . In just regard for free labor, . . . in Christian sympathy with the slave, . . . in rescue of fellow citizens now subjugated to tyrannical usurpations; in dutiful respect for the early fathers, . . . in the name of the Constitution outraged, of the laws trampled down, of justice banished, of humanity degraded, of peace destroyed, of freedom crushed to earth, and in the name of the Heavenly Father, whose service is perfect freedom,—I make this last appeal.

10.6

Dred Scott v. Sandford (1857)

In 1857, two days following James Buchanan's presidential inauguration, the Supreme Court handed down its ruling in Dred Scott v. Sandford. *The ineffectual Buchanan hoped that the decision would finally resolve the contentious slave expansion question. Instead, the case further inflamed sectional tensions.*

Dred Scott was a Missouri slave whose master took him to Illinois and the Wisconsin Territory, both of which were closed to slavery. After his master's death, friends persuaded Scott to sue for his freedom on the grounds that he resided on free soil. Ten years later, the case reached the Supreme Court. Chief Justice Roger B. Taney, appointed by Andrew Jackson in 1835, wrote the majority opinion. The Dred Scott ruling incensed Northerners and discredited the Supreme Court for decades.

FOCUS QUESTIONS

1. What does Taney identify as the central question of the Scott case?
2. How does Taney define U.S. citizenship? Why does his definition exclude slaves?
3. Why does Taney attack the Missouri Compromise?
4. Did Dred Scott win his freedom? Explain your answer.
5. Why did the *Dred Scott* decision fail to resolve the question of slave expansion?

The Question is simply this: Can a negro, whose ancestors were imported into this country, and sold as slaves, become a member of the political community formed and brought into existence by the Constitution of the United States, and as such become entitled to all the rights, and privileges, and immunities, guarantied [sic] by that instrument to the citizen? One of which rights is the privilege of suing in a court of the United States in the cases specified in the Constitution.

. . . The only matter in issue before the Court, therefore, is, whether the descendants of such slaves, when they shall be emancipated, or who are born of

SOURCE: *Dred Scott v. Sandford*, 19, *Howard*, 403–452 *passim*, in Samuel F. Miller, *Reports and Decisions of the Supreme Court of the United States* (Washington, 1875), II, 6–56.

parents who had become free before their birth, are citizens of a State, in the sense which the word citizen is used in the Constitution. . . .

The words "people of the United States" and "citizens" are synonymous terms. . . . They both describe the political body who, according to our republican institutions, form the sovereignty, and who hold the power and conduct the government through their representatives. . . . The question before us is, whether the class of persons described in the plea in abatement compose a portion of this people, and are constituent members of this sovereignty? We think they are not, under the word "citizens" in the Constitution, and can therefore claim none of the rights and privileges which that instrument provides for and secures to citizens of the United States. On the contrary, they were at that time considered as a subordinate and inferior class of beings, who had been subjugated by the dominant race, and whether emancipated or not, yet remained subject to their authority, and had no rights or privileges but such as those who held the power and the government might choose to grant them. . . .

In discussing the question, we must not confound the rights of citizenship which a State may confer within its own limits, and the rights of citizenship as a member of the Union. It does not by any means follow, because he has all the rights and privileges of a citizen of a State, that he must be a citizen of the United States. . . .

In the opinion of the court, the legislation and histories of the times, and the language used in the Declaration of Independence, show, that neither the class of persons who had been imported as slaves, nor their descendants, whether they had become free or not, were then acknowledged as a part of the people, nor intended to be included in the general words used in that memorable instrument. . . .

They had for more than a century before been regarded as beings of an inferior order, and altogether unfit to associate with the white race, either in social or political relations, and so far inferior, that they had no rights which the white man was bound to respect; and that the negro might justly and lawfully be reduced to slavery for his benefit. . . .

. . . [T]here are two clauses in the constitution which point directly and specifically to the negro race as a separate class of persons, and show clearly that they were not regarded as a portion of the people or citizens of the government then formed.

One of these clauses reserves to each of the thirteen States the right to import slaves until the year 1808, if it thinks it proper. . . . And by the other provision the States pledge themselves to each other to maintain the right of property of the master, by delivering up to him any slave who may have escaped from his service, and be found later within their respective territories. . . . And these two provisions show, conclusively, that neither the description of persons therein referred to, nor their descendants, were embraced in any of the other provisions of the Constitution; for certainly these two clauses were not intended to confer on them or their posterity the blessings of liberty, or any of the personal rights so carefully provided for the citizen. . . .

The only two provisions which point to them and include them, treat them as property, and make it the duty of the government to protect it; no other power, in relation to this race, is to be found in the Constitution; and as it is a government of special, delegated, powers, no authority beyond these two provisions can be constitutionally exercised. The government of the United States had no right to interfere for any other purpose but that of protecting the rights of the owner, leaving it altogether with the several States to deal with this race, whether emancipated or not, as each State may think justice, humanity, and the interests and safety of society, require. . . .

. . . [U]pon a full and careful consideration of the subject, the court is of opinion, that, upon the facts stated . . . , Dred Scott was not a citizen of Missouri within the meaning of the Constitution of the United States, and not entitled as such to sue in its courts. . . .

. . . [T]he plaintiff . . . admits that he and his wife were born slaves, but endeavors to make out his title to freedom and citizenship by showing that they were taken by their owner to certain places . . . where slavery could not by law exist, and that they thereby became free, and upon their return to Missouri became citizens of that State. . . .

The act of Congress, upon which the plaintiff relies, declares that slavery and involuntary servitude . . . shall be forever prohibited . . . north of thirty-six degrees thirty minutes north latitude, and not included within the limits of Missouri. And the difficulty which meets us . . . is whether Congress was authorized to pass this law under any of the powers granted to it by the Constitution. . . .

. . . [T]he right to property in a slave is distinctly and expressly affirmed in the constitution. . . . This is done in plain words—too plain to be misunderstood. And no word can be found in the Constitution which gives Congress a greater power over slave property, or which entitles property of that kind to less protection than property of any other description. . . .

. . . [I]t is the opinion of this court, that the act of Congress [The Missouri Compromise] which prohibited a citizen from holding and owning property of this kind in the territory north of the line therein mentioned, is not warranted by the Constitution, and is therefore void; and that neither Dred Scott himself, nor any of his family, were made free by being carried into this territory; even if they had been carried there by the owner. . . .

10.7

Hinton Rowan Helper, *The Impending Crisis* (1857)

In the three decades preceding the Civil War, many white Southerners vigorously defended slavery. Proslavery arguments drew inspiration from many sources, including claims of black genetic inferiority, theology, history, and contemporary criticism of Northern industrial society. Simultaneously, the South instituted laws that prevented public discussion of slavery. Abolitionist publications were seized and destroyed. Critics of slavery were intimidated and forced to leave the region.

Despite this climate, Hinton Rowan Helper (1829–1909), a white Southerner, wrote a devastating critique of Southern society. In The Impending Crisis of the South: How to Meet It *(1857), Helper attacked slavery for debasing nonslaveholding whites and retarding Southern economic progress. Although he advocated abolition, he was also a racist who called for freed slaves to be exported to Africa or Latin America.*

The Impending Crisis *sent shock waves through the nation. While Northerners applauded Helper's exposé, Southerners threatened his life and banned his book. After safety concerns forced Helper to flee the South, President Abraham Lincoln granted him a diplomatic appointment to Buenos Aries, where he served from 1861 to 1866. Upon returning to the U.S., Helper pursued a failed career as a political lobbyist. He committed suicide in 1909. (Some spelling has been modernized.)*

FOCUS QUESTIONS

1. How does Helper characterize the relationship between the North and the South?

2. How does Helper describe Southern society?

3. To what does he attribute the condition of the South? Whom does he seem to hold most responsible?

4. What is Helper's family background? Why do you think he includes this information?

SOURCE: Hinton Rowan Helper, *The Impending Crisis of the South: How to Meet It* (New York: Burdick Brothers, 1857), pp. 21–33, 120–21.

5. What is Helper's solution to problems in the South?

6. Compare Helper's views to those expressed by George Fitzhugh (Document 8.6). Give several examples. What do these differing opinions—and the Southern response to *The Impending Crisis*—demonstrate about the South on the eve of the Civil War?

It is a fact well known to every intelligent Southerner that we are compelled to go to the North for almost every article of utility and adornment, from matches, shoepegs and paintings up to cotton-mills, steamships and statuary; that we have no foreign trade, no princely merchants, nor respectable artists; that, in comparison with the free states, we contribute nothing to the literature, polite arts and inventions of the age; that, for want of profitable employment at home, large numbers of our native population find themselves necessitated to emigrate to the West, whilst the free states retain not only the larger proportion of those born within their own limits, but induce, annually, hundreds of thousands of foreigners to settle and remain amongst them; that almost everything produced at the North meets with ready sale, while, at the same time, there is no demand, even among our own citizens, for the productions of Southern industry; that, owing to the absence of a proper system of business amongst us, the North becomes, in one way or another, the proprietor and dispenser of all our floating wealth, and that we are dependent on Northern capitalists for the means necessary to build our railroads, canals and other public improvements; that if we want to visit a foreign country, even though it may lie directly South of us, we find no convenient way of getting there except by taking passage through a Northern port; and that nearly all the profits arising from the exchange of commodities, from insurance and shipping offices, and from the thousand and one industrial pursuits of the country, accrue to the North, and are there invested in the erection of those magnificent cities and stupendous works of art which dazzle the eyes of the South, and attest the superiority of free institutions! . . .

But it can hardly be necessary to say more in illustration of this unmanly and unnational dependence, which is so glaring that it cannot fail to be apparent to even the most careless and superficial observer. All the world sees, or ought to see, that in a commercial, mechanical, manufactural, financial, and literary point of view, we are as helpless as babes; that, in comparison with the Free States, our agricultural resources have been greatly exaggerated, misunderstood and mismanaged; and that, instead of cultivating among ourselves a wise policy of mutual assistance and co-operation with respect to individuals, and of self-reliance with respect to the South at large, instead of giving countenance and encouragement to the industrial enterprises projected in our midst, and instead of building up, aggrandizing and beautifying our own States, cities and towns, we have been spending our substance at the North, and are daily augmenting and strengthening the very power which now has us so completely under its thumb. . . .

[W]e feel no disposition to mince matters, but mean to speak plainly, and to the point, without any equivocation, mental reservation, or secret evasion whatsoever. The son of a venerated parent, who, while he lived, was a considerate and merciful slaveholder, a native of the South, born and bred in North Carolina . . ., a Southerner by instinct and by all the influences of thought, habits, and kindred, and with the desire and fixed purpose to reside permanently within the limits of the South, and with the expectation of dying there also—we feel that we have the right to express our opinion, however humble or unimportant it may be, on any and every question that affects the public good; and, so help us God . . .

And now to the point. In our opinion, an opinion which has been formed from data obtained by assiduous researches, and comparisons, from laborious investigation, logical reasoning, and earnest reflection, the causes which have impeded the progress and prosperity of the South, which have dwindled our commerce, and other similar pursuits, into the most contemptible insignificance; sunk a large majority of our people in galling poverty and ignorance, rendered a small minority conceited and tyrannical, and driven the rest away from their homes; entailed upon us a humiliating dependence on the Free States; disgraced us in the recesses of our own souls, and brought us under reproach in the eyes of all civilized and enlightened nations—may all be traced to one common source, and there find solution in the most hateful and horrible word, that was ever incorporated into the vocabulary of human economy—*Slavery!*

Reared amidst the institution of slavery, believing it to be wrong both in principle and in practice, and having seen and felt its evil influences upon individuals, communities and states, we deem it a duty, no less than a privilege, to enter our protest against it, and to use our most strenuous efforts to overturn and abolish it! Then we are an abolitionist? Yes! Not merely a freesoiler, but an abolitionist, in the fullest sense of the term. We are not only in favor of keeping slavery out of the territories, but, carrying our opposition to the institution a step further, we here unhesitatingly declare ourself in favor of its immediate and unconditional abolition, in every state in this confederacy, where it now exists! Patriotism makes us a freesoiler; state pride makes us an emancipationist; a profound sense of duty to the South makes us an abolitionist; a reasonable degree of fellow feeling for the negro, makes us a colonizationist. With the free state men in Kansas and Nebraska, we sympathize with all our heart. We love the whole country, the great family of states and territories, one and inseparable. . . .

That we shall encounter opposition we consider as certain; perhaps we may even be subjected to insult and violence. From the conceited and cruel oligarchy of the South, we could look for nothing less. But we shall shrink from no responsibility, and do nothing unbecoming a man; we know how to repel indignity, and if assaulted, shall not fail to make the blow recoil upon the aggressor's head. . . .

But, thanks to heaven, we have no ominous forebodings of the result of the contest now pending between Liberty and Slavery in this confederacy. Though neither a prophet nor the son of a prophet, our vision is sufficiently penetrative to divine the future so far as to be able to see that the "peculiar institution" has but a short, and as heretofore, inglorious existence before it. Time, the righter of every wrong, is ripening events for the desired consummation of our labors and the fulfillment of our cherished hopes. Each revolving year brings nearer the inevitable crisis. The sooner it comes the better; may heaven, through our humble efforts, hasten its advent.

The first and most sacred duty of every Southerner, who has the honor and the interest of his country at heart, is to declare himself an unqualified and uncompromising abolitionist. No conditional or half-way declaration will avail; no mere threatening demonstration will succeed. With those who desire to be instrumental in bringing about the triumph of liberty over slavery, there should be neither evasion, vacillation, nor equivocation. We should listen to no modifying terms or compromises that may be proposed by the proprietors of the unprofitable and ungodly institution. Nothing short of the complete abolition of slavery can save the South from falling into the vortex of utter ruin. Too long have we yielded a submissive obedience to the tyrannical domination of an inflated oligarchy; too long have we tolerated their arrogance and self-conceit; too long have we submitted to their unjust and savage exactions. Let us now wrest from them the scepter of power, establish liberty and equal rights throughout the land, and henceforth and forever guard our legislative halls from the pollutions and usurpations of proslavery demagogues. . . .

It is not so much in its moral and religious aspects that we propose to discuss the question of slavery, as in its social and political character and influences. To say nothing of the sin and the shame of slavery, we believe it is a most expensive and unprofitable institution; and if our brethren of the South will but throw aside their unfounded prejudices and preconceived opinions, and give us a fair and patient hearing, we feel confident, that we can bring them to the same conclusion. Indeed, we believe we shall be enabled—not alone by our own contributions, but with the aid of incontestable facts and arguments which we shall introduce from other sources—to convince all true-hearted, candid and intelligent Southerners, who may chance to read our book, (and we hope their name may be legion) that slavery, and nothing but slavery, has retarded the progress and prosperity of our portion of the Union; depopulated and impoverished our cities by forcing the more industrious and enterprising natives of the soil to emigrate to the free states; brought our domain under a sparse and inert population by preventing foreign immigration; made us tributary to the North, and reduced us to the humiliating condition of mere provincial subjects in fact, though not in name. We believe, moreover, that every patriotic Southerner thus convinced will feel it a duty he owes to himself, to his country, and to his God, to become a thorough, inflexible, practical abolitionist. . . .

The liberation of five millions of "poor white trash" from the second degree of slavery, and of three millions of miserable kidnapped negroes from the first degree, cannot be accomplished too soon. That it was not accomplished many years ago is our misfortune. It now behooves us to take a bold and determined stand in defense of the inalienable rights of ourselves and of our fellow men, and to avenge the multiplicity of wrongs, social and political, which we have suffered at the hands of a villainous oligarchy. It is madness to delay. . . .

Non-slaveholders of the South! Farmers, mechanics and workingmen, we take this occasion to assure you that the slaveholders, the arrogant demagogues whom you have elected to offices of honor and profit, have hoodwinked you, trifled with you, and used you as mere tools for the consummation of their wicked designs. They have purposely kept you in ignorance, and have, by molding your passions and prejudices to suit themselves, induced you to act in direct opposition to your dearest rights and interests. By a system of the grossest subterfuge and misrepresentation, and in order to avert, for a season, the vengeance that will most assuredly overtake them ere long, they have taught you to hate the abolitionists, who are your best and only true friends. Now, as one of your own number, we appeal to you to join us in our patriotic endeavors to rescue the generous soil of the South from the usurped and desolating control of these political vampires. Once and forever, at least so far as this country is concerned, the infernal question of slavery must be disposed of; a speedy and perfect abolishment of the whole institution is the true policy of the South—and this is the policy which we propose to pursue. Will you aid us, will you assist us, will you be freemen, or will you be slaves? . . .

10.8

The Lincoln-Douglas Debates (1858)

In 1858, many Americans closely watched an Illinois campaign for the U.S. Senate. The race pitted Abraham Lincoln, a relatively unknown Republican, against Stephen A. Douglas, a leading Democrat and frontrunner for the presidency. While Lincoln was a firm believer in free soil, he did not oppose slavery in the South or advocate racial equality. The architect of the Kansas-Nebraska Act, Douglas was a leading proponent of popular sovereignty—the belief that the people who lived in a territory should decide whether or not they wanted slavery. To Douglas, popular sovereignty was the best way to ensure continued economic progress for whites. Lincoln, however, opened his campaign with the famous "House Divided" address in which he declared, "I believe this government cannot endure permanently half-slave and half-free."

Lincoln and Douglas aired these opposing views in a series of seven public debates held from August to October 1858. Although Lincoln lost the Senate race, he became a national political figure. This reading includes portions of the first debate held in Ottawa, Illinois, on August 21, 1858.

SOURCE: Lincoln-Douglas First Joint Debate, Ottawa, August 21, 1858, published at Founder's Library, http://www.founding.com/library.

FOCUS QUESTIONS

1. What are Douglas's major points?
2. How does Lincoln respond to Douglas's claims?
3. Would popular sovereignty or free-soil have resolved the slave expansion issue and ended sectional tensions? Explain your answers.

LADIES AND GENTLEMEN: I appear before you today for the purpose of discussing the leading political topics which now agitate the public mind. . . .

Mr. Lincoln . . . says that this Government cannot endure permanently in the same condition in which it was made by its framers—divided into free and slave States. He says that it has existed for about seventy years thus divided, and yet he tells you that it cannot endure permanently on the same principles and in the same relative condition in which our fathers made it. Why can it not exist divided into free and slave States? Washington, Jefferson, Franklin, Madison, Hamilton, Jay, and the great men of that day, made this Government divided into free States and slave States, and left each State perfectly free to do as it pleased on the subject of slavery. Why can it not exist on the same principles on which our fathers made it? They knew when they framed the Constitution that in a country as wide and broad as this, with such a variety of climate, production and interest, the people necessarily required different laws and institutions in different localities. They knew that the laws and regulations which would suit the granite hills of New Hampshire would be unsuited to the rice plantations of South Carolina, and they, therefore, provided that each State should retain its own Legislature and its own sovereignty, with the full and complete power to do as it pleased within its own limits, in all that was local and not national. One of the reserved rights of the States, was the right to regulate the relations between Master and Servant, on the slavery question. At the time the Constitution was framed, there were thirteen States in the Union, twelve of which were slaveholding States and one free State. Suppose this doctrine of uniformity preached by Mr. Lincoln, that the States should all be free or all be slave had prevailed, and what would have been the result? Of course, the twelve slaveholding States would have overruled the one free State, and slavery would have been fastened by a Constitutional provision on every inch of the American Republic, instead of being left as our fathers wisely left it, to each State to decide for itself. Here I assert that uniformity in the local laws and institutions of the different States is neither possible nor desirable. If uniformity had been adopted when the Government was established, it must inevitably have been the uniformity of slavery everywhere, or else the uniformity of negro citizenship and negro equality everywhere.

We are told by Lincoln that he is utterly opposed to the Dred Scott decision, and will not submit to it, for the reason that he says it deprives the negro of the rights and privileges of citizenship. That is the first and main reason which he assigns for his warfare on the Supreme Court of the United Sates and its decision.

I ask you, are you in favor of conferring upon the negro the rights and privileges of citizenship? Do you desire to strike out of our State Constitution that clause which keeps slaves and free negroes out of the State, and allow the free negroes to flow in, and cover your prairies with black settlements? Do you desire to turn this beautiful State into a free negro colony, in order that when Missouri abolishes slavery she can send one hundred thousand emancipated slaves into Illinois, to become citizens and voters, on an equality with yourselves? If you desire negro citizenship, if you desire to allow them to come into the State and settle with the white man, if you desire them to vote on an equality with yourselves, and to make them eligible to office, to serve on juries, and to adjudge your rights, then support Mr. Lincoln and the Black Republican party, who are in favor of the citizenship of the negro.

For one, I am opposed to negro citizenship in any and every form. I believe this Government was made on the white basis. I believe it was made by white men for the benefit of white men and their posterity for ever, and I am in favor of confining citizenship to white men, men of European birth and descent, instead of conferring it upon negroes, Indians, and other inferior races. . . .

I do not hold that because the negro is our inferior that therefore he ought to be a slave. By no means can such a conclusion be drawn from what I have said. On the contrary, I hold that humanity and Christianity both require that the negro shall have and enjoy every right, every privilege, and every immunity consistent with the safety of the society in which he lives. On that point, I presume, there can be no diversity of opinion. You and I are bound to extend to our inferior and dependent beings every right, every privilege, every facility and immunity consistent with the public good. The question then arises, what rights and privileges are consistent with the public good? This is a question which each State and each Territory must decide for itself—Illinois has decided it for herself. We have provided that the negro shall not be a slave, and we have also provided that he shall not be a citizen, but protect him in his civil rights, in his life, his person and his property, only depriving him of all political rights whatsoever, and refusing to put him on an equality with the white man. That policy of Illinois is satisfactory to the Democratic party and to me, and if it were to the Republicans, there would then be no question upon the subject; but the Republicans say that he ought to be made a citizen, and when he becomes a citizen he becomes your equal, with all your rights and privileges. They assert the Dred Scott decision to be monstrous because it denies that the negro is or can be a citizen under the Constitution. Now, I hold that Illinois had a right to abolish and prohibit slavery as she did, and I hold that Kentucky has the same right to continue and protect slavery that Illinois had to abolish it. I hold that New York had as much right to abolish slavery as Virginia has to continue it, and that each and every State of this Union is a sovereign power, with the right to do as it pleases upon this question of slavery, and upon all its domestic institutions. . . .

Now, my friends, if we will only act conscientiously and rigidly upon this great principle of popular sovereignty, which guarantees to each State and Territory the right to do as it pleases on all things, local and domestic, instead of Congress interfering, we will continue at peace one with another. . . . Under that principle, we have grown from a nation of three or four millions to a nation of about thirty millions of people; we have crossed the Allegheny mountains and filled up the whole North-west, turning the prairie into a garden, and building up churches and schools, thus spreading civilization and Christianity where before there was nothing but savage barbarism. Under that principle we have become, from a feeble nation, the most powerful on the face of the earth, and if we only adhere to that principle, we can go forward increasing in territory, in power, in strength and in glory until the Republic of America shall be the North Star that shall guide the friends of freedom throughout the civilized world. And why can we not adhere to the great principle of self-government, upon which our institutions were originally based? I believe that this new doctrine preached by Mr. Lincoln and his party will dissolve the Union if it succeeds. They are trying to array all the Northern States in one body against the South, to excite a sectional war between the free States and the slave States, in order that the one or the other may be driven to the wall....

MR. LINCOLN'S REPLY

MY FELLOW-CITIZENS: When a man hears himself somewhat misrepresented, it provokes him—at least, I find it so with myself; but when misrepresentation becomes very gross and palpable, it is more apt to amuse him....

[T]his is the true complexion of all I have ever said in regard to the institution of slavery and the black race. This is the whole of it, and anything that argues me into his idea of perfect social and political equality with the negro, is but a specious and fantastic arrangement of words, by which a man can prove a horse-chestnut to be a chestnut horse. I will say here, while upon this subject, that I have no purpose, directly or indirectly, to interfere with the institution of slavery in the States where it exists. I believe I have no lawful right to do so, and I have no inclination to do so. I have no purpose to introduce political and social equality between the white and the black races. There is a physical difference between the two, which, in my judgment, will probably forever forbid their living together upon the footing of perfect equality, and inasmuch as it becomes a necessity that there must be a difference, I, as well as Judge Douglas, am in favor of the race to which I belong having the superior position. I have never said anything to the contrary, but I hold that, notwithstanding all this, there is no reason in the world why the negro is not entitled to all the natural rights enumerated in the Declaration of Independence, the right to life, liberty, and the pursuit of happiness. I hold that he is as much entitled to these as the white man. I agree with Judge Douglas he is not my equal in many respects—certainly not in color, perhaps not in moral or intellectual endowment. But in the right to eat the bread, without the leave of anybody else, which his own hand earns, *he is my equal and the equal of Judge Douglas, and the equal of every living man.* ...

When he [Douglas] undertakes to say that because I think this nation, so far as the question of slavery is concerned, will all become one thing or all the other,

I am in favor of bringing about a dead uniformity in the various States, in all their institutions, he argues erroneously. The great variety of the local institutions in the States, springing from differences in the soil, differences in the face of the country, and in the climate, are bonds of Union. They do not make "a house divided against itself," but they make a house united. If they produce in one section of the country what is called for by the wants of another section, and this other section can supply the wants of the first, they are not matters of discord but bonds of union, true bonds of union. But can this question of slavery be considered as among *these* varieties in the institutions of the country? I leave it to you to say whether, in the history of our Government, this institution of slavery has not always failed to be a bond of union, and, on the contrary, been an apple of discord, and an element of division in the house. I ask you to consider whether, so long as the moral constitution of men's minds shall continue to be the same, after this generation and assemblage shall sink into the grave, and another race shall arise, with the same moral and intellectual development we have—whether, if that institution is standing in the same irritating position in which it now is, it will not continue an element of division? If so, then I have a right to say that, in regard to this question, the Union is a house divided against itself; and when the Judge reminds me that I have often said to him that the institution of slavery has existed for eighty years in some States, and yet it does not exist in some others, I agree to the fact, and I account for it by looking at the position in which our fathers originally placed it—restricting it from the new Territories where it had not gone, and legislating to cut off its source by the abrogation of the slave-trade thus putting the seal of legislation *against its spread.* The public mind *did* rest in the belief that it was in the course of ultimate extinction.

But lately, I think—and in this I charge nothing on the Judge's motives— lately, I think, that he, and those acting with him, have placed that institution on a new basis, which looks to the *perpetuity and nationalization of slavery.* And while it is placed upon this new basis, I say, and I have said, that I believe we shall not have peace upon the question until the opponents of slavery arrest the further spread of it, and place it where the public mind shall rest in the belief that it is in the course of ultimate extinction; or, on the other hand, that its advocates will push it forward until it shall become alike lawful in all the States, old as well as new, North as well as South. Now, I believe if we could arrest the spread, and place it where Washington, and Jefferson, and Madison placed it, it *would be* in the course of ultimate extinction, and the public mind *would,* as for eighty years past, believe that it was in the course of ultimate extinction. The crisis would be past and the institution might be let alone for a hundred years, if it should live so long, in the States where it exists, yet it would be going out of existence in the way best for both the black and the white races....

10.9

John Brown and His Critics (1859)

By 1859, while free-soil advocates like Abraham Lincoln pledged not to disturb slavery in the South, most Southerners viewed free-soil as a crusade to destroy slavery everywhere. Their worst fears were realized in October 1859 when John Brown (1800–1859) led a raid on the federal arsenal at Harper's Ferry, Virginia. A religious zealot with a visceral hatred for slavery, Brown had gained notoriety after leading an attack on proslavery men camped at Pottawatomie Creek, Kansas, in May 1856. Brown and his followers dragged five men out of their tents, hacked them to death, and strewed their entrails in the road. Brown then fled to New England where he gained the moral and financial support of Gerrit Smith and other prominent abolitionists. In the Harper's Ferry raid, Brown hoped to incite a slave rebellion. The plan quickly fell apart when U.S. troops stormed the compound and captured or killed Brown's forces. Brown was captured and tried for murder, slave insurrection, and treason. He was found guilty and hanged on December 2, 1859.

Brown's death polarized the nation. In the North, Brown was mourned as a hero. To Southerners, Brown was the embodiment of abolitionist fanaticism. Although noted Republicans, including Lincoln and William Seward, denounced Brown's tactics, Southerners were unmoved. This selection includes Brown's last statement followed by a Georgia newspaper's reaction to his death.

FOCUS QUESTIONS

1. How does John Brown justify his actions?
2. Whom does the Georgia newspaper hold responsible for the Harper's Ferry raid? How does this reaction demonstrate growing support for secession among Southerners?
3. What is your opinion of John Brown?

John Brown:

I have, may it please the Court, a few words to say. In the first place, I deny everything but what I have all along admitted, of a design on my part to free

---

SOURCE: *6 American State Trials 700, 800* (1859).

slaves. I intended certainly to have made a clean thing of that matter, as I did last winter when I went into Missouri, and there took slaves without the snapping of a gun on either side, moving them through the country, and finally leaving them in Canada. I designed to have done the same thing again on a larger scale. That was all I intended to do. I never did intend murder or treason, or the destruction of property, or to excite or incite the slaves to rebellion, or to make insurrection. I have another objection, and that is that it is unjust that I should suffer such a penalty. Had I interfered in the manner, which I admit, and which I admit has been fairly proved—for I admire the truthfulness and candor of the greater portion of the witnesses who have testified in this case—had I so interfered in behalf of any of the rich, the powerful, the intelligent, the so-called great, or in behalf of any of their friends, either father, mother, brother, sister, wife, or children, or any of that class, and suffered and sacrificed what I have in this interference, it would have been all right, and every man in this court would have deemed it an act worthy of reward rather than punishment. This Court acknowledges, too, as I suppose the validity of the law of God. I see a book kissed, which I suppose to be the Bible, or at least the New Testament, which teaches me that all things whatsoever I would that men should do to me, I should do even so to them. It teaches me further to remember them that are in bonds, as bound with them. I endeavored to act up to that instruction. I say I am yet too young to understand that God is any respecter of persons. I believe that to have interfered as I have done, as I have always freely admitted I have done in behalf of His despised poor, is no wrong, but right. Now, if it is deemed necessary that I should forfeit my life for the furtherance of the ends of justice, and mingle my blood further with the blood of my children and with the blood of the millions in this slave country whose rights are disregarded by wicked, cruel, and unjust enactments, I say let it be done.

"The Abolition Insurrection at Harper's Ferry—The Irrepressible Conflict Begun."

Milledgeville, Georgia, *Federal Union* [Democratic]
1 November 1859

In our columns this week will be found further particulars concerning the insurrection at Harper's Ferry. There can no longer be any doubt but what this was a regularly concocted, and premeditated attempt of Abolition Fanatics to overthrow the Government, and emancipate the slaves. The form of a provisional government has been found among the papers of the prisoners, and the officers of the new Government are there named. Without such positive proof, it would be difficult to believe that such fools could be found running at large in the United States. To think that about twenty men should deliberately attempt to overthrow the Government, and commence their operations in a thickly settled portion of the country, surrounded by the chivalry of Virginia and Maryland, shows a

SOURCE: Secession Era Editorials Project, Furman University, published at http://history.furman.edu/~benson/docs/gafujb59b01a.htm.

degree of ignorance and infatuation among these fanatics never before dreamed of. If they have received direct encouragement, and have been promised assistance from any of the leaders of the Black Republican Party, it is to be hoped all these facts will come to the light. We know they have received indirect encouragement from William H. Seward, Joshua Giddings, Horace Greely, and other Republican leaders, who, by their speeches and writings, have encouraged fanatics to such deeds as this.

Perhaps the sudden and dreadful retribution that has overtaken their fanatical followers will cause these arch traitors to pause in their career. Upon their heads rests the direful responsibility of the blood that has been shed at Harper's Ferry. Will not honest and conscientious men at the north now see the necessity of putting down a party whose principles, if carried out, can lead only to civil war, murder, and rapine? The discovery and sudden overthrow of the conspiracy before it could produce much damage, shows that our country is still under the guardianship of Divine Providence. No weapon forged against our Government, whether by enemies without or traitors within has ever prospered, and we believe they never will prosper so long as the great mass of the people shall be worthy of liberty; or capable of self-government.

11

✳

The Civil War

Throughout the 1850s, debate over the expansion of slavery created bitter divisions between the North and South. The conflict fueled rapid growth of the Republican Party. Established in 1855, the Republican Party extolled Northern society and free-labor ideology. They argued that the dynamic capitalism of the North made it possible for men to attain economic self-sufficiency and enjoy social mobility. In contrast, they portrayed the South as hierarchical, static, and backward—the antithesis of the North. Convinced that the West was the key to continuing Northern prosperity and the nation's future success, the Republicans vehemently opposed the expansion of slavery.

These claims incensed Southerners. Pointing to poverty and worker exploitation in the North, they celebrated slave society as the fulfillment of the nation's political legacy. Deeply resentful of the Republicans' characterizations of the South, Southerners believed that slavery gave white people unparalleled freedom and equality. Accordingly, they believed that slavery must expand in order to ensure America's future.

With such opposing philosophies, it is not surprising that the Republicans' quick success dismayed Southerners. Selecting the explorer John C. Frémont as their presidential nominee in 1856, the Republicans campaigned on a free-soil platform and carried two-thirds of Northern states. Although Democrat James Buchanan won the election, the Republicans were quite encouraged and searched for ways to broaden their political appeal. After the Panic of 1857 created a prolonged depression, they crafted an attractive economic program designed to draw voters. As the 1860 elections neared, they rejected William H. Seward, known for his uncompromising views on slavery, in favor of Abraham Lincoln. A moderate, Lincoln opposed the expansion of slavery but not its existence in the South.

At the same time, the Democrats struggled to reconcile their sectional divisions. Failure to agree on a platform during their national convention left the party split into three factions. With the Democrats in utter disarray, Lincoln easily prevailed in the electoral vote but won only 39 percent of the popular vote. Because virtually none of Lincoln's support came from the South, Southerners faced a choice between accepting the hated Republicans or leaving the Union entirely. With slim chances of reaching a political compromise, the nation stood on the brink of civil war.

Lincoln's election provided the final push toward secession. Although he had promised not to disturb Southern slavery, Lincoln supported free-soil—the prohibition of slavery in the western territories. To Southerners who believed that slavery would die out if it could not expand, Lincoln's presidency presented a tremendous threat. Persuaded that Republican rule would bring financial devastation, racial mixing, and political subjugation, seven states of the Lower South left the Union by February 1861. While secessionists tried to convince the Upper South to join the Confederacy, Lincoln attempted to keep the nation together. His efforts failed when fighting erupted at Fort Sumter in April. Enraged by Lincoln's call for 75,000 troops to suppress the insurrection, four states of the Upper South left the Union, and the Civil War began.

Popular hopes for a quick war disappeared as the conflict became a protracted bloodbath. One in five soldiers who fought died. Those on the home front also endured great hardships. At the war's end, the South was in ruins, slavery was outlawed, and a painful reconstruction of the nation lay ahead.

THEMES TO CONSIDER

- The justifications for secession
- Each side's original war aims and the evolution of these goals over the course of the conflict
- The impact of the war on individuals' lives
- The motives for and reception of the Emancipation Proclamation
- The war's effects on women and African Americans
- The attitudes and experiences of Union and Confederate soldiers
- The war's impact on civil liberties
- Life on the Northern and Southern home fronts

11.1

John Smith Preston Advocates Secession (1861)

After decades of bitter debates over slavery and states' rights, the 1860 election of Abraham Lincoln took the nation to the brink of war with stunning speed. By early February 1861, seven slave states had left the Union and established the Confederate States of America. Despite these events, the future of the secessionist movement remained uncertain. The Upper South was more economically dependent on the North and less reliant on slavery than the Deep South. Cognizant of these factors, representatives from the Deep South made appeals for secession before state legislatures, conventions, and public gatherings throughout the Upper South. Their speeches appeared in newspapers and pamphlets across the nation.

With its impressive wealth, manpower, and prestige, no state was more important to the secessionist cause than Virginia. But many Virginians, especially those in the western part of the state, did not want to sever ties to the U.S. government. In February 1861, when the state convened a secession convention in Richmond, Unionists held a majority of the seats.

Undeterred, three secessionist commissioners from the Deep South addressed the delegates. John Smith Preston (1809–1881) was the last to speak. Born in Virginia, Preston attended the University of Virginia and Harvard and became a successful attorney. After marrying into one of the South's wealthiest families, he moved to South Carolina and earned a fortune as a sugar planter. A noted orator, Preston played a critical role in the South Carolina secessionist movement. (Some spelling has been modernized.)

FOCUS QUESTIONS

1. Why does Preston claim that the Deep South has seceded?

2. Does Preston believe that reconciliation between North and South is possible? Explain your answer.

3. How does Preston attempt to persuade Virginia to join the Confederacy?

SOURCE: Address of Hon. John S. Preston, Commissioner from South Carolina to the Convention of Virginia, February 19, 1861. Published at Documenting the American South, http://docsouth.unc.edu/imls/prestonj/prestonj.html.

4. What do you think caused the Civil War? Could the war have been avoided? Explain your answers.

I have the honor to present to you my credentials as Commissioner from the Government of South Carolina to the Convention of the people of Virginia. On these credentials being duly received by you, I am instructed by my Government to lay before you the causes which induced the State of South Carolina to withdraw from the United States, and resume the powers heretofore delegated by her to the Government of the United States of America. . . .

For nearly thirty years, the people of the non-slaveholding States have assailed the institution of African slavery, in every form in which our political connection with them permitted them to approach it. During all that period, large masses of their people, with a persistent fury, maddened by the intoxication of the wildest fanaticism, have associated, with the avowed purpose of effecting the abolition of slavery by the most fearful means which can be suggested to a subject race: arson and murder are the charities of their program. . . .

Additional millions of people, making majorities in all the States, and many of the States by legislative action, have declared that the institution of slavery, as it exists in the Southern States, is an offense to God, and, therefore, they are bound by the most sacred duty of man to exterminate that institution. They have declared and acted upon the declaration, that the existence of slavery in the Southern States is an offense and a danger to the social institutions of the Northern States, and, therefore, they are bound by the instinct of moral right and of self-preservation to exterminate slavery.

[A]fter years of earnest labor and devotion to the purpose, they have succeeded, by large majorities in all the non-slaveholding States, in placing the entire executive power of the Federal Government in the hands of those who are pledged, by their obligations to God, by their obligations to the social institutions of man, by their obligation of self-preservation, to place the institution of slavery in a course of certain and final extinction.

That is, twenty millions of people, holding one of the strongest Governments on earth, are impelled, by a perfect recognition of the most sacred and powerful obligations which fall upon man, to exterminate the vital interests of eight millions of people, bound to them by contiguity of territory and the closest political relations. In other words, the decree inaugurated on the 6th of November [the election of Abraham Lincoln] was the annihilation of the people of the Southern States. . . .

I see before me wise and learned men, who have observed and sounded the ways of human life in all its records, and many who have been chief actors in some of its gravest scenes. I ask, then, if in all their lore of human society, they find a case parallel to this? South Carolina has 300,000 whites and 400,000 slaves; the whites depend on their slaves for their order of civilization and their existence. Twenty millions of people, with a powerfully organized Government, and impelled by the most sacred duties, decree that this slavery must be exterminated. I ask you, Virginians, is right, is justice, is existence, worth a struggle? . . .

I venture to assert, that never, since liberty came into the institutions of man, have a people borne with more patience, or forborne with more fortitude, than have the people of these Southern States in their relations with their confederates [the North]. . . .

But when, at last, this fanaticism and eager haste for rapine, mingling their foul purposes, engendered those fermenting millions who have seized the Constitution and distorted its most sacred form into an instrument of our ruin, why then longer submission seemed to us not only base cowardice, but absolute fatuity [stupidity]. In South Carolina we felt that, to remain one hour under such a domination, we would merit the destruction earned by our own folly and baseness. . . .

Gentlemen of Virginia, the people of these Southern States are no noisy faction, clamoring for place and power; no hungry rabble, answering in blood to every appeal to brutal passion; no shouting mob. . . . They are a grave, calm, prosperous, religious people; the holders of the most majestic civilization; the inheritors, by right, of the fairest estate of liberty; fighting for that liberty; fighting for their fathers' graves; standing athwart their hearth-stones, and before their chamber doors. In this fight, for a time, my little State stood alone; . . . so small, so weak, so few, we began this fight alone against millions; and had millions been piled on millions, under God, in such a fight, we would have triumphed. But, sir, that God cares for Liberty, Truth and Right among His people—and we are no longer alone. Our own children from Florida and Alabama answered to the maternal call; and our great sister Georgia marshaled forth her giant progeny; the voice of Quitman came up out of his grave on the Mississippi; and Louisiana proved herself the offspring of the "Apostle of Liberty;" and, now, young Texas raises her giant form, and takes her place at the head of this majestic column of Confederated Sovereignties. . . .

Leaving out of consideration the fact, that the acquiescence, which originally founded the Union, was enforced by necessity rather than free consent, the truth seems evident, to every mind which dares to speculate advisedly on the manifest principles of that revolution we are now enacting, that they do involve fundamental and irreconcilable diversities, between the systems on which slaveholding and non-slaveholding communities may endure. We believe that these repellent diversities pertain to every attribute which belongs to the two systems, and, consequently, that this revolution—this separation—this disintegration—is no accident; that it is no merely casual result of a temporary cause; that it is no evanescent bubble of popular error or irritation; that it is no dream of philosophy; nor is it the achievement of individual ambition. It has a cause more profound and pervading than all these. It is not only a revolution of actual material necessity, but it is a revolution resulting from the deepest convictions, the ideas, the sentiments, the moral and intellectual necessities, of earnest and intelligent men. . . . No community of origin—no community of language, law or religion, can amalgamate a people whose severance is proclaimed by the rigid requisitions of material necessity. Nature forbids African slavery at the North. Southern civilization cannot exist without African slavery. None but an equal race can labor at the North. None but a subject race will labor at the South. Destroy involuntary labor, and Anglo-Saxon civilization must be remitted to the latitudes whence it sprung. . . .

We believe, as a completely logical and reasonable deduction from these repellent attributes of the Northern and Southern sections of the late Confederacy, there have arisen those constructions of the terms of confederation, which have converted a Government of consent into a Government of force; which have driven seven States to abandon that Government; which have, for sixty days, kept loaded bomb-shells bearing on the women and children of Charleston; which have turned the Federal guns on the Capitol of Virginia. . . .

Where these natural and conventional repulsions exist, the conflict is for life and death. And that conflict is now upon you. Gentlemen of Virginia, you own an empire. You are very strong. You have advanced in all the arts of life, and are very wise and very skillful. . . . But I tell you, there is no force of human power . . . which can reunite the people of the North and the people of the South as political and social equals. No, gentlemen, never; never, until by your power, your art, and your virtue, you can unfix the unchangeable economy of the Eternal God, can you make of the people of the North and the people of the South one people.

An irresistible instinct of self-preservation has forced the cotton States to recognize this absolute and imperative diversity, and they are now proceeding to erect their institutions on its present necessity. The Northern States are also manifesting their recognition of the same diversity, by preparing, with the aid of the agents of non-slavery, known as the army and navy of the United States, to attempt the subjugation of the Southern States. . . .

Believing the rights violated and the interests involved are identical with the rights and interests of the people of Virginia, and remembering their ancient amity and their common glory, the people of South Carolina have instructed me to ask, earnestly and respectfully, that the people of Virginia will join them in the protection of their rights and interests. . . .

11.2

Horace Greeley and Abraham Lincoln on Slavery and the Union (1862)

While trying to balance the various political factions in the North, Abraham Lincoln endured intense criticism. Slavery was one of the most contentious political issues. Although radical Republicans pushed Lincoln to abolish slavery, he did not want to alienate the border states or proslavery Democrats. He was therefore reluctant to embrace emancipation as a war aim despite his personal hatred of slavery. Yet, as the war continued, moral and military imperatives increased Northern support for abolition. Cognizant that slavery enabled the South to reserve its white men for fighting, the U.S. Congress passed the 1862 Confiscation Act permitting the seizure of all Confederate property and freeing all slaves who reached Union lines.

Hoping to persuade Lincoln to support emancipation publicly, Horace Greeley (1811–1872) wrote this editorial. Greeley was a journalist who began his career at the literary magazine The New Yorker. *In 1841, he founded the* New York Tribune, *a liberal newspaper known for the quality of its reporting, its advocacy of social reforms, and its criticism of slavery. Lincoln's response to Greeley follows. (Spelling has been modernized.)*

FOCUS QUESTIONS

1. What are Greeley's major arguments?
2. How does Lincoln respond to Greeley's suggestions?
3. Whose response do you find more persuasive? Was the Civil War fought primarily to end slavery? Explain your answers.

SOURCE: *New York Daily Tribune*, August 20, 1862; Abraham Lincoln, *Complete Works*, John G. Nicolay and John Hay, eds. (New York, 1894), II, 227–228.

THE PRAYER OF TWENTY MILLIONS

To Abraham Lincoln, President of the United States:

Dear Sir:

I do not intrude to tell you—for you must know already—that a great proportion of those who triumphed in your election, and of all who desire the unqualified suppression of the rebellion now desolating our country, are sorely disappointed and deeply pained by the policy you seem to be pursuing with regard to the slaves of rebels. . . .

VIII. On the face of this wide earth, Mr. President, there is not one disinterested, determined, intelligent champion of the Union cause who does not feel that all attempts to put down the rebellion and at the same time uphold its inciting cause are preposterous and futile— that the rebellion, if crushed out tomorrow, would be renewed within a year if Slavery were left in full vigor—that Army officers who remain to this day devoted to Slavery can at best be but half-way loyal to the Union—and that every hour of deference to Slavery is an hour of added and deepened peril to the Union. I appeal to the testimony of your ambassadors in Europe. It is freely at your service, not at mine. Ask them to tell you candidly whether the seeming subserviency of your policy to the slaveholding, slavery-upholding interest, is not the perplexity, the despair, of statesman of all parties, and be admonished by the general answer!

IX. I close as I began with the statement that what an immense majority of the loyal millions of your countrymen require of you is a frank, declared, unqualified, ungrudging execution of the laws of the land, more especially of the Confiscation Act. That act gives freedom to the slaves of rebels coming within our lines, or when those lines may at any time enclose—we ask you to render it due obedience by publicly requiring all your subordinates to recognize and obey it. The Rebels are everywhere . . . [trying] to convince the slaves that they have nothing to hope from a Union success—that we mean in that case to sell them into a bitterer bondage to defray the cost of the war. Let them impress this as a truth on the great mass of their ignorant and credulous bondsmen, and the Union will never be restored—never.

We cannot conquer Ten Millions of People united in solid phalanx against us, powerfully aided by Northern sympathizers and European allies. We must have scouts, guides, spies, cooks, teamsters, diggers, and choppers from the Blacks of the South, whether we allow them to fight for us or not, or we shall be baffled and repelled. As one of the millions who would have gladly avoided this struggle at any sacrifice but that of Principle and Honor, but who now feel that the triumph of the Union is indispensable not only to the existence of our country but to the well-being of mankind,

I entreat you to render a hearty and unequivocal obedience to the law of the land.

Hon. Horace Greeley

Executive Mansion, Washington, August 22, 1862

Dear Sir:

I have just read yours of the 19th, addressed to myself through the New York "Tribune." If there be in it any statements, or assumptions of fact, which I may know to be erroneous, I do not, now and here, controvert them. If there be in it any inferences which I may believe to be falsely drawn, I do not, now and here, argue against them. If there be perceptible in it an impatient and dictatorial tone, I waive it in deference to an old friend whose heart I have always supposed to be right.

As to the policy I "seem to be pursuing," as you say, I have not meant leave anyone in doubt.

I would save the Union, I would save it the shortest way under the Constitution. The sooner the national authority can be restored, the nearer the Union will be "the Union as it was." If there be those who would not save the Union, unless they could at the same time *save* slavery, I do not agree with them. If there be those who would not save the Union unless they could at the same time *destroy* slavery, I do not agree with them. My paramount object in this struggle *is* to save the Union, and *is not* either to save or to destroy slavery. If I could save the Union without freeing *any* the slaves I would do it, and if I could save it by freeing *all* the slaves I would do it; and if I could save it by freeing some and leaving others alone I would also do that. What I do about slavery, and the colored race, I do because I believe it helps to save the Union; and what I forbear, I forbear because I do *not* believe it would help to save the Union. I shall do *less* whenever I shall believe what I am doing hurts the cause, and I shall do *more* whenever I shall believe doing more will help the cause. I shall try to correct errors when shown to be errors; and I shall adopt new views so fast as they shall appear to be true views.

I have here stated my purpose according to my view of *official* duty; and I intend no modification of my oft-expressed *personal* wish that all men everywhere could be free.

Yours,

A. Lincoln

11.3

Jefferson Davis Responds to the Emancipation Proclamation (1863)

In the summer of 1862, after months of delaying, Abraham Lincoln decided to emancipate the slaves. Hoping to undermine the Southern economy and looking for moral justification for the bloody war, Lincoln drafted a preliminary emancipation proclamation. Following the Union victory at Antietam in September 1862, Lincoln published his plan to free all slaves living in Confederate territories effective January 1, 1863, unless the South renounced secession. Although the proclamation was limited in scope, it had enormous symbolic importance. In addition to placating his Northern political critics, Lincoln gained support from European liberals and invited African Americans to enlist in the Union forces.

As the following selection shows, the Emancipation Proclamation outraged most Southerners. Confederate President Jefferson Davis (1808–1889) blasted the proclamation in his annual message to the Confederate Congress. Prior to becoming the Confederacy's only president, Davis had enjoyed an impressive career as a planter, soldier, and politician. He represented Mississippi in the U.S. Senate and served as secretary of war under Franklin Pierce. After the war, he was imprisoned and served two years.

FOCUS QUESTIONS

1. Why does Jefferson Davis claim that the Confederacy finds the Emancipation Proclamation so objectionable?

2. What impact does Davis predict emancipation will have on Southern race relations?

3. How does Davis think the Emancipation Proclamation will affect the course of the Civil War?

The public journals of the North have been received, containing a proclamation, dated on the 1st day of the present month, signed by the President of the

SOURCE: "The President's Message," *Richmond Daily Dispatch,* 15 January 1863, 2.

United States, in which he orders and declares all slaves within ten of the States of the Confederacy to be free, except such as are found within certain districts now occupied in part by the armed forces of the enemy. We may well leave it to the instincts of that common humanity which a beneficent Creator has implanted in the breasts of our fellowmen of all countries to pass judgment on a measure by which several millions of human beings of an inferior race, peaceful and contented laborers in their sphere, are doomed to extermination, while at the same time they are encouraged to a general assassination of their masters by the insidious recommendation "to abstain from violence unless in necessary self-defense." Our own detestation of those who have attempted the most execrable measure recorded in the history of guilty man is tempered by profound contempt for the impotent rage which it discloses. So far as regards the action of this Government on such criminals as may attempt its execution, I confine myself to informing you that I shall, unless in your wisdom you deem some other course more expedient, deliver to the several State authorities all commissioned officers of the United States that may hereafter be captured by our forces in any of the States embraced in the proclamation, that they may be dealt with in accordance with the laws of those States providing for the punishment of criminals engaged in exciting servile insurrection. The enlisted soldiers I shall continue to treat as unwilling instruments in the commission of these crimes, and shall direct their discharge and return to their homes on the proper and usual parole.

In its political aspect this measure possesses great significance, and to it in this light I invite your attention. It affords to our whole people the complete and crowning proof of the true nature of the designs of the party which elevated to power the present occupant of the Presidential chair at Washington and which sought to conceal its purpose by every variety of artful device and by the perfidious use of the most solemn and repeated pledges on every possible occasion. . . .

The people of this Confederacy, then, cannot fail to receive this proclamation as the fullest vindication of their own sagacity in foreseeing the uses to which the dominant party in the United States intended from the beginning to apply their power, nor can they cease to remember with devout thankfulness that it is to their own vigilance in resisting the first stealthy progress of approaching despotism that they owe their escape from consequences now apparent to the most skeptical. This proclamation will have another salutary effect in calming the fears of those who have constantly evinced the apprehension that this war might end by some reconstruction of the old Union or some renewal of close political relations with the United States. These tears have never been shared by me, nor have I ever been able to perceive on what basis they could rest. But the Proclamation affords the fullest guarantee of the impossibility of such a result; it has established a state of things which can lead to but one of three possible consequences—the extermination of slaves, the exile of the whole white population from the Confederacy, or absolute and total separation of these States from the United States.

This proclamation is also an authentic statement by the Government of the United States of its inability to subjugate the South by force of arms, and as such must be accepted by neutral nations, which can no longer find any justification in withholding our just claims to formal recognition. It is also in effect an intimation to the people of the North that they must prepare to submit to a separation, now become inevitable, for that people are too acute not to understand a restoration of the Union has been rendered forever impossible by the adoption of a measure which from its very nature neither admits of retraction nor can coexist with union. . . .

11.4

Clara Barton, Medical Life at the Battlefield (1862)

Thousands of patriotic Union and Confederate women supported their respective war efforts. Women bought, made, and distributed supplies for soldiers. Assuming the duties of men away at war, they worked as farmers, clerks, and store-keepers. In rare instances, they even disguised themselves as men to serve as soldiers or spied on the enemy.

Over 3,000 women served as battlefield nurses. Pioneered by British reformer Florence Nightingale in the 1850s, nursing was a new occupation for women. Since nurses were exposed to gruesome sights and strange men, some people questioned the morality of women willing to depart from prevailing ideals of ladylike behavior. With the help of nurses and new sanitary practices, battle deaths declined from the levels of the Mexican War. Nonetheless, the medical profession still lacked an understanding of germs, and twice as many soldiers perished from disease than from combat injuries.

In this reading, Clara Barton, a Union nurse, describes a makeshift field hospital. In 1881, Barton founded the American Red Cross.

SOURCE: Perry H. Epler, *Life of Clara Barton* (Macmillian, 1915), 31–32, 35–43, 45, 59, 96–98.

FOCUS QUESTIONS

1.   Why does Barton decide to become a nurse? Why is she reluctant at first?
2.   How does Barton describe the battlefield? What types of duties does she perform?
3.   How did women's contributions to the Civil War challenge the doctrine of separate spheres?

I was strong and thought I might go to the rescue of the men who fell. . . . What could I do but go with them, or work for them and my country? The patriot blood of my father was warm in my veins. The country which he had fought for, I might at least work for. . . .

But I struggled long and hard with my sense of propriety—with the appalling fact that I was only a woman whispering in one ear, and thundering in the other the groans of suffering men dying like dogs—unfed and unsheltered, for the life of every institution which had protected and educated me!

I said that I struggled with my sense of propriety and I say it with humiliation and shame. I am ashamed that I thought of such a thing.

When our armies fought on Cedar Mountain, I broke the shackles and went to the field. . . .

Five days and nights with three hours sleep—a narrow escape from capture—and some days of getting the wounded into hospitals at Washington, brought Saturday, August 30. And if you chance to feel, that the positions I occupied were rough and unseemly for a woman—I can only reply that they were rough and unseemly for men. But under all, lay the life of the nation. I had inherited the rich blessing of health and strength of constitution—such as are seldom given to woman—and I felt that some return was due from me and that I ought to be there. . . .

. . .Our coaches were not elegant or commodious; they had no seats, no platforms, no steps, a slide door on the side the only entrance, and this higher than my head. For my man attaining my elevated position, I must beg of you to draw on your imaginations and spare me the labor of reproducing the boxes, boards, and rails, which in those days, seemed to help me up and down the world. We did not criticize the unsightly helpers and were thankful that the stiff springs did not quite jostle us out. This need not be limited to this particular trip or train, but will for all that I have known in Army life. This is the kind of conveyance which your tons of generous gifts have reached the field with the freights. These trains through day and night, sunshine and heat and cold, have thundered over heights, across plains, the ravines, and over hastily built army bridges 90 feet across the stream beneath.

At 10 o'clock Sunday (August 31) our train drew up at Fairfax Station. The ground, for acres, was a thinly wooded slope—and among the trees on the leaves and grass, were laid the wounded who pouring in by scores of wagon loads, as picked up on the field the flag of truce. All day they came and the whole hillside was red. Bales of hay were broken open and scattered over the ground littering of cattle, and the sore, famishing men were laid upon it.

And when the night shut in, in the mist and darkness about us, we knew that standing apart from the world of anxious hearts, throbbing over the whole country, we were a little band of almost empty handed workers literally by ourselves in the wild woods of Virginia, with 3,000 suffering men crowded upon the few acres within our reach.

After gathering up every available implement or convenience for our work, our domestic inventory stood 2 water buckets, 5 tin cups, 1 camp kettle, 1 stew pan, 2 lanterns, 4 bread knives, 3 plates, and a 2-quart tin dish, and 3,000 guests to serve.

You will perceive by this, that I had not yet learned to equip myself, for I was no Pallas [Greek goddess of war], ready armed, but grew into my work by hard thinking and sad experience. It may serve to relieve your apprehension for the future of my labors if I assure you that I was never caught so again.

But the most fearful scene was reserved for the night. I have said that the ground was littered with dry hay and that we had only two lanterns, but there were plenty of candles. The wounded were laid so close that it was impossible to move about in the dark. The slightest misstep brought a torrent of groans from some poor mangled fellow in your path.

Consequently here were seen persons of all grades from the careful man of God who walked with a prayer upon his lips to the careless driver hunting for his lost whip,—each wandering about among this hay with an open flaming candle in his hands.

The slightest accident, the mere dropping of a light could have enveloped in flames this whole mass of helpless men.

How we watched and pleaded and cautioned as we worked and wept that night! How we put socks and slippers upon their cold feet, wrapped your blankets and quilts about them, and when we no longer these to give, how we covered them in the hay and left them to their rest! . . .

The slight, naked chest of a fair-haired lad caught my eye, dropping down beside him, I bent low to draw the remnant of his blouse about him, when with a quick cry he threw his left arm across my neck and, burying his face in the folds of my dress, wept like a child at his mother's knee. I took his head in my hands and held it until great burst of grief passed away. "And do you know me?" he asked at length, "I am Charley Hamilton. We used to carry your satchel home from school!" My faithful pupil, poor Charley. That mangled right hand would never carry a satchel again.

About three o'clock in the morning I observed a surgeon with a little flickering candle in hand approaching me with cautious step up in the wood. "Lady," he said as he drew near, "will you go with me? Out on the hills is a poor distressed lad, mortally wounded, and dying. His piteous cries for his sister have touched all our hearts, none of us can relieve him but rather seem to distress him by presence."

By this time I was following him back over the bloody track, with great beseeching eyes of anguish on every side looking up into our faces, saying so plainly, "Don't step on us."

11.5

Tally Simpson, Letter from Fredericksburg (1862)

After the Union Army's disastrous defeat at the First Battle of Bull Run (First Manassas), President Abraham Lincoln appointed General George B. McClellan the new commander of the Army of the Potomac. A brilliant administrator, McClellan soon transformed his poorly trained men into a well-disciplined force. A proslavery Democrat, McClellan hoped that a few major victories would compel the Confederacy to rejoin the Union with slavery left intact.

McClellan's plans hinged upon his Peninsula Campaign. Circumventing Confederates stationed near the Rappahannock River, McClellan transported his men down Chesapeake Bay to the peninsula where the York and James rivers converged. Upon landing, Union troops were to begin a rear attack on Richmond, the capital of the Confederacy.

The strategy did not succeed. While McClellan awaited reinforcements, the Confederates seized the offensive. In June 1862, Robert E. Lee, commander of the South's Army of Northern Virginia, defeated a much larger Union force in the Seven Days' Battles. Alarmed by McClellan's anxious reports, Lincoln ordered the general to return to Washington.

With the Peninsula Campaign in tatters, Lee moved northward. After winning the Battle of Second Bull Run (Second Manassas), he boldly took his army into Maryland. On September 17, 1862, Lee and McClellan's armies waged the Battle of Antietam resulting in 24,000 combined Union and Confederate casualties. Although the battle was tactically a draw, Union troops forced Lee into retreat.

McClellan's failure to pursue Lee prompted Lincoln to replace him with General Ambrose E. Burnside. The decision proved catastrophic. In December 1862, Burnside led approximately 100,000 U.S. troops to Fredericksburg, Virginia. Outnumbered by 30,000 men, Lee entrenched his army on the heights west of town. After Union forces captured Fredericksburg, Burnside ordered repeated assaults on the Confederate strongholds on Prospect Hill and Marye's Heights that resulted in devastating Union losses. Sickened by the carnage, Robert E. Lee remarked, "It is well that war is so terrible—we should grow fond

SOURCE: *"From Far, Far from Home": The Wartime Letters of Dick and Tally Simpson, Third South Carolina Volunteers* by Dick Simpson and Tally Simpson, edited by Guy R. Everson and Edward H. Simpson, Jr., copyright © 1994 by Guy R. Everson and Edward H. Simpson, Jr. Used by permission of Oxford University Press, Inc.

of it." Within weeks of his defeat at Fredericksburg, Burnside was relieved of command.

In this letter, Tally Simpson, a member of the 3rd South Carolina Volunteers, writes his sisters from the Confederate camp outside Fredericksburg.

FOCUS QUESTIONS

1. How would you describe Tally Simpson's state of mind?
2. How does he describe the condition of Fredericksburg and its inhabitants?
3. How does Simpson seem to regard his Union opponents and the war in general?
4. Why do you think Simpson fought in the Civil War?

Dec 25th, 1862

My Dear Sister

This is Christmas Day. The sun shines feebly through a thin cloud, the air is mild and pleasant, a gentle breeze is making music through the leaves of the lofty pines that stand near our bivouac. All is quiet and still, and that very stillness recalls some sad and painful thoughts.

This day, one year ago, how many thousand families, gay and joyous, celebrating Merry Christmas, drinking health to absent members of their family, and sending upon the wings of love and affection long, deep, and sincere wishes for their safe return to the loving ones at home, but today are clad in the deepest mourning in memory to some lost and loved member of their circle. If all the dead (those killed since the war began) could be heaped in one pile and all the wounded be gathered together in one group, the pale faces of the dead and the groans of the wounded would send such a thrill of horror through the hearts of the originators of this war that their very souls would rack with such pain that they would prefer being dead and in torment than to stand before God with such terrible crimes blackening their characters. Add to this the cries and wailings of the mourners—mothers and fathers weeping for their sons, sisters for their brothers, wives for their husbands, and daughters for their fathers—how deep would be the convictions of their consciences.

Yet they do not seem to think of the affliction and distress they are scattering broadcast over the land. When will this war end? Will another Christmas roll around and find us all wintering in camp? Oh! That peace may soon be restored to our young but dearly beloved country and that we may all meet again in happiness.

But enough of these sad thoughts. We went on picket in town a few days ago. The pickets of both armies occupy the same positions now as they did before the battle. Our regiment was quartered in the market place while the others occupied stores and private houses. I have often read of sacked and pillaged towns in ancient history, but never, till I saw Fredericksburg, did I fully realize what one was. The houses, especially those on the river, are riddled with shell and ball. The stores have been broken open and deprived of every thing that was worth a shilling. Account books and notes and letters and papers both private and public were taken from their proper places and scattered over the streets and trampled under feet. Private property was ruined. Their soldiers would sleep in the mansions of the wealthy and use the articles and food in the house at their pleasure. Several houses were destroyed by fire. Such a wreck and ruin I never wish to see again.

Yet notwithstanding all this, the few citizens who are now in town seem to be cheerful and perfectly resigned. Such true patriots are seldom found. This will ever be a noted place in history.

While we were there, Brig Genl Patrick, U.S.A., with several of his aides-de-camp, came over under flag of truce. Papers were exchanged, and several of our men bought pipes, gloves, &c from the privates who rowed the boat across. They had plenty of liquor and laughed, drank, and conversed with our men as if they had been friends from boyhood.

There is nothing new going on. I am almost dead to hear from home. I have received no letters in nearly three weeks, and you can imagine how anxious I am. The mails are very irregular. I hope to get a letter soon. Dunlap Griffin is dead, died in Richmond of wounds received in the last battle. Capt Hance is doing very well. Frank Fleming is in bad condition. (He has been elected lieutenant since he left.)

Write to me quick right off. I wish to hear from you badly. Remember me to my friends and relatives, especially the Pickens and Ligons. Hoping to hear from you soon I remain.

Your bud
Tally

Pres Hix came for the remains of Nap his brother and Johnnie Garlington yesterday and will take them to Richmond today. They will be carried on home immediately. Tell Aunt Caroline Jim is getting on finely. Howdy to all the negroes. I have received the bundle of clothes sent to Columbia. The bundle contained one shirt, one scarf, and two pairs of socks. At least I suppose it is the one you sent to Col[umbia] to be sent to Barnwell at Richmond. I am a thousand times obliged. When is Harry coming? Oh! that peace may soon be restored to our young but dearly beloved country and that we may all meet again in happiness.

11.6

Corporal James Kendall Hosmer, On the Firing Line (1863)

The Civil War was the deadliest war in American history. More than 600,000 Americans lost their lives in the conflict—a figure nearly equal to the number of U.S. soldiers killed in all other U.S. wars combined. New weapons accounted for many casualties. The submarine, automatic gun, land mine, shrapnel, and booby trap all debuted during the Civil War. Most significantly, rifles with grooved barrels replaced muskets. By spinning a bullet as it was fired, the rifle gave soldiers unprecedented accuracy and forced commanders to change traditional military tactics. Generals grew less reliant on cavalry units and ordered soldiers to dig protective trenches. Nonetheless, commanders still ordered massive frontal assaults and charges in which scores of men died.

In this excerpt, James Kendall Hosmer, a corporal in a Massachusetts regiment, describes Civil War combat. After the war, he became a professor, author, and minister.

FOCUS QUESTIONS

1. How does Hosmer describe preparations for battle?
2. How do his emotions change throughout this reading?
3. What are his impressions of the Confederate soldiers?
4. What is the outcome of the battle?
5. What does this selection suggest about combat in the American Civil War?

June 16, 1863

We have had a battle. Not quite a week ago, we began to hear of it. . . . We knew nothing certain, however, until Saturday. (It is now Tuesday.) Toward the end of that afternoon, the explicit orders came. The assault was to be made the next morning, and our regiment was to have a share in it. We were not to go home without the baptism of fire and blood.

SOURCE: James K. Hosmer, *The Color-Guard* (Boston, 1864), 187–195.

Before dark, we were ordered into line, and stacked our arms. Each captain made a little speech. "No talking in the ranks; no flinching. Let everyone see that his canteen is full, and that he has hard bread enough for a day. That is all you will carry beside gun and equipments." We left the guns in stack, polished, and ready to be caught on the instant; and lay down under the trees. At midnight came the cooks with coffee and warm food. Soon after came the order to move; then, slowly and with many halts, nearly four hundred strong, we took up our route along the wood-paths. Many other regiments were also in motion. The forest was full of Rembrandt pictures—a bright blaze under a tree, the faces and arms of soldiers all aglow about it; the wheel of an army-wagon, or the brass of a cannon, lit up; then the gloom of the wood, and the night shutting down about it.

At length, it was daybreak.... We were now only screened from the rebels by a thin hedge. Here the rifle-balls began to cut keen and sharp through the air about us; and the cannonade, as the east now began to redden, reached its height,—a continual deafening uproar, hurling the air against one in great waves, till it felt almost like a wall of rubber, bounding and rebounding from the body,—the great guns of the "Richmond," the siege-Parrots, the smaller field-batteries; and the keen, deadly whistle of well-aimed bullets. A few rods down the military road, the column passed.... The banks of the ravine rose on either side of the road in which we had halted: but just here the trench made a turn; and in front, at the distance of five or six hundred yards, we could plainly see the rebel rampart, red in the morning-light as with blood, and shrouded in white vapor along the edge as sharpshooters behind kept up an incessant discharge. I believe I felt no sensation of fear, nor do I think those about me did....

...We climb up the path. I go between Wilson and Hardiker; keeping nearest the former, who carries the national flag. In a minute or two, the column has ascended, and is deploying in a long line, under the colonel's eye, on the open ground. The rebel engineers are most skillful opponents. Between us and the brown earth-heap which we are to try to gain today, the space is not wide; but it is cut up in every direction with ravines and gullies. These were covered, until the parapet was raised, with a heavy growth of timber; but now it has all been cut down, so that in every direction the fallen tops of large trees interlace, trunks block up every passage, and brambles are growing over the whole. It is out of the question to advance here in line of battle. It seems almost out of the question to advance in any order: but the word is given, "Forward!" and on we go.

Know that this whole space is swept by a constant patter of balls: it is really a "leaden rain." We go crawling and stooping: but now and then before us rises in plain view the line of earth-works, smoky and sulphurous with volleys; while all about us fall the balls, now sending a lot of little splinters from a stump, now knocking the dead wood out of the old tree-trunk that is sheltering me, now driving up a cloud of dust from a little knoll, or cutting off the head of a weed just under the hand as with an invisible knife.... "Forward!" is the order. We all stoop; but the colonel does not stoop: he is as cool as he was in his tent last night, when I saw him drink iced lemonade. He turns now to examine the ground, then faces back again to direct the advance of this or that flank. Wilson springs on from cover to cover, and I follow close after him. It is hard work to get the flag along: it cannot be carried in the air; and we drag it and pass it from hand to hand among the brambles, much to the detriment of its folds. The line pauses a moment. Capt. Morton, who has risen from a sick-bed to be with his command, is coolly cautioning his company. The right wing is to remain in reserve, while the left pushes still farther forward. The major is out in front of us now. He stands upon a log which bridges a ravine,—a plain mark for the sharpshooters, who overlook the position, not only from the parapet, but from the tall trees within the rebel works. Presently we move on again, through brambles and under charred trunks, tearing our way, and pulling after us the colors; creeping on our bellies across exposed ridges, where bullets hum and sing like stinging bees; and, right in plain view, the ridge of earth, its brow white with incessant volleys. . . .

. . . Down into our little nook now come tumbling a crowd of disorganized, panting men. They are part of a New York regiment, who, on the crest just over us, have been meeting with very severe loss. They say their dead and dying are heaped up there. We believe it; for we can hear them, they are so near: indeed, some of those who come tumbling down are wounded; some have their gun-stocks broken by shot, and the barrels bent, while they are unharmed. They are frightened and exhausted, and stop to recover themselves; but presently their officers come up and order them forward again. From time to time, afterwards, wounded men crawl back from their position a few yards in front of where we are. . . .

. . . We begin to know that the attack has failed. . . . We know nothing certainly. There are rumors, thick as the rifle-balls, of this general killed, that regiment destroyed, and successful attempts elsewhere. The sun goes down on this day of blood. We have lost several killed. . . .

At dusk, I creep back to the ravine, where I am to sleep. . . . For food today, I have had two or three hard crackers and cold potatoes. We have no blankets: so down I lie to sleep as I can on the earth, without covering; and before morning, am chilled with the dew and coldness of the air.

11.7

Anna Elizabeth Dickinson Describes the New York Draft Riots (1863)

The Civil War armies mobilized millions of Americans. More than 2 million men served in the Union forces while another 800,000 troops fought for the Confederacy. Although volunteers comprised significant majorities in both armies, commanders required additional manpower. In 1862, the Confederacy passed the nation's first conscription law drafting all able-bodied white men aged eighteen to thirty-five. In the latter stages of the war, the age range expanded to seventeen to fifty. An amendment exempting men who oversaw or owned twenty or more slaves drew widespread complaints about "a rich man's war but a poor man's fight."

In 1863, the Union instituted the Conscription Act drafting all fit white men aged twenty to forty-five. Like its Confederate counterpart, the law favored the wealthy. A man could escape military service by hiring a substitute or paying the U.S. government $300. Many Americans viewed the draft as a violation of their civil liberties and resented its impact on the poor. In July 1863, this discontent sparked huge riots in New York City. Years of tension between free blacks and Irish immigrants competing for the same jobs erupted in four days of violence, arson, and vandalism. Federal troops finally suppressed the uprising. Anna Elizabeth Dickinson, a famous Republican orator and writer, recounted the New York Draft riots in an 1868 novel. (Spelling and syntax have been modernized.)

FOCUS QUESTIONS

1. How does Dickinson describe the atmosphere of the riots?
2. Whom do the rioters target?
3. What is Dickinson's opinion of the rioters?
4. Whom does she hold responsible for the riots? Do you agree? Explain your answer.

SOURCE: Anna E. Dickinson, *What Answer?* (Boston, 1868), 243–257.

On the morning of Monday, the thirteenth of July, began this outbreak unparalleled in atrocities by anything in American history, and equaled only by the horrors of the worst days of the French Revolution. Gangs of men and boys, composed of railroad employees, workers in machine shops, and a vast crowd of those who lived by preying upon others, thieves, pimps, professional ruffians,—the scum of the city,—jailbirds, or those who were running with swift feet to enter the prison doors, began to gather on the corners, and in streets and alleys where they lived. . . .

A body of these, five or six hundred strong, gathered about one of the enrolling offices in the upper part of the city, where the draft was quietly proceeding, and opened the assault upon it in a shower of clubs, bricks, and paving stones torn from the streets, following it up by a furious rush into the office. Lists, records, books, the drafting wheel, every article of furniture or work in the room was rent in pieces, and strewn about the floor or flung into the street: while the law officers, the newspaper reporters,—who are expected to be everywhere,—and the few peaceable spectators, were compelled to make a hasty retreat through an opportune rear exit, accelerated by the curses and blows of the assailants.

. . . And then, every portable article destroyed,—their thirst for ruin growing by the little drink it had had,—and believing, or rather hoping, that the officers had taken refuge in the upper rooms, set fire to the house, and stood watching the slow and steady lift of the flames, filling the air with demoniac shrieks and yells, while they waited for the prey to escape from some door or window from the merciless fire to their merciless hands. One of these, who was on the other side of the street, courageously stepped forward, and, telling them that they had utterly demolished all they came to seek, informed them that helpless women and little children were in the house, and besought them to extinguish the flames and leave the ruined premises; to disperse, or at least to seek some other scene.

By his dress recognizing in him a government official, so far from hearing or heeding his humane appeal, they set upon him with sticks and clubs, and beat him till his eyes were blind with blood, and he—bruised and mangled—succeeded in escaping to the police who stood helpless before this howling crew, now increased to thousands. With difficulty and pain the inoffensive tenants escaped from the rapidly spreading fire, which, having devoured the house originally lighted, swept across the neighboring buildings, till the whole block stood a mass of burning flames. . . .

The work thus begun, continued,—gathering in force and fury as the day wore on. Police stations, enrolling offices, rooms or buildings used in any way by government authority, or obnoxious as representing the dignity of law, were gutted, destroyed, then left to the mercy of the flames. . . . Before night fell it was no longer one vast crowd collected in a single section, but great numbers of gatherings, scattered over the whole length and breadth of the city,—some of them engaged in actual work of demolition and ruin; others with clubs and weapons in their hands, prowling round apparently with no definite atrocity to perpetuate, but ready for any iniquity that might offer,—and, by way of pastime, chasing every stray police officer, or solitary soldier, or inoffensive Negro, who crossed the line of their vision; these three objects—the badge of a defender of the law,—the uniform of the Union army,—the skin of a helpless and outraged race—acted upon these madmen as water acts upon a rabid dog.

Late in the afternoon a crowd which could have numbered not less than ten thousand, the majority of whom were ragged, frowzy [unkempt], drunken women, gathered about the Orphan Asylum for Colored Children,—a large and beautiful building, and one of the most admirable and noble charities of the city.... The few officers who stood guard over the doors...were beaten down and flung to one side, helpless and stunned, whilst the vast crowd rushed in. All the articles upon which they could seize—beds, bedding, carpets, furniture,—the very garments of the fleeing inmates, some of these torn from their persons as they sped by—were carried into the streets and hurried off by the women and the children who stood ready to receive the goods which their husbands, sons, and fathers flung to their care. The little ones, many of them assailed and beaten; all—orphans and caretakers—exposed to every indignity and every danger, driven on to the street,—the building was fired....

The next morning's sun rose on a city which was ruled by a reign of terror.... Where the officers appeared they were irretrievably beaten and overcome.... Stores were closed; the business portion of the city deserted; the large works and factories emptied of men, who had been sent home by their employers, or were swept into the ranks the marauding hands. The city cars, omnibuses, hacks, were unable to run, and remained under shelter. Every telegraph wire was cut, the posts torn up, the operators driven from their offices. The mayor, seeing that civil power was helpless to stem this tide, desired to call the military to his aid, and place the city under martial law, but was opposed by the Governor....

... [E]ditors outraged common sense, truth, and decency, by speaking of the riots as an "uprising of the people to defend their liberties,"—"an opposition on the part of the workingmen to an unjust and oppressive law, enacted in favor of the men of wealth and standing." As though the *people* of the great metropolis were incendiaries, robbers, and assassins; as though the poor were to demonstrate their indignities against the rich by hunting and stoning defenseless women and children; torturing and murdering men whose only offense was the color God gave them....

It was absurd and futile to characterize this new Reign of Terror as anything but an effort on the part of Northern rebels to help Southern ones, at the most critical moment of the war,—with the State militia and available troops absent in a neighboring Commonwealth,—and the loyal people unprepared. These editors...were of that most poisonous growth,—traitors to the Government and the flag of their country,—renegade Americans. Let it, however, be written plainly and graven deeply, that the tribes of savages—the hordes of ruffians— found ready to do their loathsome bidding were not of native growth, nor American born....

11.8

James Henry Gooding, Letter to President Lincoln (1863)

During the first year of the Civil War, the U.S. government barred African Americans from the military. But after the Emancipation Proclamation was issued, thousands of African Americans were allowed to enlist. Grasping the connections between citizenship, masculinity, and military service, they eagerly joined the armed forces. By the war's end, 186,000 blacks, most of them former slaves, served in the Union army and another 29,000 were in the navy. Forty-four thousand died defending the Union and twenty-four received the Congressional Medal of Honor. All black soldiers risked re-enslavement or execution if captured by Confederates.

Despite their obvious patriotism, African Americans suffered many injustices in the military. Only white officers were permitted to lead black regiments. Until June 1864, African American troops received much lower pay than their white counterparts. Although they proved their courage in battle, they were often consigned to menial assignments like digging latrines and burying the dead. In this letter to Abraham Lincoln, James Henry Gooding protests the treatment of African American soldiers. No response from Lincoln has been documented.

FOCUS QUESTIONS

1. What are Gooding's major complaints?
2. What do Gooding's letter and Anna Elizabeth Dickinson's description of the New York Draft Riots (Document 11.7) suggest about race relations in the North?

SOURCE: *A Documentary History of the Negro People in the U.S.* ed. Herbert Aptheker (New York: Citadel Press, 1951), 482–484. All rights reserved. Reprinted by permission of Citadel Press/Kensington Publishing Corp., www.kensingtonbooks.com.

Morris Island, S.C.

September 28, 1863

Your Excellency, Abraham Lincoln:

Your Excellency will pardon the presumption of an humble individual like myself, in addressing you, but the earnest solicitation of my comrades in arms besides the genuine interest felt by myself in the matter is my excuse, for placing before the Executive head of the Nation our Common Grievance.

On the 6th of the last Month, the Paymaster of the Department informed us, that if we would decide to receive the sum of $10 (ten dollars) per month, he would come and pay us that sum, but that, on the sitting of Congress, the Regt. [regiment] would, in his opinion, be allowed the other 3 (three). He did not give us any guarantee that this would be, as he hoped; certainly he had no authority for making any such guarantee, and we cannot suppose him acting in any way interested.

Now the main question is, are we Soldiers, or are we Laborers? We are fully armed, and equipped, have done all the various duties pertaining to a Soldier's life, have conducted ourselves to the complete satisfaction of General Officers, who were, if anything, prejudiced against us, but who now accord us all the encouragement and honors due us; have shared the perils and labor of reducing the first strong-hold that flaunted a Traitor Flag; and more, Mr. President, to-day the Anglo-Saxon Mother, Wife, or Sister are not alone in tears for departed Sons, Husbands, and Brothers. The patient, trusting descendant of Africa's Clime have dyed the ground with blood, in defense of the Union, and Democracy. Men, too, your Excellency, who know in a measure the cruelties of the iron heel of oppression, which in years gone by, the very power their blood is now being spilled to maintain, ever ground them in the dust.

But when the war trumpet sounded o'er the land, when men knew not the Friend from the Traitor, the black man laid his life at the altar of the Nation,—and he was refused. When the arms of the Union were beaten, in the first year of the war, and the Executive called for more food for its ravenous maw, again the black man begged the privilege of aiding his country in her need, to be again refused.

And now he is in the War, and how has he conducted himself? Let their dusky forms rise up, out of the mires of James Island, and give the answer. Let the rich mould around Wagner's parapet be upturned, and there will be found an eloquent answer. Obedient and patient and solid as a wall are they. All we lack is a paler hue and a better acquaintance with the alphabet.

Now your Excellency, we have done a Soldier's duty. Why can't we have a Soldier's pay? You caution the Rebel chieftain, that the United States knows no distinction in her soldiers. She insists on having all her soldiers of whatever creed or color, to be treated according to the usages of War. Now if the United States exacts uniformity of treatment of her soldiers from the insurgents, would it not be well and consistent to set the example herself by paying all her soldiers alike?

We of this Regt. were not enlisted under any "contraband" act. But we do not wish to be understood as rating our service of more value to the Government than the service of the ex-slave. Their service is undoubtedly worth much to the Nation, but Congress made express provision touching their case, as slaves freed by military necessity, and assuming the Government to be their temporary Guardian. Not so with us. Freemen by birth and consequently having the advantage of thinking and acting for ourselves so far as the Laws would allow us, we do not consider ourselves fit subjects for the Contraband act.

We appeal to you, Sir, as the Executive of the Nation, to have us justly dealt with. The Regt. do pray that they be assured their service will be fairly appreciated by paying them as American Soldiers, not as menial hirelings. Black men, you may well know, are poor; three dollars per month, for a year, will supply their needy wives and little ones with fuel. If you, as Chief Magistrate of the Nation, will assure us of our whole pay, we are content. Our Patriotism, our enthusiasm will have a new impetus, to exert our energy more and more to aid our Country. Not that our hearts ever flagged in devotion, spite the evident apathy displayed in our behalf, but we feel as though our country spurned us, now we are sworn to serve her. Please give this a moment's attention.

11.9

Abraham Lincoln, The Gettysburg Address (1863)

After two years of costly defeats, the Union's prospects improved in 1863. Hoping to gain access to supplies and to force a peace settlement, General Robert E. Lee moved his forces northward into Pennsylvania. In July, Union and Confederate troops began three days of vicious fighting in Gettysburg. Both sides sustained devastating losses but the Union emerged victorious. At the same time, Ulysses S. Grant won control of Vicksburg, a crucial Confederate stronghold on the Mississippi River. Although several bloody battles lay ahead, the South never recovered from its defeats at Gettysburg and Vicksburg.

SOURCE: "Address at the Dedication of the Gettysburg National Cemetery, November 19, 1863," *Complete Works of Abraham Lincoln*, eds. John G. Nicolay and John Hay (Harrogate, TN, 1894), 9: 209–210.

On November 19, 1863, Abraham Lincoln and noted orator Edward Everett traveled to Gettysburg to dedicate a national cemetery. After Everett gave a lengthy address, Lincoln made a brief speech. The following day, Everett wrote to Lincoln, "I wish that I could flatter myself that I had come as near to the central idea of the occasion in two hours as you did in two minutes." The Gettysburg Address is widely considered a masterpiece of political rhetoric.

FOCUS QUESTIONS

1. What are the major themes of the Gettysburg Address?
2. Why do you think many Americans continue to find Lincoln's remarks so stirring?

Four score and seven years ago our fathers brought forth on this continent a new nation, conceived in Liberty, and dedicated to the proposition that all men are created equal.

Now we are engaged in a great civil war, testing whether that nation or any nation so conceived and so dedicated, can long endure. We are met on a great battle-field of that war. We have come to dedicate a portion of that field, as a final resting place for those who here gave their lives that that nation might live. It is altogether fitting and proper that we should do this.

But, in a larger sense, we can not dedicate—we can not consecrate—we can not hallow—this ground. The brave men, living and dead, who struggled here, have consecrated it, far above our poor power to add or detract. The world will little note, nor long remember what we say here, but it can never forget what they did here. It is for us the living, rather, to be dedicated here to the unfinished work which they who fought here have thus far so nobly advanced. It is rather for us to be here dedicated to the great task remaining before us—that from these honored dead we take increased devotion to that cause for which they gave the last full measure of devotion—that we here highly resolve that these dead shall not have died in vain—that this nation, under God, shall have a new birth of freedom—and that government of the people, by the people, for the people, shall not perish from the earth.

11.10

Mary Boykin Chesnut Describes Richmond at War (1863–1864)

The Civil War profoundly affected the lives of civilians. Although the North was better equipped to absorb the costs of the war, both sides confronted serious problems, including profiteering, shortages, and inflation. Northern and Southern families endured dislocations and shattering personal losses.

The economic effects of the conflict varied greatly. In the North, industries directly connected to the war flourished. The Republican-dominated Congress passed a series of probusiness measures, including protective tariffs and the Pacific Railway Act authorizing the construction of a transcontinental railroad. In deference to the party's free-soil ideals, the Republicans also helped ordinary citizens with the Homestead Act, a law granting 160 acres of public land to individuals after five years of residency on their plots. However, not all people benefited equally from the war. Corrupt contractors grew rich from selling inferior merchandise to Union troops. Ordinary workers suffered as employers cut wages and raised prices to offset the costs of tariffs and wartime taxes.

These changes paled in comparison to the economic devastation the war created in the South. With its weak central government and a populace hostile to taxation, the Confederacy struggled to fund the war effort and supply its troops. Unable to secure sufficient foreign capital or to sell enough bonds, the government financed much of the war by printing money. The tactic created enormous inflation exacerbated by widespread distribution of counterfeit Confederate currency. Where Northern prices rose eighty percent, Southern inflation rates exceeded 9,000 percent. Shortages and government seizure of private property further undermined morale. Desperate civilians rioted in several places.

Mary Boykin Chesnut (1823–1886) witnessed the war's impact on the Confederate home front. Born in South Carolina, Mary Boykin Miller was the eldest child of Mary Boykin and Stephen Decatur Miller, a prominent politician. After completing her education, Mary Miller married James Chesnut, the sole heir to a large plantation. In 1858, when Chesnut won a seat in the U.S. Senate, Mary accompanied him to Washington, D.C., and socialized with many notable people. Following the election of Abraham Lincoln, Chesnut helped draft the South Carolina secession ordinance and later served as an aide to General

SOURCE: Mary Boykin Chesnut, *A Diary from Dixie* (New York: D. Appleton and Company, 1905), 261–301.

P.G.T. Beauregard and President Jefferson Davis. During the war, Mary followed her husband throughout the South and entertained the Confederate elite. She scrupulously documented her wartime experiences in her diary. First published in 1905 as A Diary from Dixie, *her work is one of the finest firsthand accounts of life in the Confederacy.*

FOCUS QUESTIONS

1. How does Mary Chesnut describe conditions in Richmond?
2. Do you think her experiences were typical? Explain your answer.
3. What are her attitudes toward the events she describes?
4. What do these passages suggest about the war's impact upon the Confederacy?

RICHMOND, VA.

December 4th [1863]—My husband bought yesterday at the Commissary's one barrel of flour, one bushel of potatoes, one peck of rice, five pounds of salt beef, and one peck of salt—all for sixty dollars. In the street a barrel of flour sells for one hundred and fifteen dollars.

December 5th.— . . . Spent seventy-five dollars to-day for a little tea and sugar, and have five hundred left. My husband's pay never has paid for the rent of our lodgings. He came in with dreadful news just now. I have wept so often for things that never happened, I will withhold my tears now for a certainty. To-day, a poor woman threw herself on her dead husband's coffin and kissed it. She was weeping bitterly. So did I in sympathy. . . .

Christmas Day, 1863.—Yesterday dined with the Prestons. Wore one of my handsomest Paris dresses (from Paris before the war). Three magnificent Kentucky generals were present, with Senator Orr from South Carolina, and Mr. Miles. . . . Others dropped in after dinner; some without arms, some without legs; von Borcke, who can not speak because of a wound in his throat. Isabella said: "We have all kinds now, but a blind one." Poor fellows, they laugh at wounds. "And they yet can show many a scar."

We had for dinner oyster soup, besides roast mutton, ham, boned turkey, wild duck, partridge, plum pudding, sauterne, burgundy, sherry, and Madeira. There is life in the old land yet! . . .

My husband says I am extravagant. "No, my friend, not that," said I. "I had fifteen hundred dollars and I have spent every cent of it in my housekeeping. Not one cent for myself, not one cent for dress nor any personal want whatever." He calls me "hospitality run mad."

January 4th [1864]— . . . My husband came in and nearly killed us. He brought this piece of news: "North Carolina wants to offer terms of peace!" We needed only a break of that kind to finish us. I really shivered nervously, as one does when the first handful of earth comes rattling down on the coffin in the grave of one we cared for more than all who are left.

January 8th.—Snow of the deepest. . . . I was to take Miss Cary to the Semmes's. My husband inquired the price of a carriage. It was twenty-five dollars an hour! He cursed by all his gods at such extravagance. The play was not worth the candle, or carriage, in this instance. In Confederate money it sounds so much worse than it is. . . .

The Semmes charade party was a perfect success. The play was charming. . . .

Senator Hill, of Georgia, took me in to supper, where were ices, chicken salad, oysters, and champagne. The President [Jefferson Davis] came in alone, I suppose, for while we were talking after supper and your humble servant was standing between Mrs. Randolph and Mrs. Stanard, he approached, offered me his arm and we walked off, oblivious of Mr. Senator Hill. . . . Now, the President walked with me slowly up and down that long room, and our conversation was of the saddest. Nobody knows so well as he the difficulties which beset this hard-driven Confederacy. . . .

January 14th.—Gave Mrs. White twenty-three dollars for a turkey. Came home wondering all the way why she did not ask twenty-five; two more dollars could not have made me balk at the bargain, and twenty-three sounds odd.

January 20th.—And now comes a grand announcement made by the Yankee Congress. They vote one million of men to be sent down here to free the prisoners whom they will not take in exchange. I actually thought they left all these Yankees here on our hands as part of their plan to starve us out. All Congressmen under fifty years of age are to leave politics and report for military duty or be conscripted. What enthusiasm there is in their councils! Confusion, rather, it seems to me! Mrs. Ould says "the men who frequent her house are more despondent now than ever since this thing began."

Our Congress is so demoralized, so confused, so depressed. They have asked the President, whom they have so hated, so insulted, so crossed and opposed and thwarted in every way, to speak to them, and advise them what to do. . . .

February 1st.—Mrs. [Jefferson] Davis gave her "Luncheon to Ladies Only" on Saturday. Many more persons there than at any of these luncheons which we have gone to before. Gumbo, ducks and olives, chickens in jelly, oysters, lettuce salad, chocolate cream, jelly cake, claret, champagne, etc., were the good things set before us.

To-day, for a pair of forlorn shoes I have paid $85. Colonel Ives drew my husband's pay for me. I sent Lawrence for it (Mr. Chesnut ordered him back to us; we needed a man servant here). Colonel Ives wrote that he was amazed I should be willing to trust a darky with that great bundle of money, but it came safely. Mr. Petigru says you take your money to market in the market basket, and bring home what you buy in your pocket-book.

February 5th.—When Lawrence handed me my husband's money (six hundred dollars it was) I said: "Now I am pretty sure you do not mean to go to the Yankees, for with that pile of money in your hands you must have known there was your chance." He grinned, but said nothing. . . .

February 17th.—Found everything in Main Street twenty per cent dearer. They say it is due to the new currency bill. . . .

March 3d.—Hetty, the handsome, and Constance, the witty, came; the former too prudish to read *Lost and Saved*, by Mrs. Norton, after she had heard the plot. Conny was making a bonnet for me. Just as she was leaving the house, her friendly labors over, my husband entered, and quickly ordered his horse. "It is so near dinner," I began. "But I am going with the President. I am on duty. He goes to inspect the fortifications. The enemy, once more, are within a few miles of Richmond." Then we prepared a luncheon for him. Constance Cary remained with me.

After she left I sat down to *Romola*, and I was absorbed in it. How hardened we grow to war and war's alarms! The enemy's cannon or our own are thundering in my ears, and I was dreadfully afraid some infatuated and frightened friend would come in to cheer, to comfort, and interrupt me. Am I the same poor soul who fell on her knees and prayed, and wept, and fainted, as the first gun boomed from Fort Sumter? Once more we have repulsed the enemy. But it is humiliating, indeed, that he can come and threaten us at our very gates whenever he so pleases. . . .

March 7th.—Shopping, and paid $30 for a pair of gloves; $50 for a pair of slippers; $24 for six spools of thread; $32 for five miserable, shabby little pocket handkerchiefs. . . .

March 11th.—Letters from home, including one from my husband's father, now over ninety, written with his own hand, and certainly his own mind still. I quote: "Bad times; worse coming. Starvation stares me in the face. Neither John's nor James's overseer will sell me any corn." Now, what has the government to do with the fact that on all his plantations he made corn enough to last for the whole year, and by the end of January his negroes had stolen it all, Poor old man, he has fallen on evil days, after a long life of ease and prosperity. . . .

March 15th.—Old Mrs. Chesnut is dead. A saint is gone and James Chesnut is broken-hearted. He adored his mother. I gave $375 for my mourning, which consists of a black alpaca dress and a crepe veil. With bonnet, gloves, and all it came to $500. Before the blockade such things as I have would not have been thought fit for a chamber-maid.

Everybody is in trouble. Mrs. Davis says paper money has depreciated so much in value that they can not live within their income; so they are going to dispense with their carriage and horses.

March 18th.—Went out to sell some of my colored dresses. What a scene it was—such piles of rubbish, and mixed up with it, such splendid Parisian silks and satins. . . .

March 24th.—Yesterday, we went to the Capitol grounds to see our returned prisoners. We walked slowly up and down until Jeff Davis was called upon to speak. There I stood, almost touching the bayonets when he left me. I looked straight into the prisoners' faces, poor fellows. They cheered with all their might, and I wept for sympathy, and enthusiasm. I was very deeply moved. These men were so forlorn, so dried up, and shrunken, with such a strange look in some of their eyes; others so restless and wild-looking; others again placidly vacant, as if they had been dead to the world for years. A poor woman was too much for me. She was searching for her son. He had been expected back. She said he was taken prisoner at Gettysburg. She kept going in and out among them with a basket of provisions she had brought for him to eat. It was too pitiful. She was utterly unconscious of the crowd. The anxious dread, expectation, hurry, and hope which led her on showed in her face. . . .

11.11

Robert E. Lee on the Use of Slaves as Soldiers (1865)

Throughout the Civil War, white Southerners feared the three million slaves in their midst. To control slaves, whites formed patrols, spread rumors, and even relocated. Slaves often found themselves torn between their desire for freedom and their loyalties to masters. While the majority of slaves remained with their masters, thousands fled to Union lines at the first opportunity. Despite white anxieties, no large slave rebellions occurred. The Confederate army utilized slaves in many capacities, including cooking, manual labor, and nursing. Not surprisingly, the slave system deteriorated during the wartime chaos. Whites complained about lazy and undisciplined slaves. In 1864, a desperate Confederate Congress discussed offering freedom for slaves willing to fight for the South. In March 1865, they passed a bill arming 300,000 slaves as soldiers. Although the conflict ended before the plan took effect, the decision illustrated just how profoundly the war undermined slavery.

In this letter, Robert E. Lee (1807–1870) responds to a Southern senator seeking his opinion on the use of slaves in the Confederate army. One of the South's most beloved figures, Lee was born in Virginia to Ann Hill Carter and Henry "Light-Horse Harry" Lee, a former governor of Virginia and Revolutionary War hero. When his father's early death and poor business skills left his family in dire financial straits, Lee accepted an appointment to the U.S. Military Academy in order to obtain a free university education. After finishing second in his class at West Point, he joined the elite army engineering corps. His military prowess first drew notice during the Mexican War. In 1859, he led the suppression of John Brown's raid on Harper's Ferry. Two years later, when

SOURCE: *Correspondence, Orders, Reports, and Returns of the Confederate Authorities from January 1, 1864, to the End.* O.R. Series IV, Volume III [S# 129], #41.

Virginia seceded, he resigned from the U.S. Army in order to fight for his state. After becoming commander of the Army of Northern Virginia, Lee's string of sweeping victories made him a hero to many Confederates. But, by the spring of 1864, a much larger and better-supplied Union force was exacting devastating losses upon Lee's troops. With a weakened army and his own health failing, Lee ordered his men to defend Richmond and Petersburg. In April 1865, he surrendered at Appomattox. He spent his last years serving as president of Washington College (now Washington and Lee University).

FOCUS QUESTIONS

1. How has the war affected Lee's views on slavery?

2. What does Lee think that the Confederacy should do with the slaves? How does he justify this position?

3. Does Lee believe slaves will make good soldiers? What advantages does he see in enlisting them?

4. In opposing Lee's proposal, Confederate General Howell Cobb declared, "If slaves make good soldiers our whole theory of slavery is wrong." What did Cobb mean? Do you agree or disagree? Why?

5. In early 1865, what do you think the average Southerner would have said if asked, "Why are you fighting the Civil War?" Did the motives driving the war effort change from 1861 to 1865? Explain your answers.

HEADQUARTERS ARMY OF NORTHERN VIRGINIA,
January 11, 1865.

Hon. ANDREW HUNTER, Richmond, Va.:

DEAR SIR: I have received your letter of the 7th instant, and without confining myself to the order of your interrogatories, will endeavor to answer them by a statement of my views on the subject. I shall be most happy if I can contribute to the solution of a question in which I feel an interest commensurate with my desire for the welfare and happiness of our people.

Considering the relation of master and slave, controlled by humane laws and influenced by Christianity and an enlightened public sentiment, as the best that can exist between the white and black races while intermingled as at present in this country, I would deprecate any sudden disturbance of that relation unless it be necessary to avert a greater calamity to both. I should therefore prefer to rely upon our white population to preserve the ratio between our forces and those of the enemy, which experience has shown to be safe. But in view of the preparations of our enemies, it is our duty to provide for continued war and not for a battle or a campaign, and I fear that we cannot accomplish this without over-taxing the capacity of our white population.

Should the war continue under existing circumstances, the enemy may in course of time penetrate our country and get access to a large part of our negro population. It is his avowed policy to convert the able-bodied men among them into soldiers, and to emancipate all. The success of the Federal arms in the South was followed by a proclamation of President Lincoln for 280,000 men, the effect of which will be to stimulate the Northern States to procure as substitutes for their own people the negroes thus brought within their reach. Many have already been obtained in Virginia, and should the fortune of war expose more of her territory, the enemy would gain a large accession to his strength. His progress will thus add to his numbers, and at the same time destroy slavery in a manner most pernicious to the welfare of our people. Their negroes will be used to hold them in subjection, leaving the remaining force of the enemy free to extend his conquest. Whatever may be the effect of our employing negro troops, it cannot be as mischievous as this. If it end in subverting slavery it will be accomplished by ourselves, and we can devise the means of alleviating the evil consequences to both races. I think, therefore, we must decide whether slavery shall be extinguished by our enemies and the slaves be used against us, or use them ourselves at the risk of the effects which may be produced upon our social institutions. My own opinion is that we should employ them without delay. I believe that with proper regulations they can be made efficient soldiers. They possess the physical qualifications in an eminent degree. Long habits of obedience and subordination, coupled with the moral influence which in our country the white man possesses over the black, furnish an excellent foundation for that discipline which is the best guaranty of military efficiency. Our chief aim should be to secure their fidelity.

There have been formidable armies composed of men having no interest in the cause for which they fought beyond their pay or the hope of plunder. But it is certain that the surest foundation upon which the fidelity of an army can rest, especially in a service which imposes peculiar hardships and privations, is the personal interest of the soldier in the issue of the contest. Such an interest we can give our negroes by giving immediate freedom to all who enlist, and freedom at the end of the war to the families of those who discharge their duties faithfully (whether they survive or not), together with the privilege of residing at the South. To this might be added a bounty for faithful service.

We should not expect slaves to fight for prospective freedom when they can secure it at once by going to the enemy, in whose service they will incur no greater risk than in ours. The reasons that induce me to recommend the employment of negro troops at all render the effect of the measures I have suggested upon slavery immaterial, and in my opinion the best means of securing the efficiency and fidelity of this auxiliary force would be to accompany the measure with a well-digested plan of gradual and general emancipation. As that will be the result of the continuance of the war, and will certainly occur if the enemy succeed, it seems to me most advisable to adopt it at once, and thereby obtain all the benefits that will accrue to our cause.

The employment of negro troops under regulations similar in principle to those above indicated would, in my opinion, greatly increase our military strength and enable us to relieve our white population to some extent. I think we could dispense with the reserve forces except in cases of necessity.

It would disappoint the hopes which our enemies base upon our exhaustion, deprive them in a great measure of the aid they now derive from black troops, and thus throw the burden of the war upon their own people. In addition to the great political advantages that would result to our cause from the adoption of a system of emancipation, it would exercise a salutary influence upon our whole negro population, by rendering more secure the fidelity of those who become soldiers, and diminishing the inducements to the rest to abscond.

I can only say in conclusion that whatever measures are to be adopted should be adopted at once. Every day's delay increases the difficulty. Much time will be required to organize and discipline the men, and action may be deferred until it is too late.

Very respectfully, your obedient servant,
R. E. Lee, General

11.12

Abraham Lincoln, Second Inaugural Address (1865)

Although the Union had won impressive victories at Vicksburg and Gettysburg in July 1863, the Confederacy continued fighting. By early 1864, many North-erners were decrying the horrific casualties in Ulysses S. Grant's Virginia campaign. That summer, the Democrats nominated George B. McClellan on a peace platform calling for an immediate armistice followed by negotiations with the Confederacy. Lincoln expected to lose the election.

All of this rapidly changed in September when Atlanta fell to General William T. Sherman. As Sherman's men advanced and destroyed virtually everything in their path, Grant forced Robert E. Lee to entrench his troops outside Petersburg and Richmond. Buoyed by the Union victories, Lincoln easily won reelection, carrying 212 of 233 electoral votes and 55 percent of the popular vote.

SOURCE: *Inaugural Addresses of the Presidents of the United States* (Washington, D.C.: U.S. Government Printing Office, 1989).

> *By Lincoln's inauguration in March 1865, the Civil War was almost over. Standing before thousands in front of the newly completed Capitol dome, Lincoln gave this address. Its brevity and tone struck a chord with Americans eager to end the Civil War. Little more than a month later, Lincoln was assassinated.*

FOCUS QUESTIONS

1. What are Lincoln's major themes? How do they compare to those of the Gettysburg Address (Document 11.9)?
2. How does Lincoln believe the Civil War changed the nation?
3. How do you think Confederates reacted to Lincoln's remarks?

FELLOW-COUNTRYMEN: At this second appearing to take the oath of the Presidential office, there is less occasion for an extended address than there was at first. Then, a statement, somewhat in detail, of a course to be pursued, seemed fitting and proper. Now, at the expiration of four years, during which public declarations have been constantly called forth on every point and phase of the great contest which still absorbs the attention and engrosses the energies of the nation, little that is new could be presented. The progress of our arms, upon which all else chiefly depends, is as well known to the public as to myself; and it is, I trust, reasonably satisfactory and encouraging to all. With high hope for the future, no prediction in regard to it is ventured.

On the occasion corresponding to this four years ago, all thoughts were anxiously directed to an impending civil war. All dreaded it—all sought to avert it. While the inaugural address was being delivered from this place, devoted altogether to saving the Union without war, insurgent agents were in the city seeking to destroy it without war-seeking to dissolve the Union, and divide effects, by negotiation. Both parties deprecated war; but one of them would make war rather than let the nation survive; and the other would accept war rather than let it perish. And the war came.

One-eighth of the whole population were colored slaves, not distributed generally over the Union, but localized in the Southern part of it. These slaves constituted a peculiar and powerful interest. All knew that this interest was, somehow, the cause of the war. To strengthen, perpetuate, and extend this interest was the object for which the insurgents would rend the Union, even by war; while the Government claimed no right to do more than to restrict the territorial enlargement of it. Neither party expected for the war the magnitude or the duration which it has already attained. Neither anticipated that the cause of the conflict might cease with, or even before, the conflict itself should cease. Each looked for an easier triumph, and a result less fundamental and astounding. Both read the same Bible, and pray to the same God; and each invokes His aid against the other. It may seem strange that any men should dare to ask a just God's assistance in wringing their bread from the sweat of other men's faces; but let us judge not, that we be not judged. The prayers of both could not be answered—that of neither has been answered fully. The Almighty has His own purposes. "Woe unto the world because of offenses! for it must needs be that offenses come; but woe to that man by whom the offense cometh." If we shall suppose that American slavery is one of those offenses which, in the providence of God, must needs come, but which, having continued through His appointed time, He now wills to remove, and that He gives to both North and South this terrible war, as the woe due to those by whom the offense came, shall, we discern therein, any departure from those divine attributes which the believers in a living God always ascribe to Him? Fondly do we hope—fervently do we pray—that this mighty scourge of war may speedily pass away. Yet, if God wills that it continue until all the wealth piled by the bondman's two hundred and fifty years of unrequited toil shall be sunk, and until every drop of blood drawn with the lash shall be paid by another, drawn with the sword, as was said three thousand years ago, so still it must be said: "The judgments of the Lord are true and righteous altogether."

With malice toward none; with charity for all; with firmness in the right, as God gives us to see the right, let us strive on to finish the work we are in; to bind up the nation's wounds; to care for him who shall have borne the battle, and for his widow, and his orphan—to do all which may achieve and cherish a just and lasting peace among ourselves, and with all nations.

12

✳

Reconstruction

The end of the Civil War presented the nation with many difficult questions. How would the South be reintegrated into the Union? Would the president or Congress determine reconstruction policies? What rights would the federal government grant former slaves? Would women also gain new political privileges? For over a decade, such contentious issues consumed national political life.

Even before the war ended, U.S. leaders considered strategies for reuniting the country. President Lincoln proposed the "10 percent plan," allowing Southern states to reconstitute their governments after ten percent of their citizens affirmed their loyalty to the United States and renounced slavery. He made no provisions for black suffrage or the social and economic reconstruction of the South. After Lincoln's assassination in April 1865, President Andrew Johnson continued Lincoln's lenient policies. Taking advantage of a long congressional recess, Johnson pardoned many former Confederates and allowed them to create new state legislatures. Some Southern states immediately instituted "black codes" that greatly restricted the lives of former slaves.

These actions outraged many U.S. congressmen. Determined to reshape Southern society dramatically, Radical Republicans passed the Fourteenth Amendment granting freed slaves U.S. citizenship and due process of law. Opposed to these efforts, President Johnson campaigned against his own party in the elections of 1866. Dismayed by Johnson's behavior and reports of Southern intransigence, Northern voters gave the Radical Republicans sweeping victories.

Emboldened by these events, Congress instituted stronger measures in the South. With the Reconstruction Act of 1867, Congress divided the South into military districts, guaranteed freedmen the right to vote in state elections, and stripped Confederate leaders of their political powers. Republican-dominated governments now ruled the South with coalitions of carpetbaggers (Northerners who moved to the postwar South), scalawags (white Southerners who cooperated with Reconstruction officials), and blacks. Passage of the Fifteenth Amendment granted black men the right to vote. The decision to limit suffrage to men infuriated women's suffrage activists. After continued clashes with Johnson, Congress impeached the president and almost removed him from office.

Most Southern whites bitterly resented Reconstruction. Some resorted to violence through new groups like the Ku Klux Klan. Fraud and intimidation coupled with appeals to white supremacy enabled the Democrats to regain control of several state governments and to begin institutionalizing racial segregation.

In many ways, African Americans benefited from Reconstruction. Many families ripped apart by slavery reunited. New black churches and schools provided unprecedented opportunities for spiritual and intellectual fulfillment. Over 600 African-American men won political offices. Thousands acquired property and gained economic independence. Yet Reconstruction also proved disappointing. Legal and economic barriers trapped many freedpeople in sharecropping. Black attempts to exercise their political rights met white resistance. Freedom was only the first step on a long road to racial equality.

By the early 1870s, Reconstruction was faltering badly. Political corruption and economic instability overshadowed efforts to create a biracial democracy in the South. In 1877, after a hotly disputed election, Rutherford B. Hayes withdrew federal troops from the South and abandoned Reconstruction.

THEMES TO CONSIDER

- Freedpeople's responses to and interpretations of emancipation
- The benefits and limitations of emancipation
- The role of the Freedman's Bureau in helping—and sometimes hindering—the former slaves
- Southern attempts to replicate slavery and to protect white supremacy
- Freedpeople's recognition and assertion of their newly won political rights
- Clashes between presidents and Congress in formulating Reconstruction policies
- The mixed legacies of sharecropping
- The impact of emancipation and Reconstruction upon Southern whites
- The issues raised for women's rights activists by passage of the Fourteenth and Fifteenth Amendments

12.1

African Americans and the Impact of Freedom

Although they faced obstacles like poverty and illiteracy, most slaves were thrilled at their newfound freedom. Emancipation created a vast migration throughout the South. Former slaves searched for jobs, often in urban areas. Parents looked for children who had been sold. Spouses reunited after forced separations and rushed to legalize their unions. African Americans built scores of businesses, schools, and churches. They zealously pursued economic, educational, and cultural opportunities impossible under slavery.

These readings illustrate many of these changes. The first demonstrates some of the challenges former slaves encountered when trying to rebuild their families. Philip Grey, a freedman living in Virginia, tracked down his wife Willie Ann and their daughter Maria, both of whom had been sold to a Kentucky planter years earlier. Willie Ann's response is included in the following reading. In the other selections, Mingo White and Charles Davenport, two former slaves, recall emancipation and Reconstruction. Both were interviewed as part of the Federal Writers' Project, a New Deal program of the 1930s. Traveling throughout the country, federal officials collected hundreds of testimonies from former slaves. The original spelling, punctuation, and syntax of these documents have been preserved.

FOCUS QUESTIONS

1. How does Willie Ann Grey react to the letter from her husband, Philip?

2. What has Philip asked Willie Ann to do? What has changed since she was taken to Kentucky?

3. What seems to be Willie Ann's biggest concern?

SOURCES: Ira Berlin and Leslie S. Rowland, *Families and Freedom: A Documentary History of African-American Kinship in the Civil War Era* (New York: The New Press, 1997), 173, 176.

Federal Writers' Project, Slave Narratives, "A Folk History of Slavery in the United States from Interviews with Former Slaves" (Washington, D.C.: Typewritten Records Prepared by the Federal Writers' Project, 1941).

4. What does her letter suggest about the ways that slavery affected families?

5. How did Mingo White and Charles Davenport respond to news of their emancipation?

6. What problems did White and Davenport encounter?

7. What do White and Davenport's experiences reveal about Reconstruction?

Willie Ann Grey

Salvisa, KY
April 7th 1866

Dear Husband

I seat myself this morning to write you a few lines to let you know that I received your letter the 5 of this month and was very glad to hear from you and to hear that you was well this leaves us all well at present and I hope these lines may find you still in good health. you wish me to come to Virginia I had much rather that you would come after me but if you cannot make it convenient you will have to make some arrangements for me and family I have 3 fatherless little girls my husband went off under Burbridges command and was killed at Richmond Virginia if you can pay my passage through there I will come the first of May I have nothing much to sell as I have had my things all burnt so you know that what I would sell would not bring much you must not think my family to large and get out of heart for if you love me you will love my children and you will have to promise me that you will provide for them all as well if they were your own. I heard that you spoke of coming for Maria [their daughter] but was not coming for me. I know that I have lived with you and loved you then and I love you still every time I hear from you my love grows stronger. I was very low spirited when I heard that you was not coming for me my heart sank within me in an instant you will have to write and give me directions how to come I want when I start to come the quickest way I can come I do not want to be detained on the road if I was the expense would be high and I would rather not have much expense on the road give me directions which is the nearest way so that I will not have any trouble after I start from here Phebe wishes to know what has become of Lawrence she heard that he was married but did not know whether it was so or [not] Maria sends her love to you but seems to be low spirited for fear that you will come her and not for me. John Phebe['s] son says he would like to see his father but does not care about leaving his mother who has taken care of him up to this time he thinks that she needs help and if he loves her he will give her help I will now close by requesting you to write as soon as you receive this so no more at present but remain your true (I hope to be with you soon) wife.

Willie Ann Grey
To Philip Grey

Aunt Lucinda sends her love to you she has lost her Husband & one daughter Betsy she has left 2 little children the rest are all well at present. Phebe's Mary was sold away from her she heard from her the other day she was well.
Direct your letter to Mrs. Mollie Roche Salvisa Ky

Mingo White
Interviewed at Burleson, Alabama
Interviewed by Levi D. Shelby, Jr.
Age when interviewed: 85–90

De day dat we got news dat we was free, Mr. White called us niggers to the house. He said, "You are all free, just as free as I am. Now go and get yourself somewhere to stick your heads."

Just as soon as he say dat, my mammy hollered out, "Dat's 'nough for a yearlin'." She struck out across de field to Mr. Lee Osborn's to get a place for me and her to stay. He paid us seventy-five cents a day, fifty cents to her and two bits for me. He gave us dinner along with de wages. After de crop was gathered for that year, me and my mammy cut and hauled wood for Mr. Osborn. Us left Mr. Osborn dat fall and went to Mr. John Rawlins. Us made a sharecrop with him. Us'd pick two rows of cotton and he'd pick two rows. Us'd pull two rows of corn and he'd pull two rows of corn. He furnished us with rations and a place to stay. Us'd sell our cotton and open corn and pay Mr. John Rawlins for feedin' us. Den we moved with Mr. Hugh Nelson and made a sharecrop with him. We kept movin' and makin' sharecrops till us saved up 'nough money to rent us a place and make a crop for ourselves.

Us did right well at dis until de Ku Klux got so bad, us had to move back with Mr. Nelson for protection. De mens that took us in was Union men. Dey lived here in the South but dey taken us part in de slave business. De Ku Klux threat to whip Mr. Nelson, 'cause he took up for de niggers. Heap of nights we would hear of de Ku Klux comin' and leave home. Sometimes us was scared not to go and scared to go away from home.

One day I borrowed a gun from Ed Davis to go squirrel huntin'. When I taken de gun back I didn't unload it like I always been doin'. Dat night de Ku Klux called on Ed to whip him. When dey told him to open de door, he heard one of 'em say, "Shoot him time he gets de door open." "Well," he says to 'em, "Wait till I can light de lamp." Den he got de gun what I had left loaded, got down on his knees and stuck it through a log and pulld de trigger. He hit Newt Dobbs in de stomach and kilt him.

He couldn't stay round Burleson any more, so he come to Mr. Nelson and got 'nough money to get to Pine Bluff, Arkansas. The Ku Klux got bad sure 'nough den and went to killin' niggers and white folks, too.

Charles Davenport
Interviewed at Natchez, Mississippi
Interviewed by Edith Wyatt Moore
Age at interview: About 100

Like all de fool niggers o'dat time I was right smart bit by de freedom bug for awhile. It sounded powerful nice to be told: "You don't have to chop cotton no more. You can throw dat hoe down and go fishin' whensoever de notion strikes you. And you can roam 'round at night and court gals just as late as you please. Ain't no marster gwine to say to you, "Charlie, you's got to be back when de clock strikes nine."

I was fool 'nough to believe all dat kind o' stuff. But to tell de honest truth, most o' us didn't know ourselfs no better off. Freedom meant us could leave where us'd been born and bred, but it meant, too, dat us had to scratch for us ownselfs. Dem what left de old plantation seems so all fired glad to get back dat I made up my mind to stay put. I stayed right with my white folks as long as I could.

My white folks talked plain to me. Dey say real sadlike, "Charlie, you's been a dependence, but now you can go if you is so desirous. But if you wants to stay with us you can sharecrop. Dey's a house for you and wood to keep you warm and a mule to work. We ain't got much cash, but dey's de land and you can count on havin' plenty o'victuals. Do just as you please."

When I looked at my marster and knowed he needed me, I pleased to stay. My marster never forced me to do nary thing about it. . . .

Lord! Lord! I knows about de Kloo Kluxes. I knows a-plenty. Dey was sure 'nough devils a-walkin' de earth a-seekin' what dey could devour. Dey larruped de hide off de uppity niggers an' drove de white trash back where dey belonged.

Us niggers didn't have no secret meetin's. All us had was church meeting in arbors out in de woods. De preachers would exhort us dat us was de chillen o'Israel in de wilderness an' de Lord done sent us in to take dis land o'milk and honey. But how us gwine-a take land what's already been took?

I sure ain't never heard about no plantations bein' divided up, neither. I heard a lot o'yaller niggers spountin' off how dey was gwine-a take over de white folks' land for back wages. Dem bucks just took all dey wages out in talk. 'Cause I ain't never seen no land divided up yet.

In dem days nobody but niggers and "shawlstrap" folks voted. Quality folks didn't have nothin' to do with such truck. If dey hada wanted to de Yankees wouldn'ta let 'em. My old marster didn't vote and if anybody knowed what was what he did. Sense didn't count in dem days. It was powerful ticklish times and I let votin' alone. . . . [O]ne night a bunch o'uppity niggers went to a entertainment in Memorial Hall. Dey dressed deyselfs fit to kill and walked down de aisle and took seats in de very front. But just about time dey got good set down, de curtain dropped and de white folks rose up without a-sayin' a word. Dey marched out de buildin' with dey chins up and left dem niggers a-sittin' in a empty hall.

Dat's de way it happen every time a nigger tried to get too uppity. Dat night after de breakin' up o'dat entertainment, de Kloo Kluxes rode through de land. I heard dey grabbed every nigger what walked down dat aisle, but I ain't heard yet what dey done with 'em.

12.2

Elizabeth Hyde Botume, A Northern Teacher's View of the Freedmen (1863–1865)

Early in the Civil War, Union troops occupied the islands off the coast of South Carolina. Under the "contraband" policy, all property—including land and slaves—was confiscated and placed under the jurisdiction of the U.S. government. Cognizant that soldiers could not care for war refugees and slaves, Secretary of the Treasury Salmon P. Chase authorized charitable organizations to send aide workers and teachers into the occupied territory. In October 1863, the New England Freedmen's Aid Society dispatched Elizabeth Hyde Botume to educate former slaves. She later recounted her experiences in First Days Amongst the Contrabands, *excerpted below.*

FOCUS QUESTIONS

1. How does Botume describe the condition of the freedmen she encounters?
2. Describe white attitudes toward the freedmen.
3. Describe the freedmen's attitudes toward whites and their newfound freedom.

Contrabands were coming into the Union lines, and thence to the town, not only daily, but hourly. They came alone and in families and in gangs,—slaves who had been hiding away, and were only now able to reach safety. Different members of scattered families following after freedom, as surely and safely guided as were the Wise Men by the Star of the East.

On New Year's Day I walked around amongst these people with Major Saxton. We went to their tents and other quarters. One hundred and fifty poor refugees from Georgia had been quartered all day on the wharf. A wretched and most pitiable gang, miserable beyond description. But when we spoke to them, they invariably gave a cheerful answer. Usually to our question, "How do you do?" the response would be, "Thank God, I live!"

SOURCE: Elizabeth Hyde Botume, *First Days Amongst the Contrabands* (Boston, 1893), 78–79, 82–83, 117–118, 168–169, 176–177.

Sometimes they would say, "Us ain't no wusser than we been."

These people had been a long time without food, excepting a little hominy and uncooked rice and a few ground-nuts. Many were entirely naked when they started, and all were most scantily clothed and had already had some extremely cold days, which we, who were fresh from the North, found hard to bear.

It was the same old story. These poor creatures were covered only with blankets, or bits of old carpeting, or pieces of bagging, "crocus," fastened with thorns and sharp sticks. . . .

I went first to the negro quarters at the "Battery Plantation," a mile and a half away. A large number of Georgia refugees who had followed Sherman's army were quartered here. Around the old plantation house was a small army of black children, who swarmed like bees around a hive. There were six rooms in the house, occupied by thirty-one persons, big and little. In one room was a man whom I had seen before. He was very light, with straight red hair and a sandy complexion, and I mistook him for an Irishman. He had been to me at one time grieving deeply for the loss of his wife, but he had now consoled himself with a buxom girl as black as ink. His sister, a splendidly developed creature, was with them. He had also four sons. Two were as light as himself, and two were very black. These seven persons occupied this one room. A rough box bedstead, with a layer of moss and a few old rags in it, a hominy pot, two or three earthen plates, and a broken-backed chair, comprised all the furniture of the room. I had previously given one of the women a needle and some thread, and she now sat on the edge of the rough bedstead trying to sew the dress she ought, in decency, to have had on. . . .

The winter of 1864–1865 was a sad time, for so many poor creatures in our district were wretchedly ill, begging for help, and we had so little to give them. Many of the contrabands had pneumonia. Great exposure, with scanty clothing and lack of proper food, rendered them easy victims to the encroachments of any disease. I sent to Beaufort for help. The first doctor who came was exasperatingly indifferent. He might have been a brother of a "bureau officer," who was sent down especially to take care of the contrabands, and who wished all the negroes could be put upon a ship, and floated out to sea and sunk. It would be better for them and for the world. When we expressed our surprise that he could speak so of human beings, he exclaimed, "Human beings! They are only animals, and not half as valuable as cattle."

When a doctor came, I went from room to room and talked with the poor sick people, whose entire dependence was upon us. Finally I could endure his apathy and indifference no longer.

"Leave me medicines, and I will take care of people as I can," I said. . . .

I could not, however, excuse the doctor, a man in government employ, drawing a good salary with no heart in his work. Beaufort was reported to be a depot for officials whom government did not know what to do with. . . .

Early in February we went to Savannah with General and Mrs. Saxton, and members of the general's staff, and other officers. How it had become known that we were to make this trip I cannot tell, but we found a crowd of our own colored people on the boat when we went aboard. To our exclamations of surprise they said with glee—

"Oh, we're goin' too, fur us has frien's there."

We found the city crowded with contrabands who were in a most pitiable condition. Nearly all the negroes who had lived there before the war had gone away. A large number went on with the army; those left were the stragglers who had come in from the "sand hills" and low lands. The people from the plantations too had rushed into the city as soon as they knew the Union troops were in possession.

A crowd of poor whites had also congregated there. All were idle and destitute. The whites regarded the negroes as still a servile race, who must always be inferior by virtue of their black skins. The negroes felt that emancipation had lifted them out of old conditions into new relations with their fellow beings. They were no longer chattels, but independent creatures with rights and privileges like their neighbors. . . .

Nothing in the history of the world has ever equaled the magnitude and thrilling importance of the events then transpiring. Here were more than four millions of human beings just born into freedom; one day held in the most abject slavery, the next, "de Lord's free men." Free to come and to go according to the best lights given them. Every movement of their white friends was to them full of significance, and often regarded with distrust. Well might they sometimes exclaim, when groping from darkness into light, "Save me from my friend, and I will look out for my enemy."

Whilst the Union people were asking, "Those negroes! what is to be done with them?" they, in their ignorance and helplessness, were crying out in agony, "What will become of us?" They were literally saying, "I believe, O Lord! help thou mine unbelief."

They were constantly coming to us to ask what peace meant for them? Would it be a peace indeed? Or oppression, hostility, and servile subjugation? This was what they feared, for they knew the temper of the baffled rebels as did no others.

12.3

The Louisiana Black Code (1865)

Most former Confederates bitterly resented racial integration and the emancipation of the slaves. Accordingly, every Southern state passed "black codes" designed to protect white supremacy and to replicate the slave system. While the laws granted freedmen some civil rights, such as marriage and property ownership, the statutes

SOURCE: Louisiana Black Code, 1865, Senate Executive Document No.2, 39th Cong., 1st Sess., p. 93.

greatly restricted the lives of ex-slaves. To ensure a servile labor force, states barred African Americans from many businesses and trades. Under broadly defined vagrancy laws, unemployed freedmen could be arrested, fined, imprisoned, and bound out as laborers. Some states instituted segregation and most prohibited interracial marriage. Former slaves were forbidden to carry firearms, travel freely, or to testify in court against whites. The black codes and white violence against ex-slaves outraged Northerners and prompted more rigorous Reconstruction policies.

FOCUS QUESTIONS

1. What were some of the ways Louisiana restricted the lives of African Americans?

2. What do these laws suggest about the white response to the end of the Civil War?

3. Compare life under the black codes to life under slavery. What did African Americans gain from emancipation? What areas of their lives could not be constrained by Black Codes?

Sec. 1 *Be it ordained by the police jury of the parish of St. Landry*, That no negro shall be allowed to pass within the limits of said parish without special permit in writing from his employer. Whoever shall violate this provision shall pay a fine of two dollars and fifty cents, or in default thereof shall be forced to work four days on the public road, or suffer corporeal punishment as provided hereafter....

Sec. 3 ...No negro shall be permitted to rent or keep a house within said parish. Any negro violating this provision shall be immediately ejected and compelled to find an employer; and any person who shall rent, or give the use of any house to any negro, in violation of this section, shall pay a fine of five dollars for each offence.

Sec. 4 ...Every negro is required to be in the regular service of some white person, or former owner, who shall be held responsible for the conduct of said negro. But said employer or former owner may permit said negro to hire his own time by special permission in writing, which permission shall not extend over seven days at any one time....

Sec. 5 ...No public meeting or congregations of negroes shall be allowed within said parish after sunset; but such public meetings and congregations may be held between the hours of sunrise and sunset, by the special permission in writing of the captain of patrol, within whose beat such meetings shall take place....

Sec. 6 ...No negro shall be permitted to preach, exhort, or otherwise declaim to congregations of colored people, without a special permission in writing from the president of the police jury....

Sec. 7 ... No negro who is not in the military service shall be allowed to carry firearms, or any kind of weapons, within the parish, without the special written permission of his employers, approved and endorsed by the nearest and most convenient chief of patrol....

Sec. 8 ... No negro shall sell, barter, or exchange any articles of merchandise or traffic within said parish without the special written permission of his employer, specifying the article of sale, barter or traffic....

Sec. 9 ... Any negro found drunk within the said parish shall pay a fine of five dollars, or in default thereof work five days on the public road, or suffer corporeal punishment as hereinafter provided.

Sec. 11 ... It shall be the duty of every citizen to act as a police officer for the detection of offences and the apprehension of offenders, who shall be immediately handed over to the proper captain or chief of patrol.

12.4

African Americans Seek Protection (1865)

Although no longer enslaved, the freedmen faced significant obstacles. With limited education and economic resources, many ex-slaves found themselves at the mercy of their former masters. Nonetheless, they seized the opportunity to organize and express themselves politically. Many African Americans attended conventions held throughout the South in order to discuss possible methods for protecting themselves. In this passage, a group of African Americans in Virginia describe their plight and request assistance from the U.S. Congress.

FOCUS QUESTIONS

1. Why is it significant that these delegates are meeting?
2. What are the delegates' major concerns? What protections do they request?

SOURCE: "The Late Convention of Colored Men," *The New York Times*, 13 August 1865, 3.

3. Why are the delegates dissatisfied with Andrew Johnson's Reconstruction policies?

4. What does this reading suggest about race relations and Reconstruction policies in the immediate aftermath of the Civil War?

We, the undersigned members of a convention of colored citizens of the State of Virginia, would respectfully represent that, although we have been held as slaves, and denied all recognition as a constituent of your nationality for almost the entire period of the duration of your government, and that by your permission we have been denied either home or country, and deprived of the dearest rights of human nature; yet when you and our immediate oppressors met in deadly conflict upon the field of battle—the one to destroy and the other to save your government and nationality, we, with scarce an exception, in our inmost souls espoused your cause, and watched, and prayed, and waited, and labored for your success. . . .

When the contest waxed long, and the result hung doubtfully, you appealed to us for help, and how well we answered is written in the rosters of the two hundred thousand colored troops now enrolled in your service; and as to our undying devotion to your cause, let the uniform acclamation of escaped prisoners, "Whenever we saw a black face we felt sure of a friend," answer.

Well, the war is over, the rebellion is "put down," and we are declared free! Four-fifths of our enemies are paroled or amnestied, and the other fifth are being pardoned, and the President [Andrew Johnson] has, in his efforts at the reconstruction of the civil government of the States, late in rebellion, left us entirely at the mercy of these subjugated but unconverted rebels, in everything save the privilege of bringing us, our wives and little ones, to the auction block. He has, so far as we can understand the tendency and bearing of his action in the case, remitted us for all our civil rights, to men, a majority of whom regard our devotions to your cause and flag as that which decided the contest against them! This we regard as destructive of all we hold dear, and in the name of God, of justice, of humanity, of good faith, of truth and righteousness, we do most solemnly and earnestly protest. Men and brethren, in the hour of your peril you called upon us, and despite all time-honored interpretation of constitutional obligations, we came at your call and you are saved; and now we beg, we pray, we entreat you not to desert us in this the hour of our peril!

We know these men—know them well—and we assure you that, with the majority of them, loyalty is only "lip deep," and that their professions of loyalty are used as a cover to the cherished design of getting restored to their former relation with the Federal Government, and then, by all sorts of "unfriendly legislation," to render the freedom you have given us more intolerable than the slavery they intended for us.

We warn you in time that our only safety is keeping them under Governors of the military persuasion until you have so amended the Federal Constitution that it will prohibit the States from making any distinction between citizens on account of race or color. In one word, the only salvation for us besides the power of the Government, is in the possession of the ballot. Give us this, and we will protect ourselves. No class of men relatively as numerous as we were ever oppressed when armed with the ballot. But, 'tis said we are ignorant. Admit it. Yet who denies we know a traitor from a loyal man, a gentleman from a rowdy, a friend from an enemy? . . .

. . . All we ask is an equal chance with the white traitors varnished and japanned with the oath of amnesty. Can you deny us this and still keep faith with us? "But," say some, "the blacks will be overreached by the superior knowledge and cunning of the whites." Trust us for that. We will never be deceived a second time. "But," they continue, "the planters and landowners will have them in their power, and dictate the way their votes shall be cast." We did not know before that we were to be left to the tender mercies of their landed rebels for employment. Verily, we thought the Freedmen's Bureau was organized and clothed with power to protect us from this very thing, by compelling those for whom we labored to pay us, whether they liked our political opinions or not! . . .

We are "sheep in the midst of wolves," and nothing but the military arm of the Government prevents us and all the truly loyal white men from being driven from the land of our birth. Do not then, we beseech you, give to one of these "wayward sisters" the rights they abandoned and forfeited when they rebelled until you have secured our rights by the aforementioned amendments to the Constitution.

Let your action in our behalf be thus clear and emphatic, and our respected President, who, we feel confident, desires only to know your will, to act in harmony therewith, will give you his most earnest and cordial cooperation; and the Southern States, through your enlightened and just legislation, will speedily award us our rights. Thus not only will the arms of the rebellion be surrendered, but the ideas also.

12.5

Thaddeus Stevens Attacks Presidential Reconstruction (1865)

In the wake of the Civil War, politicians sharply disagreed over the best way to rebuild the nation. Their differences sparked clashes between Congress and presidents. Where Presidents Abraham Lincoln and Andrew

SOURCE: "Reconstruction," *Congressional Globe*, 39th Congress, 1st Session, part 1 (18 December 1865), 72–74.

Johnson offered lenient plans designed to readmit the Southern states quickly, a small group of Radical Republicans demanded a more punitive policy. In this speech, Senator Thaddeus Stevens (R-PA), a strong advocate for racial equality, calls for harsh punishment of former Confederates. He later played significant roles in drafting the Fourteenth Amendment and the military reconstruction acts of 1867.

FOCUS QUESTIONS

1. Why does Stevens believe that Congress should control Reconstruction?
2. What proposals does he offer for governing the postwar South? What is his attitude toward the former Confederates?
3. What is his attitude toward the freedmen?
4. How do you think white Southerners responded to Stevens's remarks?

December 18, 1865

The President assumes, what no one doubts, that the late rebel States have lost their constitutional relations to the Union, and are incapable of representation in Congress, except by permission of the Government. It matters but little, with this admission, whether you call them States out of the Union, and now conquered territories, or assert that because the Constitution forbids them to do what they did do, that they are therefore only dead as to all national and political action, and will remain so until the Government shall breathe into them the breath of life anew and permit them to occupy their former position. In other words, that they are not out of the Union, but are only dead carcasses lying within the Union. In either case, it is very plain that it requires the action of Congress to enable them to form a State government and send representatives to Congress. Nobody, I believe, pretends that with their old constitutions and frames of government they can be permitted to claim their old rights under the Constitution. They have torn their constitutional States into atoms, and built on their foundations fabrics of a totally different character. Dead men cannot raise themselves. Dead States cannot restore their existence *"as it was."* Whose especial duty is it to do it? In whom does the Constitution place the power? Not in the judicial branch of Government, for it only adjudicates and does not prescribe laws. Not in the Executive, for he only executes and cannot make laws. Not in the Commander-in-Chief of the armies, for he can only hold them under military rule until the sovereign legislative power of the conqueror shall give them law. . . .

Congress alone can do it. . . . Congress must create States and declare when they are entitled to be represented. Then each House must judge whether the members presenting themselves from a recognized State possess the requisite qualifications of age, residence, and citizenship; and whether the election and returns are according to law. . . .

It is obvious from all this that the first duty of Congress is to pass a law declaring the condition of these outside or defunct States, and providing proper civil governments for them. Since the conquest they have been governed by martial law. Military rule is necessarily despotic, and ought not to exist longer than is absolutely necessary. As there are no symptoms that the people of these provinces will be prepared to participate in constitutional government for some years, I know of no arrangement so proper for them as territorial governments. There they can learn the principles of freedom and eat the fruit of foul rebellion. Under such governments, while electing members to the territorial Legislatures, they will necessarily mingle with those to whom Congress shall extend the right of suffrage. In Territories Congress fixes the qualifications of electors; and I know of no better place nor better occasion for the conquered rebels and the conqueror to practice justice to all men, and accustom themselves to make and obey equal laws.

They ought never to be recognized as capable of acting in the Union, or of being counted as valid States, until the Constitution shall have been so amended as to make it what the framers intended; and so as to secure perpetual ascendancy to the party of the Union; and so as to render our republican Government firm and stable forever. The first of those amendments is to change the basis of representation among the States from Federal numbers to actual voters.... With the basis unchanged the 83 Southern members, with the Democrats that will in the best times be elected from the North, will always give a majority in Congress and in the Electoral College.... I need not depict the ruin that would follow....

But this is not all that we ought to do before inveterate rebels are invited to participate in our legislation. We have turned, or are about to turn, loose four million slaves without a hut to shelter them or a cent in their pockets. The infernal laws of slavery have prevented them from acquiring an education, understanding the common laws of contract, or of managing the ordinary business of life. This Congress is bound to provide for them until they can take care of themselves. If we do not furnish them with homesteads, and hedge them around with protective laws; if we leave them to the legislation of their late masters, we had better have left them in bondage.

12.6

President Johnson Opposes Black Suffrage (1867)

Thrust into presidency after the assassination of Abraham Lincoln, Andrew Johnson inherited the contentious question of how to reconstruct the Union. The only Southern Senator to remain in Congress following secession, Johnson had long opposed the planter class and slavery. But as a lifelong Democrat, Johnson's political agenda differed greatly from that of the Radical Republicans.

In May 1865, while Congress was in recess, Johnson implemented a lenient Reconstruction policy. Johnson's program included few provisions for protecting the freedmen and enabled many unrepentant former Confederates to regain political power. When Congress reconvened in December 1865, outraged Radical Republicans refused to recognize newly elected Southern congressional representatives. In the following months, Congress overrode Johnson's vetoes of the Civil Rights Act and the Supplementary Freedmen's Bureau Act. In March 1867, Congress passed a Reconstruction Act requiring Southern states to permit black male suffrage in order to reenter the Union. In many intense debates, Johnson alienated many moderate Republicans and lost control over Reconstruction. In this message to Congress, Johnson explains why he opposes enfranchising African-American men.

FOCUS QUESTIONS

1. Why is Johnson opposed to granting Southern black men the right to vote?

2. Compare Johnson's racial attitudes to those of Thaddeus Stevens (Document 12.5).

3. If you had been one of the architects of federal Reconstruction policy, what would you have proposed? How would you have punished the South for secession? What provisions would you have made for the former slaves?

SOURCE: Andrew Johnson, "Third Annual Message," December 3, 1867, James D. Richardson, ed. *A Compilation of the Messages and Papers of the Presidents, 1789–1908* (Washington, D.C.: Bureau of National Literature and Art, 1909), Vol. VI, pp. 564–565.

It is manifestly and avowedly the object of these laws to confer upon negroes the privilege of voting and to disfranchise such a number of white citizens as will give the former a clear majority at all elections in the Southern States. This, to the minds of some persons, is so important that a violation of the Constitution is justified as a means of bringing it about. The morality is always false which excuses a wrong because it proposed to accomplish a desirable end. We are not permitted to do evil that good may come. But in this case the end itself is evil, as well as the means. The subjugation of the States to negro domination would be worse than the military despotism under which they are now suffering. It was believed beforehand that the people would endure any amount of military oppression for any length of time rather than degrade themselves by subjection to the negro race. Therefore they have been left without a choice. Negro suffrage was established by act of Congress, and the military officers were commanded to superintend the process of clothing the negro race with the political privileges torn from white men.

The blacks in the South are entitled to be well and humanely governed, and to have the protection of just laws for all their rights of person and property. If it were practicable at this time to give them a Government exclusively their own, under which they might manage their own affairs in their own way, it would become a grave question whether we ought to do so, or whether common humanity would not require us to save them from themselves. But under the circumstances this is only a speculative point. It is not proposed merely that they shall govern themselves, but they shall rule the white race, make and administer State laws, elect Presidents and members of Congress, and shape to a greater or less extent the future destiny of the whole country. Would such a trust and power be safe in such hands?

The peculiar qualities which should characterize any people who are fit to decide upon the management of public affairs for a great state have seldom been combined. It is the glory of white men to know that they have had these qualities in sufficient measure to build upon this continent a great political fabric and preserve its stability for more than ninety years, while in every other part of the world all similar experiments have failed. But if anything can be proved by known facts, if all reasoning upon evidence is not abandoned, it must be acknowledged that in the progress of nations negroes have shown less capacity for government than any other race of people. No independent government of any form has ever been successful in their hands. On the contrary, wherever they have been left to their own devices they have shown a constant tendency to relapse into barbarism. In the Southern States, however, Congress has undertaken to confer upon them the privilege of the ballot. Just released from slavery, it may be doubted whether as a class they know more than their ancestors how to organize and regulate civil society.

12.7

A White Planter Responds
to Emancipation (1866)

The Civil War destroyed much of the South. Cities, factories, farms, and railroads lay in ruins. 260,000 Confederate soldiers died. Ratification of the Thirteenth Amendment ended slavery nationwide. These losses devastated the Southern economy. Many whites found themselves fighting with former slaves for scarce land and resources. Unwilling to accept such humiliation, Southern states passed black codes designed to force freed people back onto plantations and deny them basic civil liberties.

Whenever possible, former slaves resisted white subjugation. Eager to demonstrate control over their households, freedmen took their wives out of the fields and placed them at home raising children and keeping house. Black men struggled to preserve their economic independence and avoid white supervision. But, with no redistribution of Southern lands, many found it impossible to rent or buy their own property.

At the same time, whites desperately searched for ways to replace slave labor. They persuaded freedmen to sign labor contracts that were often unfair. For blacks looking for alternatives to wage labor under white bosses, sharecropping seemed like a good solution. Sharecropping, however, proved a mixed blessing. Unable to absorb the production costs and living expenses between harvests, sharecroppers of both races were trapped in a vicious cycle of debt and dependency in which all family members spent long hours farming. Overproduction of cotton depleted soil and depressed prices. While wealthier Southerners pursued new business opportunities in mining, lumber, and textiles, poor Southerners working in agriculture battled bad weather, unstable markets, and ill health.

In this letter, M. C. Fulton, a Georgia planter, offers the Freedmen's Bureau suggestions for improving the Southern economy.

FOCUS QUESTIONS

1. How does M. C. Fulton describe the lives of the freedpeople in his community?

SOURCE: Ira Berlin and Leslie S. Rowland, *Families and Freedom: A Documentary History of African-American Kinship in the Civil War Era* (New York: The New Press, 1997), 185–187.

2. What do his comments suggest about the former slaves' reactions to emancipation?

3. What does Fulton want the Freedmen's Bureau to do? Do racial and gender stereotypes inform his remarks? If so, provide examples.

4. What do Fulton's suggestions indicate about the economic impact of emancipation? How were the economic needs of whites and blacks interconnected?

5. How does Fulton seem to be responding to emancipation? Do you think his reactions were typical? Explain your answers.

Snow Hill near Thomson Georgia April 17th 1866

Dear Sir—Allow me to call your attention to the fact that most of the Freed-women who have husbands are not at work—never having made any contract at all—Their husbands are at work, while they are nearly idle as it possible for them to be, pretending to spin—knit or something that really amounts to nothing for their husbands have to buy them clothing I find from my own hands wishing to buy of me—

Now these women have always been used to working out [in the fields] & it would be far better for them to go to work for reasonable wages & their rations—both in regard to health & furtherance of their family wellbeing—Say their husbands get 10 to 12—or 13$ a month and out that feed their wives and from 1 to 3 or 4 children—& clothe the family—It is impossible for one man to do this & maintain his wife in idleness without stealing more or less of their support, whereas if their wives (where they are able) were at work for rations & fair wages—which they can all get; the family could live in some comfort & more happily—besides their labor is a very important percent of the entire labor of the South—& if not made available, must affect to some extent the present crop—Now is a very important time in the crop—& the weather being good & to continue so for the remainder of the year, I think it would be a good thing to put the women to work and all that it is necessary to do this in most cases is an order from you directing the agents to require the women to make [labor] contracts for the balance of the year—I have several that are working well—while others and generally younger ones who have husbands & from 1 to 3 or 4 children are idle—indeed refuse to work & say their husbands must support them. Now & then there is a woman who is not able to work in the field—or who has 3 or 4 children at work & can afford to live on her children[']s labobor [labor]—with that of her husband—Generally however most of them should be in the field—

Could not this matter be referred to your agents They are generally very clever men and would do right I would suggest that you give this matter your favorable consideration & if you can do so to use your influence to make these idle women go to work. You would do them & the country a service besides gaining favor & the good opinion of the people generally—

I beg you will not consider this matter lightly for it is a very great evil & one that the Bureau ought to correct—if they wish the Freedmen & women to do well—I have 4 or 5 good women hands now idle that ought to be at work because their families cannot really be supported honestly without it This should not be so—& you will readily see how important it is to change it at once—I am very respectfully Your obt [obedient] servant

M. C. Fulton

I am very willing to carry my idle women to the Bureau agency & give them such wages as the Agent may think fair—& I will further garanty [guarantee] that they shall be treated kindly & not over worked—I find a general complaint on this subject everywhere I go—and I have seen it myself and experienced its bad effects among my own hands—These idle women are bad examples to those at work & they are often mischief makers—having no employment their brain becomes more or less the Devil's work shop as is always the case with idle people—black or white & quarrels & Musses among the colored people generally can be traced to these idle folks that are neither serving God—Man or their country—

Are they not in some sort vagrants as they are living without employment—and mainly without any visible means of support—and if so are they not amenable to vagrant act—? They certainly should be—I may be in error in this matter but I have no patience with idleness or idlers Such people are generally a nuisance—& ought to be reformed if possible or forced to work for a support—Poor white women . . . have to work—so should all poor people—or else stealing must be legalized—or tolerated for it is the sister of idleness—

12.8

Howell Cobb, A White Southern Perspective on Reconstruction (1868)

Congressional Reconstruction policies drastically changed Southern politics and society. Under the supervision of federal troops, existing governments were dismantled and replaced with new governments dominated by Republicans. Coalitions

SOURCE: Howell Cobb to J. D. Hoover, 4 January 1868, *Annual Report of the American Historical Association for the Year 1911: Vol. 2. The Correspondence of Robert Toombs, Alexander H. Stephens, and Howell Cobb*, ed. U. B. Phillips (Washington, DC, 1913), 690–694.

of African Americans, newly arrived Northerners (carpetbaggers), and Southern whites (scalawags) passed ambitious social reforms and expensive public works programs. Horrified by these changes, many former Confederates attacked Reconstruction as intrusive and corrupt.

Howell Cobb (1815–1868) was one of the best-known opponents of Reconstruction. Born into an elite Georgia family, Cobb studied at the University of Georgia and became a lawyer. After entering politics, Cobb served in the U.S. House of Representatives, became governor of Georgia, and was secretary of the treasury under President James Buchanan. Following Abraham Lincoln's election, Cobb resigned his cabinet post and became a leading secessionist. After chairing the Confederate constitutional convention, he commanded a military regiment. Following the war, Cobb distanced himself from politics but assailed Reconstruction in private letters like the one excerpted here.

FOCUS QUESTIONS

1. Why is Howell Cobb so critical of Reconstruction policies? Which policies does he find most upsetting?

2. How does Cobb describe the postwar South?

3. Describe Cobb's attitudes toward Northerners and African Americans. Do you think attitudes like Cobb's were common among white Southerners? Explain your answer.

Macon [GA] 4 Jany., 1868

We of the ill-fated South realize only the mournful present whose lesson teaches us to prepare for a still gloomier future. To participate in a national festival would be a cruel mockery, for which I frankly say to you I have no heart, however much I may honor the occasion and esteem the association with which I would be thrown.

The people of the south, conquered, ruined, impoverished, and oppressed, bear up with patient fortitude under the heavy weight of their burdens. Disarmed and reduced to poverty, they are powerless to protect themselves against wrong and injustice; and can only await with broken spirits that destiny which the future has in store for them. At the bidding of their more powerful conquerors they laid down their arms, abandoned a hopeless struggle, and returned to their quiet homes under the plighted faith of a soldier's honor that they should be protected so long as they observed the obligations imposed upon them of peaceful law-abiding citizens. Despite the bitter charges and accusations brought against our people, I hesitate not to say that since that hour their bearing and conduct have been marked by a dignified and honorable submission which should command the respect of their bitterest enemy and challenge the admiration of the civilized world. Deprived of our property and ruined in our estates by the results of the war, we have accepted the situation and given the pledge of a faith never yet broken to abide it.

Our conquerors seem to think we should accompany our acquiescence with some exhibition of gratitude for the ruin which they have brought upon us. We cannot see it in that light. Since the close of the war they have taken our property of various kinds, sometimes by seizure, and sometime by purchase, and when we asked for remuneration have been informed that the claims of rebels are never recognized by the Government. To this decision necessity compels us to submit; but our conquerors express surprise that we do not see in such ruling the evidence of their kindness and forgiving spirit. They have imposed upon us in our hour of distress and ruin a heavy and burthensome tax, peculiar and limited to our impoverished section. Against such legislation we have ventured to utter an earnest appeal, which to many of their leading spirits indicates a spirit of insubordination which calls for additional burdens. They have deprived us of the protection afforded by our state constitutions and laws, and put life, liberty and property at the disposal of absolute military power. Against this violation of plighted faith and constitutional right we have earnestly and solemnly protested, and our protests have been denounced as insolent, and our restlessness under the wrong and oppression which have followed these acts has been construed into a rebellious spirit, demanding further and more stringent restrictions of civil and constitutional rights. They have arrested the wheels of State government, paralyzed the arm of industry, engendered a spirit of bitter antagonism on the part of our negro population towards the white people with whom it is the interest of both races they should maintain kind and friendly relations, and are now struggling by all the means in their power both legal and illegal, constitutional and unconstitutional, to make our former slaves *our masters*, bringing these Southern states under the power of *negro supremacy*.

To these efforts we have opposed appeals, protests, and every other means of resistance in our power, and shall continue to do so until the bitter end. If the South is to be made a pandemonium and a howling wilderness the responsibility shall not rest upon our heads. Our conquerors regard these efforts on our part to save ourselves and posterity from the terrible results of their policy and conduct as a new rebellion against the constitution of our country, and profess to be amazed that in all this we have failed to see the evidence of their great magnanimity and exceeding generosity. Standing today in the midst of the gloom and suffering which meets the eye in every direction, we can but feel that we are the victims of cruel legislation and the harsh enforcement of unjust laws.... We regarded the close of the war as ending the relationship of enemies and the beginning of a new national brotherhood, and in the light of that conviction felt and spoke of constitutional equality.... We claimed that the result of the war left us a state in the Union, and therefore under the protection of the constitution, rendering in return cheerful obedience to its requirements and bearing in common with the other states of the Union the burdens of government, submitting even as we were compelled to do *to taxation without representation*; but they tell us that a successful war to keep us in the Union left us out of the Union and that the pretension we put up for constitutional protection evidences bad temper on our part and a want of appreciation of the generous spirit which declares that the constitution is not over us for the purposes of protection.... In such reasoning is found a justification of the policy which seeks to put the South under negro supremacy. Better, they say, to hazard the consequences of negro supremacy in the south with its sure and inevitable results upon Northern prosperity than to put faith in the people of the south who though overwhelmed and conquered have ever showed themselves a brave and generous people, true to their plighted faith in peace and in war, in adversity as in prosperity....

With an Executive who manifests a resolute purpose to defend with all his power the constitution of his country from further aggression, and a Judiciary whose unspotted record has never yet been tarnished with a base subserviency to the unholy demands of passion and hatred, let us indulge the hope that the hour of the country's redemption is at hand, and that even in the wronged and ruined South there is a fair prospect for better days and happier hours when our people can unite again in celebrating the national festivals as in the olden time.

12.9

Equal Rights Association Proceedings (1869)

The politics of Reconstruction strained long-standing partnerships between abolitionists and women's rights activists. Radical Republicans refused to link black suffrage and women's suffrage. In 1869, Congress passed the Fifteenth Amendment prohibiting the denial of suffrage on the basis of race, color, or previous condition of servitude. It did not, however, extend voting rights to women of any race. The decision ignited heated debates among social reformers and prompted a split in the women's movement that lasted over twenty years. In this reading, members of the American Equal Rights Association, an interracial coalition, try to reconcile African American and women's demands for voting rights.

SOURCE: Elizabeth Cady Stanton, Susan B. Anthony, and Matilda Joslyn Gage, eds. *History of Woman Suffrage* (New York: Fowler & Wells, 1882), 2:382, 391–92, 397, and Proceedings, American Equal Rights Association, New York City, 1869; *Stanton-Anthony Papers*, reel 13, frame 0504.

FOCUS QUESTIONS

1. Compare the arguments of Frederick Douglass and Susan B. Anthony. With whom do you most agree? Explain your answer.

2. How does Lucy Stone attempt to reconcile Douglass and Anthony's points of view?

3. What do these proceedings suggest about nineteenth-century America? Was Reconstruction the appropriate time to enfranchise women as well as black men? Explain your answers.

Mr. [Frederick] Douglass: I must say that I do not see how any one can pretend that there is the same urgency in giving the ballot to woman as to the negro. With us, the matter is a question of life and death, at least, in fifteen States of the Union. When women, because they are women, are hunted down through the cities of New York, and New Orleans, when they are dragged from their houses and hung upon lampposts; when their children are torn from their arms, and their brains dashed out upon the pavement; when they are objects of insult and outrage at every turn; when their children are not allowed to enter schools; then they will have an urgency to obtain the ballot equal to our own. (Great applause.)

A Voice: Is that not all true about black women?

Mr. Douglass: Yes, yes, yes; it is true of the black woman, but not because she is a woman, but because she is black. (Applause.) Julia Ward Howe at the conclusion of her great speech delivered at the convention in Boston last year, said "I am willing that the negro shall get the ballot before me." (Applause.) Woman! Why, she has 10,000 modes of grappling with her difficulties. I believe that all the virtue of the world can take care of all the evil. I believe that all the intelligence can take care of all the ignorance. (Applause.) I am in favor of woman's suffrage in order that we shall have all the virtue and vice confronted. Let me tell you that when there were few houses in which the black man could have put his head, this woolly head of mine found a refuge in the house of Mrs. Elizabeth Cady Stanton, and if I had been blacker than sixteen midnights, without a single star, it would have been the same. (Applause.)

Miss [Susan B.] Anthony: The old anti-slavery school says women must stand back and wait until the negroes shall be recognized. But we say, if you will not give the whole loaf of suffrage to the entire people, give it to the most intelligent first. (Applause.) If intelligence, justice, and morality are to have precedence in the Government, let the question of woman be brought up first and that of the negro last. (Applause.) While I was canvassing the State with petitions and had them filled with names for our cause to the Legislature, a man dared to say to me that the freedom of women was all a theory and not a practical thing. (Applause.) When Mr. Douglass mentioned the black man first and the woman last, if he had noticed he would have seen that it was the men that clapped and not the women. There is not the woman born who desires to eat the bread of dependence, no matter whether it be from the hand of father, husband, or brother; for any one who does so eat her bread places herself in the power of the person from whom she takes it. (Applause.) Mr. Douglass talks about the wrongs of the negro; but with all the outrages that he to-day suffers, he would not exchange his sex and take the place of Elizabeth Cady Stanton. (Laughter and applause.). . . .

MRS. LUCY STONE: Mrs. Stanton will, of course, advocate the precedence for her sex, and Mr. Douglass will strive for the first position for his, and both are perhaps right. If it be true that the government derives its authority from the consent of the governed, we are safe in trusting that principle to the uttermost. If one has a right to say that you can not read and therefore can not vote, then it may be said that you are a woman and therefore can not vote. We are lost if we turn away from the middle principle and argue for one class. . . . Over in New Jersey they have a law which says that *any* father—he might be the most brutal man that ever existed—*any* father, it says, whether he be under age or not, may by his last will and testament dispose of the custody of his child, born or to be born, and that such disposition shall be good against all persons, and that the mother may not recover her child; and that law modified in form exists over every State in the Union except Kansas. Woman has an ocean of wrongs too deep for any plummet, and the negro, too, has an ocean of wrongs that can not be fathomed. There are two great oceans; in one is the black man, and in the other is the woman. But I thank God for that XV Amendment, and hope that it will be adopted in every State. I will be thankful in my soul if *any* body can get out of the terrible pit. But I believe that the safety of the government would be more promoted by the admission of woman as an element of restoration and harmony than the negro. I believe that the influence of woman will save the country before every other power. (Applause.) I see the signs of the times pointing to this consummation, and I believe that in some parts of the country women will vote for the President of the United States in 1872. (Applause.). . . .

12.10

Susan B. Anthony
on Women's Rights (1873)

Incensed when neither the Fourteenth nor Fifteenth Amendments granted women suffrage, some women's rights activists began challenging state laws barring women from voting. In November 1872, Susan B. Anthony (1820–1906) and thirteen other women persuaded officials in Rochester, New York, to allow them to vote in the presidential election. After gaining national attention, the women were arrested for illegal voting, but only Anthony was put on trial. Henry R. Selden, Anthony's attorney, made a strong case for women's suffrage based on the Fourteenth Amendment. But his efforts failed. Without allowing the all-male jury to deliberate, Judge Ward Hunt directed them to find Anthony guilty. In imposing sentence, Hunt ordered Anthony to pay a $100 fine as well as court costs. Their fiery exchange follows. Anthony never paid a cent of her fine. But, in order to prevent her from appealing to the U.S. Supreme Court, Hunt refused to imprison her.

FOCUS QUESTIONS

1. Describe the interchange between Judge Hunt and Susan B. Anthony.
2. What are Anthony's major complaints? Do you find her arguments persuasive? Explain your answer.

JUDGE HUNT: The prisoner will stand up. Has the prisoner anything to say why sentence shall not be pronounced?

ANTHONY: Yes, your honor. I have many things to say; for in your ordered verdict of guilty, you have trampled underfoot, every vital principle of our government. My natural rights, my civil rights, my political rights, are alike ignored. Robbed of the fundamental privilege of citizenship, I am degraded from the status of a citizen to that of a subject; and not only myself individually, but all of

SOURCE: U.S. Circuit Court for the Northern District of New York, *United States v. Anthony* (January 1873).

my sex, are, by your honor's verdict, doomed to political sub-jection under this so-called republican government.

HUNT: The Court can not listen to a rehearsal of arguments the prison-er's counsel has already consumed three hours in presenting.

ANTHONY: May it please your honor, I am not arguing the question, but simply stating the reasons why sentence can not, in justice, be pronounced against me. Your denial of my citizen's rights to a vote is the denial of my consent as one of the governed, the denial of my representation as one of the taxed, the denial of my right to a trial of my peers as an offender against the law, therefore, the denial of my sacred rights to life, liberty, property, and—

HUNT: The Court can not allow the prisoner to go on.

ANTHONY: Of all my prosecutors, . . . not one is my peer, but each and all are my political sovereigns; and had your honor submitted my case to the jury, as was clearly your duty, even then I should have had cause of protest, for not one of those men was my peer; but, native or foreign, white or black, rich or poor, educated or ignorant, awake or asleep, sober or drunk, each and every man of them was political superior; hence, in no sense, my peer. . . . Jury, judge, counsel, must all be of the superior class.

HUNT: The Court must insist—the prisoner has been tried according to the established forms of law.

ANTHONY: Yes, your honor, but by forms of law all made by men, interpreted by men, administered by men, in favor of men, and against women; and hence, your honor's ordered verdict of guilty, against a United States citizen for the exercise of "that citizen's right to vote," simply because that citizen was a woman and not a man. But, yesterday, the same man-made forms of law declared it a crime punishable with a $1,000 fine and six months imprisonment, for you, for me, or any of us, to give a cup of cold water, a crust of bread, or a night's shelter to a panting fugitive as he was tracking his way to Canada. And every man or woman in whose veins coursed a drop of human sympathy violated that wicked law, reckless of consequences, and was justified in so doing. As then the slaves who got their freedom [had to] take it over, or under, or through the unjust forms of law, precisely so now must women, to get their right to a voice in this Government, take; and I have taken mine, and mean to take it at every possible opportunity.

HUNT: The Court orders the prisoner to sit down. It will not allow another word.

ANTHONY: When I was brought before your honor for trial, I hoped for a broad and liberal interpretation of the Constitution and its recent amendments, that should declare all United States citizens under its protecting aegis—that should declare equality of rights the national guarantee to all persons born or naturalized in the United States. But failing to get this justice—failing, even to get a jury of my peers—I ask not leniency at your hands—but rather the full rigors of the law.

HUNT: The Court must insist—The prisoner will stand up. The sentence of the Court is that you pay a fine of one hundred dollars and the costs of the prosecution.

ANTHONY: May it please your honor, I shall never pay a dollar of your unjust penalty. All the stock in trade I possess is a $10,000 debt, incurred by publishing my paper—*The Revolution*—four years ago, the sole object of which was to educate all women to do precisely as I have done, rebel against your man-made laws, unjust, unconstitutional forms of law, that tax, fine, imprison, and hang women, while they deny them the right of representation in the Government; and I shall work on with might and main to pay every dollar of that honest debt, but not a penny shall go to this unjust claim. And I shall earnestly and persistently continue to urge all women to the practical recognition of the old revolutionary maxim, that "Resistance to tyranny is obedience to God."

HUNT: Madam, the Court will not order you committed until the fine is paid.

12.11

Ku Klux Klan during Reconstruction (1872)

Some white Southerners used terrorist tactics to thwart Reconstruction. In spring 1866, a group of Confederate veterans organized the Ku Klux Klan, a social club based in Pulaski, Tennessee. The club adopted elaborate costumes and secret rituals. It soon evolved into a protest movement directed at Republicans and

SOURCE: U.S. Congress, *Testimony Taken by the Joint Select Committee to Inquire into the Condition of Affairs in the Late Insurrectionary States* (Washington, DC, 1872), 12: 1133–1134.

African Americans. Determined to preserve white supremacy and impede Reconstruction, Klansmen targeted "uppity" African Americans, Republicans, and people who cooperated with the Reconstruction governments. While Klan activity was limited to certain areas, state officials were unable to control the vigilantes and asked the federal government for assistance. In 1871, Congress investigated Klan activities and passed three Enforcement Acts that successfully suppressed the Klan. In this selection, Edward "Ned" Crosby, an African American, describes Klan actions in Mississippi.

FOCUS QUESTIONS

1. What types of Klan activities does Crosby describe?
2. How did Klansmen attempt to influence elections?
3. Why do you think someone would have joined the Klan during Reconstruction?

Columbus, Mississippi, November 17, 1871

EDWARD CROSBY (colored) sworn and examined.
By the Chairman:

QUESTION: Where do you live?

ANSWER: Right near Aberdeen—ten miles east of Aberdeen.

QUESTION: State whether you were ever visited by the Ku-Klux; and, if so, under what circumstances.

ANSWER: I have been visited by them. They came to my house, and came into my house.... It looked like there were thirty-odd of them, and I didn't know but what they might interfere with me, and I just stepped aside, out in the yard to the smokehouse. They came up there and three of them got down and came in the house and called for me, and she told them I had gone over to Mr. Crosby's.... She didn't know but they might want something to do to me and interfere with me and they knocked around a while and off they went.

QUESTION: Was this in the night-time?

ANSWER: Yes, sir.

QUESTION: Were they disguised?

ANSWER: Yes, sir.

QUESTION: Had you been attempting to get up a free-school in your neighborhood?

ANSWER: Yes, sir.

QUESTION: Colored school?

ANSWER: Yes, sir.

QUESTION: Do you know whether their visit to you had reference to this effort?

ANSWER: No, sir; I know only this; I had spoken for a school, and I had heard a little chat of that, and I didn't know but what they heard it, and that was the thing they were after.

QUESTION: Were their horses disguised?

ANSWER: Yes, Sir. . . .

QUESTION: Did you know any of the men?

ANSWER: No, sir; I didn't get close enough to know them. I could have known them, I expect, if I was close up, but I was afraid to venture.

QUESTION: Did they ever come back?

ANSWER: No, sir.

QUESTION: What do you know as to the whipping of Green T. Roberts?

ANSWER: Only from hearsay. He told me himself. They didn't whip him. They took him out and punched him and knocked him about right smart, but didn't whip him.

QUESTION: Was he a colored man?

ANSWER: He was a white man—a neighbor of mine.

QUESTION: Who took him out?

ANSWER: The Ku-Klux. . . .

QUESTION: What if anything do you know of any colored men being afraid to vote the republican ticket and voting the democratic ticket at the election this month, in order to save their property, and to save themselves from being outraged?

ANSWER: Well sir, the day of the election there was, I reckon, thirty or forty; I didn't count them, but between that amount; they spoke of voting the radical [Republican] ticket. It was my intention to go for the purpose. I had went around and saw several colored friends on that business. . . . I know some of the party would come in and maybe they would prevent us from voting as we wanted to. I called for the republican tickets and they said there was none on the ground. I knocked around amongst them, and I called a fellow named Mr. Dowdell and asked if there would be any there; he said he didn't know; he asked me how I was going vote; I told him my opinion, but I was cramped for fear. They said if we didn't act as they wanted they would drop us at once. There is only a few of us, living amongst them like lost sheep where we can do the best; and they were voting and they stood back and got the colored population and pushed them in front and let them vote first, and told them there was no republican tickets on the ground. I didn't see but three after I voted. Shortly after I voted, Mr. James Wilson came with some, and a portion of the colored people had done voting. I met Mr. Henderson; I was going on to the other box at the Baptist church. He asked if there were any colored voters there; I told him there was thirty or forty, and there was no republican tickets there. Mr. Wilson had some in his pocket, but I didn't see them. I saw that I was beat at my own game, and I had got on my horse and dropped out.

QUESTION: Who told you that unless the colored people voted the democratic ticket it would be worse for them?

ANSWER: Several in the neighborhood. Mr. Crosby said as long as I voted as he voted I could stay where I was, but he says, "Whenever Ned votes my rights away from me, I cast him down."

QUESTION: Was he a democrat?

ANSWER: A dead-out democrat.

QUESTION: Did you hear any other white men make the same declaration?

ANSWER: Not particular; I only heard them talking through each other about the colored population. I heard Mr. Jerome Lamb—he lived nigh Athens—tell a fellow named Aleck that lived on his place, he spoke to him and asked him if he was going to vote as he did; Aleck told him he was—he did this in fear, mind you—and Aleck went and voted, and after he voted he said, "Aleck, come to me;" says he, "Now, Aleck, you have voted?" Aleck says, "Yes sir;" he said, "Well, now, Aleck, you built some very nice houses. Now, I want you to wind your business up right carefully. I am done with you; off of my land."

QUESTION: Had Aleck voted the republican ticket?

ANSWER: Yes, sir.

QUESTION: Did all the colored men except these three vote the democratic ticket that day?

ANSWER: Up at Grub Springs all voted the democratic ticket. There was no republican ticket given to the colored people at all.

QUESTION: Did they vote the democratic ticket from fear that they would be thrown out of employment or injured?

ANSWER: That was their intention. You see pretty nigh every one of them was the same way I was, but there was none there; and them they were all living on white people's land, and were pretty fearful. The Ku-Klux had been ranging around through them, and they were all a little fearful.

QUESTION: Do you think they were all radical in sentiment, and would have been glad to have voted the radical ticket if uninfluenced?

ANSWER: They would. They had a little distinction up amongst themselves—the white and colored people. One of the said, "Ned, put in a republican ticket." Well, there was none on the ground and I remarked, "If there is any radical tickets on the ground I will take one of them, and I will not take a democratic ticket, and I will fold them up and drop that in the box, and they will never tell the difference," and it got out that I had voted the radical ticket, and some were very harsh about it.

QUESTION: Would the colored people of your county vote the radical ticket if left alone?

ANSWER: Well, sir, I suppose they would have done it.